RENAISSANC

FRANK KERMODE

RENAISSANCE ESSAYS

Shakespeare, Spenser, Donne

*

COLLINS
FONTANA BOOKS

First published in Great Britain
by Routledge & Kegan Paul 1971
First published in Fontana 1973
Copyright © 1971 Frank Kermode

Printed in Great Britain
Collins Clear-Type Press
London and Glasgow

CONTENTS

PREFACE   vii

INTRODUCTION   1

1   SPENSER AND THE ALLEGORISTS   12

2   'THE FAERIE QUEENE', I AND V   33

3   THE CAVE OF MAMMON   60

4   THE BANQUET OF SENSE   84

5   JOHN DONNE   116

6   THE PATIENCE OF SHAKESPEARE   149

7   SURVIVAL OF THE CLASSIC   164

8   SHAKESPEARE'S LEARNING   181

9   MATURE COMEDIES   200

10   THE FINAL PLAYS   219

11   ADAM UNPARADISED   260

INDEX   299

PREFACE

A great part of this book was written during my tenure of the
John Edward Taylor Chair at Manchester University. Chapter 3,
eventually published in the Stratford-on-Avon Studies volume on
Elizabethan Poetry, was given as a lecture in the University.
Chapters 2, 4 and 8 were lectures delivered at the John Rylands
Library and eventually published in its *Bulletin*. Chapter 1, the
British Academy Warton Lecture for 1962, was also written during
the same period; so were Chapters 9, 10 and 11, though first
published in the Stratford-on-Avon Studies volume *The Early
Shakespeare*, in the British Council series 'Writers and their Work'
and in the collection called 'The Living Milton'. Since Chapter 6,
though delivered as a lecture at Columbia University on the
occasion of the quatercentenary in 1964, also belongs to these
same years, this is in most ways a Manchester volume, and I want
to express my gratitude to all friends and colleagues there. Older
and even dearer debts call for acknowledgment: to Professor D. J.
Gordon, of Reading University, without whose aid few of these
projects would ever have been conceived, and to Mr. J. B. Trapp,
Librarian of the Warburg Institute, who took a hand in their
rearing. For imperfections of constitution or education the parent
is, naturally, responsible.

London   FRANK KERMODE
December 1970

INTRODUCTION

Of these essays the earliest was written in 1956, the latest in 1970. Some—the first four and, I suppose, the eighth—look like what is known as 'research', and the remainder look like what is known as 'criticism', though they all felt rather alike in the writing. It does seem absurd of people to suppose that only the first kind or only the second can be good—especially teachers, who are paid to do both and to range between library and classroom. The difference is that the 'research' pieces are intended to apply new information to, or contest existing solutions of, problems of the sort that exercise scholars, whereas the others are of a more explanatory nature and intended, in the first instance, for non-professors. I suppose the scholarly and pedagogical extremes might be represented by Chapters 4 and 9. But I very much hope that there is nothing here that does not contain something new, and nothing that defies the attention of all save the erudite.

In so flourishing a business as criticism it is not to be thought that scholarly topics remain untouched for a decade or more, and a good deal has happened since I wrote some of these essays. It would be folly to try and bring them all up to date by rewriting them, or to summarize crowded years of work on Shakespeare, Milton and Donne. Here and there, where something has happened to make me think I was wrong, I have changed a word or, rarely, a sentence, in Chapters 5–11; for the most part these changes relate to matters of fact. But the case seems different for the first four essays, which are narrower in focus and on less popular authors. Spenser and Chapman are the concern of specialists and of too few others; all will quite rightly ask that these pieces should not be reprinted without some mention of later work in the same areas which perhaps overthrows or qualifies their arguments, or even strengthens them.

For this reason I will here briefly survey the relevant literature.

It seems better to do it all in one piece than write a set of after-words, because interrelated questions arise, particularly in relation to Spenser. It will be perfectly obvious that one of my interests is in allegory and that I believe Spenser to have been, on occasion, what Chapman was more consistently and indisputably, a dark and conceited allegorist.

Over the past decade or so there has been a rather curious split in Spenser studies: on one hand we have a new interest in occult aspects of structure and imagery, on the other, a strong distaste for such matters accompanied by new definitions and valuations of allegory.

The party of darkness is typically interested in iconography, assuming in general that this is not a simple matter but one that challenges the reader's knowledge and ingenuity; a complex of images represents a new image, not just an aggregation of old ones, and the new meaning, not fully understandable from a survey of the context, is what one has to determine, in full awareness of the possible range of component meanings, astrological and so on. It is not surprising that Dr. A. D. S. Fowler, one of the most learned of Spenserian iconographers, is also a leader of the new school of arithmological Spenserians. This approach, first applied to *Epithalamion* by Professor Kent Hieatt in his *Short Time's Endless Monument* (1960) and extended to the whole of *The Faerie Queene* by Fowler in *Spenser and the Numbers of Time* (1964), has stiffened the resistance of the other party; contemptuous of old-style 'historical allegory', suspicious of newfangled iconography, they were hardly likely to welcome the most exorbitantly occult interpretations so far proposed. There is a good deal of indignation about Fowler's methods, which involve statistical procedures of a gravely inhumane variety and are backed by great iconographical learning—more indignation, indeed, than counter-attack. For Fowler has made some important and some incontrovertible discoveries, and these are embarrassing to all who detest the notion of a poem containing puzzles. The danger is that, as Fowler himself puts it, Spenser's poem may come to seem 'an overwrought and excessively patterned work' (p. 255), and the opposition would argue that it is Fowler, not Spenser, who has made it so.

The anti-puzzlers, some of whom are mentioned in the early pages of Chapter 2 below, have been formidably strengthened over the past few years, and I shall have to look at one or two of them in some detail. Here it would be tedious to mention all the scholars who subscribe to some version of the party line, and I think none of them would be offended if I said that their general doctrine is most authoritatively set forth in Rosemond Tuve's posthumous *Allegorical Imagery* (1966). This is a formidable yet temperate work by a distinguished scholar whose too early death we all deplore, and it complains with justice, where some others of the party tend to make undiscriminating mock, of interpretations which, though oversimple in themselves, result in a spurious complexity: that is, ingenious but partial allegorical readings which ignore literal meanings or fail to allow that in the full context one image qualifies another. Her concern was to treat allegory in terms of 'what was involved in reading allegorically . . . at a given time' (p. 33), namely Spenser's. This, of course, entailed investigation into earlier allegory and criticism of later allegorical readings, many of which (Fowler's, for example) Miss Tuve found to be unhistorical and methodologically awry, in that they seek what is not to be found, and others (A. C. Hamilton's, for example) in that they react too sharply against the methods thus abused and emasculate allegory in order to enhance narrative. Her own position may be illustrated by this comment on the Cave of Mammon:

> Mammon's cave is most surely a moral allegory showing the evils of concupiscentia (in its most embracing sense, as well as covetousness in a narrower sense). But both the imagery of the canto and the extraordinary freedom and grace of the following vision of Guyon's angelic protector prove us right in our feeling that we have been in hell, where there was nothing *but* concupiscentia, and have seen the Beast himself, who thinks he is a god. It is better not to dilute these poetic experiences to moral allegory only—fictions which convince us we should fight greed or strive for chaste love in marriage; they portray men faced with the death of soul or learning what its freedom depends upon.
>
> (p. 51)

An allegory, thus conceived, is not a static moralization, and Miss Tuve therefore distinguished it from moral allegory, 'though Spenser does not separate the two in practice; perhaps no poet could' (p. 332).

Miss Tuve most closely resembles her supporters in her impatience with *historical* allegory. Here, I think, she was uncharacteristically and fashionably injudicious; for even if one finds historical allegory less interesting than allegory in general (and no doubt it has been badly done and boring in the past) a lack of interest in the critic is insufficient to abolish whatever it is he declines to attend to; it is no use pretending the historical allegory is not there when it so obviously is, and especially in Books I and V. This is a point I stress in the first two essays printed here; it seems to me that we are more likely to lose grip on the poem by failing to attend to this allegory than by doing so. *The Faerie Queene* is, among other things, a very topical poem about events that were always seen as given meaning by reference to those great myths of religious and national history which provided structures for all time and the whole world; and in setting all that aside as of minor interest we deprive the work of a special density and relevance to the nature of human fictions without which it will always seem to the ordinary reader lacking in precisely this application to the human condition.

However that may be, it is certain that the party of which I have been speaking scorns to consider, much less develop, historical readings. I can discover nothing published in the intervening years which makes any difference to, or even seriously considers, my remarks on the First Book in Chapters 1 and 2. The Fifth Book has been the subject of two full-length studies, many allusions and one important article. These I must now speak to.

First in time and importance is René Graziani's 'Elizabeth at Isis Church' (*P.M.L.A.*, 1964, 376 ff.), the writing and publication of which were almost exactly contemporary with those of my Chapter 2. It would be possible, and possibly fruitful, to quarrel about the detail of this piece, but it is in general learned and right-minded. Graziani remarks that the quality of the work itself will prevent our taking a 'stingy monistic view of the allegorical possibilities of Isis Church', adding quite properly that 'the historical allegory has been neglected lately, surprisingly in view of the topical allusiveness of much of Book V'. Graziani thinks the Church is Parliament, and Britomart's dream an allegory of Elizabeth's differences with Parliament in the case of Mary Queen of Scots.

The drift of this argument is of course away from mine, but

Graziani also points out that Mary was tried 'in what was in effect a special court of Chancery, a Commission of English peers headed by the Chancellor of the Realm and "Keeper of the Queen's Conscience", Thomas Bromley'. She herself was reminded of this when the Court informed her that 'they were to proceed according to Equity and Reason, and not upon any cunning niceties of Law . . .'; she would be heard 'according to Equity with Favour' (these quotations are from Camden's *History of the Princess Elizabeth*). Elizabeth, after much hesitation, saw that equity required the death of Mary; her final decision is represented, as presumably no one denies, in the Mercilla episode of the poem.

Graziani reminds us that Spenser was himself an officer of the Irish Court of Chancery; he would presumably be interested in the more general constitutional issues as well as in the particular case of the Queen of Scots. It is a characteristic assimilation of particular historical event to general principle. Graziani even conjectures that Spenser had a particular place in mind, namely the Commons' Chamber, once a splendid chapel; and that the statue of Isis recalls the figure of the Virgin standing on the Serpent which formerly stood in the smaller chapel called Our Lady of the Piews, next door. These minute topographical details seem to me neither implausible nor necessary to the truth of the general proposition. The equity courts, incidentally, were adjacent to the Great Hall at Westminster. Graziani and I cannot, presumably, both be right in detail, nor yet in our account of the Church generally; but surely our common principle is right: we know the *kind* of thing to look for.

This, however, is exactly what the authors of two monographs either deny or ignore. T. K. Dunseath (*Spenser's Allegory of Justice*, 1968) mentions Graziani's piece without examining it, satisfied that because the 'search for historical possibilities has diminished' (p. 4) he need not bother about them. But neither this truth nor the fact that 'the meaning of Book V encompasses and transcends the historical allegory' (pp. 15–16) entails that there is no such allegory, nor that it ought to be neglected. Mr. Dunseath's mistaken inference explains why he was able to write 240 pages about Book V without saying more than a few unilluminating words about what after all remains one of the most mysterious and baffling passages in the whole poem. Jane Aptekar (*Icons of Justice*, 1969) takes a somewhat similar tone, calling Graziani's piece odd, but not saying why or explaining why she herself, in ignoring what is there but unfashionable, does not deserve that epithet or worse.

So much for historical allegory and for the fashionable dislike of it. The Cave of Mammon, being without historical dimension, is presumably a problem more congenial to such exegetes, and Mr. Paul Alpers, in an entertaining, argumentative and learned work which has nothing to do with historical allegory, devotes a good deal of space to the Seventh Canto of Book II (*The Poetry of The Faerie Queene*, 1967).

Generally speaking Alpers is a Tuvian, emphasizing the diffusion of effect we should look for in allegories such as Spenser's and taking a dead set against what he regards as the overcurious iconography and, *a fortiori*, the arithmology of Fowler. He doesn't, however, refute Fowler, dismissing him merely as one head of a hydra it would be tedious and unprofitable to fight; another and less learned head, attributable to the same beast, is mine, and as we shall see he does pause long enough to take a cut at this one. Miss Tuve, as I understand her, cautiously approved the general ideas of my Chapter 3 (p. 32 of her book), but then I doubt whether she would have subscribed to some of Alpers' extensions of her principles, such as this: 'In reading *The Faerie Queene* one apprehends the depths only by staying on the surface' (p. 157). This unenterprising method does not seem to have helped much when the poem is really dark; and of course the meaning of the remark depends on what you mean by 'depths', as well as upon a proof that diving is always fruitless. Alpers illustrates his point by a neat handling of Occasion in Book II (pp. 229 ff.), but it cannot be held that all the iconography is of this kind or that all the allegory is similarly on the surface; in fact, it is of course part of the opposing case that there are very different thicknesses of allegory in the poem, and it is not pretended that Occasion is very thick or very dark. If we maintain that all Spenser's allegory is like this, or like the House of Alma, we shall have to ask ourselves why there are parts of the poem which remain puzzling, which obviously mean something and we cannot say what. An instance would be the Church of Isis, but Alpers does not so much as mention it in his long book.

However, he does stand and fight on the Cave of Mammon, my reading of which he rightly regards as inconsistent with the theory that superficial readings are alone defensible. Of that reading Alpers observes, with enviable confidence, that it is opposed to 'Spenser's sense of the reality his poem has' (pp. 200-1). To know that is admittedly to possess a weapon against which commonplace shields are no defence, but having displayed it Mr. Alpers chivalrously abstains from using it. Instead, having explained that the notes left by early readers—Fowler (who collected them) to the contrary—either support his view of the matter or nobody's, he undertakes to show that looking for any but simple iconographical and structural principles is bound to be wrong by lengthily examining the Cave of Mammon and two of its interpreters.

I can't do justice to the passage (pp. 235-78) in which Professor Harry Berger and I, who had thought ourselves poles apart on this issue, are neatly clapped into Mr. Alpers' good-natured pillory; and naturally I do not speak for Berger. What Alpers dislikes, I gather, is not so much my general conclusion as my method of reaching it, which allows images to be enigmatic. This, of course, he will not have. I wish he had thought to say more about another allegorist, Chapman, who was, after all, Spenser's exact contemporary and also, though admittedly more ostentatiously, a learned poet; Chapman was enigmatic and proud of it, but all Alpers says is that he was working in 'a less strict and coherent tradition' (p. 104). This does seem like another instance of abolishing inconvenient instances by uttering judgments founded on magical insights rather than evidence.

Why, asks Alpers, did Spenser, if he went in for enigmas, create in the passage on the Golden Chain something that looks very like one, and then give its meaning away at the end of stanza 49? The answer is that in this very limited instance Spenser thought it proper to do so; it did not conflict with his sense of the reality of the poem (a criterion available to us all, in the end) to be explicit about this very small part of a complicated scheme. It is, I repeat, no part of the 'dark' argument that *everything* is enigmatic; Spenser is less reader-repellent than Chapman, and did not want to be so in any degree. It is, after all, easy to do what Alpers the doctrinaire always denies to be possible, namely, to distinguish between passages in which Spenser is being enigmatic and passages in which he isn't. Different demands are made on us, different kinds of attention are elicited. This is why everybody feels how different he is from Chapman: not that they are in different traditions, but that Chapman is always as obscure as Spenser is only sometimes. This elementary difference, which does not eliminate the resemblances, is perfectly evident to all who have read both poets, unless they happen to have committed themselves to a theory which prevents them from seeing it. Anyway, the example of the Golden Chain is not only very negative ('isn't this the kind of thing Kermode says Spenser doesn't do?'), it is also totally inapposite, since I never said anything of the sort.

More positively, Alpers objects to my interpretation of the Garden of Proserpina. He prefers, at a risk he does little to insure against, to treat it as yet another image of avarice. It not only calls for unconvincing demonstrations that the tediously repetitive need not be tedious, but destroys the parallel between the temptations of Guyon and those of Christ, a parallel which Alpers, without substituting more plausible evidence for it, appears to accept. In such a scheme the Garden must have a place, and to seek to determine it is not the same as 'making a case for a conclusion already determined' (p. 241), unless one says that of any attempt to support an hypothesis. For there is a plausible hypothesis, as he admits; and if it is to be validated, one has to explain much material which, if it simply continues to lie around, accounted for on some sophistical *ad hoc* theory of repetitiousness, will tell strongly against it.

The association, in the scheme of temptations, between avarice and other kinds of concupiscence, including mental varieties, is simply much stronger than Alpers understands. Thus it is true, as he remarks, that in the passage where Comes speaks of the Hesperidian apples as signifying astronomical knowledge, Comes also remarks, giving the whole thing a more homely turn, that the serpents which guarded these apples were sleepless, like avaricious men. It is hard to see why the comparison, which relates to the keepers of the apples and not to the apples, should strike Alpers as qualifying the signification of the apples; or why he would not take this as a possible further demonstration of the association, in Comes, of *curiositas* with greed, rather than as a confutation of that association in my piece. (Fowler, incidentally, notes the Saturnian element in the temptations, and remembers that 'curious learning was the especial domain of Saturn' [p. 113], and I do not see why I should not mention this.)

8

INTRODUCTION

Finally, Alpers thinks for some reason that I failed to observe of the myths in stanzas 54–55 that they all involve a golden fruit (though how I contrived to proceed as I did without knowing this is a question) and that, having picked this up, we should linger on the surface to admire its subtlety. Further, to question the schematic character of my reading, he claims that I have got the tree wrong; it is a good tree, and its fruit, unlike everything else Guyon sees on his visit to Mammon, offers 'a genuine human good' (p. 243). This is the sort of surface contradiction and complexity he wants to find; it is convenient to ignore, in so good a cause, the fact that the branches of this tree, borne down by their fruit, dip into a hellish river, full of souls in torment. 'The way to read Spenser's verse,' advises Mr. Alpers, 'here and everywhere, is to pay the fullest and most detailed attention to the surface of the verse' (p. 244). Quite so; one begins there. To have done so would have prevented the nonsense about the tree, and perhaps raised a doubt as to whether the most boring and obvious reading is necessarily the right one. The main difficulty, if having been advised I may offer some advice in return, is that Alpers, holding the views here so energetically propagated—that Spenser is always simple and always the same, that the surface is where we ought to stop—has quite unnecessarily limited his vision. Whenever he is faced with a passage which can't obviously be reconciled with the theory, he has to do one of two things: forbear to discuss them (Church of Isis) or trivialize them (Cave of Mammon).

I think the opening pages of my piece may be too emphatic; the aim was simplicity, and I may have overdone it. But on the reading of the Cave I am unrepentant. There may be errors of emphasis and detail, but the general drift of it is right, or at any rate substantially unchallenged so far.[1]

I have been talking about Chapters 1, 2, and 3 of this book, and it may occur to some readers that they look like an abandoned foundation of a book on Spenser. This would be a shrewd guess. My reasons for abandoning the project, which occupied me off and on for a long time, were, I suppose, ultimately temperamental. The Spenser who exercised my imagination was a maker

[1] Professor Maurice Evans ('The Fall of Guyon', ELH, A Journal of English Literary History, xxviii (1961), 215–24) feels that my interpretation is inconsistent with the view he holds, that Guyon is 'Christianized' in this canto, and that this determines the structure of the whole book.

9

of dark conceits, and I had less to say of the rest of the poem than of I, II and V. However, I had my say about the Garden of Adonis in Book III, and the Mutability Cantos, in *The Sense of an Ending* (1967) and wrote a more broadly based introduction and commentary in the small *Spenser* edited for the New Oxford English series (1965).

A word now about 'The Banquet of Sense', Chapter 4, below, which contains a reading of Chapman's most obscure poem, *Ovids Banquet of Sence*. Here the number of critics is smaller, and none of them is a simple-lifer. Professor Millar MacLure (*George Chapman*, 1966) adopts a view close to mine and opposed to the old 'Ideal Beauty' reading; he says that 'the whole poem is an extended exercise in paradox in theme and figures, and that the paradoxes are intended covertly to undermine the Ovidian "philosophy" of the senses. This is the "judiciall perspective" which Chapman asks of his readers' (p. 53). He adds another possible source, the *Hypnerotomachia*, 'in which Poliphilo meets five maidens representing the senses, which incite him to lust and then appease it' (p. 51), Poliphilo being rather luckier than Ovid. He also indicates thematic parallels in Barnabe Barnes's *Parthenophil and Parthenope* (1593), and usefully adds to my list four more Elizabethan instances of the banquet-of-sense *topos*, from Drayton, Constable and Jonson, its chief proponent.

In an article called 'This curious frame: *Ovid's Banquet of Sense*' (*Studies in Philology*, 1965, 192 ff.), J. P. Myers, Jr., makes another attack on the Ideal Beauty readings and, while endorsing mine, offers to strengthen and patch it where necessary. He surveys the so-called 'epyllia' of the period, with the elaborate and structurally relevant digression, and finds the announced digression of stanzas 51-55 to be consonant with them. Myers also points out that my struggle about Chapman's order of the senses would have been less arduous had I noticed that he puts them in the same order in *Hero and Leander*, V. 42-46, and that others had adjusted the order similarly; the placing of Hearing at the head of the list may derive from Aristotle's *Parva Naturalia*, 437a. Good. Myers also thinks I have misunderstood stanza 19. I do not agree that the statue of Niobe is a 'perspective sculpture' on the analogy of the perspective picture; whether there were such sculptures I do not know and much doubt, but all Chapman can have meant at this point is that you had to stand at a distance from the statue to make out what it represented. I accept correction on other details of the statuary: the obelisks do not represent Apollo and Artemis, as I said, but only support representations of them; and the children are carved in ivory, not marble. On the whole I think Myers still agrees with me about the sculpture, rejecting Elizabeth Donno's interpretation in her *Elizabethan Minor Epics* (1963), a version of the old Ideal Beauty reading which says that close-up Ovid can see something secret and good, whereas afar off the profane multitude see only Niobe. He is rather sad to have to turn this down, but in fact it makes nonsense of the iconography and indeed of the poem.

So far from challenging my reading, Mr. Raymond B. Waddington (*Review of English Studies* (1968), pp. 158 ff.) thinks I missed an important and rather obvious bit of evidence in its favour. This is its epigraph from Persius: *Quis haec lege? Nemo. Hercule nemo,* | *Vel duo vel nemo*: 'Who'll read such stuff?' asks a friend. 'Nobody, by God,' replies Persius, 'one or two or none at all.' Mr. Waddington suggests that *Hercule*, a slangy oath in the Latin, is used seriously by Chapman, who had a great deal of time for Hercules and used him in various capacities, including those of the cleanser of dirty worlds and the enemy of lust. He also represented the labours of scholarship, on which Chapman also dwelt; and so 'reading by Hercules' is very deep reading. Since Persius was making satirical attacks on sensuality, he was an appropriate source. There may be something in this; one had thought the motto more restricted in application, another way of saying what Chapman said in his Preface, namely that he would be rather disgusted if he found many readers; but it is true that the name of Hercules might start a train of obscure reflections.

So far, then, though it may need shoring up here and there, as Mr. Myers remarks, this ten-year-old piece seems to be withstanding the scholarly weather. The first four chapters of the book contain the material most likely to need patching so I have attended to them here. The others must take their chance, or solicit the imagination of the reader to mend them.

I

SPENSER AND THE ALLEGORISTS

There is no 'Spenser controversy', Spenser has been 'dislodged' with no fuss at all. Why? What follows hints at one possible answer.

Spenser is a known maker of allegories. If you believe, as many people appear to, that allegory is necessarily superficial, *The Faerie Queene* is dull in so far as it is simple, and a failure in so far as it is difficult. Coleridge, perhaps, first specified that allegory was a mode inferior to 'symbolism', and this is now commonplace. Blake's distinction between Vision and Allegory—which is 'formed by the Daughters of Memory'—was accepted, for instance, by Yeats, who blames Spenser and Bunyan for the unhappy vogue of allegory in England. A German Symbolist friend of his—probably Dauthendey, the man who hated verbs —won Yeats's approval by observing that 'Allegory said things which could be said as well, or better, in another way'.[1] As such views gain ground, Spenser's fortunes wilt; and in our own day we may find a critic of distinction, Professor Yvor Winters, willing to dismiss *The Faerie Queene* in a few derisive words.[2] From Hazlitt reading the poem in 'voluptuous indolence', we progress easily to Winters not reading it at all.

On the other hand, though we tend to associate allegory with grey abstraction, we are all fascinated by what Goethe called 'the green and golden archetype'.[3] There are the archetypes of Miss Bodkin, which are Jungian, and those of Professors Wheelwright

[1] *A Book of Images* drawn by W. T. Horton and introduced by W. B. Yeats (London, 1898), p. 8. (Partially reprinted in *Ideas of Good and Evil*, 1903, and in *Essays and Introductions*, 1961.)

[2] *The Function of Criticism* (1957), p. 44.

[3] Quoted in Philip Wheelwright, *The Burning Fountain* (1954), p. 89.

and Frye, which are not. There is a general and an increasing interest in the exposure of radical myth-structures in works of literature. But Spenser does not come well out of this. The interpreters of Melville and Hawthorne and Kafka welcome every new subtlety of method; but Spenser seems fated to suffer at best a criticism of reduction, a dubious salvation by archetypes.

It is pointless to discuss criticism which, in the teeth of scholarly evidence, finds Spenser too simple. My concern is with reductive criticism, which works by the abolition of contexts, by the sacrifice of the poem's *presence* to its radical myths and types. These are, of course, to be found in the poem, and at the present moment they confer prestige; but much damage may be done in the process of isolating them in their primitive glory. *The Faerie Queene* is, after all, an heroic poem, extremely conscious of its peculiar relation to history—to 'now and England'. To reduce it to a 'Biblical quest-romance',[4] as Northrop Frye does, is, however brilliant the work, not to glorify but to impoverish it. The mistake, in short, is 'to be led away into exploring the possible significance the myths used may be thought to possess in themselves, into infinite speculations about their archetypal patterns and analogies, instead of the realized meaning of the work itself'. It is not without interest that the excellent book from which I borrow these words[5] is not about Spenser but about Joyce; whose work, it may be thought, deliberately invites such speculations, whereas Spenser's does not.

Perhaps there will always be enmity between those who believe symbols and archetypes to have value in themselves, and those who think it obvious that the value of a symbol, however much traditional significance it may accrete, is finally determined by its context; much as the meaning of redness in a sign varies from 'hot water' to 'stop!' or 'Manchester United'. For example, the most superficial inquiry into the history of the principal figures of the book of Revelation will reveal that for all their antiquity they alter their meanings with their context. Professor E. H. Gombrich has more than once castigated the 'mystical antiquarianism' which treats images as if they were possessed of inalienable meanings. To do so is to abandon a complex civility in favour of a dubious *sapientia veterum*. Now the context in which

---

[4] *Anatomy of Criticism* (1957), p. 194.
[5] S. L. Goldberg, *The Classical Temper* (1961), pp. 201–2.

Spenser's archetypes acquire value is not easy to describe; but I think we may gather something of the importance of the attempt if we can find a group of images used in his own way by Spenser and in a revealingly different way by a modern author. Such are the apocalyptic images used by Spenser in the first book of *The Faerie Queene*; and I shall first speak of the use to which Spenser puts them. Later I shall look at the contexts provided by a well-thought-of twentieth-century writer, D. H. Lawrence.

Spenser would have been happy to call the book of Revelation 'a continued Allegory, or darke conceit'. Like his own poem, it has a spiritual as well as an historical aspect; for if, according to St. Augustine, it is an allegory of the soul's escape from bonds of sin,[6] it is also, by weight of tradition, a prophecy to be fulfilled by events in time. Spenser's first book has intentions closely parallel to these, for it proceeds on the old assumption that the history of mankind is the history of man's soul writ large. Book I might fairly be designated a Tudor Apocalypse.

Upton first observed the frequent allusions to Revelation (and Warton, I am sorry to say, was shocked by them). Little was added to the subject until recently, when Mrs. J. W. Bennett and Professor J. E. Hankins looked into it again and transformed it. Mrs. Bennett[7] noticed that the use made of Revelation by Reform theologians was very relevant to Spenser's purposes; and Mr. Hankins brought to bear the patristic commentaries.[8] Certain identifications are now, I suppose, beyond dispute. St. George and Arthur share qualities of the Christ of Revelation—a point made vivid by those medieval Apocalypses which show the Knight 'faithful and true' bearing, in his battle with the demonic host, a white shield with a cross *gules*.[9] Una is the 'woman clothed with the sun' of Rev. xii. 1, traditionally identified with the true

[6] *De Civitate Dei*, xx. vii.

[7] *The Evolution of the Faerie Queene* (1942), cap. ix.

[8] 'Spenser and the Revelation of St. John', *Publications of the Modern Language Association of America*, lx (1945), 364–81.

[9] See, for example, M. R. James, ed., *The Apocalypse in Latin*, MS. 10 in the collection of Dyson Perrins, 1927, plate 81; or the corresponding plate in *L'Apocalypse en Français au XIIIe siècle* (Bib. Nat. fr. 403), ed. L. Delisle et P. Meyer, 1900. According to the influential commentary of Beatus, the horse is the body of Christ, the rider 'Dominus maiestatis . . . verbum patris altissimi . . . id est, divinitas incarnata'. (*Beati in Apocalypsin Libri X*, ed. H. A. Sanders, 1930, p. 591.)

church, which Tertullian called *integram . . . incorruptam virginem*,[10] to be echoed down the centuries to Newton.[11] Another glance at some illuminated Apocalypse that shows the Woman with her glory of sunshine will help to explain why Spenser, at the climax of the book, speaks of

> The blazing brightness of her beauties beame,
> And glorious light of her sunshyny face.

Duessa, though she is all doubleness and multiplicity, all departures from a primal integrity, is also the Whore of Babylon; and Spenser's Eighth Canto is perfectly illustrated in medieval illustrations of Rev. xvii. 4.[12] Archimago is associated with antichrist, a person who does not occur in Revelation, but was early attracted into its ambience from the Epistles of John. According to that source there were many antichrists, and the list of historical characters so named by their enemies must be very long; it is a common error, which Mrs. Bennett repeats, that Wyclif first applied the term to a pope. In any case, the application of the word to the papacy in general is the important one for our purposes; this was the work of Luther.[13] Archimago is antichrist in this sense. He is also the false prophet and the beast from the land. Arthur has traits of the knight *fidelis et verax*, but the first account of him is a development in chivalric terms of the angel in Rev. xviii. He wears the seal of the spouse (Cant. viii. 6) and shares the angel's satisfaction at the catastrophic prospects of Babylon, which is Rome.

Many minor allusions to Revelation I here ignore; the structural resemblances are sufficient to establish the point. When Red

[10] As quoted by Jewel, *Apologia Ecclesiae Anglicanae*, 1562, pars vi, cap. xvi, div. 1; in *The Works of John Jewel* (Parker Society, 1848), iii. 41.

[11] Sir Isaac Newton, *Observations upon the Prophecies of Daniel and the Apocalypse of St. John* (1733), p. 279: 'the woman . . . clothed with the sun, before she flies into the wilderness, represents the primitive Church catholick. . . .'

[12] The beast she rides on has seven heads, standing for the deadly sins, and ten horns, representing—according to Hugh of St. Victor—the violated commandments (Migne, *Patrologia Latina*, cxcvi. 799; quoted by M. W. Bloomfield, *The Seven Deadly Sins*, 1952, p. 85).

[13] *Preface to the Revelation of St. John* (1545); in *Works of Martin Luther*, 1932, vi. 479–88. This is Luther's second Preface to the book; in his first (1522) he had found it 'neither apostolic nor prophetic' (ibid., p. 488). The second Preface had much influence. See E. L. Tuveson, *Millennium and Utopia* (1949), pp. 24 ff.

Cross deserts Una, Spenser is remembering Rev. ii. 4: 'for thou hast left thy first love'.[14] He means that England deserted the true catholic church. Una lost is the woman clothed with the sun who suffers forty-two months in the wilderness (the primary reference is to the typical wanderings of the Israelites). The overthrow of the dragon is closely associated with the battle of Christ against Satan, and so with the Passion, the Resurrection, and the Harrowing of Hell.[15] The tree and the water which refresh Red Cross during the three-day battle are from Rev. xxii, and signify the two sacraments of the Reformed Church. The book presented by Red Cross to Arthur, the Babylonian House of Pride, the two Jerusalems—Cleopolis, and the city of Red Cross's vision—are further instances.[16]

Spenser was evidently conscious of iconographic and exegetical traditions; it is part of his method to telescope significations by glancing back at them: thus Red Cross, not only England but a saint imitating Christ, dissolves into the object of his imitation. Nevertheless, it remains clear that Mrs. Bennett was right in thinking that his use of apocalyptic material was strongly coloured by recent anti-Romanist versions of Revelation. But her emphasis on extreme Protestantism is itself extreme. The apologists of the English settlement give the whole matter a new Anglican interest; and to leave Foxe and Jewel out of account is to miss what is most important to Spenser. I think it is part of the same mistake that Mrs. Bennett discourages attempts to give the allegory a clear historical application. I do not mean that we ought to go back to calling Una Anne Boleyn; only that Scott was near the truth when he argued that the adventures of Red Cross 'bear a peculiar and obvious, though not a uniform, reference to the history of the Church of England'.[17] Not, be it noted, to the events of the English Reformation; but more broadly, so that the destruction of Error suggests to Scott the early Church purging itself of such heresies as Arianism, and the victory over Sansfoy Constantine's defeat of paganism.[18] The only commentator to develop Scott's

[14] Hankins (loc. cit.) relates this episode to Cant. viii.

[15] As Hankins (loc. cit.) suggests.

[16] Hankins relates the House of Coelia to the Earthly Jerusalem.

[17] Quoted in *The Works of Spenser: a Variorum Edition*, ed. E. Greenlaw, C. G. Osgood, F. M. Padelford, and R. Heffner, i (1932), 450.

[18] This last idea is all the more probable in the light of the report that Constantine owed his victory to British troops (Foxe, *Acts and Monuments of the Church*, ed. M. H. Seymour, 1838, p. 76).

suggestion was Thomas Keightley almost a century ago; and the Variorum editors report his views without approval.[19]

I do not agree with Keightley's detailed interpretation; but that there is in the text of the First Book a body of allusion to the history of the Church seems to me inescapable, though it requires a detailed demonstration which this hour will not contain. The poem is addressed to the 'only supreme governor' of the Church; this title in itself required historical justification, and so did the claim that English Christianity was older than the Roman church. In fact all the apologists of the Settlement made the appeal to history as a matter of course. And whoever agreed that the English was the true primitive catholic church had to think of her history as beginning, not with the convulsions of Henry VIII's reign, but, as Jewel put it, 'after the first creation of the world'[20] or, more practically, with the arrival in England of Joseph of Arimathea. For Christianity came here not from Rome, but from the East; and Una is descended from kings and queens whose 'scepters stretcht from East to Westerne shore' (i. 5). 'Neither did the east and the west, nor distance of place, divide the church', says Foxe; but 'this catholic unity did not long continue.'[21] Thanks, of course, to the papacy; and Foxe enables us to recognize in Spenser's text the features of certain especially guilty popes, who were the progenitors of Duessa. Her father has the West under his rule, 'And high hath set his throne where *Tiberis* doth pas' (ii. 22). Rome has divided the world and exiled the catholic church. Who will restore and re-establish it?

The answer is, of course, the Supreme Governor and her agents. But by what right does she undertake to do so? To answer that, one has only to recall that the most insistent of all complaints against the papal antichrist is, probably, that which concerns the usurpation of temporal authority. Thus Foxe, like Luther,[22] is always on the emperor's side against the pope, and, like Jewel, holds that the emperor has the power to call General Councils and the right to exact temporal obedience from the Bishop of Rome; an argument of great importance to the English. The

---

[19] *Variorum*, i. 454–5.   [20] Ed. cit. iii. 49.   [21] Foxe, p. 168.
[22] For Luther, the third woe of Rev. xiii is the papal assumption of temporal power in the Bull *Unam sanctam* of Boniface VIII (1302). See *Works of Luther*, vi. 484, and F. Saxl, 'Reformation Pamphlets', in *Lectures* (1957), i. 255 ff.

self-aggrandizement of that bishop—helped by various donations, genuine and false—led not only to the humiliation of emperors but to persistent interference in the English state; the presumption of Gregory VII, the schemes of Becket, the ordeal of John, the need for such measures as the statutes of Praemunire and Provisors, were all chronicled and noted. The right and duty of restoring the Church to her pre-Hildebrandine purity (Canterbury independent of Rome, the sacrament administered in both kinds to the laity, no transubstantiation, proper respect for Romans xiii) belonged to the heiress of Empire, to Elizabeth, whom Spenser in the dedication of his poem calls 'most high, mightie and magnificent Empresse'.

In throwing off the yoke of the papacy, runs the argument, the English had not only reasserted the primitive values of the Church but restored the authority of the Empire. Satan is still loose for a season; the struggle against the false prophet and the wounded beast will go on. But in England there will be a proper balance of spiritual and temporal power. This is like enough to the situation of Spenser's poem; and neither the poem nor the political realities of the time could have been quite as they were, Foxe could not have spoken of 'the whole church of Christ, namely . . . the church of England',[23] had not the queen inherited the imperial authority.

Miss Frances Yates has connected the revival of chivalry at court (which is clearly relevant to Spenser's procedures in his poem) with a rather elaborate emperor-cult of Elizabeth.[24] This is not an easy matter. Somewhere in the cult there is a nucleus of serious political theory; hence the appearance in lists of early Reformers of such names as Marsilius of Padua and Dante, who called upon the emperor to reform the Church and gave him a certain authority over the pope. But other elements of the cult are harder to define. Miss Yates connects the image of Elizabeth as Astraea with the return of England to 'Constantinian imperial Christianity'; the Virgin returns to the Empire, as Virgil prophesied.[25] Thus the Queen, after the example of her predecessor, had

[23] *Acts and Monuments*, p. 998.

[24] 'Queen Elizabeth as Astraea', *Journal of the Warburg and Courtauld Institutes*, x (1947), 27–82.

[25] Constantine officially recognized this application of *iam redit et Virgo*; see Harold Mattingly, *Journal of the Warburg and Courtauld Institutes*, x (1947), 19.

united Church and Empire; and the astrological associations of the Astraea figure were available and ingeniously used for imperial propaganda, as, for example, in *Faerie Queene* V.

Similar cults of Charles V, Henri III, and Henri IV and others, indicate that the political value of this theme had been noticed elsewhere. It is expounded not only by Foxe but in the Preface to Erasmus's paraphrases on the New Testament, both books ordered to be placed in English churches. Elizabeth is not likely to have overlooked the special propriety of the theme to herself. 'Let Virgo come from heaven, the glorious star. . . . Let her reduce the Golden Age again', says a character in *The Misfortunes of Arthur*, prophesying the reign of Elizabeth, though in 1588. It is even possible that the eirenic implications of the myth could have helped to conciliate the remaining English Romanists, much as the historians' proof of the ancient liberties of the English church seems to have contented them, at least before the arrival of the Jesuit missions.[26] However that may be, we must obviously allow for the pressure of such a cult on Spenser's poem. The myth of the queen as Astraean empress is inseparable from the use of apocalyptic figures with historical significations, and itself involves a strong sense that the whole history of the Empire, from Aeneas to Constantine, from Charlemagne to Elizabeth, culminated in the present moment.

And there is, I believe, another tradition of Empire to be considered. Constantine was venerated as a Messianic king, and after him—such was the potency of Apocalypse and the Sibylline Books —Christians imagined, for more than a thousand years, that 'the figure of the warrior-Christ was doubled by another, that of the Emperor of the Last Days'.[27]

The Church, influenced by Augustine, had in 431 condemned chiliastic interpretation of Apocalypse. So far as learned writers are concerned, it then lay dormant until it was adapted by Joachim and in the pseudo-Joachite writings. Foxe and his contemporaries took the Augustianian view, and Spenser seems to have shared it. He had no feeling for the earthly rule of the saints, for all that he

---

It is worth observing that the Woman of Revelation can be related, in terms of Johannine astrology, to the zodiacal Virgo (see Austin Farrer, *A Rebirth of Images*, 1949, pp. 202–3).

[26] M. Powicke, *The Reformation in England* (1961), p. 143.

[27] Norman Cohn, *The Pursuit of the Millennium* (1962), p. 209.

writes of the Golden Age; mutability will end only with the great Sabbath. There was to be a remarkable revival of millennial sentiment in the next century; but Spenser's learned contemporaries seem not to have given it much thought. There is, however, a more popular tradition, which we should no more ignore than we ignore the popular versions of the St. George legend. It is part of the material which the great epic includes and subdues to its purposes.

Here St. John joins forces with Sibylla, a witness of sufficient authority to be classed, in the *Dies irae*, with David. After Constantine, the Sibylline writings repeatedly identify the emperor with the warrior *fidelis et verax*. Thus, after the murder of Constans I, the *Tiburtina* foretold the reign of another Constans, who would bring back the Age of Gold, reunite the Empire—divided by the Arian Constantius—destroy heresy, and convert the Jews.[28] Thenceforth the Emperor of the Last Days was an imperial archetype to which heroes might strive to conform. His enemy, antichrist, was readily identified with the current pope.

Professor Cohn, from whose remarkable book I derive many of these facts, shows that certain social and economic conditions favour the rise of such eschatological fantasies. The aspirations of the medieval urban poor—whose social conditions were not so different from those obtaining in the great towns of England in Spenser's time—seem spontaneously to have assumed sibylline-apocalyptic form. The *prophetae*, leading hordes in quest of the holy city, called every large town Jerusalem and saw the Heavenly Jerusalem in the sky.[29] The whole terrible story—the popular emperor-cults, the massacres, the crazy anti-Semitism—testifies not only to the power, but also to the durability of these images. Cohn can explicitly connect the Brethren of the Free Spirit with modern Nietzschean primitivism, and explain the Nazi revival of a chiliast known as the Revolutionary of the Upper Rhine.[30] One other element in medieval millennialism I will mention now because it also has modern counterparts, to which I

[28] Norman Cohn, *The Pursuit of the Millennium* (1962), p. 16.
[29] See also Mircea Eliade, *The Myth of the Eternal Return*, trans. W. R. Trask, Bollingen Series, xlvi (1954), p. 8.
[30] Ruth Kestenberg-Gladstein argues that the expression 'Third Reich' is a translation of the Joachite *tertius status* (*Journal of the Warburg and Courtauld Institutes*, xviii, 1955, 245–95).

shall allude later: sexual naturalism, sometimes involving secret 'Adamite' modes of intercourse. We know that Spenser shared the official horror of sects suspected of libertinism—Anabaptists, for instance, and the Family of Love—but he cannot have been insensitive to this popular apocalyptism, so closely related to the images he himself was using. Whether he wrote of Apocalypse, of Arthur, or of the St. George all knew from folk-play and pageant, he was dealing with cultural and historical forces of much vaster scope than academic commentary on the Bible.

I mean that his Arthur is not merely a Tudor ancestor, not merely a mirror of that chivalry which preserves the virtues in a troubled time, but also a Tudor version of that ancient eschato-logical dream, the emperor of the Last Days. Arthur's relation to Charlemagne is well known,[31] and Charlemagne made possible the identification of the eschatological warrior with the emperor of the West, and united the myth of the returning emperor with that of the great champion against Islam. But perhaps we should also see behind him all those eschatological emperors, sometimes mere fanatics, sometimes real emperors assuming the role, some-times kings, like Louis VII of France, forced into it. And, of course, Arthur here does duty for the queen, whose sex is one cause of the extreme diversity of allegorical method in Spenser's poem. When we think of this aspect of Spenser's imperial myth, we might do worse, I think, than to remember the rough side of it: those marches of flagellants and paupers, those inspired impostors. These fantastic eschatological archetypes were not confined to poems; they could be expressed in action.

Now it must be confessed that Spenser *complies* with the arche-types. If the archetype of the hero insists that he fight a dragon, Spenser obliges. Mircea Eliade, arguing from many instances, calls this 'the conversion of event into myth',[32] part of the means by which 'archaic humanity . . . defended itself . . . against all the novelty and irreversibility of history'.[33] And perhaps all the apocalyptic material I have mentioned could be related to this archaic retreat from event into fantasies of perpetual renewal which defeat the terrors of history, or provide an escape from

[31] E. K. Chambers, *Arthur of Britain* (1927), p. 56. For the confusion of the coming of Arthur with the Second Coming of Christ, see Lord Raglan, *The Hero* (1949), p. 41.

[32] *Eternal Return*, p. 39.   [33] Ibid., p. 48.

history into myth. If Spenser sacrifices actuality, contemporaneity, to the archetypes; if, celebrating his Astraea, his *renovatio mundi*, he sinks out of history into sibylline fantasy; then he deserves all the reductive criticism he gets. But to believe that, one would have to forget the whole effort of imagination and reason which conferred upon archetypes complex interrelated meanings for that poem and for that time. The achievement of Spenser in that heroic First Book is not to have dived into the archetypes, but to have given them a context of Virgilian security—to have used them in the expression of an actual, unique, critical moment of a nation's culture and history. He looks backward only to achieve ways of registering the density of the central situation: the reign of Elizabeth. Iam *redit et Virgo*. He does not convert event into myth, but myth into event. His mood is acceptance; he welcomes history, not seeking to lose his own time in some transhistorical pattern. Such patterns of course exist; but only the unique and present moment can validate them. As to that moment, Apocalypse prophesied and history foreshadowed it; the mind of Europe—not merely that of Virgil and Constantine, Dante and Marsilius, Ariosto and Foxe, but of the people— expected its coming. Spenser celebrates the Elizabethan *renovatio* with something of Virgil's sober exaltation. It is a phase of no temporal cycle but a once-for-all historical event, like the Incarnation itself—however cruel the claims of Mutability and the certainty of suffering in the Last Days.

This acceptance of history—this reduction of dream to providential event—is very remote from the popular chiliasm, which, in Eliade's formula, amounts to a prohibition of history 'through a reintegration of human societies within the horizon of archetypes and their repetition'.[34] One might say that Spenser, like Virgil, celebrates the end of the need for such subterfuge: there will be no *ekpyrosis*, the city is eternal. The consequences are not all gay. At the end of Eliade's book the dilemma is projected as a dialogue between archaic and modern man; the passage bears a striking though unconscious resemblance to the *Mutabilitie* cantos, and ends with a choice between Christianity and despair which echoes Spenser's fragmentary last stanzas. To reject the archetypes is to live in the existential complexity of a hard world.

We have experienced in our own times a tendency for the

[34] *Eternal Return*, p. 153.

22

archetypes and cycles to reassert their attractiveness. Cohn records the rebirth of the medieval eschatological fantasies, for instance in Nietzscheanism and Nazism, where, among other symptoms, there was the kind of anti-Semitism which identifies the Jews as the demonic host which must be destroyed in the Last Days before the *tertius status* or thousand-year Reich. Eliade also notices this panic flight into archaism. In literature, as I have argued elsewhere, it is especially evident that the old patterns recur; Yeats, for example, has his archetypes and cycles, his eschatological fantasies of violence upon horses in the Last Days, his harsh masculine millennium of princes and viziers, his numerological speculations about the year 1927. (The bewilderment he felt in common with A. E., at the failure of that year to be sufficiently catastrophic has many medieval parallels.) Yeats speaks of his systematized fantasy, in a famous phrase, as an attempt 'to hold in a single thought reality and justice';[35] it is a saying much more relevant to *The Faerie Queene* than to *A Vision*, that headlong flight into archetype and cycle (though it applies to some of the poems). Joyce borrowed his cycles from Mme Blavatsky.[36] Henry Miller testifies to the continuance of these tendencies in the *avant-garde* of our own time.

I remember at this point the character Lebedev in Dostoevsky's *The Idiot*. In his view, the European railway system was a disastrous consequence of the fall of 'the star called Wormwood' (Rev. viii. 11). 'The whole spirit of the last few centuries, taken as a whole, sir, in its scientific and practical application, is perhaps really damned, sir!' But as Lebedev, comic expositor of antichrist, proceeds, the fun dies away. Things, we feel the message coming through, really are falling apart. In *War and Peace*, on the other hand, apocalyptic prophecy is only a whimsical trick of characterization. Now, in the books which pour out to prove that the great English poets were all 'adepts' of the 'tradition', we hear the voice of Lebedev, not that of Tolstoy. And in seminal works of modernist poetry, in *The Waste Land* and *The Cantos*, we find ourselves comfortably close to the archetypes.

This is a position very unfavourable to Spenser. His poem is not a decorated anteroom through which initiates pass on their

---

[35] *A Vision* (1961), p. 25.
[36] See Clive Hart, *Structure and Motif in Finnegan's Wake* (1962), especially cap. 2.

way to some inner chamber where they will find the archetypes, or Mr. Joseph Campbell's 'monomyth'.[37] Professor Frye, acting on his belief that 'myths explain the structural principles behind familiar literary facts',[38] provides a brief and brilliant account of *Faerie Queene* I. There is, I think, little to be said against it, considered as part of his classification of the world of literature in terms of a physics of archetype; but in so far as this is all he will say about the work, there is a huge, indeed fatal, reduction of the work's actual complexity, its 'presence'. My objection is very similar to that brought by Miss Helen Gardner against Dr. Austin Farrer's archetypal reduction of St. Mark's Gospel: she says that it 'evaporates St. Mark's sense of what we mean by historical reality'.[39] In Spenser this is equally a sense of the uniqueness of the moment celebrated; it acquires a timeless and unrepeatable quality, and the event transcends the archetype.

In the last part of this paper I will try to sharpen the contrast between Spenser's acceptance of history, and the modern rejection of it in favour of the archetypes, by returning to the themes of Apocalypse and their use by a single eminent modern author who was obsessed by them, namely D. H. Lawrence.

Lawrence's interest in the theme, as he observes in his last book, *Apocalypse*,[40] was lifelong. It began with the chapel hymns of his childhood. During the war the language of apocalypse colours his constant lamentation, which has a strong flavour of seventeenth-century puritanism: the world is in a rapid decline; it will be renewed; God's Englishmen will have much to do with the *renovatio* that follows the disasters of the Last Days.[41] In a letter to Bertrand Russell he is positive about the coming resurrection.[42] As for himself, he is 'drowning swiftly', he informs Lady Ottoline Morrell, 'under this last wave of time, this bursten flood'.[43] In the Irish Rebellion of 1916 he hears 'the passing bell of this present death'.[44]

I ought to explain that I am here concerned with what I consider

[37] *The Hero with a Thousand Faces* (1949); and see E. Honig, *Dark Conceit* (1960), especially cap. 3.
[38] *Anatomy of Criticism*, p. 215.
[39] *The Limits of Literary Criticism* (1956), p. 33.   [40] 1932.
[41] See the sermon-like letter to Lady Cynthia Asquith in *Collected Letters*, ed. H. T. Moore (1962), p. 342; and the predictions of doom in another to the same correspondent, p. 378.
[42] Ibid., p. 346.   [43] Ibid., p. 378.   [44] Ibid., p. 451.

to be the shabbiest aspect of Lawrence's mind, its dark side; and I hope I may ask you to assume that I have a proper respect for him when, in his true vein, he celebrates life and quickness. Yet, as Frederick Carter observes, occultism is 'an important and significant side of his genius',[45] however it may be glossed over by some expositors. And the fact is that he was more susceptible to than critical of ideas, especially if they were antiscientific; for instance, the passages on archaic sculpture in *Women in Love* are very early, very close to Hulme and Worringer. He moved easily in the current of such ideas. But at that very time he was writing to Gordon Campbell about Celtic and Latin symbolism in a way that makes it clear that he was becoming an adept of the archetypes.[46] Had he been able to bring himself to it, he would have found congenial some such brotherhood as the Golden Dawn. He studied Jane Harrison, Frazer, and G. R. S. Mead; he read in Theosophy: 'the esoteric doctrines are marvellously illuminating, historically',[47] he says, thinking probably of the cyclical doctrines. And from Mme Blavatsky and James Pryse and others, especially the painter Frederick Carter, he developed, in the early 1920's, a new interest in the occult meanings of Revelation.

Mme Blavatsky taught that the author of this work was 'a Jewish kabalist *pur sang*, with all the hatred inherited by him from his forefathers towards the Mysteries', and that this distinguished him from the Apostle John, whom Jesus himself had initiated into the 'Pythagoreo-Essenian mysteries'.[48] I suppose this is the key to Lawrence's theory that Revelation as we have it is deformed by successive Jewish and Christian sophistications, and that the original text described a Mystery ritual: he could have found support in G. R. S. Mead.[49] In the remaining years of his life the need to understand the ur-Apocalypse grew more and more urgent, and he sought the help of Carter.

Lawrence did not, in Carter's view, have a complete grasp of

---

[45] *D. H. Lawrence and the Body Mystical* (1932), p. 5.

[46] *Collected Letters*, pp. 302–4; see, for 'non-human' sculpture, an earlier letter to Campbell, p. 291.

[47] Ibid., p. 519.

[48] *Isis Unveiled* (1950), ii. 91, 147. The assumption of separate authorship is common; Farrer questions it in *Rebirth of Images*, pp. 22 ff.

[49] See, for example, *Fragments of a Forgotten Faith* (1900), p. 431. He also borrowed Dupuis's *Religion Universelle* from Carter; this takes Revelation to be an account of Mithraic initiations.

the occult material;[50] but he worked over it restlessly, and in a long letter to Carter in 1923 began to offer detailed interpretations of Revelation.[51] In 1924 he wrote some articles about it. His special interest in apocalyptic symbolism colours *The Plumed Serpent* (1926). He was much taken with such matters as the relation of the zodiac to the Great Year, and the heavenly macrocosm, the Man in the Sky, which is a planetary version of the seven seals of consciousness or sequence of ganglia.[52] He began to read commentaries on the book, including the commentary of Loisy,[53] and the authoritative two-volume work of Archdeacon Charles,[54] whom he derided for suggesting that the Kaiser was antichrist. The text of the work as it stands he hated, because it was 'Jewy' and 'chapel' and offered an underdog's view of religion; but behind the corruptions, the 'Judeo-Roman screen' concealing the myths, he had to admit that Revelation gave him what he could not find in Ezekiel or Daniel or the apocryphal apocalypses: an indispensable pagan document, a guide to the life of image-thinking, to 'a kind of Golden Age', as Carter says, 'his Hesperidean garden with girls and apples and the dragon all complete'.[55]

As early as 1923 he was saying that the Seals are the sympathetic ganglia and the vials 'the corresponding voluntary ganglia' of which Sagittarius stands for the 'most secret, and the most potent . . . the first and last'.[56] Revelation was, when you got down to the real Mystery ritual, a guide to 'emotional-passional knowledge'.[57] Eventually Lawrence gave the theme full treatment in *Apocalypse*.

Richard Aldington, in his preface to that book, affirms incorrectly that Lawrence really cared little for this kind of thing, but adds, rightly, that like the Etruscans, Revelation offered Lawrence another way of saying something he believed to be of

[50] *D. H. Lawrence and the Body Mystical*, pp. 17, 60.

[51] *Collected Letters*, pp. 744 ff.

[52] Learnt, perhaps, from James Pryse; the notion is fully expounded in his *A New Presentation of the Prometheus Unbound of Aischylos* (1925); see especially p. 100.   [53] *L'Apocalypse de Jean* (1923).

[54] R. H. Charles, *A Critical and Exegetical Commentary on Revelation of St. John* (1920).   [55] *D. H. Lawrence and the Body Mystical*, p. 56.

[56] *Collected Letters*, pp. 745–6. Lawrence at this stage was more certain of the truth than of the details of the sevenfold system, which he had learnt from the Vedantists. For a clear exposition, see Carter, pp. 20 ff.

[57] *Collected Letters*, p. 749.

extreme importance, something he had often tried to express before: this was the hostility between modern man and the Cosmos in the Christian era, and especially since the Reformation, when Protestants 'substituted the non-vital universe of force and mechanistic order, and the long slow death of the human being set in'.[58] So, under the veil of the Christian, power-envying, logic-loving sophistries of the present text, he found a mystery ritual, a *katabasis*, a Magna Mater split by the meddling editors into two: the woman clothed with the sun and the Scarlet Woman (for under the bad dispensation 'the colour of life becomes the colour of abomination').[59] The first half of Revelation is the great text of archaic sense-knowledge, a set of images associated not by logic but by intuition. Some such text he had been seeking from his earliest days; he told Jessie Chambers there would never be another Shakespeare because his was an integrated age, whereas 'Things are split up now';[60] and this is a view given its ultimate and most elaborate expression in the 'Introduction to his Paintings' of 1929.[61]

I do not deride *Apocalypse*—it is in some ways a beautiful performance, alive and thoroughly Lawrentian both in its assault on the modern failure to 'connect' and in its final celebration of 'quickness'. My purpose is historical description. In any case, as I have said, Lawrence was not unique in this flight from actuality into the primitive. But he was, perhaps, unique in the thoroughness with which he developed his views and gave himself to them. He sometimes behaved more like a medieval *propheta* than a man of his time, irresistible to disciples, willing to seek the New Jerusalem; even, like those tortured visionaries, advocating sexual practices of an archaic or Adamite character.[62]

---

[58] *Apocalypse*, p. 54.   [59] Ibid., p. 175.

[60] Quoted in H. T. Moore, *The Intelligent Heart* (1960), p. 94.

[61] In *A Propos of Lady Chatterley's Lover* (1962), pp. 13 ff.

[62] The Brethren of the Free Spirit claimed to possess 'modum specialem coeundi, non tamen contra naturam', identical with that of Adam in Paradise. According to Wilhelm Fränger's study of Bosch's connexion with this sect (*The Millennium of Hiéronymus Bosch*, 1952, p. 129) this *modus specialis* was the practice of *coitus reservatus*, which has persisted in later sects, and now enjoys the advocacy of Mr. Aldous Huxley. But in the 'Hell' part of Bosch's triptych there is, according to Fränger, an attack on rival sects in which the Adamite doctrines had degenerated, and he leaves us in little doubt as to the nature of their secret sexual practices.

This aspect of the matter suggests a final confrontation between the first book of *The Faerie Queene* and the only modern work of fiction known to me which also comments upon the state of the nation in terms of Apocalypse. This is *Lady Chatterley's Lover*, first published in 1928, when Lawrence was in the midst of his apocalyptic studies, though only recently made available for mature consideration. It is clear enough that the novel echoes those earlier Cyprianic prophecies of Lawrence about the rottenness and death of England, the world of the new logos, of 'mechanized greed'. 'Our old show will come flop', as Dukes puts it;[63] and Mellors himself, 'There's a bad time coming, boys, there's a bad time coming!'[64] It is equally clear that the famous passage about red trousers means little without reference to Lawrence on apocalyptic red.[65] (Lawrence could hardly be expected to believe that the value of symbols is determined by context, and he believed red to be the life-colour.) What is less obvious—yet it follows from his belief in using symbols that are not only archaic but veiled—is the direct relation between the amorous action of *Lady Chatterley* and Lawrence's exposition of the Opening of the Seals. These seals, he held, were the seven centres or gates of 'dynamic consciousness'. The old Adam dies in seven stages; at the climactic seventh he is also reborn.[66] Lawrence develops this idea in terms of initiation ritual: the opening of the last seal is compared to 'a stark flame . . . clothed anew' in Hades.[67] 'Then the final flame-point of the eternal self of a man emerges from hell';[68] and, finally, this moment is related to the emergence of the initiate from the goddess's temple, dazed and ecstatic. 'The cycle of individual initiation is fulfilled. . . . The initiate is dead, and alive again in a new body.'[69] Then there is a silence in heaven.

The seals stand for the ganglia, and this rite represents the 'awakening' of a human body; which, as expert witnesses asserted, is a theme in *Lady Chatterley's Lover*. Lady Chatterley dies into life. Indeed, the parallels between her association with Mellors and the Opening of the Seals are very close. There are seven significant sexual encounters in the novel (the eighth occurs during a brief reunion in London, out of series; there has been a pause in heaven). I am glad to have my counting confirmed by the

[63] Ed. of 1960, p. 77.   [64] *Lady Chatterley's Lover*, p. 315.
[65] Ibid., p. 229; *Apocalypse*, p. 175.   [66] *Apocalypse*, pp. 108–9.
[67] Ibid., p. 117.   [68] Ibid., pp. 119–20.   [69] Ibid., p. 124.

Warden of All Souls, who also observes that the seventh is 'for his purposes', as it is for mine, 'the significant episode'.[70] For reasons made clear by Warden Sparrow, this encounter is different from its predecessors: 'the reckless, shameless sensuality shook her to her foundations, stripped her to the very last, and made a different woman of her . . . burning the soul to tinder . . . the passion licked round her, consuming, and when the sensual flame of it pressed through her bowels and her breast, she really thought she was dying: yet a poignant, marvellous death'. She has the 'deep organic shame' burnt out, and reaches 'the core of the physical jungle'.[71] The act is anal, Adamite. All this is surely concerned with the seventh seal, the secret, potent Sagittarius, Governor of the organs of Generation, by means of which the sacred fire is stolen.[72] The astrology of this may be, to the eye of the profane, obscure. What is beyond doubt is that the seventh stage of the process represents the mystic descent into Hades.[73] Connie, like the postulant of the Mysteries, must die in this seventh stage. She dies into life, is initiated. The Mysteries, we remember, represented this rebirth by a sexual act. So the modern Dragon, the dirty-white Dragon of the modern Logos, as Lawrence calls it, which reduces the human consciousness and nervous system to a condition of death, is defeated. Connie, whom the vulgar may call a Scarlet Woman, is really the Woman clothed with the Sun.

In one respect, at any rate, Lawrence's method here resembles Spenser's; for it is surely obvious that although the allegory is a spiritual allegory, dealing with the regeneration of one woman, it is also historical, and prophesies, or prays for, the regeneration of England. England, he explains in *A Propos of Lady Chatterley's Lover*, knows only bad or 'white' sex, 'the nervous, personal, disintegrative sort'[74]—the sort, in fact, that Lady Chatterley knew

---

[70] 'Regina *v.* Penguin Books', *Encounter*, 101 (February 1962), pp. 35–43.

[71] *Lady Chatterley's Lover*, pp. 258–9.

[72] Pryse, *Prometheus*, pp. 100–1.

[73] Clearly explained by Carter, p. 21 and p. 31 (discussing the physiological facts).

[74] p. 115. One may note that Lawrence's preoccupation with 'bad' sex also echoes that of the Brethren of the Free Spirit. Lawrence would have understood Fränger's explanation of the man buried upside down to his waist in Bosch's 'Hell' (*The Millennium of Hieronymus Bosch*, p. 119). The triptych has many other emblems of sterile or egotistic sexuality, consequence of the

before she met Mellors. 'We can have no hope of the regeneration of England from such sort of sex. . . . And the other, the warm blood-sex that establishes the living and revitalizing connexion between man and woman, how are we to get that back? I don't know. Yet get it back we must . . . or we are lost.' And he goes on to speak of this necessary regeneration of England, the religious restoration of 'the ancient seven-cycle' and so on.[75] The two ideas—of personal and national rebirth—melt into each other, in the commentary as in the novel itself. Connie is England and Mellors is Lawrence's Arthur, emperor of the Last Days.

Quoting a passage from *Apocalypse* on the old familiar theme— 'We are unnaturally resisting our connection with the cosmos, etc.'—Helen Corke remarks: 'The passage changes into the singular as I read it.'[76] This is shrewd; and it must count against Lawrence in this comparison that his apocalyptic researches and applications are secret, 'isolate' to use a favourite word of his, and very remote from the main goings-on of the world. A well-known observation of Mr. Eliot's that 'a man does not join himself with the Universe so long as he has anything else to join himself with',[77] applies closely to Lawrence. But we must not forget that in some ways, as I suggested earlier, Lawrence simply develops *à outrance* tendencies of some importance in the literary culture not only of his own time but of ours. He is not alone in that garden of archetypes; not only poets but even as Miss Gardner observed, theologians are to be found there. For example, in his study of Mark, Dr. Farrer treats Revelation[78] very much in the fashion reprehended by Miss Gardner, and asks us to think of the book as made up of images which 'live the life of images, not of concepts' and obey 'imagery laws', not 'the principles of conceptual system'—such images being 'the stuff of revelation' with which theology and metaphysics meddle in vain; they are sealed within the horizon of archetypes, inaccessible to reason.[79] Such a view certainly seems to entail a total rejection of history, and Lawrence would have found it more to his taste than

divorce of 'spirit and instinct' which 'causes a withering of the vegetation forces and an over-development of the brain' (Fränger, p. 101).

[75] Pp. 116–17. [76] *Lawrence and Apocalypse* (1933), pp. 127–8.
[77] *Selected Essays* (1932), p. 131.
[78] *The Rebirth of Images* (1949).
[79] *The Glass of Vision* (1948), pp. 45, 51.

Archdeacon Charles. Even in *Lady Chatterley*, where it has its place, history becomes part of a private myth. This is despair and flight and unreason; Spenser is hope, acceptance, and intellect.

It is clear, then, that a Lawrentian sacrifice of *presence* to *type* is no way to approach *The Faerie Queene*. Hence we mistakenly assume that the poem is allegorical in the sense of superficial, or, in uprooting the archetypes, we destroy its texture. Lawrence himself, as it happens, mentions *Faerie Queene* I at the beginning of *Apocalypse*. 'I hated, even as a child, allegory: people having the names of mere qualities, like this somebody on a white horse, called "Faithful and True". . . . When as a small boy I learned from Euclid that "The whole is greater than the part", I immediately knew that that solved the problem of allegory for me. A man is more than mere Faithfulness and Truth. . . . Though as a young man I almost loved Spenser and his *Faerie Queene*, I had to gulp at his allegory.'[80] This has very little to do with Spenser; but we may be sure that had Lawrence studied *The Faerie Queene* in detail it would have been by some method akin to that which he used on Revelation, a peeling away of Christian and imperial sophistications to reach the valuable mystery beneath. Such is Lawrence's horror of allegory that he cannot bring himself to say right out what the symbols of *Apocalypse* mean, though in fact they had rather precise significance for him: 'Symbols mean something: yet they mean something different to every man. Fix the meaning of the symbol, and you have fallen into the commonplace of allegory.'[81] Yet this is the place where he needs to show that 'The book . . . of seven seals . . . is the body of man'.[82]

The warrior 'faithfull true' means more in Spenser than Lawrence could conceive; and in making of him what he did, Spenser assumed that men can keep their heads above the tide of time, and find in the present moment senses which are enriched, but not absorbed, by the ancient images. We need a better understanding of this sober and confident humanity, of the methods by which Spenser provided contexts in which the archetypes find a present meaning. Such an understanding requires a double effort—we must study the causes of Spenser's exclusion from our serious reading as well as the texts and contexts of *The Faerie Queene*

[80] *Apocalypse*, p. 7.   [81] Ibid., p. 109.   [82] Ibid., p. 108.

itself. Since I have used Lawrence as typical of beliefs and attitudes I deplore, I may well end with one sentence in *Apocalypse* which my argument endorses: 'The Apocalypse is still a book to conjure with.'[83] Perhaps the spirit of Spenser will one day consent to be called.

[83] *Apocalypse*, p. 297.

2

'THE FAERIE QUEENE', I AND V[1]

To speak of the 'world' of a particular poet is to use a figure no one will find unfamiliar. It is a question of the natural uniformity, cohesion and interrelation of a body of work, however various, however divided into continents and elements. It is to assert that in Wordsworth, for example, there is a force universally at work, like gravity. And indeed the study of such worlds has sometimes been held to be analogous to physics. It would seem, on the face of it, that to make such a world (and poets have not scrupled to claim that they imitated God in doing so) is the labour of a major poet. For one thing, there is a requirement of size; a world has bulk before it has this kind of complexity. There is also a requirement of order and continuity, qualities one senses in a Shakespeare as well as in a Dante or a Milton, in the artist who seems to have no explicit philosophical or theological programme as well as in the poet whom we think of as in some way 'committed'.

Literate persons bring to such worlds certain expectations. These are the product of civilized conversation, of allusions encountered in literary comment. But the first thing that happens when they reach the new world is that these expectations are falsified and have to be dismantled. It is something like the experience Keats describes in his sonnet on Homer. The unaffected reader of Milton has a similar experience; he approaches Eden with certain expectations of severity and is disarmed by pleasure and human beauty, two features often omitted from maps of Milton. This dismantling process tends to be more violent with Spenser than with almost anybody else, partly because his poem is less

[1] See Preface.

well known than *Paradise Lost* or *Hamlet*, even to people who admire it. It is long, unfinished, and darkly related to the learning
and images of an age fundamentally strange to us. It is true that
there is an abundance of scholarly guidance to be had; but in the
end that also creates, as guides to public monuments usually do,
expectations not always to be exactly realized. Furthermore, the
guide one employs will always omit to mention what to the un-
conditioned eye may seem very striking features, so that there are
not only unattained but unexpected experiences.

What I have now to say takes issue with some learned and acute
modern guides to Spenser; but I say it not in a spirit of conten-
tion, but with proper gratitude for the help I have accepted from
them. Spenser is very diverse, and lends support to many generali-
zations which seem flatly counter to one another. Thus, as everybody knows, *The Faerie Queene* fluctuates from a philosophical
extreme—as in The Garden of Adonis, and the Mutability Cantos
—to relatively naïve allegory such as the House of Alma. It
contains passages—such as Guyon's stay in the Cave of Mammon,
or Britomart's in the Church of Isis—which seem to deal with
high matters, but deliberately conceal their full meaning; yet it
also contains transparent historical allusions to the trial of Mary
Queen of Scots and the campaigns in the Netherlands. Its mood
varies from the apocalyptic in Book I to the pastoral in Book VI.
Sometimes, as with Florimel, one senses the need to complete
Spenser's allegory for him, and sometimes one feels that he has
for the time being almost forgotten about it; yet there are other
times when one wonders at the density of meanings the fiction
is made to bear. Readers of Spenser's own epoch seem to have
enjoyed the allusions to great men of the age as well as the moral
allegories;[2] but later there was some danger of his sinking under
the explanations of scholars, and in recent years there has been
a noticeable trend towards simplicity of interpretation.

Obviously, we should not cumber his world with our own
planetary ingenuities; but I think this process has gone too far.
I shall now briefly characterize some of these simplifications, and
then examine some aspects of the poem which seem to me to
remain stubbornly what the simplifiers do not wish them to be.

At the beginning of this century it was assumed by all who

[2] See A. D. S. Fowler, 'Oxford and London Marginalia to *The Faerie
Queene*', *Notes and Queries*, ccvi (1961), 416-19.

considered Spenser's more philosophical passages that he knew Plato's dialogues, and that he may have interested himself in Renaissance Neo-Platonism. Later there came a different under-standing; philosophical sources were found in Lucretius, in Empedocles, in 'old religious cults'. And it became a common-place of scholarship that Spenser could be illuminated by reference to the learning of Ficino, Benivieni, or Bruno.[3]

The picture of Spenser as a very learned man is not in itself absurd, since he understood that the heroic poet should be a 'curious and universal scholar'. But perhaps only an unfamiliarity with the conditions of Renaissance scholarship could have per-mitted anyone to imagine him to be systematically acquisitive of learning. Also there was prevalent an oversimple view of the Renaissance as a clean new start, which implied a failure to understand the extent to which medieval syntheses—including much Aristotle and Plato which scholars have misguidedly traced back to the original—persisted in the learning of Spenser's time. Thus the Garden of Adonis, which has attracted much speculation, possibly contains little philosophy that would have surprised an educated reader in any age between that of Spenser and that of Boethius. Not surprisingly there has been a reaction, and such influential books as those of W. L. Renwick (1925) and C. S. Lewis (1936) presented a more credible philosopher-poet, Lewis even labelling him, in a famous passage, 'homely' and 'churchwardenly'.[4] Whether or no we accept this provocative formula, it remains true that Spenser used compendia, handbooks of iconography and so on; that he learnt from popular festivals; and that it would have been harder than used to be supposed to catch him working with an ancient classic open before him.

Yet we should not make the mistake of thinking that what

[3] Robert Ellrodt, *Neoplatonism in Spenser* (1961)—a book which argues admirably for a Spenser simplified philosophically by the elimination of Renaissance Neoplatonism from *The Faerie Queene*—opens with an account of this development.

[4] *The Allegory of Love* (1936; references to edition of 1958). 'Popular, homely, patriotic' (p. 311) is Lewis's description of the allegory of Book I. 'We have long looked', he says, 'for the origins of *The Faerie Queene* in Re-naissance palaces and Platonic Academies, and forgotten that it has humbler origins in the Lord Mayor's Show, the chap-book, the bedtime story, the family Bible, and the village church' (p. 312). 'Churchwardenly', 'honest', 'domestic', belong to a list of epithets on p. 321.

seems exotic or far-fetched to us necessarily seemed so to Spenser. It is enough, perhaps, to remind ourselves of the great differences between his map of knowledge and ours—to remember, for instance, the continuing importance of astrology; the over-riding authority of theology; and a view of classical antiquity which seems to us simply fantastic. Spenser's mind was trained in forms of knowledge alien to us, and habituated to large symbolic systems of a kind which, when we read of them in Huizinga's *The Waning of the Middle Ages*, are likely to strike us as almost absurdly frivolous. Yet he was very serious in his wish to 'make it new' —'it' being the sum of knowledge as it appeared to an Englishman at what seemed to be a great crisis of world history. It is hard for us to remember that Spenser served a queen whom he regarded as technically an empress, and whose accession was regularly thought of as the sounding of the seventh trumpet in the Book of Revelation.[5] Spenser saw this world as a vast infolded, mutually relevant structure, as inclusive as the Freudian dream; but he also saw it as disconnected, decaying, mutable, disorderly. We should expect to find his mind, especially when he deals with systematic ideas of order, very strange to us; and we should not easily allow this strangeness to be lost in learned simplifications.

I turn now to a second device for reducing the proportion of relatively inaccessible meaning in *The Faerie Queene*. This is to minimize the importance of a characteristic which had certainly appealed to Spenser's contemporaries, namely the element of historical allegory. Dryden thought that each of Spenser's knights represented an Elizabethan courtier; even Upton, who in his way knew so much more about *The Faerie Queene* than we do, stressed the historical allegory and elaborately explained allusions to Elizabethan history. This way of reading Spenser persisted and, perhaps, reached its climax in the work of Lilian Winstanley half a century ago. But it was dealt a blow from which it has not recovered at the hands of the great American Spenserian, Edwin Greenlaw, in his book *Studies in Spenser's Historical Allegory* (1932).

Greenlaw's object is, broadly, to subordinate historical to ethical allegory. Historical allegory, he says, has reference principally to general topics; it refers to specific persons only moment-

---

[5] This apocalyptic strain persisted into the next reign in the posthumous portraits of Elizabeth; see Roy C. Strong, *Portraits of Queen Elizabeth I* (1963). And see T. Brightman, *The Revelation of St. John Illustrated* (1616), pp. 490 f.

arily and with no high degree of organization. This is now, I think, the received opinion, and it certainly makes sense to relieve Spenser of barrenly ingenious commentary relating his poem to obscure, forgotten, political intrigues. But if we apply Greenlaw's criteria indiscriminately we are likely to be left with a Spenser drained of that historical urgency which seems to be one of his most remarkable characteristics; it is the adhesive which binds the dream image to immediate reality. And certainly one consequence of the modern simplification of Spenser has been to loosen the bond between his great First Book and an actual world by denying the complexity of his historical allegory.

Finally, there is a third and very sophisticated mode of simplification, and this we can represent by reference to two critics, Mr. A. C. Hamilton in his *The Structure of Allegory in the Faerie Queene* (1961) and Mr. Graham Hough in his *Preface to the Faerie Queene* (1962). Mr. Hamilton is an enemy of 'hidden allegorical significance', at any rate in Spenser, though of course he knows how much Renaissance critical theory has to say about 'dark conceits'. He suggests that we have now established 'a fatal dichotomy' between poet and thinker, and that the despised old romantic habit of reading the poem for the beauties of its surface was no more harmful than the modern way of looking straight through to the emblematical puzzles beneath. We have, he argues, made the poem a kind of Duessa 'whose borrowed beauty disguises her reality'. Or, ignoring the fiction, we seek historical allusion, treating Book I, for example, as a concealed history of the English Reformation; or we devise some 'moral reading yielding platitudes which the poet need never have laboured to conceal'. Offering some instances of this, he asks, 'Is this the morality which More found divine? . . . The "conceit as passing all conceit?" ' And he proposes his 'radical reorientation': by concentrating upon the fiction—the image—he will show that the poem is not like Duessa but like Una, who 'did seem such, as she was'. He finds support for his policy of subordinating all allegorical meanings to the literal in some remarks of Sidney, and asks us to see the moral senses not as kernels of which the fiction is the shell, but as the expanding petals of a multifoliate rose—the meaning 'expanding from a clear centre'.[6]

[6] A. C. Hamilton, *The Structure of Allegory in The Faerie Queene* (1961), pp. 5, 7, 10, 11, 17.

Mr. Hamilton shows much skill and sensibility in developing a reading along these lines. But the method, attractive as it sounds, will not serve. We lose too much. Not that I deny the pre-eminence of the literal meaning, which Aquinas himself would have accepted; only it does not mean quite what Mr. Hamilton thinks. The praise of Henry More, for example, which was not in the least extravagant, depended upon a well established view that images could combine old truths to make a new one; the whole was greater than its parts, and if you broke down the 'icon' into its original constituents the parts together would have less meaning than the whole icon. The pleasure and instruction, you may say, is double: it is the intellectual delight of breaking down the icon and the intuitive benefit of perceiving its global meaning. In short, although we may welcome the figure of the multifoliate rose, we still need the idea of the kernel and the shell, or of the fiction as a means of concealment: it will not, in Spenser, be as perversely opaque as it is in Chapman, but it may well be as elaborate as the sixth book of Aeneid, as read by Renaissance mythographers.

What you find under the surface depends upon your learning and penetration. Behind the Garden of Adonis are philosophic constituents; behind the First Book, constituents of world history; behind the Fifth Book and especially the elaborate dream of Brito-mart, high matters of imperial and national legal theory. I want, so far as it is possible to have the best of both worlds, to enjoy the fiction much as Mr. Hamilton does, but also to deny his conten-tion that the 'universal reference prevents our translating events into historical terms'. Thus I am sure that Book V is impoverished if the Church of Isis passage is treated simply as a figurative render-ing of the love-relationship of Artegall and Britomart; and this is how Mr. Hamilton, following a note in A. S. P. Woodhouse's famous essay, would have us read it.[7]

Mr. Hough tries, in his very agreeable book, to satisfy the con-testants in his kind of quarrel by arguing that there are interme-diate stages in literature between complete 'realism' and naïve allegory; Shakespeare is equidistant between these extremes, his magic fully absorbing his theme so that one might speak of an 'incarnation'. Nobody, I suppose, using Mr. Hough's chart,

[7] 'Nature and Grace in The Faerie Queene', E.L.H., xvi (1949), 216, n. 42.

would care to put Spenser—so far as the epic poem is concerned—anywhere save where he puts him, between Shakespeare and 'naïve' allegory, as a maker of 'poetic structures with various degrees of allegorical explicitness'. And Mr. Hough's insistence that the allegory is 'relaxed and intermittent' ought to remind us of the constantly varying 'thickness' of Spenser's thematic meanings. But I do not think he serves us so well in asking us to depend in our reading upon our 'general sense' of how 'mythical poetry' works.[8] *The Faerie Queene* is an epic and so historical; we simply do not have an instinct which enables us to participate in historical myths relating to the religious, political and dynastic situations of Spenser's day. And our feeling for 'mythical poetry' tells us nothing relevant to the juristic imperialism of his Church of Isis.

I have respect for both of these books; each in its way says that Spenser is a great poet who can mean much to modern readers; and I have given only a very partial account of them. But I quarrel with them, as with the others, because they habitually ignore what I think may be the peculiar strength of Spenser. Probably no other English poet has ever achieved so remarkable a *summa* as his. And it seems to me that we must not modernize him at the cost of forgetting this. 'Poetry is the scholar's art'. We should be glad to find in *The Faerie Queene* not only the significances of dream, but that fantastic cobweb of conscious correspondences, running over all the interlinked systems of knowledge, which a scholar-poet and a courtier might be expected to produce. Leaving out of account the philosophical simplification I began with, I intend now to speak of two parts of the poem: the historical allegory of Book I, and the allegory of justice in two parts of Book V. In each case, I myself find that the hidden meanings contribute to the delight of the fiction, because some of this delight arises from recognition of the writer's complex intent. And I do not think it does the dreamlike narrative any harm to include in it elements recognizable by conscious analysis.

The First Book of *The Faerie Queene* is well known to be apocalyptic, in the sense that it presents a version of world history founded rather closely upon the English Protestant interpretation of the Book of Revelation. I have elsewhere[9] tried to explain how

---

[8] Graham Hough, *A Preface to The Faerie Queene* (1962), p. 107.

[9] In Chapter 1, above.

the force of the book—as I see it—stems from a peculiarly subtle and active interplay of actual history with apocalyptic-sibylline prophecy. In its more political aspect, Book I is a celebration of the part of Elizabeth Tudor, the Protestant Empress, in the workings of providence. This a writer sufficiently sympathetic to Spenser—Milton, for example—would take in at a glance; and nothing in Milton is more Spenserian than the apocalyptic exhortations to England in the pamphlets *On Reformation* and *Areopagitica*, with their emphasis on God's manner of dealing with the nations, and the special role chosen for his Englishmen in the overthrow of antichrist. The Puritan commentators on Revelation, especially Bullinger and Bale, had long insisted upon the degree to which the text foretold the history of the Church, now reaching a climax; and for the better part of a century English opinion accepted Foxe's reading of ecclesiastical history as prefigured in the flight of the woman clothed with the sun—the true catholic church —into a wilderness from which, after forty-two months, she returns to her own as the Church of England. Discussing elsewhere the profusion of references to Revelation in Spenser's text, I expressed some surprise that the very scholars who, by the citation of patristic and Reformist commentaries, have made these identifications so sure, should, under the inhibition of Greenlaw, have forborne to study them in their obvious historical dimension. The text of *The Faerie Queene*, Book I is admittedly studded with the prophetic emblems of Revelation; it admittedly suggests that the Elizabethan settlement—the *renovatio mundi* brought by the Phoenix, the Astraean Elizabeth—fulfils the plan of history laid down in the Bible. Would it not seem likely that the narrative should allude to the history of the Church in the wilderness—that the story of Una and Duessa should, like Foxe's history of the Church, demonstrate the culmination of the divine plan in Elizabeth's accession?

It is clear that the limited series of allusions admitted by most editors to the course of English Reform under Henry VIII and Edward VI would not be enough for the apocalyptic-historical purpose Spenser announces with his imagery from Revelation. If you once identify the English with the primitive Catholic Church, you begin its history, as Jewel said, 'after the first creation of the world'.[10] After that, Joseph of Arimathaea brought Eastern

[10] John Jewel, *Works* (Parker Society, 1848), iii. 79.

Christianity to England; later there was a Christian king, Lucius; hence the early splendours and purity of the English Church, and the historic English independence of Rome and the 'ten-horned beast' or Latin Empire, impaired only by the treachery of Hildebrand and his successors.[11] The imperial claims of Elizabeth, however, defined the papal power and were traced back to Constantine.

Now the celebration in image and allegory of the Foxian version of history is not a remote and learned fancy; just as *The Faerie Queene* had her 'yearly solemne feaste', so had Elizabeth. Her Accession day (17 November) was celebrated with increasing fervour, especially after the Armada, so that the Papists called it blasphemous and a parody of the adoration of the Virgin. Mr. Roy C. Strong has well surveyed the main themes of sermon, tract, ballad and entertainment relating to this feast.[12] Elizabeth is *rarissima Phoenix, ultima Astraea*, the renewer of the Church and faithful true opponent of antichrist. She has undone the work of the wicked popes who usurped the emperor's power and rights; she inherits both Lucius' recognized position as God's vicar, and the imperial power of Constantine and Justinian. Antichrist, the murderous sorcerers of the see of Rome, stands finally exposed. The queen is the defender of the true Church in an evil world. In a sense she *is* that Church. When Mr. Strong's preacher speaks of her as the sun shedding beams of religion, he is remembering 'the woman clothed with the sun', who turns into the Una of whose sunshiny face Spenser speaks, 'glistening euery way about the light of the euerlasting Gospel'.[13] As Mr. Strong observes, 'the complexities of eschatological and imperial theory are never far away from the Accession Day themes'.[14] Foxe's book, available with the Bible in every church, had become part of the body of patriotic thought, a textbook of English imperialism.

Now 'homely Spenser' made, in the First Book of his poem, an epic of these very Accession Day themes, and he too chains up Foxe beside the Bible. An appeal to history was a prerequisite not only of the claims of the Catholic Church of England to antiquity

[11] John Napier, *A Plaine Discovery of the Whole Revelation* (1593), p. 36.
[12] 'The Popular Celebration of the Accession Day of Queen Elizabeth I', *Journal of the Warburg and Courtauld Institutes*, xxi (1958), 86–103.
[13] M. Augustine Marlorat, *A catholike exposition upon the Revelation of Saint John* (1574), p. 167 verso.   [14] Strong, 'Accession Day', 101.

and purity, but also of the queen's claim to possess imperial power over the bishops. *The Faerie Queene* may be mythical poetry; but its myths are the myths of English polity in the fifteen-eighties and nineties. Greenlaw himself observed that the use of Arthurian legend was for the Elizabethans not a Tennysonian archaism, but an argument from antiquity. The Elizabethans in fact saw Arthur's not as Malory's world, but as a unified Britain, and Arthur himself as king of the whole island, which, under the diadem of Constantine, was an empire according to *Leges Anglorum*.[15] Greenlaw observed also that it was commonplace in popular pageants to present the queen as True Religion; and that Spenser's poem reflects the view that her greatest service was the establishment of true religion in England.[16] We are speaking of an age that venerated Foxe—the age of Archbishop Parker, of Sandys, of a queen who herself insisted upon her role as head of a church founded by Joseph of Arimathaea and a State that inherited the powers of the Constantinian Empire. Indeed she had, the claim ran, reunited the two.[17] Spenser could not avoid allusion to the whole of church history according to Foxe in describing the struggle between Una and antichrist.

Earlier interpretations of this kind—such as those of Scott and Keightley—have been ignored or coldly dismissed by Spenser's modern editors.[18] I think Scott and Keightley were wrong in detail, since they did not look at the history of the church through the medium of Elizabethan propaganda; but they had the right instinct. Any apologist of the Elizabethan settlement was obliged to produce historical arguments, and Spenser, as an allegorical poet, did so by means of hidden meanings in his fiction.

No one is in much doubt about the relationship of Una and Duessa. Una is pure religion, which came to England direct from the East: she is descended from 'ancient Kings and Queenes, that had of yore | Their scepters stretcht from East to Westerne shore' (I. i. 5). Duessa, on the other hand, claims descent only from an

[15] See E. Kantorowicz, *The King's Two Bodies* (1957), p. 346.

[16] E. Greenlaw, *Studies in Spenser's Historical Allegory* (1932), cap. I.

[17] Thus the queen is shown in portraits not only as wearing the imperial diadem and trampling on the Pope (so revenging the indignity of Frederick Barbarossa) but also as the woman clothed with the sun, or True Church. See Roy C. Strong (p. 126, n. 1 *supra*).

[18] See *The Works of Spenser: a Variorum Edition*, ed. E. Greenlaw, C. G. Osgood, F. M. Padelford, and R. Heffner, i (1932), 450.

Emperor 'that the wide West under his rule has | And high hath set his throne, where *Tiberis* doth pas' (I. ii. 22). Her false description of her father as emperor alludes to papal usurpations on the imperial power, a constant source of Protestant complaint. As Miss Frances Yates rightly says, Duessa and Una 'symbolize the story of impure papal religion and pure imperial religion'.[19] The success of the Tudors against the papacy is a restoration of Una, of imperial rights over the *sacerdotium*. The emperor, or empress, is, as Jewel says,[20] the Pope's lord and master; Rome is not directly descended, he adds, from the primitive Eastern church, whereas the reformed Church of England can make exactly this claim. Duessa is in fact a representative of a religion not only anti-christian but also anti-imperialist, anti-universalist. Duessa's very name accuses her of schism.

The Red Cross Knight has dealings with both ladies, appearing first with Una in his capacity of defender of the true faith. It is part of the dreamshift technique of the poem that he begins thus, and as *miles Christi*, to end as the knight *fidelis et verax* or Christ himself (whose bride Una is the Church)—after a career of error typical of the human pilgrimage and also of the history of England. In confronting him with Error in the opening Canto, Spenser fulfils a multiple purpose, having in mind not only Christ's victory over sin in the wilderness, but Una's great enemy, heresy, against which the early English Church protected her. Scott thought Error stood for Arianism; it probably corresponds more generally to that series of heresies which Bale associates with the opening of the second and third apocalyptic seals: Sabellianism, Nestorianism, Manichaeism, as well as Arianism.[21] Modern heresy, for which Jewel firmly places the responsibility on Rome, is the brood of these earlier errors. The locusts of stanza xiv derive, as Upton pointed out, from Revelation ix. 7, and were traditionally associated with heretical teaching—a point made by that herald of reform, Matthew of Paris, whom Foxe quotes approvingly.[22] The association is also remembered by Bale.[23] The

[19] 'Queen Elizabeth as Astraea', *Journal of the Warburg and Courtauld Institutes*, x (1948), 68.   [20] Jewel, *Works*, iii, 76, 85–86.
[21] John Bale, *The Image of Both Churches*, *Select Works*, ed. Christmas (Parker Society, 1849), pp. 322 ff.
[22] *Acts and Monuments of the Church*, ed. M. H. Seymour (1838), p. 221.
[23] Bale, *Image of Both Churches*, p. 352.

enemies of Una had existed as long as there had been a Roman antichrist; Red Cross is her champion, since God had entrusted her, as Milton thought it natural, to 'his Englishmen'. The victory of Constantine, which made possible the Christian Empire, was achieved, according to Foxe, with the aid of British troops; he thought it represented the end of 294 years since the Passion, and the binding of Satan for a thousand years. Constantine was himself of course British, born of St. Helena at York.

Archimago, as is generally agreed, corresponds to the false prophet and the beast from the land, and so to antichrist. But it is worth observing that Spenser gives him a name which suggests that he is a magician; and this is a charge incessantly made against popes by Foxe and many others. Marlorat's compendious commentary on Revelation, published in 1574, says, on Rev. xiii. 15 (where the dragon seeks by supernatural means to destroy the woman clothed with the sun), that popes were often 'nigromancers'. He cites Cardinal Buno, who, in a life of Gregory VII, 'writeth that many obtained the Popedom by divelish arts', especially Sylvester II, John XVIII, John XX, Benedict VIII, and Benedict IX. Gregory VII himself, 'erst called Hildebrand', was a 'notable nigromancer, who with the shaking of his sleeues woulde make as it were sparks of fire to flye abroad as often as he liked'.[24] Boniface VII and VIII, and most of the sixteenth-century popes, are also on the list. Napier the mathematician, in his commentary of 1593, finds allusion to popish necromancy in the Sibylline books, and says on the evidence of 'Platina, the Popes own secretarie', that there have been twenty-two 'Necromantick Popes and . . . eight Atheists'.[25]

Sylvester II, who is frequently said to have sold his soul to the devil, was in fact a man of learning, a mathematician, and one who had a good try at reconciling papacy with empire; but doubtless the special odium reserved to him may be accounted for by his having been Pope in A.D. 1000, when according to some accounts (not Foxe's) Satan was loosed after a thousand years of bondage. The other Pope most persistently charged with necromancy is Gregory VII, who was specially detested because, having gained authority in England through the Conqueror, he began that

[24] Marlorat, op. cit., p. 199 recto.
[25] Napier, *Plaine Discovery*, Appendix (unpaginated). See also Jewel, *Works*, ii, 85.

interference with English government which disfigured so many subsequent reigns, notably those of Henry II (who claimed judicial authority over the clergy) and John. Foxe singles him out as the Pope who started the encroachment on the rights of the temporal governor 'whereby the Pope was brought to his full pride and perfection of power in the fourteenth century'.[26] I have little doubt that Spenser was thinking chiefly of Hildebrand when he made Archimago a master of magic arts and described his plots against Red Cross.

We hear of Archimago's arts in xxxvi, and in xlviii he produces a succubus, a false church 'most like that virgin true' until her real nature is revealed. She deceives Red Cross with her claim to be *una sancta ecclesia*, and makes outrageous demands on his body. Spenser may not have been thinking only of the troubles of the eleventh to the fourteenth century; the Synod of Whitby, where, according to Foxe,[27] Wilfrid first led England into the power of Rome, may also have been in his mind. But Gregory VII, who first claimed control of both the swords, ecclesiastical and temporal,[28] and so usurped the power of the emperor (Foxe has a woodcut illustrating the incident of Henry IV waiting Hildebrand's pleasure in the snow), was the greatest papal villain. The powers resigned by Henry IV and later by Barbarossa, upon whose neck Alexander III set his foot, were recovered and refurbished by Spenser's empress, a point upon which Jewel is explicit.[29] So Spenser allows Archimago to conjure up the demonic church which tried to rule the world, and which the British Tudors were to exorcise. But the disgrace of Red Cross, which begins here, represents the long misery of the English Church from the time of Gregory VII until the first stirrings of reformation with Wyclif.

Other crucial events in the Anglican version of church history are reflected in Spenser's narrative. The presumptions of Boniface III coincided with the rise of Islam, and a monk called Sergius gave aid and comfort to these new enemies. The Turks were part of antichrist, said Foxe,[30] taking the contemporary threat

[26] *Acts and Monuments*, p. 112.   [27] Ibid., p. 663.
[28] Ibid., p. 112.   [29] *Works*, iii, 75, 76, 99, 116.
[30] *Acts and Monuments*, p. 391. Foxe does not name Sergius, but see Wyclif, *De pontificium Romanorum Schismate, Select Works*, ed. Arnold (1869–71), iii. 245, and E. L. Tuveson, *Millennium and Utopia* (1949), p. 23.

from this quarter to be the loosing of the angels of the river Euphrates (Rev. xvi. 12); it reached its present form and strength at the end of the thirteenth century, just when papal power was greatest. Now Spenser has this, or something very like it, in mind when he makes Sansfoy an ally of Archimago. Red Cross first meets Duessa in the company of the infidel Sansfoy (ii. 13). She is adorned with a Persian mitre which, together with the bells and flounces of her 'wanton palfry', signify the union of popish flummery and oriental presumption. Sansfoy is the pagan anti-christ, defeated by Red Cross as Arthur defeated the pagan Saxons and the crusades the Saracens. I do not say he does not, with his brothers, make a triad opposed to that of the Theological Virtues; the readings are perfectly consistent with one another. Sansloy and Sansjoy are also aspects of antichrist and paganism. It all goes back to Boniface and the Turks—even, perhaps, Duessa's lie about her past when she claims[31] to have been betrothed to a great prince who was murdered, which might be an allusion to the establishment by Boniface III of the puppet emperor Phocas.

There is surely reason to suppose that Spenser would think along these lines. Let me, to avoid tedium, spare analysis of the Fraelissa and Fradubio episode, clearly another allegory of the wrong choice of faith, and pass on to the story of Kirkrapine, Abessa and Corceca. Corceca is obviously blind devotion. Abessa, as Sr. Mary R. Falls established,[32] is not an abbess but absenteeism, from *abesse*. The main difficulty is with Kirkrapine. I agree with Sr. Mary Falls that he cannot refer to the evils of monasticism; she argues, with some force, that the reference to church-robbing is more likely to apply to the behaviour of English bishops and courtiers after the Reformation. She cites much evidence, and more could be adduced. Sandys, for example (though himself not innocent of the charges he brings against others), asked the queen to end the abuses of the 'surveyors'[33] 'that trot from one diocese to another, prying into churches. The pretence is reformation; but the practice is deformation. They reform not offences, but for money grant licences to offend.' And he asks the queen—'our most mild Moses'—to stay the hand of these 'church-robbers'.

[31] *F. Q.*, II. ii. 23.
[32] 'Spenser's Kirkrapine and the Elizabethans', *Studies in Philology*, i (1953), 457–75.
[33] *Sermons*, ed. John Ayre (Parker Society, 1842), p. 122.

But he also calls this a perpetuation of a characteristic antichristian practice; and this is really our clue. Spenser is not thinking exclusively of a topical issue; what he has in mind is the duty of the newly restored church to abolish a practice typical of popery, that of using the goods of the church for personal and temporal purposes. Luther gloomily foresaw that church-robbers would not be checked till Armageddon.[34] Long afterwards Milton echoed him in *Of Reformation*,[35] speaking fiercely of prelates: 'How can these men not be corrupt, whose very cause is the bribe of their own pleading, whose mouths cannot open without the strong breath and loud stench of avarice, simony and sacrilege, embezzling the treasury of the church on painted and gilded walls of temples, wherein God hath testified to have no delight, warming their palace kitchens, and from thence their unctuous and epicurean paunches, with the alms of the blind, the lame, the impotent, the aged, the orphan, the widow?' Milton accuses the prelates of theft in several kinds; Jewel specifically calls the Roman hierarchy *sacrilegos*, which is in the contemporary translation 'church-robbers', for refusing the laity the wine at communion. Clearly any act which impoverished the church could be called church-robbing; there were contemporary instances, but Spenser has in mind the long record of antichrist and his misdeeds. In *The Shepheardes Calender* 'September'[36] he is more specifically attacking contemporary misappropriations; but when he speaks of the foxes replacing the wolves in England he is thinking of the clergy as having taken over the role of thieves from the pagans. To compare the antichristian clergy to foxes is an old device stemming from Christ's description of Herod as a fox, and from a gloss on Cant. ii. 14; Sandys uses it[37] and so does Spenser when he gives Duessa, revealed in all her ugliness, a fox's tail (I. vii. 48). What is scandalous is that this ancient wrong should have survived in the reformed church. Kirkrapine, incidentally, lives in concubinage with Abessa. This certainly suggests the unholy relation between simony and absenteeism in Spenser's time, but also suggests that it is a leftover from an earlier period; for Abessa reproaches Una with unchastity, which hints at the Romanist distaste

[34] *Preface to the Revelation of Saint John*, 1545; in *Works* (1932), vi. 479–88.
[35] *Prose Works* (Bohn edition, 1895), ed. J. A. St. John, ii. 415.
[36] See Paul E. Maclane, *Spenser's Shepheardes Calender* (1961), p. 127.
[37] *Sermons*, p. 64.

for the married priesthood of the reformed church,[38] and again associates Kirkrapine with the bad religion before reform.

Archimago, disguised as Red Cross and having Una in his charge, represents a bogus English church betraying true religion. That Sansloy should bring Archimago near to death suggests the self-destructive follies of Urban VI (1318–89, Pope from 1378), who seems in fact to have been more or less insane; Wyclif said that he destroyed the authority of the papacy; after him 'there is none to be received for the pope, but every man is to live after the manner of the Greeks, under his own law'.[39] This lawless folly, and the contemporary inroads of the Turks, probably account for the episode. The rescue of Una from Sansloy by satyrs, as Upton noticed,[40] means the succour of Christianity by primitivist movements such as the Waldensian and Albigensian; some primitives fall into idolatry (hence the follies of some puritan heretics) but the true Reformation line is represented by the well-born primitive Satyrane, who instantly knows the truth and opposes Sansloy.

The subjection of Red Cross to Orgoglio is the popish captivity of England from Gregory VII to Wyclif (about 300 years, the three months of viii. 38). The *miles Christi*, disarmed, drinks of the enervating fountain of corrupt gospel and submits to Rome. He is rescued by Arthur, doing duty for Elizabeth as Emperor of the Last Days, saviour of the English Church. The viciously acquired wealth of Duessa is confiscated. In ix. 17 Red Cross places Una under the charge of Gloriana, head of the Church. In this warp of allegory the capitulation to Despair must mean the Marian lapse; after that Red Cross is assured of his Englishness, and shown the New Jerusalem, of which Cleopolis or London, capital of the Earthly Paradise,[41] seat of the empress, is the earthly counterpart. Only then does he assume the role of the warrior *fidelis et verax* and, with the aid of the two sacraments of the true church, enact the slaying of the beast, the harrowing of hell, the restoration of Eden and the binding of Archimago. The English settlement—to which, as Revelation proved, all history

[38] It must be admitted that Spenser himself, like the queen, felt some distaste for married priests, at any rate in the *Shepheardes Calender*.

[39] Quoted in Foxe, *Acts and Monuments*, p. 227.

[40] *Variorum*.

[41] See J. W. Bennett, 'Britain among the Fortunate Isles', *Studies in Philology*, liii (1956), 114 ff.

tended—is a type of that final pacification at the end of time. Spenser makes it clear that it is *only* typical; but the boldness with which he conflates history and the archetype in Revelation proves how fully he accepted Foxe's bold formula, 'the whole church of Christ, namely . . . the church of England'.[42]

I have tried, in making this sketch of the allegory of ecclesiastical history in Book I, not to forget that Spenser's historical view was that of Anglican church historians. This, after all, is rather to be expected than not, in view of the apocalyptic and protestant-imperialist nature of Spenser's poem. What I suggest, in short, is that given the apocalyptic character of Book I—which cannot be denied—allegories of the kind I propose *must* be present in the poem; consequently the historical allegory is not the flickering, limited affair it is sometimes said to be; nor can we pick it up in all its depth by a learnedly ignorant contemplation of the surface of the fiction.

I now turn to a different aspect of Spenser's allegory, the episodes of Mercilla and the Church of Isis in Book V. I take it that the allegory is both juristic and imperialist. Obviously Justitia is here presented as superior to the private virtue treated by Aristotle, and of course also to *ius*, which is one of its servants. Thus it is in the great fourteenth-century fresco at Siena, and thus it is in the commonplaces of Roman law.

There is no longer any need to prove the existence of Spenser's imperial theme; Miss Yates has clearly established it. Elizabeth claimed imperial status, adapting with the Emperor Charles V and others a view of empire that goes back to the Ghibellines. She was the world-leader who maintained the imperial peace, and renewed the time, preparing her people for the coming of Christ. This was the official role of Spenser's Virgin, the Empress-Astraea.[43] And this Protestant and nationalist imperialism denies what even Frederick II admitted, that the Pope has a complementary task. In the empress the *potestates distinctae—imperium* and *sacerdotium*—of medieval law are united.

The opening lines of Book V describe how very far we have got from the age of gold. Spenser's poem throughout maintains

[42] *Acts and Monuments*, p. 998.
[43] F. A. Yates, 'Queen Elizabeth as Astraea', see note 19 of this chapter; and 'Fêtes et Cérémonies au temps de Charles Quint', *Les Fêtes de la Renaissance*, n.d., pp. 57-97.

a tension between the ideal and the actual, and he knows that the return of the Imperial Virgin, first prophesied for Constantine, has occurred only in a figurative and restricted sense. Yet he is prepared to maintain this tension, and to present his Elizabeth as Iustitia or Astraea.[44]

He speaks thus of Justice:

> Most sacred virtue she of all the rest
> Resembling God in his *imperiall* might:

And thus of Elizabeth:

> Dread Souerayne Goddesse, that doeth highest sit
> In seate of judgement, in th'Almighties stead . . .

First we hear of the agents of justice, of Arthegall as pupil of Astraea and disciple of Bacchus and Hercules, dispensing justice with the aid of Talus. The allegory proceeds simply enough until Arthegall falls victim, Hercules-like, to Radigund; and although there is much of political interest in these cantos, and we see instances of Injustice, we have not yet encountered the formal Iustitia. This we do when Britomart, at the beginning of Canto vii, enters the Church of Isis to prepare for the liberation of Arthegall.

We shall understand neither the Church of Isis nor the Court of Mercilla unless we have some notion of the contemporary connotations of the word 'Equity', and its relation to Justice. Spenser, though in translating Plutarch's 'Iseion' he probably borrowed the expression 'Isis Church' from Adlington's Apuleius,[45] obviously intended in this part of the Fifth Book to make a formal *Templum Justitiae*.[46] In doing so he is remembering a tradition at

---

[44] For Astraea as Justice (in a temple) see the lines addressed by Sir Robert Whittington to Sir Thomas More: they allude to *Astraeae criticae mystica chrismata | et Aeris fixa tholo verba minantia*. See R. S. Sylvester's transcription of the lines in *Huntington Library Quarterly*, xxvi (1963), 147 ff.

[45] *Variorum*, v. 216.

[46] As in Bartolomeo Delbene, *Civitas Veri* 1609 (written in the fifteen-eighties). There are Temples of Justice and of Injustice in this book, which was dedicated to Henry III and reflects the mode of the philosophical discussions held in the Palace Academy (see F. A. Yates, *The French Academies of the Sixteenth Century* (1947), pp. 111 ff.).

least as old as Augustus, whom Ovid congratulated on raising a
temple to Iustitia. Ulpian called judges the priests of Justice;
Justinian speaks of the 'most holy temple of Justice' and of 'the
temple of the Roman Justice'. Statues were made showing
governors as Justice embodied, with Dike, Eunomia and Themis
beside them.[47] The twelfth-century glossator Placentinus elaborately describes an allegorical Temple of Justice: Justitia is a
dignified figure with Ratio over her head, many Virtues about
her, and Equity in her embrace.[48]

This figuration developed along with the Roman law. The
Neapolitan lawyer Lucas de Penna held that Iustitia, properly conceived, is identical with equity.[49] Equity is indeed the source of
law, that which makes Justice just; for *summa ius, summa iniuria* is
an old saying. Penna's jurisprudence was influential in sixteenth-
century France,[50] and the allegorical representations of Justice and
Equity were modified accordingly. Thus Delbene shows Equity
controlling Justice with a rod (*obtemperatio quasi virgula*).[51] Equity
is the mother of law, the mediator between natural and human
law; and this point was given cosmological significance by the
equation between *mater* and *materia* in the dicta of late medieval
jurisprudence.[52] In this way the justification of cosmic inequalities
and of human law—perhaps even of human salvation, since the
Billigkeit of Luther is related to these conceptions of equity[53]—
are all related, and Spenser's choice of the Plutarchan myth of
Isis begins to have the look of a very rich allegorical invention.

Imagery of this kind formed a part of that juristic myth which,
as Kantorowicz showed, replaced earlier liturgical conceptions of
the emperor after the death of Frederick II.[54] It is therefore intimately associated with the imperial mythology cultivated at the

[47] See E. Kantorowicz, 'ΣΥΝΘΡΟΝΟΣ ΔΙΚΗΓ', *American Journal of
Archaeology*, lvii (1953), 65 ff.

[48] H. Kantorowicz, *Studies in Glossators of the Roman Law* (1938), pp. 183 ff.

[49] W. Ullmann, *The Medieval Idea of Law* (1946), p. 43, quoting de Penna:
Ius simpliciter sumptum est aequitas.

[50] Ullmann, *Medieval Idea of Law*, pp. 183 ff.

[51] *Civitas Veri*, pp. 168 and 174 (illustration).

[52] Ullmann, p. 50.

[53] This large suggestion I make in the hope that someone may pursue it.
It was put to me by Professor Gordon Rupp after my lecture. It does not
seem improbable that Luther should apply to theology doctrine associated
with the emperor.

[54] E. Kantorowicz, *The King's Two Bodies*, cap. IV.

court of Elizabeth I. The emperor, as a fount of equity, directly mediates divine law, without the intervention of the Pope. But even if it is allowed (as it must be) that the Elizabethan propaganda borrowed freely from European imperialist mythology, it is also evident that the imagery so far spoken of is related to Roman law, and not to English. This calls for a word on the contacts between the two systems.

The prospect of a Reception of Roman law in England seems to have existed but briefly during the reign of Henry VIII. More, Elyot and Starkey admired Roman law, largely because of its superior equity; the king's cousin Cardinal Pole was its advocate. The king himself, when he abolished the study of canon law in England, set up Chairs of Civil Law at Oxford and Cambridge, and Gentile at Oxford, an Italian refugee, was a learned Roman civilian. Maitland, who at one time held the view (now disputed) that a Reception came very near to occurring, notes that Roman law 'made pleasant reading for a King who wished to be a monarch in church as well as state: pleasanter reading than could be found in our ancient English law-books'.[55] But the common lawyers prevailed. How then could the king's daughter develop her imperial mythology in terms of the Roman law? Admittedly, the close relationship between English and French courts in the fifteen-eighties, when there were high hopes of a *politique* agreement, might alone have ensured that the French mystique of *imperium* should affect English practice. Of course it was possible to maintain that even 'by the common law of England, a Prince can do no wrong', as Bacon put it to the Council during the examination of Essex in 1600.[56] And the Tudors had always founded their rights in the common law. But they were certainly not unwilling to improve their security by reference to another system (appropriate, after all, to the re-embodiment of Augustus and Constantine) in which the Prince was not merely *legibus solutus* but also *lex animata* and a god on earth.

That Elizabethan England was conscious of a double standard in law is suggested by the contemporary debate on English equity. Formerly it had been considered an aspect of the common law, and since 1873 it has returned to the common law; but in the

[55] F. W. Maitland, 'English Law and the Renaissance', in *Historical Essays* (1957), p. 140.
[56] See G. B. Harrison, *Robert Devereux, Earl of Essex* (1937), pp. 263-4.

time of Elizabeth it was the province of the queen. The prerogative courts, especially those of Chancery and Star Chamber, represented the queen's justice independent of the common law
courts. The Chancellor in Chancery was not bound by common
law precedent but by equity and conscience; Hatton called himself
the queen's conscience, and when Hamlet speaks of 'the conscience of the King' he is presumably remembering a familiar
expression, 'the conscience of the Queen', which was the motive
of Chancery. The positive function of the Court was to remedy
injustices that had no remedy in common law. This might be for
many reasons, and not only because the common lawyers were
bound by rule and precedent, and the common law incompetent
in certain causes, such as those relating to uses and trusts. The
plaintiff might be a poor man, or the defendant a magnate with
power to bribe, threaten or persuade a jury. (One remembers that
the earl of Leicester was surprised to be told that it was an offence
to influence a juryman.)[57] The increased use of this court brought
many protests from Elizabethan lawyers, who saw in the growing
activity of the courts of equity a usurpation of their authority.[58]
Already, in fact, Chancery was building up the colossal backlog
of business and the concern for precedent that made it, for
Dickens, not so much a court of equity as a death-trap for innocent litigants. But in Spenser's time it was still the court of the
queen's conscience; and inevitably the judgements of the chancellor, which were unrelated to the common law, touched the older
tradition of the Roman law at many points.

So did the Court of Star Chamber. This court grew out of the
Council, and dealt equity in criminal cases, notably those touching
the security of the queen. Thus it punished scandals, seditions,
riots, and, in this reign, recusancy; for which reason, and because
of its brutal examinations and punishments, it was hated by
Puritans and abolished when the Long Parliament came to power
in 1641. Chancery had its enemies also. Star Chamber was a
court in which the monarch was present, either symbolically (as in
Elizabeth's reign) or in person, as at least twice in the reign of

---

[57] W. S. Holdsworth, *A History of English Law* (1924), i. 505.
[58] Evidence for this in Holdsworth, i. 508-9, and in George Spence, *The
Equitable Jurisdiction of the Court of Chancery* (1846), i, Part 2, Book i. For a
useful recent summary see John W. Dickinson, 'Renaissance Equity and
Measure for Measure', *Shakespeare Quarterly*, xiii (1962), 287-97.

James I.[59] The association of this court with absolutism was strong in the minds of its enemies, and absolutist doctrine was in turn associated with the Roman law.[60] In 1610 Cowell, a Cambridge law professor, argued that Roman law and absolute monarchy went hand in hand; and Bacon on the other side assured James I that the Court of Chancery was the court of his absolute power, as well as the conscience of the realm.[61] It is hardly surprising, then, that when Parliament triumphed so did the common law; when Star Chamber was put down Chancery narrowly escaped. In the reign of Elizabeth a Roman absolutism would affect not only the imagery of a poet but the speculations of jurists. Raleigh argued that the capacity of Parliament was merely advisory;[62] and later Lord Ellesmere, known as the great enemy of the common law, could declare that the judges had no rights of equity since these belonged to the chancellor in his capacity as the king's conscience.[63]

In the native English conception, law is logically prior to equity, hence the maxim 'Equity follows law'. In Roman law, as we have seen, equity can be called the source or foundation of law: *lex est super aequitate fundata; ius simpliciter sumptum est aequitas.*[64] Without equity law has nothing to do with justice: *summa ius, summa iniuria.* In the England of Elizabeth there was a conflict between the common and the imperial interpretation, and Spenser favours the latter. The fount of imperial equity is the emperor; and the relation of *lex scripta* to his will is analogous to the relation of Scripture to the will of God.[65] On this view the object of a court of equity is to enable the emperor to *justify* the law (even when it proceeds like Star Chamber, to do so, by ear-lopping and other mutilation). The theological parallel is intimate. Like her father, Elizabeth, as head of Church and State, must have found comfort in the Roman law; she wielded the two swords, and was charged with all the powers of *imperium* and *sacerdotium.*

With all this in mind, let us look at the Church of Isis, Spenser's *Templum Iustitiae.* He begins with a conventional assertion of the

---

[59] Holdsworth, i. 500.   [60] Maitland, p. 147.

[61] Maitland, p. 134. *Works of Francis Bacon,* ed. Spedding, Ellis and Heath (1861), xiv. 292.

[62] Quoted by C. H. McIlwain, *The High Court of Parliament* (1910), p. 330.

[63] McIlwain, p. 294.   [64] Ullmann, p. 43.   [65] Ullmann, p. 53.

pre-eminence of Justice over the other virtues, and approves the ancient custom of establishing temples to Justice (*Iustitiam namque colimus quasi Deam sanctissimam* says an old jurist, who cannot think of Justice as merely a virtue).[66] But what he then celebrates is not Justice but Equity—'that part of Iustice, which is Equity'; and in the end he will show it to be the better part. The choice of Plutarch's myth has all Spenser's subtlety of invention. Plutarch notices that at Hermopolis Isis was identified with Justice.[67] She is also associated with Astraea; with the moon, emblem of the *imperium*; and with matter.[68] He wants us to remember that Justice and Equity reflect a vast cosmic process; that Equity is like matter, and that Justice gives it mutable forms. But he also means that Osiris is the common law considered in isolation from the equity courts. The priests of Isis are Ulpian's learned civilians, servants of the imperial equity (their long hair distinguishing them from the tonsured canonists) and they practise in such prerogative courts as Chancery and Star Chamber. (Spenser apparently borrowed the detail of their long hair from an account of the priesthood of Rhea.)[69] Their slightly feminine appearance may also be appropriate to the service of an empress, and their asceticism to the intense virginity cult which attached to this inheritor of the titles *vicarius Iustitiae* (from the Empire) and *vicarius Christi* (from the British King Lucius). But chiefly their abstinence from wine, the blood of the rebellious Titans, alludes to their implacable opposition to innovation and recusancy (we recall the earlier association of the giant with Anabaptism). The foot set on the crocodile and the foot fast on the ground (vii) reflect the criminal equity of Star Chamber; the wand, like the one in Delbene which signified the control of Justice by Equity, stands for the power of Chancery in civil cases. Why does the crocodile enwreath her waist with his tail? (For I assume we must emend vi. 9: 'That with *his* wreathed tail . . .') In Plutarch the crocodile is Typhon, an evil force, destroyer of Osiris. Here the Plutarchian sense is present also; Plutarch speaks of Typhon as discord and heat.

[66] Kantorowicz, *King's Two Bodies*, p. 111, n. 70.

[67] *De Iside et Osiride*, in *Moralia*, ed. Babbitt (1936), v. 11.

[68] See F. A. Yates, 'The Religious Policy of Giordano Bruno', *Journal of the Warburg and Courtauld Institutes*, iii (1939–40), 183–4. The Egyptian goddess could conceivably also suggest the ancient Church of England, which Bruno called 'Egyptian'.   [69] *Variorum*, v. 214–15.

Crocodiles were engendered by the sun on the mud of the Nile, and were in consequence a product, like wine, of the earth,[70] and so in Spenser's allegory associated with rebellion and injustice. Here the crocodile is purely human law: *summa ius, summa iniuria*. Its tail suggests an impotent enmity towards imperial Equity; but the foot of Isis controls it as firmly as, in the woodcuts, that of Elizabeth controls the papacy.

In her dream, Britomart becomes a priest, but is at once (xiv) transformed into an empress, robed in imperial purple and crowned with the sun symbol. In view of what we already know about her as progenitress of the Tudors, we see that Britomart is now, in a vision, the imperial power of the dynasty. The Typhonic tempest and fire that follow are rebellion against this power, as established by the settlement—rebellion both political and religious, and suppressed by the common laws of England, here represented by the crocodile. The presumption of the crocodile after this can represent the impatience of the common lawyers with absolutist claims, and with the increased use of prerogative courts; and the strange union of Britomart and the crocodile is the full union of justice and equity in the imperial dispositions of the queen. Human law, according to medieval jurisprudence, can attain to natural law only in union with equity; and the source of equity is the empress. According to the priestly interpreter of the dream, the crocodile is Arthegall, who throughout the Book has stood for Justice considered independently of Equity; and from the union springs a lion, symbol of the natural law. Thus the empress, maintaining a proper relation between the common law and equity, is making proper use of her prerogative courts for the purpose of controlling the habitual and inevitable injustice of the law, and the forces tending to rebellion. Spenser, in short, has refashioned the traditional figures of Justice allegories in order to intervene in the current controversy between the courts of law and the courts of equity; and this in its turn implies a defence of the imperial claims of Elizabeth, which necessarily involve the Roman law.

We turn now to the Court of Mercilla. It is often said that Spenser's methods are not truly pictorial; but sometimes *The Faerie Queene* has the air of a great fresco, where one part should be seen in a simultaneous spatial relation with another, as in

[70] *Moralia*, v. 133.

Lorenzetti's great allegories for the Palazzo Pubblico in Siena. So it is here. We remember that Britomart, fortified by her night in Isis Church, goes off to overthrow Radigund, the type of female tyranny. This is exactly echoed in Canto ix; for Mercilla is an aspect of Isis. They are related to one another much as are Iustitia and Buon Governo in Lorenzetti.[71] And in Mercilla's presence we are once more in the prerogative courts of England. Overseen by Awe, regulated by Order, the people seek the true justice denied them in the common law, a justice not perverted by 'brybes, or threates' (xxiv). A poet punished by the nailing of his tongue to a post has committed slander (he accused the queen of 'forged guile', which is a quotation from the Isis Church canto [VII. vii. 3] and there associated with the rebellious Typhon-crocodile). His offence and its punishment remind us of the juris-diction and also of the penalties of the Court of Star Chamber. The queen's throne, with the lions and fleurs-de-lys of England and France, recall the obligatory presence of her State in that court. Above her is a cloud-like canopy borne up by angels, perhaps a deliberate reminiscence of the *maestà*.[72] She has two swords—the sceptre of peace and clemency and the rusted sword of justice; the *imperium* demands clemency,[73] but equity is not merely a matter of mercy, and the rusted sword is sometimes used. The presence of two swords can, in addition, hardly fail to suggest the *potestates distinctae* of medieval political theory; she embodies both the *imperium* and the *sacerdotium*.[74]

She is surrounded by the daughters of Jove, the Litae, pro-perly the *horai* of Hesiod, whose function is equity. They are Dike (Justice, and sometimes called Astraea), Eunomia, Ius, and Irene (Pax). With them are Temperance and Reverence. These are im-perial virtues. Long before Elizabeth, the emperor has been

---

[71] See George Rowley, *Ambrogio Lorenzetti* (1958); N. Rubenstein, 'Politi-cal Ideas in Sienese Art', *Journal of the Warburg and Courtauld Institutes*, xxi (1958), 179 ff; E. Kantorowicz, *The King's Two Bodies*, pp. 112–13. For Iustitia and the emperor represented as equally enthroned—as might be said of Isis and Mercilla—see the article of E. Kantorowicz cited in n. 47 of this chapter.

[72] H. Kantorowicz compares Placentinus' Iustitia with a Renaissance *maestà* (*Glossators*, p. 186); but E. Kantorowicz contests this (*King's Two Bodies*, p. 112, n. 76). For elements of Mariolatry in the Elizabeth cult see Yates, 'Queen Elizabeth as Astraea', pp. 76 ff.

[73] Yates, 'Queen Elizabeth as Astraea', p. 62.

[74] Ullmann, p. 170.

enthroned with Dike and Eunomia; the other virtues echo those represented in Lorenzetti's Sienese frescoes. The lion at the feet of Mercilla—and reminding us of the statue at Nonsuch of Henry VIII trampling a lion—again fulfils Britomart's dream, but is the common law in bondage to equity.

The tone of this passage is that of a courtly version of the popular Queen's Day celebrations, wherein Elizabeth was thanked for delivering the realm from the evil power of the Pope, and for maintaining the peace and security of the state. Her accession day God had ordained as a Holy Day 'next to that of his sonne Christ',[75] and Spenser, though he thinks of her as Astraea and as Isis, also thinks of her as the Blessed Virgin. Being herself Justice incarnate as Equity, she proceeds, as Britomart proceeded to the suppression of Radigund, to the trial of Duessa. Duessa is frankly Mary Queen of Scots, the most distinguished victim of Elizabeth's prerogative courts; and the book moves on to an easy historical allegory of the Netherlands campaign against the Spanish supporters of antichrist. We are reminded of III. iii. 49, and the prophecy of a universal peace under a royal virgin who 'shall Stretch her white rod over the Belgicke shore'—the rod, we see, was the rod of Isis-Equity in the seventh canto of the Book of Justice.

It would seem, then, that the Fifth Book has, at its critical points, a most elaborate juristic-imperialist allegory. I have not explained it in full; for my immediate purposes I shall be satisfied if it appears that scholars are wrong to reduce the Isis Church episode to a 'marriage debate', and explain the vision of the crocodile threatening Britomart as a recapitulation of the rape of Amoret. Even Woodhouse's elaborate and rather fine interpretation[76] makes it only a dream allegory of the future union of Britomart and Arthegall. I have tried to put the episode into a context of juristic allegory, and restore its links with Spenser's dominant heroic theme, the vision of Empire.

I have said enough, perhaps, in arguing for Protestant-imperialist ecclesiastical history in Book I, and for Protestant-imperialist equity in Book V, to show that I believe in a Spenser more rather than less historical in his allegory, a Spenser more susceptible than it has lately been fashionable to believe, to historical analysis. In fact I do not think one can enter fully into his

[75] Strong, 'Accession Day', p. 99.   [76] *E.L.H.* (1949), p. 216, n. 42.

long dream without the kind of knowledge such analysis has provided, and should provide. Spenser followed the antique poets heroical in this: he excluded no learning that would subserve his national theme, and enable him to show knowledge and history as they are related to a vision of his country as the heir of Empire and of Eden.

3

THE CAVE OF MAMMON

The object of this chapter is to expound the seventh canto of the Second Book of *The Faerie Queene*. There is little agreement as to its interpretation, so the topic has its own interest. But it cannot be treated in isolation from the Second Book as a whole; and since the relation between this mysterious episode and the remainder of the Legend of Temperance seems to be characteristic of Spenser's method throughout *The Faerie Queene*, what I have to say, in so far as it is correct, has a bearing upon the conduct of the entire poem, and in the long run upon certain obscure aspects of Renaissance poetry in general. So I begin with some remarks on that larger topic.

Any reader who has even a slight familiarity with Renaissance allegorical habits will see that Spenser's epyllion *Muiopotmos* is concerned with the descent of the soul into the captivity of matter as a result of sensuality. He may see other related meanings, some of them debatable; but I think he will not have much doubt about this one. On the other hand, a reader who has no such familiarity will be quite in the dark. He will see, of course, that the story must be allegorical, but at best will invent some sort of historical key for it; as a matter of fact, commentary on *Muiopotmos* was, until quite recently, of this kind. With *The Faerie Queene* the position is incalculably more difficult; there is historical allegory; there is very simple allegory as in the House of Alma and the Castle of Medina passages in this Second Book; but there is also allegory of the kind represented by the Temple of Isis in Book V, the Garden of Adonis in Book III, and the Cave of Mammon. These are not 'face-value' allegories, and the confusion of commentary is adequate testimony to the fact. Spenser seems to be assuming a special kind of reader, or rather a special kind of information, and he may also be held to believe that even this community of information will not, however complete and subtle, provide absolute explanations, full translations of image into discourse. The efforts of poets who wrote like this was not merely to discover wisdom but to create it—not merely to benefit by the power of extant mythologies, but to make significant myths of their own. It is a mythopoeic power that we must deal with; if we cannot see Spenser as a myth-maker we shall make very little of his poem. It is all the more important to see this need because Spenser, though he characteristically refers to his whole work as a 'dark conceit', does not, like Chapman, boast of the secrecy of his meanings.

Yet he is, in his way, an esoteric poet; like all poets in the Neo-Platonic tradition, not only the guardian of secrets but the creator of new secret wisdom. The position is one that was so familiar to Renaissance poets that to put it out of one's mind is almost certainly to distort one's reading not only of a Chapman or a Spenser but even in some degree of Shakespeare; for it was taken for granted that one of the properties of a fiction, however exoteric it might appear, was the possession of occult significance. This will not seem strange to anyone who considers the currency, the commonplaceness indeed, of commentaries on the Scriptures —the myriad works on Genesis, the expositions of the Psalms and Job and the Song of Songs—that strike the modern eye as merely curious or fantastic. Given certain assumption about its relation to revealed truth, these methods of allegoresis were equally applicable to pagan wisdom. On the boundary between the two stood the always influential Macrobius, who deplored fables as a means of entertainment, but believed *narratio fabulosa* to be a proper means of veiling holy truths:

> A frank, open exposition of herself is distasteful to Nature, who, just as she has withheld an understanding of herself from the uncouth senses of men by enveloping herself in variegated garments, has also desired to have her secrets handled by more prudent individuals through fabulous narratives. Accordingly, her secret rites are veiled in mysterious representations so that she may not have to show herself even to initiates.[1]

[1] *Commentary on the Dream of Scipio*, trans. W. H. Stahl (1952), pp. 85-7.

The extant Pythagorean *logia* are an instance, nonsense phrases which preserved wisdom *a vilitate secretam*, for *amat divina natura celari*.[2] Such phrases have a skin everybody can see and a marrow a few can extract; they are not meant for the profane. *Sub verborum tegmine vera latent*, in John of Salisbury's words.[3] This is a twelfth-century Platonist; in the Renaissance such views grew in strength and complexity. How could Erasmus say that a pagan fable, allegorically interpreted, might be more valuable than scripture read literally (*si consistas in cortice*)?[4] How could Ronsard speak of ancient poetry as 'une Theologie allegorique, pour faire entrer au cerveau des hommes grossiers par fables plaisantes et colorées les secrets qui'ils ne pouvoient comprendre, quand trop ouvertement on descouvroit la vérité'?[5] Or Chapman plant obscurity at the core of his fictions? 'Obscuritie in affections of word, & indigested concets, is pedanticall and childish; but where it shroudeth it selfe in the hart of his subject . . . with that darknes will I still labour to be shaddowed . . .' (Dedication of *Ovids Banquet of Sence*). Were they not aware that there was an inherent contradiction in making public what they wished to keep secret? Even Chapman, with his talk of writing for two or three only, sought publication. And this is, as Wind points out, 'the basic paradox of cryptic art . . . it frequently addresses itself to the very audience from which it professes to be hidden' (Wind, pp. 157 and 20; Seznec, pp. 102–3). But the paradox ceases to be troublesome if provision can be made for two classes of reader, one which stops at the skin, the other which penetrates to the marrow.

Of the complex tradition of secret ancient wisdom, much has recently been written, not only in learned papers on the *icones symbolicae*, Orphism, and the like, but also in the authoritative

[2] L. G. Gyraldus, *Philosophi Pythagorae Symbolorum Interpretatio*, in *Opera Omnia* (1696), pp. 637–8; see further Edgar Wind, *Pagan Mysteries of the Renaissance* (1958), Chap. I, and for 'screening allegories . . . coined to hide from exoteric view the facts of an esoteric rite, while suggesting symbolically the rite's spiritual sense' in primitive societies, see Joseph Campbell, *The Masks of God* (1959), pp. 96 ff.

[3] *Entheticus*, quoted in Curtius, *European Literature and the Latin Middle Ages*, trans. W. Trask (1953), p. 206.

[4] *Enchiridion militis Christi*, quoted in Seznec, *The Survival of the Pagan Gods*, trans. by B. F. Sessions (1953), pp. 98–9.

[5] *Abbregé de l'Art Poetique Francoys*, 1565, quoted by D. P. Walker, 'The Prisca Theologia in France', *Journal of the Warburg and Courtauld Institutes* (1954), p. 224.

general studies of Seznec and Wind. The earlier *Genealogia* of Boccaccio was supplemented in the middle of the sixteenth century by the manuals of Giraldi, Conti, and Cartari, and these became the source of a great many allegorical programmes, both pictorial and literary. The medieval element, as Seznec shows, remains in all these works; but there was some attempt, however perfunctory, to use ancient texts (Philostratus, Pausanias) and ancient coins and statues. And the Orphic strain in Renaissance Neo-Platonism ensured a respect for mystery as well as straightforward allegory. We have also to remember the syncretism of the movement; Christian themes could be given pagan expression, Ovid was habitually moralized, the view that Plato had learned the wisdom of Moses opened a path to the most elaborate discoveries of truth in ancient mythology and religion. Christian truth is hidden in pagan story. 'But have a care in speaking of these things. They should be hidden in silence as are the Eleusinian mysteries; sacred things must needs be wrapped in fable and enigma' (Mutianus Rufus, quoted in Seznec, p. 99). '*Universam poesim aenigmatum esse plenam docet Plato.*'

It is a short step from this creative exploration of mythology to the new making of enigmatic myths. The differences between a modern and a Renaissance view of the ancient world and its divinities are vast. As D. J. Gordon has said of Chapman's having invented mythological deities such as Teras, Eronusis, and Ceremony, his was not the familiar Olympic pantheon;

> the elaborate abstractions of late antiquity were far more familiar to sixteenth century writers than they are to us. The syncretism of Plutarch in his *Isis and Osiris*, and the mixture of Greek and Egyptian cults in Diodorus Siculus were as present to their minds as the marbles of the Olympians. . . . A glance through the pages of Cartari or at the illustrations to his text is enough to show how wild, how 'unclassical' . . . this pantheon was.[6]

When a man set out to imitate antique models—and that was the key to most Renaissance artistic activity—he assumed the right to amplify and to change the model. He would *invent*, though in the Renaissance sense of the word; he would create new figures and

[6] 'Chapman's *Hero and Leander*', *English Miscellany* (1954), pp. 53–4; see also p. 42, and Seznec, p. 321.

new meanings by adapting and re-combining any fragmentary or scattered evidence he could find. He would make new mysteries, and the material of them would be 'classical' in his sense; their meaning would be of universal import because, in so far as they were authentic, truth lay enigmatically within them. Such are Wind's 'Pagan Mysteries of the Renaissance'. Such are the 'programmes' of Renaissance art, recombinations of old myth and allegory to reveal truth. The material may derive from well-thumbed manuals, the contributory themes from the allegorical fantasies of Platonic academists; but the result will be an enigma calling for explication by adepts. So, for example, with the still-disputed interpretation of Botticelli's *Primavera*.[7]

My assumption is that the Cave of Mammon had such a programme and that it is similarly enigmatic; that it is an invention of this kind, requiring the sort of attention given by art-historians to the *Primavera*. One may make this assumption without at all disputing that Spenser's allegory is frequently medieval, that he is staid, 'churchwardenly', openly didactic. Underneath all that, there is a profounder mythopoeic activity; the great allegorical centres of his poem are planned like enigmatic pictures. The audience of an epic is likely to be uneven in learning;

> while it was no doubt best for people as a whole to continue to accept the traditional teachings with naïve faith, learned men . . . should be able to discern the inevitable part played in Christianity, as in pagan belief, by the weaving of fables (Seznec, p. 99).

The marrow of a Spenserian allegory is designed to be extracted by the same enlightened method as that of an Orphic mystery, an Egyptian hieroglyph, a Renaissance emblem, or indeed an ancient epic.

Guyon is the hero of the legend of Temperance. In the sixth canto he is parted from his guide, the Palmer, but resists the temptations of Phaedria, 'immodest Mirth'. He then proceeds, though without his Palmer, 'as Pilot well expert in perilous wave' through a wilderness. After a long journey during which he comforts himself with reflecting upon his own virtues, he comes to 'a gloomy glade' where, in the darkness sits 'an uncouth, salvage, and

---

[7] See E. H. Gombrich, 'Botticelli's Mythologies', *Journal of the Warburg and Courtauld Institutes* (1954), pp. 7–60; Seznec, pp. 112 ff., and Wind, pp. 100 ff.

uncivile wight'. This is Mammon. All about him are heaps of gold, which, at the sight of Guyon, he pours down a hole into the earth. Guyon, however, stops him, and asks him who he is. After complaining of Guyon's presumption, Mammon explains that he is 'God of the world and worldlings', dispenser of everything for which men 'swinck and sweat incessantly':

> Riches, renowne, and principality;
> Honour, estate, and all this worldes good.

He offers Guyon limitless wealth if he will serve him. Guyon rejects this 'worldly mucke'. Mammon points out that money is a way to greatness; but Guyon scorns him, and attributes much of the world's misery and wrongful government to the love of money. He will not in any case 'receave | Thing offred till I knew it well be got'. Guyon then asks in what secret place all this mass of treasure is kept; and Mammon leads him down through a hole into the earth. Soon they come to 'an ample plaine' through which runs 'a beaten broad high way' that leads 'to Plutoes griesly raine'. Beside this road sit Pain and Strife, Revenge, Despight, Treason, Hate, Gealosie, Feare, Sorrow, Horrour, with Owls and Night-ravens, and 'sad *Celeno*' a harpy, to signify rapacity, but sitting and singing as she does in *Aeneid* iii. They arrive at a 'little dore . . . that to the gate of Hell . . . was next adjoyning'. This is the house of Richesse. Before it sits 'selfe-consuming Care'. The door opens, and they enter, Guyon undismayed by the darkness and danger. As soon as he gets in, and thenceforth during his stay, he is followed by a monstrous fiend; if Guyon should covet anything or lay hand or lip or lustful eye on anything, or sleep, so transgressing 'the fatall *Stygian* lawes', this fiend that hovers over him would rend him in pieces. The house is full of gold, roofed over by a spider's web and covered in dust; there is but 'a faint shadow of uncertain light, Such as a lamp, whose life does fade away'. The skulls and bones of dead men lie around. They pass through an iron door, Guyon not speaking, and find there a show of riches such 'As eye of man did never see before' —all the wealth of the world, above and below ground: 'Loe here the worldes blis, loe here the end, To which all men do ayme'. Guyon rejects it;

> Another blis before mine eyes I place,
> Another happinesse, another end.

Mammon gnashes his teeth; Guyon has escaped. But he takes him into his furnace room, where fiends make gold; 'Here is the fountaine of the worldes good.' Guyon easily rejects him.

Now Mammon leads the knight to the Temple of Philotime, which is guarded by Disdayne. In a large room supported by golden pillars, all inscribed with emblems of mortal glory, sits Philotime, surrounded by her adorers. Her beauty is great, but 'wrought by art and counterfetted shew':

> Nath'lesse most heavenly faire in deed and vew
> She by creation was, till she did fall.

She holds a chain stretching from heaven to hell and called Ambition, upon which men fight for advantage. Mammon explains that Philotime is his daughter, and that

> Honour and dignitie from her alone
> Derived are, and all this worldes blis.

She has been thrust out of heaven from envy; and he offers her to Guyon, who politely refuses, calling himself unworthy, but also explaining that he has plighted his troth to another lady.

Mammon, inwardly angry, now conducts him down a sombre path into a garden full of black flowers and fruit: Cypress, Gall, Heben, Poppy, Hellebore, Cicuta (the hemlock of Socrates). This is the Garden of Proserpina. In an arbour in the midst she has a silver seat, and beside it is a tree laden with glistering fruit. This tree is the source of certain mythological apples: those of the Hesperides, that by which Atalanta was defeated, that which Paris awarded to Venus. The boughs overhang Cocytus, in which stream groan the damned. Two of these are described: Tantalus, who begs drink and is sternly refused it by Guyon; and Pilate. Mammon roughly asks Guyon to eat of the fruit and rest on the silver stool; should he do either the fiend would rend him in pieces. But he does not suffer 'lust his safetie to betray'. By now he is weak for lack of food and sleep; he has been with Mammon for three days. He requests immediate escort back to 'living light'; Mammon has to grant it, as no man may spend more than three days below the earth. Guyon at once falls into a deep faint. There ends the seventh canto. The eighth opens with the famous 'And is there care in heaven?' giving praise for God's mercy in sending angels 'to serve to wicked men'. A voice summons the

Palmer, who finds sitting beside the prostrate Guyon an angel sent to save him from a threatening danger.

This is the picture. It makes much allegorical sense without elaborate explanation; I have mentioned a great many simple personifications with an obvious function in an allegory of this kind. But there is evidently something pretty mysterious about some details; and these are so important that commentators disagree radically about the true meaning of the allegory, and its place in the second Book as a whole. For example, there is a general dispute as to whether Guyon stands for Aristotle's Temperance or his Continence; more particularly, whether his going with Mammon in the first place is not parallel to the Red Cross Knight's submission to Pride and Despair in the first Book. Thus V. K. Whitaker sees the significance of the events in the separation from the Palmer (Prudence), after which Guyon 'is tempted by Phaedria [and] weakened almost to death by Mammon'.[8] Harry Berger, in his recent impressive study of Book II, argues that Guyon descends of his own free will, and is guilty of curiosity. Once in the cave, he has no difficulty with Mammon's crudely material enticements; he surveys them all coldly, with scientific detachment. His faint is a direct result of his mental intemperance (*curiositas*) for he has neglected his human needs in order to serve it (H. Berger, *The Allegorical Temper*, 1957, pp. 17 ff.). The more general view is, roughly, Milton's, though he made the odd and famous mistake of sending the Palmer into the cave with Guyon:

> our sage and serious Poet *Spencer*, whom I dare be known to think a better teacher then *Scotus* or *Aquinas*, describing true temperance under the person of *Guion*, brings him in with his palmer through the cave of Mammon, and the bowr of earthly blisse that he might see and know, and yet abstain.[9]

[8] *That Soueraine Light*, ed. W. R. Mueller and D. C. Allen (1952), p. 77.
[9] *Areopagitica, Complete Prose Works*, Vol. II, ed. Sirluck, 1959, p. 516. Sirluck argues that Milton's own convictions led him unconsciously to revise Spenser's passage, which must have seemed to him to place too much confidence in the Aristotelian doctrine of habitual temperance. This assumes that the Palmer is Reason. If he were Prudence, another common interpretation, one might equally expect him to go with Guyon into the Cave, since Prudence is *conduttrice delle virtù morali*.

So Ernest Sirluck, seeking to re-establish the contact, which some recent speculation has questioned, between *Faerie Queene* II and the *Nicomachean Ethics*, finds that Guyon here represents 'the virtuous man with reference to wealth and honour' as part of Spenser's larger purpose, which is to show the good life with reference to moral virtue, just as in the first book he showed it with reference to faith.[10]

These wide disagreements do not, however, preclude general consent that the ordeal in the cave is the crisis of Guyon's quest, the character of which is to be understood in accordance with the interpretation placed upon the crucial seventh canto. It is argued, for instance, that Guyon overgoes Achilles in the first half of the book by demonstrating the conquest of wrath, and Ulysses in the second by his conquest of concupiscence;[11] or that he moves out of the sphere of Fortune into that of creative love, so dramatizing the insufficiency of Aristotelian temperance—'the innocence and limited wisdom resulting from reflexes so easy'—in comparison with the Christian temperance—'supernaturally infused, accessible to all, but gained by each with difficulty' (Berger, pp. 62–3). It is, at all events, essential to understand what is meant by the Cave of Mammon passage if one is to get Book II right.

Is Guyon in the cave committing a sin, merely resisting temptations which are scarcely troublesome to the habitual temperance of Aristotle, or undergoing some kind of initiation? I shall argue for the last of these interpretations. To begin with, what precisely does Mammon offer Guyon? The usual answer is Wealth, or perhaps, Wealth and Honour. Mammon offers the inducements of the World, as against those of the flesh and the Devil. And this is, doubtless, a good explanation, *si consistas in cortice*; the fact that it is insufficient is amply shown by the allegorical details it leaves unexpounded, and notably by the Garden of Proserpina, the final stage of Guyon's temptation, which has indeed never been explained. I hope to show that the temptation, understood as a whole, is of a kind that makes it certain that the canto does in fact describe an initiation, and that what Guyon undergoes is a *total* temptation parallel to that of Christ in the wilderness.

[10] 'The Faerie Queene, Bk. II, and the Nicomachean Ethics', Modern Philology (1952).
[11] A. C. Hamilton, 'A Theological Reading of The Faerie Queene, ii', English Literary History (1955).

Mammon is not merely a money-god; in *Paradise Lost*, for instance, Milton associates him with vainglory as well as money (ii. 229 ff.) and elsewhere, speaking of the Cave of Mammon with Spenser in mind, he expressly adds to these venal learning (*Animadversions on the Remonstrant's Defence to Smectymnuus*, xiii). Now commentators have noticed, without explaining, certain similarities between Spenser's Cave and the temptations in *Paradise Regain'd*. There Christ rejects a magic banquet of potent appeal to the senses; and then, in turn, temptations of wealth, power, honour, and forbidden learning. Satan at this point is 'quite at a loss, for all his darts are spent' (*Paradise Regain'd*, iv. 366). According to exactly this scheme Marvell constructed his 'Dialogue between the Resolved Soul and Created Pleasure'. Each sense is tempted in turn and the temptation rejected on the ground that the reward of abstinence will be superior. There is a break in the poem there, marked by a chorus, and the tempter passes on to the temptation of female beauty, rejected by Satan as unlikely to succeed with Christ; the temptations of gold, military and civic glory, and finally of knowledge. These resisted, the Chorus proclaims the soul triumphant. 'The World has not one Pleasure more'. This insistence on the totality of the temptation as set forth in a literary scheme is ultimately based on Luke, iv. 13, 'And when the devil had ended *all* the temptation, he departed from him for a season'. In the normal intensity of biblical commentary the word *all* becomes significant; accordingly Augustine in his remarks on the text, writes as follows:

. . . these three kinds of vice, namely, the pleasures of the flesh, and pride, and curiosity, include all sins. And they appear to me to be enumerated by the Apostle John, when he says, *Love not the World: for all that is in the world is the lust of the flesh, and the lust of the eyes, and the pride of life*. For through the eye especially prevails curiosity. To what the rest indeed belong is clear. And that temptation of the Lord Man was threefold: by food, that is, by the lust of the flesh, where it is suggested, *command these stones that they be made bread*: by vain boasting, where, stationed on a mountain, all the kingdoms of the earth are shewn Him, and promised if He would worship; by curiosity, where, from the pinnacle of the temple, He is advised to cast Himself down, for the sake of trying whether He would be borne up by angels. And accordingly after the enemy could prevail with Him by none of these temptations, this is said of him, *When the devil had ended all his temptations.*

This occurs in the Homily on Psalm 8,[12] in which, incidentally, occur the words, 'What is man that thou art mindful of him? or the son of man, that thou visitest him?', to which Spenser alludes in the opening of canto viii when treating of Guyon's angelic helper. An understanding of this would have saved much bewildered commentary.

The Cave of Mammon canto is not concerned with the concupiscence of the flesh; that is dealt with in the Phaedria episode. It provides the remainder of the total temptation. Guyon is offered and rejects money, even as a means to greatness. Milton's Christ, who will accept benefits only in so far 'as he likes the giver' (*Paradise Regain'd*, ii. 321-2) is anticipated in the refusal of Guyon to 'receave thing offred till I know it well be got'. Spenser intensifies the temptation of riches by leading up to a point where Guyon is offered literally all the riches of the world, as the demon hovers over him. But he knows of a higher reward 'another bliss, another happiness, another end'. He then rejects Philotime, the daughter of Mammon. Since Mammon was equated with Pluto by the mythographers,[13] Philotime is the daughter of Dis and Persephone, and virtually the same person as Pride in I. iv (Lucifera, daughter of Pluto and 'sad *Proserpina* the Queene of hell') patroness of the other deadly sins. Her beauty is counterfeit, because she stands for an earthly idea of honour not a heavenly; the honour of the pagans which resides in human values, not that of the Christian which goes by 'perfect witness of all-judging Jove'. Behind this choice of a heavenly honour there lies the authority of St. Augustine; for reasons connected with the whole design of *The City of God* he spent much time on the antithesis between the two honours. The pagan, even at its most virtuous,

[12] *Enarrationes in Psalmos; Exposition of the Book of Psalms*, trans. Tweedy, Scratton, and Wilkins (1847), I, pp. 70 ff. Aquinas, citing Ambrose, also asserts the inclusiveness of the temptation (*S.T.*, III, 41, 4), and Lancelot Andrewes said that 'under these three heads come all temptations' (*The Wonderfull Combate ... between Christ and Satan*, 1592, p. 23).

[13] See Gyraldi, p. 202; Ben Jonson, *Love Restored, Workes* (1640), pp. 203 ff.; Lotspeich, p. 20.

rests on Opinion, not Truth. The exalted Roman honour commended by Sallust, for instance, and exemplified by Scipio Africanus, is only a shadow of the Christian honour, which is achieved more by suffering than by action, and rewarded in the next world, not this.[14] Guyon, then, temperately rejects the false honour in favour of the true, the earthly in favour of the heavenly city. The Christian honour depends upon self-conquest. In Marvell's poem, Pleasure offers Glory:

> Wilt thou all the Glory have
> That War or Peace commend?
> Half the World shall be thy Slave,
> The other half thy Friend.

But the reply of the Resolved Soul is clear as to the falsity of the thing offered:

> What Friends, if to myself untrue?
> What Slaves, unless I captive you?

If the analogy with Marvell and Milton is correct, Spenser should include a temptation to vain learning. And this brings us to the Garden of Proserpina, the unexplained part of the Mammon episode.

The principal literary sources of this Garden are *Odyssey*, x. 509 ff., and Claudian, *De Raptu Proserpinae*, where Pluto consoles his captive with talk of the benefits she will enjoy in his realm:

> est etiam lucis arbor praedives opacis
> fulgentis viridi ramos curvata metallo
>
> (ii. 290–1)

('And there is a rich tree in the dark groves, the curving branches of which gleam with bright gold'.) The spider also derives from Claudian, perhaps by way of *Muiopotmos*. But Spenser, as Warton noticed, omits the beautiful flowers and fruits of Claudian's garden, and instead combines this tree of golden fruit with the Homeric Grove of Persephone. The result is a picture like that of Polygnotus in the Lesches at Delphi, to which I shall recur, and

---

[14] *City of God*, V, xii–xx; see F. Kermode's 'Milton's Hero', *Review of English Studies*, 1953, pp. 317–30.

which shows the grove of Proserpina as a place where 'black poplars and willows grow' (Pausanias, *Description of Greece*, x. 30). Homer does not say they are black. The herbs in Spenser's garden are all deadly poisons, appropriate to Proserpina in her character as Hecate, patroness of poisons (N. Comes, p. 570). One of these, Cicuta, killed Socrates, devotee of true knowledge.

What is the meaning of the apples on Spenser's tree? They are in the first place the fruit that must not be eaten in the underworld; and in so far as they represent a temptation to be resisted under severe penalties, they are related to Eve's apple, which was eaten out of appetite, vain-glory, and curiosity. But Spenser complicates this by saying that all the famous apples of mythology grew on this tree. So they mean rather more than merely *mala Punica*.[15] The apples mentioned are related: those with which Hippomenes deceived Atalanta were said to be Hesperidean (N. Comes, p. 637) and given to him by Venus, who also, according to Ovid, gave Acontius his apple (*Heroides*, xxi. 123–4). Whatever they signify it is not avarice, as the commentators say; we have left that behind. The apples of the Hesperides were emblems of astronomical knowledge. The story of Atalanta was sometimes interpreted as a warning against blasphemy, since she desecrated the shrine of the Great Mother (Comes, p. 738). Comes says that the apple offered by Discord to the goddesses was the symbol of an insane contempt for the divine wisdom (p. 670). For the apple of Acontius I can find no mythographical source; this may be one that Spenser made up himself. Acontius, enamoured of Cydippe, won her by a trick. He wrote on an apple, 'I swear by Artemis that I will marry Acontius' and threw it in the girl's way. She picked it up and read the message aloud; and as she did so in the precincts of the temple of Artemis the words had the force of a solemn oath. Attempts to marry her to another man were thwarted by the gods, and in the end she married Acontius. It may be this trifling with an oath that made the story seem to Spenser another illustration of the danger of blasphemy; certainly the apple-stories all indicate intemperance of mind not body.

Spenser's Cocytus contains many sinners, but only two are

[15] The pomegranate, associated with Proserpina and the food of the dead, was widely diffused in Greek myth and folklore, and the motif exists also in Celtic folklore.

named. The first is Tantalus. He is normally taken as a type of avarice, not without support from the mythographers; but he is much more certainly a type of blasphemous or intemperate knowledge. 'Lo, Tantalus, I here tormented lye: Of whom high Jove wont whylome feated bee.' Tantalus served the gods with a dish made of the body of his son Pelops; as Fulgentius says, in order to test their immortality (*Fabularum liber*, ed. Helm, 1898, p. 57)—a *curious* thing to do. Others, with Pindar, say that being a guest of Jove, Tantalus grew arrogant, and reported to men the secrets of divine knowledge. Comes says he suffers '*ob loquacitatem, quia secreta Deorum mortalibus diuulgaveret*', 'for his loquacity, in that he revealed to mortals the secrets of the Gods' (pp. 633 ff.) and quotes Cornelius Gallus saying that Tantalus 'published what should not be spoken'. 'Why,' asks Comes, 'was Tantalus called a son of Jupiter? Because he was held to be a man deeply versed in divine and natural knowledge, and this, as the Pythagoreans understood, is not every man's having, but pertains only to those whose souls have been especially summoned from the sphere of Jupiter to inhabit these bodies' (Comes, p. 637). Tantalus, in short, revealed to the profane the innermost secrets of religion. Similarly Ovid says that Tantalus was punished for revealing or despising the Eleusinian mysteries, and got an appropriate punishment for his fault (*Ars Am.*, ii. 601–6); and Pausanias in his account of Polygnotus' painting shows Tantalus suffering in hell among those who showed disrespect for these mysteries (X. xxxi). Guyon refusing him help, says he must be an example of the *mind's* intemperance, not the body's. Tantalus, like the apples, stands for a blasphemous ambition of divine knowledge, a subject both traditional, and, in Spenser's time, acutely topical, for the limits of permitted inquiry were a matter of interest to theologians, scientists, and magicians alike.

The companion of Tantalus is Pontius Pilate, and one confesses to feeling less certain here. He calls himself 'the falsest judge alas, and most unjust' and certainly as a magistrate he corrupts my law by falsifying it. As an archetype of judicial corruption he was presented in the Towneley plays as a questmonger, an unambiguously vile and corrupt lawyer.[16] Here he admits that he 'delivered up the Lord of life to die, And did acquite a murder felonous, The whiles my hands I washt in puritie.' His question

[16] A. Williams, *The Characterization of Pilate in the Towneley Plays* (1950).

'what is truth?' would in the circumstances fall under the Augustinian *curiositas*; and he abuses knowledge.[17]

There is small doubt, then, that Guyon undergoes the temptations of wealth, glory, and inordinate or blasphemous curiosity. There remains, at this stage, one obscure and important detail, Proserpina's silver seat or stool, in which Mammon urges the weary knight to rest and eat an apple. Had he done so, the fiend would have seized him. What are we to make of this stool? It cannot be, in common sense, what the commentators say, an invitation to sloth. Upton wrote an interesting but unsatisfactory note relating the stool to the seat upon which Theseus sits for ever in *Aeneid*, vi: *Sedet, aeternumque sedebit | Infelix Thesus* (617–18). This is traditionally moralized in the manner of Tertullian: 'to sit too long is laborious in itself; the poet Virgil treats it as a punishment . . .' (quoted in Gronovius, *Thesaurus*, X, 16). And Spenser alludes to Theseus in *F.Q.* (I. v. 35) describing the damned in the course of his passage on Aesculapius in the underworld: 'Theseus condemned to endlesse slouth by law'. But Theseus was condemned *to* sloth, not *for* sloth; in fact he had just been attempting with some vigour the rape of Proserpina. Upton gets nearer the point when he adds, 'This stoole, on which it was unlawful to sit, our poet imaged from the forbidden seat in the Eleusinian mysteries'; and he refers us to the standard seventeenth-century work on these mysteries, the *Eleusinia* of J. Meurs or Meursius, and to Warburton's famous disquisition on the sixth *Aeneid* in *The Divine Legation of Moses*, adding, 'Our knight has now gone through a kind of initiation, and passed all the fiery trials; and comes out more temperate and just, as silver tried in the fire' (*Variorum* Spenser, ii, 239).

I think Upton was right about the stool, and about the initiatory nature of Guyon's ordeal; but the points need proving. The Homeric *Hymn to Demeter* has a stool covered with a silver fleece, on which Demeter, after Iambe has made her smile, consents to sit; but the Hymn was not known, save for a few lines, until 1780. However, as Allen points out in his edition (p. 151), this seat was often related to the sorrowful stone, *agelastos petra*, on which Ceres sat by a well on the road to Eleusis; and this stone has a well-established place in the ritual as a forbidden seat. Clement of

<hr />

[17] Spenser's Pilate cries out in the manner of Virgil's Theseus, '*discite iustitiam moniti et non temnere divos*', *Aeneid*, vi. 620.

Alexandria knew that the *mystes* might not sit in a certain seat, 'lest they should appear to be imitating the mourning Ceres' (*Protrepticon*), and Meursius repeats this '. . . *ne lugentem imitari viderentur*' (*Eleusinia* (1619), p. 10). This forbidden seat of the mysteries was associated with Theseus, who, either by his descent or in the course of a preparatory initiation like that of Hercules, had violated the secret knowledge they confer. He duly appears in the Polygnotus painting, in his Chair of Forgetfulness, as it was called; he is to pass eternity forgetting what it would have been better for him not to know (Pausanias, xxix. 9). I should like to produce, but cannot, Spenser's immediate source for this placing of a punitive chair of oblivion in the garden of Proserpina;[18] it is in Meurs—too late, of course, and in a scholium on Aristophanes, perhaps too obscure. However, it seems certain enough that this chair or stool fits the general pattern of the Garden temptations; they are all associated with the sin of forbidden knowledge, and the related sin of revealing or perverting divine knowledge.

In its general conception, the underworld in which this total temptation is enacted derives from *Aeneid*, vi, of which a normal Renaissance allegorical interpretation was that Aeneas underwent certain trials to strengthen his own virtues that they might collaborate with divine grace in bringing him to a final spiritual consummation.[19] But Spenser drew also on Homer and Claudian; and he seems to me to have used also the Delphic murals as described by Pausanias. These were an important source of Renaissance mythography (Seznec. pp. 232 ff.), and contain, as does Claudian, Eleusinian elements. For example, Polygnotus depicted the basket of Demeter which was an important ritual object; he showed, as we have seen, the fate of the profaner of the mysteries. Pausanias gives a detailed account of the fiend Eurynomus (X. xxviii) amplified by Cartari in his *Imagini de i Dei*, a standard manual (1581 ed., p. 235). Cartari describes the practice Eurynomus had of tearing his victims to pieces, and he seems to be the same fiend

---

[18] Persephone is represented visually as sitting on a silver chair holding up a pomegranate (V. Magnien, *Les Mystères d'Eleusis*, 1950, p. 136).

[19] As in the *Disputationes Camaldulenses* of Landino, of the Florentine Academy; see M. Y. Hughes, *Virgil and Spenser* (University of California Publications in English) (1929), pp. 263–418, especially pp. 399 ff.

described by Spenser as continually threatening Guyon. In the Eleusinian rite the suppliant was followed by a fury, and was forbidden to turn round.[20] There is a concurrence of detail to suggest that Spenser was doing what had been done before; so Michelangelo in his *Bacchus* may have celebrated the mysteries of Dionysius (Wind, pp. 147 ff.) suggesting an initiatory rite based upon ancient mysteries.

There is, naturally, an ambiguity in the attitude of the Renaissance to these mysteries. They were pagan, and the early fathers strenuously condemned them; but the Neo-platonists valued them highly, and their influence in Spenser's day was powerful. Even Clement, an important source of information on Eleusis, saw that they were in some respects parallel to Christian teaching (*Stromata*, V. ii); an initiate exchanges a human for a divine *phronesis*; he spends three days in 'hell'. Tertullian, commenting on the rite in which Mithraic initiates were offered, and were required to refuse, a crown, the ceremony taking place in a cave, argued that this was the devil imitating divine things (*De Corona*, xv). The celebrated initiation of Apuleius was regularly given a Christian application,[21] and Meurs himself insists, as do many others, that the aim of the mysteries was the correction of life, the achievement of a perfection which would bring happiness in this life and honour in the next (Meursius, pp. 12, 47; taking the hint from Cicero, *De Legibus*, xi). The Platonic interpretation of the rite as representing the descent of the soul into matter and its liberation therefrom was not hostile to Christian teaching, especially under the conditions I described earlier; the veiling of truth under the shows of pagan myth and religion is assumed in allegories of Spenser's kind, and it seems likely that he has reinforced the theme of Guyon's initiation with a series of occult allusions to the Eleusinian rite.

What makes this the more likely is the fact that Hercules was an Eleusinian initiate; he had to be, before he could descend to the underworld for Cerberus—a labour allegorized as the conquest of the passions (Meursius, p. 12). There is no space to speak of the strong element of Hercules in Guyon, as in most of Spenser's knights. It is another subject. Suffice it that Guyon even in his

[20] Iamblichus, *Protrepticon*, p. 340; see also Lucian, *Cataplus*.
[21] See the commentary of Beroaldus; and A. D. Nock, *Conversion* (1933), Chap. IX.

lapse when he sees the nymphs in the fountain, is imitating
Hercules, who had become as a result of the allegorization of his
Choice and his Labours, a type of heroic virtue, and indeed of
Christ.[22] There is nothing to be wondered at in the consequence
of what I have argued: that Guyon in the cave is imitating both
Hercules and Christ, particularly in their initiatory ordeals.

I return now to the original total temptation of Christ in the
desert. We have seen that Guyon's corresponds in its general
pattern; but a consideration of a few more aspects will suggest an
answer to the questions, what is Guyon initiated into? How is he
different when he comes out of the Cave? Let us take up the
resemblances between his temptation and that of Christ.

Christ wished to be tempted 'that he might strengthen us
against temptation' (*Summa Theologica*, III. 41. 1); this was, as
St. Gregory said, 'not unworthy' in him, and Guyon's openly
encountering Mammon is parallel. Christ's resistance is exemplary; so is Guyon's. 'Christ of his own freewill exposed himself
to be tempted by the devil . . . the devil prefers to assail a man
who is alone . . . And so it was that Christ went out into the
desert, as to a field of battle, to be tempted there by the devil.' So
Aquinas, adding that Christ actually provoked the devil. The distinction between a proper avoidance of the occasion of sin and a
proper acceptance of the good temptations which strengthen a
man for great achievements is as clear in Spenser, who makes
Occasio a character in the Second Book, as it is in Aquinas. The
difference is between an external temptation, like Job's or Christ's,
and a temptation caused internally by concupiscence. The former
variety is without sin (Heb., iv. 15: Christ 'was *in all points*
tempted like as we are, yet without sin'). 'And hence,' adds St.
Thomas, 'Christ wished to be tempted by an enemy, but not by
the flesh.' The proper resistance to such temptation is *passive*. This
is the familiar paradox of Christian warfare, that the soldier puts

[22] See M. Y. Hughes, 'The Christ of *Paradise Regained* and the Renaissance
Heroic Tradition', *Studies in Philology* (1938), pp. 254–77; also Hallett Smith,
pp. 290 ff. That Guyon could partake simultaneously of the nature of Christ
and Hercules is suggested by this observation of Comes (*Mythologia*, 1588,
p. 1056), 'In order to show that wisdom is the gift of God, and that there
can be no virtue without this divine will, they [the ancients] feigned that
Hercules, that is to say fortitude and honesty and greatness of soul in over-
throwing vice and trampling down pleasures, was the Son of God.'

on the whole armour of God, but merely suffers himself to be tempted; and this disposes of Berger's objection, that Guyon is quite untroubled by Mammon's inducements and merely pandering to his own vanity (Berger, pp. 17 ff.). Augustine had distinguished at length between the passive Christian and the active pagan heroism; Aquinas reaffirms this in the present context: 'Christ came to destroy the works of the devil not by powerful deeds, but rather by suffering' (*S.T.*, III. 41. 1). Milton says he conquered 'by humiliation and strong sufferance'; his Christ replies 'temperately', 'sagely', 'unmoved', etc., to all temptation, and defeats the final temptation of violence by complete immobility on the pinnacle.

Christ's temptation took place at the end of his time in the wilderness; so did Guyon's. He allowed this because at such a time the devil would dare to approach him; he 'abandoned his manhood to its nature' that he might conquer the devil 'not by God, but by the flesh' (*S.T.*, III. 41. 4). Similarly Guyon undertakes Mammon as natural man (without his palmer) and vanquishes him 'not as by God, but as by man' (*S.T.*, III. 41. 4). After the temptation Christ, in the weakness of his human nature, receives the ministrations of angels; so does Guyon. According to Luke, iv. 13, the devil then 'departed from him for a time', and this was interpreted as meaning 'until his Passion'. Guyon's next temptation is at the climax of his quest in the Bower of Bliss. After his Herculean faltering over the nymphs[23] in the fountain he proceeds to the active destruction of the evil Acrasia. Milton undoubtedly thinks of the temptation in the wilderness as a kind of initiation; having passed through it, say the angels, Christ is now ready for his work:

> Queller of Satan, on thy glorious work
> Now enter, and begin to save mankind.
>
> (*P.R.*, iv. 634–5)

---

[23] Guyon (unlike his colleague in Book V) does not succumb to pleasure as Hercules did to Omphale. On this aspect of Hercules, cf. Comes, p. 713, 'Magis periculosum est ne voluptatibus, quam difficultatibus, plerumque vincamur', which is echoed by Spenser in the opening of the sixth Canto of Book II:

> A Harder lesson to learn Continence
> In joyous pleasure, then in grievous paine.

Hercules, after his own (passive) initiation, became actively heroic and dragged Cerberus, the passions, from hell. Hercules was the pagan type of heroic virtue, and, as I have said, he was Christianized. If Guyon's temptation was a prelude to an active heroic virtue, we should now ask what this virtue was.

The classic exposition is in a book upon which Spenser certainly drew, the *Nicomachean Ethics*. Aristotle, at the end of his Sixth Book, distinguishes between 'natural' and 'proper' virtue; we are born with the first, but the second is what we aspire to, and it cannot exist without prudence. Book VII, which is mostly about the lower virtue Continence, opens with some distinctions. Three things are to be avoided; vice, incontinence, brutality. The contraries of the first two are virtue and continence; the contrary of the third is Heroic Virtue, which places men above others, in the likeness of gods. Aristotle says very little about Heroic Virtue but it is enough, in the context of so famous a book, to have provoked a long debate, in which the virtue of Hercules also plays its large part. Augustine made it a suffering virtue: Isidore of Seville applied the idea to poetry. Milton has the virtue in mind when he writes in *Areopagitica* of the true warfaring Christian as one who, like Hercules, 'can apprehend and consider vice with all her baits and seeming pleasures, and yet abstain' (*ed. cit.*, p. 514); and *Paradise Lost*, ix opens with an excursus on his 'Sad task, yet argument | Not less but more Heroic then the wrauth | Of stern *Achilles*', and a defence of a new kind of heroism—not of wars, 'hitherto the onely Argument | Heroic deem'd' but 'the better fortitude | Of patience and Heroic Martyrdom'. The frontispiece of Sandy's *Ovid* and the verses prefatory to the work illustrate the association of Heroic Virtue with Pallas Athene and the control of appetite, as against voluptuous indulgence as represented by Circe or, in some manifestations, Venus: choose Heroic Virtue and you undertake 'the Path and Toyles of *Hercules*'. The formal confrontation of pagan and Christian heroic virtue may be found in Dryden, where it occurs at length in a debate between St. Catherine and a heathen philosopher Apollonius in *Tyrannic Love*, II. iii. And, more remarkably, Dryden uses the idea of Christianized heroic virtue elliptically in a witty passage of *Annus Mirabilis*. Prince Rupert, refusing the tactical bait by which the Dutch admiral tried to lead him on to the sandbanks, declines the engagement and joins the main fleet instead.

> Heroic Virtue did his Actions guide,
> And he the substance not th'appearance chose.
>
> (l. 166)

In this instance the normally impetuous Rupert displayed the true heroism of abstinence, which incidentally requires the ability to distinguish between apparent and real goods.

The idea, then, is common enough, especially in an age ambitious of Christian epic. The reconciliation of Aristotle's Heroic Virtue with Christianity had been undertaken by Aquinas and elaborated in the process of distinguishing between the virtues and the gifts of the Holy Ghost (*S.T.*, II–I. 68.1):

> The virtues perfect man according as it is natural for him to be moved by his reason in his interior and exterior actions. Consequently man needs yet higher perfections whereby to be disposed to be moved by God. These perfections are called gifts, not only because they are infused by God, but also because by them man is disposed to become amenable to the Divine inspiration. . . . Even [Aristotle] says that for those who are moved by Divine Instinct, there is no need to take counsel according to human reason, but only to follow their inner promptings, since they are moved by a principle higher than human reason. . . . The gifts perfect men for acts which are higher than acts of virtue. . . . Hence Aristotle above virtue commonly so called, places a kind of *heroic* or *divine* virtue.

This reconciliation of Aristotle's Heroic Virtue with the gifts is brought about partly through the agency of a third party unnamed, Macrobius, whose treatment of the Virtues in the *Commentary* on Cicero's *Somnium Scipionis* was the second great ancient source for medieval and Renaissance treatments of the subject. Following Plotinus (*Enn.*, I. ii) the Commentary 'arranges the grades of the virtues according to a proper and natural classification: the first, political virtues, the second "cleansing" or purgatorial virtues; the third the virtues of the purified mind, the fourth, the exemplary virtues. Virtues of the first grade are proper to man as a social animal; virtues of the second type are found only in the man who is capable of attaining the divine, "the man who has resolved to be purged of all contamination with the body", and by an escape from mortal things, as it were, to mingle solely with the divine.' In this grade, Temperance is abstinence 'from everything that the habits of the body seek, as far as nature will permit'. The third type 'includes the virtues of the purified and serene mind, completely and thoroughly cleansed from all taint of this world'. The fourth type is inaccessible to men, consisting of the virtues 'that are present in the divine mind itself'. Macrobius sums up: 'The first type of virtue mitigates the passions, the second puts them away, the third has forgotten them, and to the fourth they are anathema.'

When Aquinas speaks of 'those who are moved by Divine instinct'—the most striking example of this kind of heroic virtue in literature is Milton's Samson at the end of his life—he presumably has in mind the man who possesses the Macrobian virtues of the third type. One may see the conflation of Aristotle and Macrobius in Benedict xiv's treatment, which the *Catholic Encyclopedia* calls 'classical', of heroic virtue: 'a habit of good conduct that has become a second nature, a new motive power stronger than all corresponding inborn inclinations, capable of rendering easy a series of acts each of which, for the ordinary man, would be beset with great, if not insurmountable, difficulties'. And Benedict distinguishes between the 'social virtues', which are the political virtues of Macrobius related to Matthew, v. 48, and the exemplary or divine virtues, adding that 'it is . . . necessary to posit certain intermediate virtues which are between the social, which are human, and the exemplary, which are divine. These intermediate virtues are of two degrees of perfection; the lesser in the soul still struggling upwards from a life of sin to a likeness with God—these are called the purifying virtues (*virtutes purgatoriae*): the greater in the souls which have already attained to the divine likeness—these are called the virtues of the purified soul (*virtutes jam purgati animi*) . . . this is a perfection rare in this life.' The distinction between heroic virtue, so Christianized, and sanctity, is a fine one; but it is demonstrated in the parallel careers of Guyon and the Red Cross Knight. The progress of Guyon towards heroic virtue is from *virtutes purgatoriae* to *virtutes jam purgati animi*; and the inclusive temptation of the Cave of Mammon is a divine aid to this progress.

To bring the matter of the virtues nearer to Spenser, one may mention Tasso's brief and direct treatment of it in his discourse *Della Virtù Heroica e della Carità*. Cicero, he says—but he means Macrobius—placed above the moral virtues 'le purgatorie, e quelle d'anima giàpurgata, e l'esemplari'. He places Heroic Virtue as far above the moral virtues as heroes are above men, between the human and the divine. Aristotle he finds in some ways unhelpful, since there must be more to say about the virtue than that it is abstention from vice and bestiality; it is a perfection of good, and it has its own *soggetto*, as temperance has pleasure and fortitude danger. It contains all the other virtues, as the heavens the elements, in a nobler and more eminent mode. The nearest of the virtues to the Heroic is Magnanimity; heroic virtue is to magnanimity as glory is to honour. Above all the other virtues it involves prudence. Is it a way of keeping the affections in bounds, or does it on occasion use their vehemence? It both reins and employs the passions; for, as Plato says, 'anger is the warrior of the reason'. It has to do more with action than speculation. Finally, it resembles Charity in that Charity contains the other theological virtues; and it has no limited end; and controls the affections efficaciously; and looks for the reward of glory. But Heroic Virtue is inferior to Charity not only in that the hero is inferior to the martyr in fortitude, but in its end; for it achieves acts of fortitude, whereas Charity benefits others (*Opere di Torquato Tasso* (1823), xi, 169 ff.). Elsewhere, Tasso calls proper to heroic poetry the virtues acquired by long exercise and also those infused by divine grace (xii, 7). The *Aeneid* is the pagan model of an epic in which both kinds of virtue are represented; and it is balanced on the mysterious sixth book, in which Aeneas descends into Hell.

Guyon is concerned with Heroic Virtue, as the Red Cross Knight with Charity. In the course of his quest, the Red Cross Knight errs, suffers, is purged, and attains to sanctity and a vision of the Heavenly City. Guyon passes from the lower temperance of natural habit to the virtue of a hero, which includes all the cardinal virtues. His achievement is active, indeed destructive; he makes his anger the warrior of his reason. He passes not from temperance to continence, as they argue who relate Spenser too narrowly to the *ipsissima verba* of Aristotle, but through a purgatorial process from human to semi-divine virtue, from a human to a divine *phronesis*. He becomes one of the purified souls described by Benedict, rare in this life; not a saint but a hero, like Hercules after his initiation. But the initiation of Guyon is modelled upon the temptation of the great exemplar of Christian heroic virtue, Christ in the wilderness. After his succour by the angels he can proceed, 'all his great work before him set'. He destroys the Bower without reflection, as if by an inner prompting. His initiatory temptation in the Cave of Mammon is the necessary preparation for his assault on Acrasia, just as the temptation of Christ was the necessary prelude to the final victory over Satan.

The Cave of Mammon is a mystery of the sort that labours to be shadowed with obscurity. We have first to see that the temptations to which Guyon is subjected are tacitly based upon those of Christ, and that they represent all possible temptations. The passive resistance of Guyon is related, by a typical syncretist device, to the pagan mysteries as well as to Christ as hero. Guyon undergoes, like Aeneas in the allegorized *Aeneid*, a purgatorial experience, and emerges no longer a knight of mere temperance but an exemplar of heroic virtue and direct instrument of providence. At the beginning of Book II, there is a meeting between the Red Cross Knight and Guyon. When they part the Palmer says:

> Joy may you have, and everlasting fame,
> Of late most hard atchiev'ment by you donne,
> For which enrolled is your glorious name
> In heavenly Registers above the Sunne,
> Where you a Saint with Saints your seat have wonne:
> But wretched we, where ye have left your marke,
> Must now anew begin, like race to runne.

'Like race'—it is notorious that the two Books run in parallel. That is because of the parallelism between Charity and Heroic Virtue. The trials of each knight differ in accordance with their ends; but each is tried and purged. As Upton said, 'Our knight has now gone through a kind of initiation, and passed all the fiery trials: and comes out more temperate and just, as silver tried in the fire.' The state into which he passes is that of heroic virtue; he is no longer a temperate man but an active instrument of God.

4

THE BANQUET OF SENSE[1]

I use the term 'Banquet of Sense' to describe a theme in Renaissance art and literature: one of those patterns, literary and iconographical, that recur more frequently than is supposed; which import into the context in which they are found meanings that the modern eye can miss; and which can alter and deepen what seems to be the obvious significance of even familiar passages. It is permissible, since the publication of Curtius's book,[2] to call such elements, *topoi*, though this strains the original rhetorical sense of the term. Perhaps the vaguer 'theme' will serve. The expression 'banquet of sense' is probably most familiar from the title of Chapman's poem *Ouids Banquet of Sence*, but that is one of the most difficult poems in the language, and I shall come to it last, when I have tried to provide some idea of what the theme implies in other contexts. It may be useful to consider first a familiar poem of which the structure, a very rigid one, is perhaps not generally understood, and which includes a rather full literary banquet of sense—Marvell's *Dialogue between the Resolved Soul and Created Pleasure*.

This work is divided into two sections. In the first, the resolved soul, the true warfaring Christian, successfully resists a sensual temptation or trial. In the second he overcomes the temptations of women, wealth, glory and improper learning. In its entirety this scheme, rarely found in such purity, but also present in Spenser and in *Paradise Regain'd*, represents a totality of possible

[1] See Preface.
[2] *European Literature and the Latin Middle Ages*, trans. W. Trask, London, 1953.

temptations: 'Triumph, triumph, victorious Soul, The World has not one Pleasure more.' At the back of this is the common interpretation of Luke iv. 13 as signifying that the temptations undergone by Christ in the desert included all that were possible, and so indicated to the Christian the whole strategy of the devil.[3] Translated to literature, and contaminated with the Renaissance myth of the Christianized Hercules, with help from St. Augustine in the discrimination between Christian and pagan Heroic Virtue, the theme of total temptation assumes the form given it by Marvell, and the defeat of sensual temptation is related to that of the Choice of Hercules. The rejection of Pleasure may take other forms (as, for example, the refusal to drink of Circe's cup, which is equivalent to choosing Heroic Virtue, whereas to drink of it is to fall into bestiality, called the opposite of Heroic Virtue in Aristotle's seminal chapter, *Nicomachean Ethics*, VII. i). But Marvell chooses to open with a Banquet of Sense, properly rejected. The senses are treated in ascending order; from Taste and Touch, which operate only in direct contact with the object of sense; to Smell, which is a kind of mean between these and the higher senses, and to Sight and Hearing, the highest, which operate at a distance without contact. Then he proceeds to treat the other parts of the total temptation, until with its final temptation of forbidden learning rejected, the Soul completes its imitation of Christ.

The Banquet of Sense has both Christian and pagan sources. The Christian source is the passage on the Eucharist in 1 Corinthians x. Its interpretation was obviously of central spiritual and political importance in the seventeenth century. St. Paul speaks first of manna as a type of the Eucharist, observing that the backslidings of the Israelites in the desert teach us that, being allowed spiritual meat and drink, we should not 'sit down' to unspiritual. Partakers of the body and blood of Christ, we should not with the Gentiles sacrifice to devils: 'Ye cannot drink of the cup of the Lord, and the cup of devils; ye cannot be partakers of the Lord's table, and of the table of devils. . . . If any man say unto you, this is offered in sacrifice unto idols, eat not. Whether therefore ye eat, or drink, or whatsoever ye do, do all to the glory of the Lord.'

---

[3] See Frank Kermode, 'Milton's Hero', *R.E.S.* (n.s.), iv (1953), 317–30, and Chapter 3, above.

And in the same chapter is the assurance that God 'will not suffer you to be tempted above that you are able'. The direct use of this passage in devotional writing may be illustrated by Jeremy Taylor's recommendation of prayer before and after food so that we may 'remove and carry up our mind and spirit to the celestial table, often thinking of it, and desiring it, that by enkindling thy desire to heavenly banquets, thou mayst be indifferent, and less passionate for the earthly'.[4]

The pagan shadow of the Eucharist is the banquet, or *Symposium*, of Plato; and its opposite, the shadow of the Pauline 'table of devils', is 'nature's banquet', or 'the banquet of sense'.[5] As a matter of fact, the easily achieved association of a sense-by-sense temptation with the tale of the temperate man's resistance to evil occurs very early, in the primal source of the Choice of Hercules motif, Xenophon's account of the myth told by the sophist Prodicus; κάκια promises the young man ease and pleasure: 'You shall taste all of life's sweets and escape all bitters. In the first place, you shall not trouble your brain with war or speculation; other topics shall engage your mind; your only speculation, what meat or drink you shall find agreeable to your palate; what delight of ear or eye; what pleasure of smell or touch; what darling lover's intercourse shall most enrapture you; how you shall pillow your limbs in the softest slumber; how cull each individual pleasure without alloy of pain.'[6] This treatment of the senses seems, however, to have been neglected by Xenophon's earlier imitators,[7]

---

[4] *Holy Living*, ii. 7. See also Colet on 1 Cor. xxii, '. . . at the table of the Lord the case is this, that the communicants of Christ are turned into him, whereas, at the table of the devils, they either change the devils unto themselves; or are changed into the devils' (*Colet's Lectures on 1 Corinthians*, ed. J. H. Lupton, London, 1874, p. 108). But Colet allegorizes: the good banquet is Scripture, the bad pagan learning.

[5] The two could have been associated by a recollection of the early Christian ἀγάπη, mentioned by Chrystostom (in 1 Cor. xi. 17, *Hom.* xxvii) and Tertullian (*Apol.* xxxix). It was familiar from religious controversy. See Hooker, *Laws of Ecclesiastical Polity*, Preface, iv. 3; Everyman ed., London, 1907, i. 110–11, and n. 3.

[6] *The Works of Xenophon*, trans. Dakyns (1890–7), iii (i) 4.

[7] For example, Silius Italicus, *Punica* xv, where Scipio is tempted. Voluptas urges him to shun war, offering him ease instead. The argument of Virtus prevails: 'quis aetheris servatur seminis ortus | coeli porta patet'. Silius perhaps avoided the senses because in Book XI he had already shown the demoralizing effect of feasting and pleasure-seeking in Hannibal and his

and to have been re-attached later to the theme of the temptation of Pleasure; and then the senses were given a more regular sequence, so that, as a rule, good love proceeded from the highest senses up to intellect, and bad to the lowest sense, touch. In short, like Circe's cup, the natural temptations of the senses as represented in a banquet of sense serve to distinguish clearly between men who aspire to Heroic Virtue (or to the love of God) and men who sink into bestiality, preferring the creature to the Creator. The passage on the senses in Augustine's *Confessions* no doubt remained in people's minds: it is indeed echoed in Marvell's language.[8]

The schematic presentation of the senses as a group with clearly defined iconographical attributes relating to a banquet is a late invention.[9] It does not seem to occur in Italian painting, though it is common in Netherlandish art, where it perhaps flourished by association with the popular theme of the Prodigal Son. Unluckily no art historian has provided a professional description of the material, and this is a very amateur account of the way it was used. An engraving by Adrian Collaert bears the legend: 'Accipe homo quae quinque ferunt munera Sensus | Accipe, & oblatis prudentius utere donis; | Ne te quos tibi cernis famularier ultro, | His famulum adfectus reddat mala suada cupido', emphasizing the need for temperance, lest the senses should become not servants but masters; for, in Chapman's favourite expression, 'dati sunt sensus ad intellectum excitandum'. The senses are 'the five gates through which ideas and apprehensions enter to inhabit the soul', as Ripa puts it in his standard handbook.[10] The danger is that the

---

troops at Capua. For a complete history of the Prodician Choice from antiquity forward, see Erwin Panofsky, *Hercules am Scheidewege*, Berlin, 1930. Elizabethan treatments of the theme are discussed in Hallett Smith, *Elizabethan Poetry* (1952), p. 296. The statement that in England the theme was 'ignored until it was made widely known by Shaftesbury's thesis' (W. Wells, *Leeds Art Calendar*, iii, 1953, 27) is false.

[8] *Confessions* x. ii *et seq.* Augustine on the pleasures of hearing ('voluptates aurium tenacius me implicaverant et subiugaverant') may have suggested Marvell's 'none can chain a mind That this sweet chordage cannot bind'.

[9] 'Banquet' here has the usual sixteenth- and seventeenth-century sense of a light collation, not a main meal.

[10] *Iconologia* (ed. of 1603), p. 499: 'I cinque porti, per li quali entranno l'idee, & l'apprensioni ad habitar l'anima.'

gratification of the senses should become an end in itself, so that a sensual Voluptas is mistaken for the highest good. In the Collaert engraving the senses are given their symbolic attributes, more or less according to Ripa: Sight with a looking-glass held up to the banqueter, an eagle and a burning cresset; Hearing, with a lute and a fawn; Smell with flowers and a hunting-dog; Taste with a basket of fruit and a cup of wine, a fruit-eating monkey[11] above; Touch in contact with the banqueter and attended by falcon and tortoise, emblem of venereal pleasure. Touch is embraced by the diner, for whom Hearing is playing, and to whom Taste and Touch offer wine and flowers.

In Collaert the emphasis is on danger rather than on dissipation; sometimes the banquet setting seems little more than a way of treating pastime and good company, as in Teniers. But there is normally a moral in it. As a phase of the Prodigal Son story it is, of course, highly moralized by its context, even in so naturalistic a portrayal as Murillo's. On the whole the banqueter is in great danger, is being offered a seductive and disastrous benefit, like Circe's cup. Another way of putting the same case is in the ordinary Choice of Hercules: in the version of Annibale Carracci (called by Panofsky 'canonical') Virtue points to her height, which is attained only by a steep road; on it stands a white horse, emblematic of Virtus, manly glory (sometimes it is Pegasus). She is supported by a figure with a Bible. Pleasure wears a revealing gown, and has about her emblems of idle delight—theatrical masks, instruments of music, and so on. There are innumerable variations, Virtue shading over into Pallas, Pleasure into Venus.[12] An engraving after a lost picture by Peter Potter gives a christianized version: Hercules has become the Christian pilgrim choosing between Truth and the World, whom the devil inspires. The way of Truth, who carries a Bible, passes through a strait gate; it is a *via crucis*, not a way of fame; the angel stands by to crown the man who chooses right. The World offers pleasure and power; an orb in her hair, at her feet the minted gold of wealth;

---

[11] For the pejorative association of monkeys with the sense of taste, see H. W. Janson, *Apes and Ape Lore in the Middle Ages and the Renaissance* (1952), pp. 239 ff.

[12] Shaftesbury says 'the shape, countenance, and person' of Pallas may be given to Virtue and those of Venus to Pleasure. (*Characteristicks*, 1714, iii. 364).

roses, drinking glasses, instruments, and a cushion represent the
sensual appeal. Behind her one sees suggested orgies of various
sorts, and behind them burning Sodom; Death leads the dance
with his drum. Now this takes us very near to a point where the
Choice of Hercules and the Banquet of Sense come together; and
they do so in an anonymous etching after Sanraedam's Choice.
Virtue, attired as Minerva, shows the hero a painting in which one
distinguishes the virtues of Fortitude with her column, Justice
with scales, Temperance with mixing bowl, and Charity with
children. These are on the hill of Virtue. On the other, the hell
side, is Vice, displaying a grotesque banquet of sense. The
association of this theme with bestiality as opposed to heroic
virtue is here extremely obvious. It is 'nature's banquet'—to it
Comus urges the Lady, and Satan Christ. The contrast, explicit in
Paradise Regain'd, is with a heavenly banquet.

I come now to examples of the theme in English poetry, first in
Ben Jonson, who uses it at least three times, first in Act IV of
Poetaster. We hear of a 'heavenly banquet' that Ovid arranges
for his friends. Ovid in the play is a poet of talent, but dangerously
immoral, and strongly contrasted with Horace whom, a little
earlier, we have heard commending the frugal feasts of Scipio
Africanus. We see that the term 'heavenly banquet' is a deliberate
irony; the company, drawn from a loose aristocracy and a court-
aping merchant class, dress up as gods and goddesses. Ovid, playing Jove, proclaims that, 'of his licentious goodness', he is 'willing to make the feast no fast from any manner of pleasure'
(IV. v. 15–17). The party takes its rather lascivious course, until
music is called for; there is a song, and then another, 'to revive
our senses' (207). The object of this song, we gather, is:

> To celebrate this feast of sense,
> As free from scandall, as offence.
> Here is beautie, for the eye;
> For the eare, sweet melodie;
> Ambrosiack odours, for the smell;
> Delicious nectar for the taste;
> For the touch, a ladies waste;
> Which doth all the rest excell!

(212–19)

The banquet is interrupted by the arrival of Emperor Augustus, who is shocked by the blasphemous representation of the gods in pursuit of sensual pleasure; Ovid as a poet, with all the special responsibilities of a poet, is particularly to blame.

> O who shall follow virtue and embrace her,
> When her false bosome is found nought but aire?
> Who shall, with greater comfort, comprehend
> Her unseen being, and her excellence,
> When you, that teach, and should eternize her,
> Live, as shee were no law unto your lives?
>
> (IV. vi. 40-7)

The association of Ovid with the Banquet theme has no source in the poet himself, and must have arisen from Chapman or from the more emancipated reading of the *Ars Amatoria* and *Amores*. The writers of Elizabethan epyllia had gained a certain new freedom in erotic expression; Ovid seems to have become a sort of counter-Plato; and the formal opposition between the two could be expressed very economically in the contrast between the Banquet of Sense and the Banquet of Heavenly Love derived from the *Symposium*.

The clearest example of this collocation is also to be found in Jonson's late play, *The New Inn*. Lovel, 'a complete gentleman, a soldier, and a scholar' is a melancholy guest in the New Inn where are also found the supposed Lady Frampul and her servants. Prudence, the chambermaid, is elected 'sovereign of the sports' at the inn, and she sets up a court of love at which Lovel woos Frances, the supposed Lady, by giving her a full exposition of the true Florentine Art of Love. But Lord Beaufort, a less scholarly gentleman, is seized with an un-Platonic desire for Laetitia, and in this the contrast resides. Lovel delivers a fairly pure version of some passages in the *Symposium*, modified by Ficino's Commentary upon it. First he is asked to define Love:

> . . . by description,
> It is a flame, and ardor of the minde,
> Dead, in the proper corps, quick in anothers;
> Trans-ferres the Lover into the Loved . . .
> It is the likenesse of affections,
> Is both the parent, and the nurse of love.

> Love is a spirituall coupling of two soules,
> So much more excellent, as it least relates
> Unto the body . . .
>
> (III. ii. 95–102)

But Lord Beaufort disagrees:

> I relish not these philosophicale feasts;
> Give me a banquet o' sense, like that of *Ovid*:
> A forme, to take the eye; a voyce, mine eare;
> Pure *aromatiques* to my sent; a soft,
> Smooth, deinty hand, to touch; and, for my taste,
> *Ambrosiack* kisses to melt downe the palat.
>
> (III. ii. 125–30)

Here the Plato-Ovid opposition is as clear as anyone could wish, and here too the association of the banquet with Ovid and sensual love is so casual as to seem conventional. It is interesting to note that Jonson was disgusted at the failure of this play, and clearly did not believe that its inner meanings were beyond the scope of the common reader, whom he addresses thus: 'If thou canst but spell, and join my sense, there is more hope of thee than of a hundred fastidious impertinents who were there present the first day, yet never made piece of their prospects in the right way'— as we should say, never got the right angle on it.[13] The theme was less esoteric than we might suppose.

Beaufort's praise of Ovidian love, of the anti-Platonic Banquet, is at once censured by Lovel; those who indulge it, he says

> Are the earthly, lower forme of lovers,
> Are only taken with what strikes the senses,
> And love by that loose scale.
>
> (III. ii. 131–3)

The distinction is basically that between the two Aphrodites of the *Symposium*—Lovel speaks for Ourania, Beaufort for Pandemos, illustrating his case with kisses stolen from Laetitia, which are qualitatively very different from that formal, licensed, Platonic kiss, mixture of souls,[14] which is to be Lovel's reward from Lady

---

[13] It may be noted that Chapman uses precisely this figure in his Preface to *Ovids Banquet of Sence*.

[14] 'All chaste lovers covet a kisse, as a coupling of soules together. And therefore Plato the devine lover saith, that in kissing, his soull came as far as

Frampul. We may, says Lovel, be attracted by 'what's fair and graceful in an object'; but love must seek out the soul within, that which 'can love me again', return love—the Anteros complementary to Eros.

Lovel: My end is lost in loving of a face,
An eye, lip, nose, hand, foot or other part,
Whose all is but a statue, if the mind
Move not, which only can make returne.
The end of love is, to have two made one
In will, and in affection, that the mindes
Be first inoculated, not the bodies.
Beaufort: Gi' me the body, if it be a good one.

(III. ii. 148–55)

Lovel censures this remark; Beaufort's kind of love is

A mere degenerate appetite,
A lost, oblique, deprav'd affection,
And beares no marke, or character of Love;

(III. ii. 168–70)

and he concludes with a plea for purity, making the absence of sensuality a condition of true love. The words in which Lady Frampul signifies her approval sum up the whole theme:

O speake, and speake for ever! let mine eare
Be feasted still, and filled with this banquet!
No sense can ever surfeit on such truth!

(III. ii. 201–3)

There is in this passage a clear and formal distinction between the two banquets of love. One is divine, one natural; one uplifting, one degenerate; one a banquet of the soul, which employs the

---

his lippes to depart out of the bodie' (Castiglione, *The Courtier*, trans. Hoby, Everyman edn., 1928, p. 315). For kissing in cult-Platonism, see Nesca A. Robb, *Neoplatonism of Italian Renaissance* (1935), p. 191. The Lovel-Beaufort opposition in Jonson may have taken from *trattati d'amore*, perhaps indeed from *The Courtier*, where Bembo's exposition of Platonic love is interrupted by the sardonic comments of Morello, who thinks that 'the possessing of this beautie which he prayseth so much, without the bodie, is a dreame' (ed. cit. p. 307). Also Lovel is an older man than Beaufort, which is again part of Castiglione's position.

senses properly, as agents of the mind; the other a banquet of sense which can only corrupt, which is a yielding to Voluptas or degrading natural pleasure rather than the food of the soul.[15]

Jonson does not allow the high-minded view all its own way, and there may be ironic references to the cult-Platonism of the contemporary court; but this need not prevent us from tracing back the banquet-debate to a philosophical source in Ficino's Commentary on the *Symposium*.[16]

Ficino distinguishes Venus Ourania and Venus Pandemos. The former is divine beauty, the object of the love of the contemplatives, belonging to the sphere of Mind. The latter is the vulgar or natural Venus, Venus Genetrix, the associate of the *anima mundi*; the force that urges men to procreate, and so to continue the earthly simulacra of divine beauty. The former is 'quella intelligenzia, la quale nella Mente Angelica ponemmo' (that intelligence we attribute to the Angelic Mind); 'l'altra e la forza del generare, all'Anima di Mondo attribuita' (the other is the generative power we attribute to the Soul of the World). Venus Vulgaris, though baser than the other because it finds satisfaction through the senses and the fancy, is not evil. But there is a third kind of love, which Ficino, as a physician, considers a form of madness, and calls 'bestial love'.[17] This is not properly love at all, and should not be called by 'il sacratissimo nome di Amore'. It is merely an affair of the senses. About this kind of love we hear most in the Sixth and Seventh Orations; Tommaso Benci introduces it thus:

Da queste celesti vivande adunque state discosto, state discosto, o empii; i quali involti nelle fecce terrene, è al tutto a Bacco, è a Priapo divoti, lo Amore, che e dono celeste, abbassate in terra è in loto a uso di porci. Ma voi, castissimi convitate, etc.

[15] Jonson again returns to the Banquet of Sense in his *Loves Welcome. The King and Queenes Entertainment at Bolsover* (1634), where it is combined with the myth of Eros and Anteros (*Works*, ed. Herford and Simpson, vii 807 ff.).

[16] This influential work, written in Latin in 1474, reports the remarks of seven Platonists of the Medici circle on the *Symposium*, supposed to have been made at the annual banquet on Plato's reputed birthday (7 November). The text used here is Ficino's own Italian translation (ed. Rensi, 1914).

[17] For Ficino's differences from Pico della Mirandola on this point, see Panofsky, *Studies in Iconology* (1939), p. 144.

Throughout the book there is, of course, a strong association of heavenly love with the Banquet of Plato's work, 'il quale e Convito di Amore intitolato'. Further, the three kinds of love correspond to the three ways of life; Celestial Love to the Contemplative Life, Terrestrial Love to the Active Life, Bestial Love to the Voluptuous Life. If a man chooses the last of these, there is a sudden fall 'dal vedere . . . nella concupiscenzia del tatto'. Such a fall indicates vileness and dishonour; but those who do not so fall 'pascendosi eglino delle vere vivande dell'Animo, s'empione più e con più tranquillità amano'. What can be worse than that a man should fall thus? Through such madness he becomes a beast. 'Il vero Amore non e altro che un certo forza di volare à la divina bellezza. Lo Amore adulterato e una rovina da'l vedere à'l tatto.'

Ficino draws these strong contrasts between the extremes of bestial and heavenly love with reference to the banquet—the banquet of heavenly love—which the man who abandons himself to voluptuousness is giving up. Bestial love involves this collapse from the highest to the lowest of the senses, from sight to touch; for, in Ficino's work, the senses exist in a fixed hierarchy which he explains as follows:

> Il senso per li cinque sentimenti del suo corpo sente le immagini e qualità de corpi, i colori per gli occhi, per gli orecchi le voci, gli odori per il naso, per la lingua i sapori, per i nervi le qualità semplici degli Elementi . . . Si che quanto appartiene al nostro proposito, sei potenzia della Anima . . . La ragione si assomiglia à Dio, il Viso al fuoco, l'Udito all'aria, l'Odorato à'vapori, il Gusto all'acqua, è il Tatto alla terra.

Reason, which seeks the Celestial, has no seat in the body; Sight, as the noblest of the senses, is placed highest in it. Next come Hearing and Smell, and then Taste and Touch, corresponding to the lowest of the elements. Counting reason as a sense, three senses appertain to Body and Matter, and three to the Soul. Reason, Sight and Hearing nourish the Soul; Touch, Taste and Smell the body.[18]

[18] Aristotle (*De Anima* II. vi–xii) establishes the order Vision–Hearing–Smell–Taste–Touch; in *De Sensu* (441a) he calls taste a form of touch, which may explain why in literary treatment the order of these two is sometimes reversed.

Questa grazia di virtù, figura, o voce, che chiamo lo animo à
se e rapisce per il mezzo della ragione, viso è audito,
rettamente si chiama Bellezza. Queste sono quelle tre Grazii
di li quali così parlò Orfeo; Splendore, Veridità, è Letizia
abbondante.

The intellect, vision and hearing are concerned with beauty, and
so alone have to do with love; the others are concerned with the
opposite of beauty and bring about the collapse into the badness
of touch.

Love is engendered in the eye; this is the first step in his progress towards the divine, un-material condition, through the
stages which are familiar from Castiglione and Spenser's *Hymns*.
The Imagination idealizes the beauty sensed; the Reason interprets it, seeing it as a type not of visual but of moral beauty,
and finally relates it to the one universal truth and beauty, which
completes the 'spiritual circuit' of the emanation and return of
beauty to its source, a basic theme in Ficino and in philosophers
and poets such as Spenser, who follow him. But if this primary
ocular impression makes one yield to a desire to gratify the lower
senses, and in particular Taste and Touch, that is the 'love' that
turns man into beast; the love symbolized, for example, in the
story of Circe. In contradistinction to the Banquet of Intellect, or
Heavenly Love, the gratification of the lower soul is justly represented as a voluptuous feast, a debauch of created pleasure, a
banquet of sense.

It is now, I think, clear that Jonson expected one to see his Court
of Love scene as an exercise in this 'topic'. It occurs, less schematic-
ally, in other plays, for example in Massinger's *A New Way to
pay Old Debts* (III. i), where the Prodician Hercules is associated
with the formal scheme of temptation. This use is merely episodic.
In the exceptionally interesting academic play *Lingua* (1602–3?)
attributed to Thomas Tomkis, there is an extended allegory concerning the senses which appear with standard allegorical attributes: one of them must be shown to be best; a crown is awarded
to Visus and a robe to Tactus, which decision is celebrated in a
banquet given by Gustus which reduces all the senses to wild
and brutal uselessness.

Thirty years later Randolph alludes to the topic in *The Muses*

Looking-Glass, in the speech of Acolastus, 'a voluptuous epicure', which is balanced by that of Anaisthetus, representing the other of two extremes between which Temperance is a mean. (Colax, the flatterer, applauds them both, the first in a speech which, failing to discriminate between the senses, and between satisfaction and indulgence, has been preposterously attributed to Randolph's own 'Cyrenaic' philosophy by those who suppose that Milton was 'answering' him in *Comus*.) The casualness of such allusions to the Banquet proves the currency of the idea;[19] and it is not surprising to find that Shakespeare used it more than once.

In a simple form it occurs in Sonnet 141:

> In faith I do not love thee with mine eyes,
> For they in thee a thousand errors note;
> But 'tis my heart that loves what they despise,
> Who in despite of view is pleas'd to dote,
> Nor are mine ears with thy tongue's tune delighted,
> Nor tender feeling to base touches prone;
> Nor taste nor smell desire to be invited
> To any sensual feast with thee alone.

The senses are treated in order (eye and ear first, smell, taste and touch, the lower triad, last) and followed in the eighth line, as it were inevitably, by the expression 'sensual feast'. The theme recurs also in *Timon of Athens*. Timon's honour and nobility, much insisted upon, are firmly associated with his bounty and his lavish entertainments. There are two banquets in the play. At the first, Timon says grace, and a masquer dressed as Cupid enters to announce the arrival of his fellow-masquers.

> Hail to thee, worthy Timon, and to all
> That of his bounties taste! The five best Senses
> Acknowledge thee their patron, and come freely
> To gratulate they plenteous bosom. The Ear,
> Taste, Touch, Smell, pleas'd from thy table rise;
> They only now come but to feast thine eyes.

[19] Compare the absence of detail in Harington's marginal note on Ariosto's account of the behaviour of Ruggiero ('this new Hercules') with Alcina: 'This lascivious description of carnall pleasure needs not offend the chaste eares or thoughts of any, but rather shame the unchast, that have themselves been at such kind of bankets' (*Orlando Furioso in English Heroical Verse*, 2nd edn., 1634, p. 409). Ruggiero yields all to the sense of touch, and is debased as Hercules was by Omphale.

And he introduces 'a masque of Ladies as *Amazons*, with lutes in their hands, dancing and playing', who feast the eyes of Timon. There seems no doubt that this little entertainment is intended as part of that acute unspoken criticism of Timon's misconception of Honour and Nobility which runs through the finely composed early scenes of the play. At the second banquet, when Timon understands his self-deceit, and is about to meet the consequence of his having so mistaken the nature of Honour, he offers his guests, with a misanthropic grace, dishes containing nothing but warm water—without smell, taste or colour—in token of his awareness that he had been wrong to calculate Honour in terms of gold and the sensuous delights it makes available. Timon is wrong about Magnanimity; failing in Heroic Virtue he sinks to bestiality.

In *Venus and Adonis* Venus has many of the attributes of Voluptas or Vice tempting the young man. Her rival is not Pallas but the martial sport of hunting. The splendid horse represents the active life, military virtue, as in Rubens's *Choice of Hercules* in the Uffizi. Adonis wants to hunt the dangerous boar not the timid hare. But Venus assails him as the Voluptas-figure assails Hercules in some Baroque 'Choices'—and the breaking away of the horse allows it to be used as an emblem of 'natural' desire. The bridle, as we see in the Rubens picture and in Shaftesbury's study of the theme, is an emblem of Temperance; under its control the horse was Manly Virtue, without it, natural lust. The hare likewise has a double function; it is not merely that which Adonis is ashamed to hunt, but also, as often iconographically, a symbol of voluptuousness. (When Venus, lost in the labyrinth of passion, rushes about the world in search of Adonis, her movements are described in language that deliberately recalls the passage about the hare.) If we are in doubt about the kind of love advocated by this Venus, there is a Banquet of Sense to satisfy us. Adonis has spoken, though coldly, after long silence.

What! canst thou talk? quoth she, Hast thou a tongue?
O would thou hadst not, or I had no hearing!
Thy mermaid's voice hath done me double wrong;
I had my load before, now press'd with bearing;
    Melodious discord, heavenly tune harsh sounding,
    Ear's deep-sweet music, and heart's deep-sore wounding.

Had I no eyes but ears, my ears would love
That inward beauty and invisible;
Or were I deaf, thy outward parts would move
Each part in me that were but sensible.
    Though neither eyes nor ears, to hear nor see,
    Yet should I be in love by touching thee.

Say that the sense of feeling were bereft me,
And that I could not see, nor hear, nor touch,
And nothing but the very smell were left me,
Yet would my love to thee be still as much;
    For from the stillitory of thy face excelling
    Comes breath perfum'd, that breedeth love by smelling.

But O, what banquet wert thou to the taste,
Being nurse and feeder of the other four!

This scheme is worked out with great care; it is perfectly proper
that the ear should apprehend and love the inward beauty, having
the power to do so only to a lesser extent than the eye—in fact,
some would have called it the superior organ—but after that the
sensual stimuli mentioned by Venus are all blind and deaf. A love
which is 'still as much' without the action of eye and ear, which
can subsist on the lower senses, is bestial love. She comes finally
to taste, which supports only the body, and calls Adonis a banquet to the taste alone. The implied contrast with true love and
the true convivium of love is firmly established.[20]

[20] There are also allusions to the theme in *Antony and Cleopatra*. They
suggest the use of banquets for the temptation of the 'new Hercules' of Renaissance epic. There is a conflict, taken over from Plutarch, between heroic
virtue and sensuality; and Shakespeare is at pains to emphasize the Herculean
aspect of Antony. Plutarch says 'he was thought to be discended from one
Anton, the sonne of Hercules', and adds, 'this opinion did Antonius seeke to
confirme in all his doings', (*North's Plutarch*, Tudor Translations, 1896, vi. 4).
In the comparison with Demetrius he says that Antony at the mercy of
Cleopatra resembled Hercules made effeminate by Omphale (vi. 91). (Cf.
Antony and Cleopatra, II. vi. 21-3.) The portents of Antony's fall include the
striking by lightning of the Temple of Hercules in Patras (vi. 13). Shakespeare
stresses the Herculean side of Antony (I. iii. 84; I. v. 23, where 'demi-Atlas'
means 'the substitute of Atlas'; IV. xii. 43-7) to the degree that he converts
the god who deserts Hercules (IV. iii. 12-17) from Plutarch's Bacchus into
Hercules, and makes no mention of Bacchus, though to Plutarch's Antony

Before undertaking Chapman's poem it may be useful to have a summary of the theme as it occurs elsewhere. The Platonic Banquet represents love, the ascent from sense to the higher powers of the soul, and ultimately the apprehension of the divine beauty. The Banquet of Sense represents a descent from sight to the senses capable of only material gratification—what Ficino calls 'bestial love'. Theologically the parallel is with the Eucharist and the 'devil's table'; and sometimes this Christian sense is very active, as when Bembo rejects sense in order to achieve 'the feast of angels'.[21] There are distinctions that ought to have been introduced, had space permitted; the body must be served, and Renaissance Platonism made provision for the service of the terrestrial Venus, witness the treatises of Leone Ebreo and Mario Equicola, among others.[22] But in general the Banquet of Sense is not regarded as a good thing, and is concerned with love of the counter-Platonic or Ovidian variety. The blandishments it represents are trials to be overcome. Is it so or otherwise used by Chapman? To find out it is necessary to 'passe through Corynnas Garden'[23] with the aid of such lanterns as may be had. The Dedication seems to promise deliberate obscurity, but clarity at the heart of the matter. Poetry must not be as plain as oratory. With that appeal to the sister-art which renaissance criticism had made habitual, Chapman compares the poetical presentation of

---

he was at least as important as Hercules. Octavius makes it clear that Antony was familiar with the hard Prodician road to glory (I. iv. 55–64); but he prefers to Roman *gravitas* that Egypt which is represented throughout as gluttonous feasting and sensual indulgence. Shakespeare also stresses the connections between Cleopatra and Venus, which Plutarch had also foreshadowed; but for Plutarch Cleopatra in the barge is Venus coming 'to play with the god Bacchus' (vi, 25); for Shakespeare she is Venus approaching to betray Hercules.

[21] *The Courtier*, ed. cit., p. 322.

[22] Equicola, for instance, defends corporeal pleasure and glorifies the sense of touch (*Libro di natura d'amore* (1525), pp. 297–8, 165, 170). Marino (*Adone*, viii) echoes this, calling Touch the superior of the other senses, and copulation 'il primo godimento della voluttà'. For the Epicurean element in Renaissance Platonism see D. C. Allen, 'The Rehabilitation of Epicurus in the early Renaissance', *S.P.* XIV (1944), 1–5; Edgar Wind, *Pagan Mysteries of the Renaissance* (1958), especially Chap. V; A. J. Smith, 'The Metaphysic of Love', *R.E.S.* n.s. ix (1958), 362–75.

[23] Dedication, in *Poems*, ed. P. B. Bartlett (1941), p. 50.

his theme with the painter's use of technical devices to give his work a depth and vitality impossible to mere outlines; his skill will be evident to the trained observer. It is with this controlled obscurity that Chapman intends to compose; the trained auditor, he says, will have means to 'sound the philosophical conceits'. In the 'Justification' of *Andromeda Liberata* (Bartlett, p. 327) he nevertheless claims a poet's right to 'Ambiguity in the sence'.

It would appear that the story of Ovid in Julia's garden, the fiction which does the 'varying' of the 'Schema', is intended to adorn and give utility, or affective force, to the philosophic material. Now the scheme is a treatment of the senses in descending order: first, the three which act through a medium, without contact with what is sensed, and then taste and touch, the senses of necessity, which in the Ficinian scheme are at best base servants of the higher soul. Although Chapman heretically treats Visus third in order and ignores the intermediate position given to Gustus in the orthodox scale, the scheme of the poem, as Bush pointed out,[24] presumably derives ultimately from Ficino, and should, as we have seen, be concerned with the collapse of the soul into bestiality, the descent to Tactus. It is therefore strange that Chapman should write in his fiction an apparent glorification of the sensual stimulation of the counter-Plato, Ovid.

My own view is that this is ironical; that Chapman is here portraying the Ovid whom Apollo called 'lasciui . . . praeceptor Amoris' (*Ars Amatoria*, ii. 497). It must be confessed that a theory which treats the poem as having a persistent irony blended with its didactic tone makes it even more difficult, but that is no reason, in the case of Chapman, for rejecting the theory. It is an objection, certainly, that Chapman complained, in *The Shadow of Night*, of 'fleshly interpretations' of myth, and preferred the older moralized Ovid: but this can be met, I think, by asserting his hostility to the contemporary erotic mythological genre exemplified by *Venus and Adonis*. Shakespeare's poem has a moral scheme cast into a fiction which is erotic in tone; but it betrays its 'matter' by playing up the comic and erotic elements for their own sakes. It is this kind of subtle subversion of morality that Marston makes a show of objecting to in *Pygmalions Image*. Chapman, in *Ouids Banquet*, turns the screw once more and

[24] *Mythology and the Renaissance Tradition* (1934), p. 204.

restores the 'utility' of the poetry. He too has an erotic fiction in support of a philosophical scheme; but that scheme is itself an ironical sham, a learned defence by Ovid (the Ovid of the Elizabethan epyllion) of the counter-Platonic Banquet, the Ovidian Banquet of sophisticated sensual indulgence.

But this is not the opinion of Chapman's commentators, despite the fact that his hostility to the erotic sense and to Shakespeare has long been suspected on other grounds. Miss J. Spens, one of the pioneers, holds that 'Chapman's subject is the sublimation of the senses', and even considers whether Julia is not 'merely a name for what Shelley called Intellectual Beauty'; she thinks that Chapman's purpose is 'to reach a spiritual ecstasy by means of the senses'. Miss M. C. Bradbrook explains that Chapman evokes 'a scene of extreme sensual delight only to reject the expected conclusions and to present his Ovid and Julia as models of Platonic chastity, who could extract all the delights of the senses without succumbing to their lure'. And she quotes in support of this view, which seems to me frankly untenable, stanzas 35 and 36, without observing that they are spoken by Ovid and not by Chapman *in propria persona*. Mr. Hallett Smith is more cautious, and reminds us of the rejection of erotic poetry in the *Coronet for his Mistress Philosophy*, published with *Ouids Banquet*; but he so far supports Miss Spens and Miss Bradbrook as to say that 'Chapman rejects the idea that heaven can only be gained by labours of the soul and of continence', which is certainly not what is meant by stanza 63. M. Jean Jacquot sees the difficulty, but argues that the apparently contradictory attitudes of the poet in *The Shadow of Night* and *Ouids Banquet* find their reconciliation in Platonism, and argues for Chapman's adherence to a Platonic scheme exalting a sensual ecstasy of the sort some writers find in Donne's 'Extasy'; but I think he ends with a reconciliation of opposites impossible even to sixteenth-century Platonism when he says that 'Corinna représente à la fois la Vénus céleste et la Vénus terrestre dont parle Platon'.[25] If this is so we may as well give Chapman up as hopeless.

[25] *Essays and Studies*, xi (1925), 159; *Shakespeare and Elizabethan Poetry* (1951), p. 19; *Elizabethan Poetry* (1952), p. 97; *George Chapman, sa vie, sa poésie, son théâtre, sa pensée* (1951), pp. 65, 67–8, 227, 252; E. Rees (*The Tragedies of Chapman*, 1954) calls the poem 'a tortured attempt to reconcile the sensual with the spiritual' (p. 21).

One does not forget that there was a strain of Florentine Neo-Platonism, sponsored by Leone Ebreo, which condoned sensual indulgence to a degree beyond what Ficino (in whom of course the senses have their place as excitants of the mind) would have countenanced. But even if Chapman, on the evidence improbably, did subscribe to this how is the *Coronet* to be read? As a palinode? For his own *Banquet* would then have to be regarded as the product of 'Muses that sing loues sensuall Emperie'.

The truth is surely that Chapman cannot be writing the kind of poem he obviously and explicitly deplored, and against which he writes in the *Coronet*.[26] His love, Philosophy, 'teaches by passion what perfection is . . . all powre and thought of pridefull lust depriuing'.

> Her mind (the beam of God) drawes in the fires
> Of her chaste eyes, from all earths tempting fewell.

He takes Ovid, for the present purpose, as the master of lascivious arts and Julia as a libertine. (How, incidently, could this lady, of all ladies, represent Intellectual Beauty?) Ovid, in fact, is the counter-Plato, and Julia his sensual banquet, his anti-convivium. What we are told of, despite the curious fictional disguise, is the Circean fall into bestiality. This is the Ovid of Jonson's *Poetaster*; an Ovid associated not only with blasphemous banquets but with the view that love is of the blood, not of the soul (IV. ix. 31ff.).

There is no question there that Ovid's views are reprehensible; and indeed the *Poetaster* as a whole is concerned to establish that Ovid desecrates poetry and truth; a condemnation which, as Mr. A. H. King has shown, includes the 'Ovidians', poets of the period.[27] I am certain that if we hold on to this clue we shall get somewhere near the sense of Chapman's poem.

Ovid's treatment of each sense in turn is, basically, Aristotelian,

[26] Cf. *Hero and Leander* (Sestiad iii, 35), 'Joy grauen in sence, like snow in water wasts'; the passage on the avoidance of 'vulgare Raptures' in *Euthymiæ Raptus* (ll. 504–24); and the distinction between two poetic 'furies'—one divine, the other degenerately human—in the Dedication of the *Odysseys* to Somerset (Bartlett, p. 408). These all suggest that Chapman would have used the Banquet scheme with the normal moral value. See also the congratulatory poems preceding *Ovids Banquet of Sence*.

[27] *The Language of the Satirized Characters in Jonson's 'Poetaster'* (Lund Studies in English, x, 1941).

with the usual accretions; for the most part it is not much unlike what a Renaissance Platonist might have said. But the object of his argument is, in the narrative context, to convince himself of the rightness of, and to persuade Julia to, sexual indulgence. In doing so he is abusing learning, as, on the view probably held by Chapman, the Shakespeare of *Venus and Adonis* was doing; for *Venus and Adonis* is also full of morality, but it is an erotic poem, and read as such; it had a contemporary reputation as a 'luscious marrowbone pie', an aphrodisiac dangerous to women.

In fact Jonson, as M. Jacquot has seen, uses another *topos*; this is associated with seduction, and cannot very well be associated with anything else. Laumonier thought the scheme must have originated with a troubadour; but Curtius traces its origin to Donatus's commentary on Terence, *Eunuchus* IV. ii. 10: 'Quinque lineae sunt amoris, scilicet visus, allocutio, tactus, osculum sive suavium, coitus'. Sometimes 'partes' replaces 'lineae'. The *topos* is of frequent occurrence in medieval Latin verse and the theme was still in use by French poets of the sixteenth century, including Marot and Ronsard. It turns up in the well-known song of 'Come again, sweet love doth now invite', with the usual pun on 'die', which here means what the French politely called the 'don de mercy', the last part of love;

> To see, to speak, to touch, to kiss, to die
> With thee again in sweetest sympathy.

Professor Baldwin finds it in *Venus and Adonis*.[28]

It is interesting that this *topos* is also used in the *Illustrations de Gaule* of Jean Lemaire des Belges (1509–12); for there are in that work hints also of the scheme of the Banquet of Sense. This was

---

[28] See P. Laumonier, *Ronsard poète lyrique* (1909), p. 514; J. Hutton, 'Spenser and the *Cinq Points en Amour*', *M.L.N.* lvii (1942), 657–61; E. Curtius, op. cit., pp. 512 ff.; T. W. Baldwin, *The Literary Genetics of Shakespeare's Poems and Sonnets* (1950), p. 16; A. Adler, 'The topos *quinque lineae amoris* as used by Ronsard', *Bibliothèque d'Humanisme et de la Renaissance*, xv (1953), 220–5. Curtius mistakenly reports (p. 514, n. 10) that Doutrepont, *Jean Lemaire de Belges et la Renaissance* (1934), gives Annius as a source for *Illustrations de Gaule*, i. 25, which contains the *topos*. He takes as a chapter reference what is in fact a page reference to Stecher's edition of Lemaire (1882). Doutrepont gives no source for the *cinq points* as used in the *Illustrations*; his reference to Ubertin's edition of the *Heroides* as the general source of the twenty-fifth chapter is not relevant to the present issue.

noticed by Schoell (as reported by Miss Bartlett, ed. cit. p. 431) and M. Jacquot pursued the line of enquiry. The *Illustrations* describes how Paris (associated, by the way, with the wrong choice of the voluptuous life) meets at the side of a fountain a nymph who offers him a banquet of fruits. We are told, with considerable learning, how his (higher) senses are ravished by her; and then the scheme passes into an exposition of the five degrees of love—'le regard, le parler, l'attouchement, le baiser; Et le dernier qui est le plus desiré, et auquel tous les autres tendent, pour finale resolution . . .' The 'don de mercy' is granted, and the nymph 'soccombe volontairement sur les tapis verds de l'herbe'.[29] Now it is clear, allowing for the same degree of variation in the order of the *lineae amoris* that we have seen already in these examples, that from the moment when Ovid *sees* Corinna, and she him, the course of the poem, by accident or design, follows this scheme. He speaks, he kisses, he touches; and he does not die only because some 'other Dames' (116) interrupt him. Chapman explicitly informs us that in this case we shall have to take the will for the deed; 'intentio animi actio', he concludes. It would appear that Chapman deliberately conflates the schemes of Banquet and *lineae*, and that this is on the whole evidence that Ovid's intention is not, *au fond*, Platonic.

Corinna's garden contains a fountain with an elaborate piece of statuary erected by Augustus, and consisting of a statue of Niobe which he had brought from Mount Sipylus, so named after one of Niobe's sons. As Schoell pointed out, the description of the statue as a rock which looked like a woman only from a distance, is lifted out of Comes' account of Pausanias' description of the rock *in situ*; what is more important is that Chapman has invented the story of Augustus transferring it to this garden and surrounding it with statues of Niobe's fourteen children (3–5). He also adds the obelisks representing Apollo and Artemis, with an optical device by means of which they seem eternally to be wreaking their vengeance on the children, on whose marble breasts they throw purple shadows. (These divinities, as children of the Titaness Leto, killed Niobe's children because she boasted equality with Leto on account of their number.) Now Niobe signifies presumption, as her father Tantalus signifies the abuse of knowledge. There is a Florentine engraving dated 1541, of Apollo and

[29] *Oeuvres*, ed. Stecher, i. 177 ff.; Jacquot, op. cit., p. 66.

Latona striking the Niobides, with the legend 'Discite quam nulli
tutum contemnere divos'.[30]

This group, then, has the moral intention of warning mortals
against presumption; and it is unlikely to be a coincidence that,
as we are explicitly told, Augustus went to the trouble of having
it put where the poem says it is.[31] We also know the tradition that
Augustus deplored the libertinism of Ovid, and outlawed him for
it. The statue is there to warn Ovid off; it is caution against the
rash act we see him about to commit. I do not see why we should
forget that Julia did grant the 'don de mercy', and that Ovid
suffered in consequence the wrath of the divine emperor. Then
why is Corinna referred to as 'this Romaine *Phoebe*'? Because the
tears of Niobe fall upon her; or because Ovid is behaving like
Actaeon. A little earlier (8) she is compared to Venus.

Corinna's garden is a paradise of pleasure; but this in itself, like
the fountain in which Corinna bathes, is a two-handed emblem.
The nature of the garden depends upon the character of Corinna
herself, and I take it as a dangerous *hortus deliciarum*.

Having bathed, Corinna takes her lute and sings (12). Her song
is not at all easy to follow, but the sense of it is something like
this: It is better to despise than to love. It is also better to be
beautiful than to be wise, because it is through the sense of sight
that the souls of admirers are to be won rather than through any
intellectual sympathy. The eagle of Jove (signifying perspicacity
in Comes, II. i, as well as natural supremacy) is taken by the dove
of Venus (universally accepted as a symbol of lust). It is a woman's
right and privilege to enjoy the mischievous transformations
wrought by beauty. This magic makes men follow them more the
more they flee, as destiny follows the man who flies it; and it
enables foolish woman to be praised as wise (because the man
wastes his learning in the praise and pursuit of her, as Ovid is
about to do) and also to mock the man for this waste of wisdom.
In love, he calls female beauty wise, which is like calling profane-
ness holy; just as he tries to show that mere natural desire is a

---

[30] See Rodolfo Lanciani, *Il gruppo dei Niobidi nel giardino di Sallustio* (1906),
p. 24.

[31] Augustus had, in the Renaissance, a reputation as a maker of pithy
mottoes, based on the report (Aulus Gellius, *Noctes Atticae* X. xi; Erasmus,
Adagia, s.v.—with increasing emphasis in succeeding editions) of his having
invented the motto *festina lente*.

solemn matter of fate, and human wisdom mere foolishness because it is against this sort of love. I am not sure that I have construed the last part right, and 'Nature, our fate' may have some connection with the Theophrastian quotation in the Margin at stanza 84: 'Natura est uniuscuiusque Fatum'. (Chapman also uses 'fate' sometimes to mean 'character' or 'disposition'.) But this does not affect the truth that the song of Corinna is a very improper song for Intellectual Beauty to sing, and would come better from a cultivated courtesan, which, of course, is nearer to the usual idea of Julia.

Ovid, who does not yet know that Corinna is going to be 'mercifull' (13), overhears the song, and is immediately down to his ears in love: 'loues holy streame Was past his eyes, and now did wett his eares' (14). He moralizes this with great expense of wit and learning. His hearing, he says, is 'sette on fire With an immortall ardor' and the music 'My spirits to theyr highest function reares' (17). This is unexceptionable, and so, one supposes, is Ovid's desire to transfer his life into the inventive faculty of his lady, as the intellect passes into what it apprehends. So, he says, his life could be exhausted in harmony:

> Thus sense were feasted,
> My life that in my flesh a Chaos is
> Should to a Golden Worlde be thus dygested.   (25)

This is the golden world imposed upon chaos at the creation by the 'deus et melior natura' of the opening lines of Ovid's *Metamorphoses*. A divine, harmonious, principle of order reduced the microcosmic chaos to the same unexampled happiness and regularity. All this, says Ovid in his conceit, would happen if I could inhabit the harmony of her invention. It is a harmless wish. Indeed the section on Hearing is for the most part an exceptionally brilliant set of variations on the 'laus musicae', which would go quite well into any true *convivium*, though perhaps there is sufficient learned amorous hyperbole to hint that even here the presumptuous and wrongly-learned Ovid is sophisticating this knowledge and applying it to bad ends. The song ended, we are told that its accents 'in this Banquet his first seruice were' (30).

The second service is Smell (31–40). The delicacy and power of this 'course of Odors' (40) is also given a tremendous eulogy, with

learning from Theophrastus; but when Ovid ceases to speak and
the poet comments, it is thus:

> So vulture loue on his encreasing liuer,
> And fruitfull entrails eagerly did feede. (41)

The passion of Ovid is obviously having the outrageous physiological effects of the bestial kind of love. I do not understand the
penultimate line of the stanza, but the meaning of the allusion to
Diana is simple. From Apuleius on, the fable of Actaeon torn to
pieces by his own hounds was used as a warning against becoming
the victim of one's own passions. As the sight of Diana in similar
circumstances brought Actaeon to this end, Ovid must beware.
He is in danger of yielding not to Intellectual Beauty but the
madness of lust.

Immediately Chapman inserts an explicit rhetorical warning to
Ovid not to proceed to Sight, for if he does so he will

> be prickt with other sences stings,
> To tast, and feele, and yet not there be staide. (43)

The Banquet is about to follow its downward course, and Touch
implies the _dernière pointe_. Ovid, in doubt as to his most successful
course of action (he is not thinking of withdrawal), prays to
Juno, somewhat disrespectfully, as the goddess who since she
rules 'all Nuptiale rites', can 'speede Such as in Cyprian sports
theyr pleasures fix' (47). This is a frank prayer for help towards
sensual satisfaction. He decides to be bold, observing that it is
'Attempts, and not entreats get Ladies larges, And grace is sooner
got of Dames than graunted' (48)—maxims he might have derived from his own highly practical _Art of Love_, though not
from the _Symposium_.

Chapman's discourteous syntax, with its disregard for the
normal amenities of exposition, must be held responsible for the
disturbances in the next section. The sight of Corinna strikes
Ovid 'to the hart with exstasie' (49). This must be the ecstasy of
'thoughts cupidinine' described and condemned in the _Coronet_;
relating to the love which can 'eate your [i.e. "sensual amorists" ']
entrails out with exstasies' (_Coronet_ 5.9; 2.4). It is love for a beauty
that deceives,

> 'tempting men to buy
> With endless showes, what endlessly will fade.' (51)

unless there is a true exchange of intellectual qualities, and this, from what we have heard Ovid and Julia say already, is not to be the case here, for the only intellectual activity is Ovid's squandering his 'mine of knowledge' in beautifying a calculating coquette.

The opening lines of the next stanza (52) have, I think, misled commentators, and consequently the relationship between stanzas 52–55 and the remainder of the poem has been completely misunderstood. Chapman makes it quite clear that this passage is to be read as a digression; stanza 56 begins:

> With this digression, wee will now returne
> To Ouids prospect . . .

This digression is not about Ovid's kind of love, but the opposite kind, which exists not when men yield to the shows which tempt them to buy 'what endlessly will fade', but when souls are exchanged; the beauty that causes this (for all love is an appetite of beauty) is sacred, and 'the feast of soules' (52) not a carnal banquet. This is the first stage of the Platonic ascent. This sacred beauty stands in obvious contrast to the other kind, which Ovid is advised not to venture upon. The digression has nothing to do with Ovid except to show what is wrong with him; in looking at Corinna he is yielding to the wrong kind of beauty; and this, I think, is clear enough despite incidental obscurities.

At stanza 56 Chapman returns to Ovid, and describes what he saw. The lady's beauty is warmly extolled and called a miracle of nature; as she lies there she resembles a soul in Elysium, of which, indeed, her beauty makes her an emblem.

> She lay at length, like an immortall soule
> At endlesse rest in blest *Elisium*:
> And then did true felicite enroule
> So fayre a Lady, figure of her kingdome.
>   Now *Ouids* Muse as in her tropicke shinde,
> And hee (strooke dead) was meere heauen-born become,
>   So his quick Verse in equal height was shrinde . . . (57)

Chapman here has a marginal note which is more than usually irresponsible in its syntax:

The amplification of this simile, is taken from the blisfull state of soules in *Elisium*, as *Virgill* faines: and expresseth a regenerate beauty in all life and perfection, not intimating any rest of death. But in place of that eternall spring, he poynteth to that life of life thys beauty-clad naked Lady.

(Miss Bartlett reads 'peace of that eternall spring' and records no variants, but this seems to me the safest of several possible emendations I should like to make in her text). Now this certainly sounds as if Corinna were the subject of a comparison with Elysium,[32] but what the note really means is this:

> The Elysium to which I compare the lady is that of Virgil. Elysium is not death, but a new life of beauty and perfection. The state to which seeing her reduced Ovid may be compared to the condition of Elysium in that he was, as it were, struck dead with wonder when he saw her and, when he recovered from the shock, was reborn into a condition of ecstatic pleasure at her beauty. But the comparison applies in that respect only; for what Ovid was dealing with was not Elysium but the vital beauty of this lady.

It is not the simile, but Virgil's Elysium, that 'expresseth a regenerate beauty'; in place of regenerate beauty Ovid is concerned with this 'beauty-clad naked Lady'. The candid reader who is familiar with Chapman's ways will agree that this is the likeliest interpretation. If his note means that Corinna stands for a regenerate, heavenly beauty, it is in conflict with everything that has gone before and comes after. Even Ovid realizes that Corinna is not this kind of Elysium. At first he says she is, and tries to prove it by a series of elaborate conceits (58–60); she is different from Elysium only in that she can move about (61). But the comparison breaks down in the end:

> 'Elisium must with vertue gotten bee,
> With labors of the soule and continence,
> And these can yield no ioy with such as she,
> Shee is a sweet Elisium for the sence . . .'   (62)

In stanza 58 Ovid begins to carve with his eyes this un-Socratic feast of feasts; the terms in which he first praises what he sees are

---

[32] This is admittedly a *topos* in itself; one source is Dante, *Convivio*, Ode ii ('Amor, che nell mente mi ragiona') stanza iv, and the commentary in Treatise iii. cap. 8.

the amplification of this Elysium-simile. Having called Corinna an '*Elisium* for the sence' he attempts to justify this incontinent joy by arguing that the senses are not to fust in us unused. The 63rd stanza:

> The sence is giuen vs to excite the minde,
> And that can neuer be by sence excited
> But first the sence must her contentment finde,
> We therefore must procure the sence delighted,
>   That so the soule may use her facultie;
> Mine Eye then to this feast hath her inuited,
>   That she might serue the soueraigne of mine Eye,
> Shee shall bide Time, and Time so feasted neuer
> Shall grow in strength of her renowne for euer.   (63)

is often taken to be the 'moral' of the poem, and Ovid's sensual exercise upon Corinna's beauty a mere fictional demonstration of it. Unless the senses are contented, their mistress, the soul, cannot 'use her facultie': 'else a great Prince in prison lies'. Furthermore, Chapman happens to give evidence elsewhere that he approves of the sentence with which the stanza begins, for in his note on the Vice-Virtue passage in Hesiod ('But before Virtue do the Gods rain sweat') he quotes it in a Latin version, the source of which I have not traced: '. . . by the worthily exercis'd and instructed organs of that body, her Virtue's soul received her excitation to all her expressible knowledge (for *dati sunt sensus ad intellectum excitandum*)'.[33]

It would be surprising if Chapman did not hold this view, which is perfectly orthodox; the end of the senses is to inform, and to stimulate the mind. But Ovid is, as usual, disingenuous; he is expending his knowledge to 'set wise glosses on the fool'. Again, as usual, Chapman does not make it evident that the 'her' of line 6 refers to 'sence' rather than to Corinna or the soul, but it is so; the Eye invites the 'sence' to the feast that it might serve the soul (the sovereign of mine Eye). The 'sence' here must mean touch-taste. Much of Chapman's cloudy stuff could have been

---

[33] *Poems*, ed. cit., p. 219. The precise origin of this expression I have not traced, but the notion is familiar; cf. Aquinas, *Summa Theologica* I. lxxxiv. 6; 'Secundum Platonis opinionem . . . sensibilia excitant animam sensibilem ad sentiendum, et similiter sensus excitant animam intellectivam ad intelligendum.'

clarified by attention to the elements of exposition. What the last two lines mean I cannot say; but it remains clear that Ovid is using this learning about the ends of sense dishonestly, because it is not the *mind* he is in process of exciting. And the example he chooses of the attractive force of beauty is Helen, the beauty which pulled the towers of Troy about its ears (68), a disaster which was regarded as archetypal. Shakespeare uses it to enforce the universality of Lucrece's horror—Helen is 'the strumpet that began this stir'. (Here it is Ovid's fall that is presaged.)

After this we are told of Corinna's binding up her hair, and of the emblematic jewels she arranges in it. One has the sense, 'Decrescente nobilitate, crescunt obscuri' (70)—perhaps a reference to Ovid's presumption. Another is an 'Eye in Saphire set and close upon it a fresh Lawrell spray'—with the posy *Medio caret* (71). In the margin Chapman explains that 'Sight is one of the three sences that hath his medium extrinsecally, which now (supposed wanting) lets the sight by the close apposition of the Lawrell: the application whereof hath many constructions'. The construction in the text is that the emblem shows 'not eyes, but meanes must truth display'. Perhaps this means that the poet is improperly relying on the visual stimulus which, without the intervention of wisdom, is powerless to see truth. The last emblem is of Apollo and his team, with the motto *Teipsum et orbem*, which is surely a counsel of self-control; we remember that he killed the children of Niobe for a similar ignorant presumption. If these are warnings they are neglected; for in stanza 72 Ovid, despite his earlier philosophizing, is clearly bent on the baser sensual achievements.

> To taste and touch, one kisse may worke the same:
> If more will come, more then much more I will.

And he shows himself to Corinna. She chides him for compromising her honour: 'Thought Sights childe Begetteth sinne' (78), she says, apparently in no doubt that from Visus the development is, in this case, downwards. Ovid, of course, has his answer; this is an error of Opinion, for Reason would see that any harm done by looking at naked beauty is done to the looker (79 f.). But Love has entered his brain, and taken command of his actions; wherefore he must beg a kiss to satisfy *Gustus* and have the fourth course of his Banquet. He even makes this sound like

a moral obligation, the motive of his soul (87) being incomplete
while two senses remain unsatisfied. The *communis sensus* requires
to be furnished with the remainder of the Banquet. Corinna very
properly chides Ovid for his presumption and folly:

> I see unbidden Guests are boldest still,
> And well you showe how weake in soule you are
> That let rude sence subdue your reasons skil ... (89)

and, significantly, mentions the difference of their station; Ovid
is not noble. He has his easy, orthodox reply to this: 'Vertue
makes honor' (91). Corinna responds with a purely Platonic
argument:

> Pure loue (said she) the purest grace pursues,
> And there is contact, not by application
> Of lips or bodies, but of bodies vertues,
> As in our elementale Nation
> Stars by theyr powers, which are theyr heat and light
> Do heauenly works, and that which hath probation
> By vertuall contact hath the noblest plight,
> Both for the lasting and affinitie
> It hath with naturall diuinitie. (92)

This is worthy of Lovel in the *New Inn*. Ovid's reply settles any
remaining doubt about his idealism; he caps Corinna's philosophy,
explaining that her virtual influence proceeds from form not substance, and that his present longings can only be satisfied by the
latter (93). This frank preference for matter over form is surely
the position of Beaufort in Jonson's play: 'Gi' me the body, if it
be a good one.' And in the next stanza his argument for a kiss is
conducted by an analogy so ingenious that Corinna, delighted
with his learning, yields; she will not, she says,

> coylie lyft *Mineruas* shielde
> Against *Minerua*.

And she resumes the tone of her song; the whole episode is for
her only a problem in the craft of wooing, such as the *Art of Love*
examines from both male and female points of view. So Ovid
gains his kiss, the fourth course in the Banquet and the third
Point of Love.

But the satisfaction of *Gustus* only renders the plea for *Tactus*

more urgent; the transition from one sense to another is worked
out in six surprisingly intelligible stanzas (97–102). Now Ovid is
well on the way he says, to having the Golden World established
out of the chaos of his flesh. But 'with feasting, loue is famisht
more' (101) and the touch must be brought into play.

> Loue is a wanton famine, rich in foode,
> But with a richer appetite controld,
> An argument in figure and in Moode
> Yet hates all arguments: disputing still
> For sence, gainst Reason, with a senceless will.   (101)

This is explicit enough. To dispute for Sense against Reason,
which this kind of love must do, is 'senceless'; 'will', as often in
Shakespeare, is here virtually 'lust'. The subjugation of Reason to
Sense is, of course, the precise opposite of the discipline of the
true *convivium*. And Ovid's praise of *Tactus* removes any remaining
vestige of suspicion that this is more than a philosophical seduction, ironically described so that the true Platonic Banquet may be
praised by implication. Touch he first says, is the 'sences ground-
worke' (102); but then he calls it 'the sences Emperor':

> is't immodestie
> To serue the sences Emperor, sweet Feeling
> With those delights that fit his Emperie?   (103)

A sensual empery, indeed. Touch is the fundamental sense; but to
the Platonist, a base drudge, not an emperor. The position of
Ficino is completely reversed. Since, continues Ovid, the mind
cannot be corrupted by the actions of the body; since he means
well, and *abusus non tollit usum*, he hopes he may touch Corinna.
The lady is 'glad his arguments to heare' (105) and, preparing for
this act, exposes 'Latonas Twinns, her plenteous brests'. I do not
see why they should be called Latona's twins unless it is to
remind us that Latona's twins slew the presumptuous Niobides,
and that Ovid, for all his ingenuity, is courting the same fate.
Anyway, the favour is granted, and Ovid makes much of the
hand which is to have the honour, calling it, among other things,
'king of the king of sences' (107), that is, master of the sense of
touch. Stanza 109 revives the conceit of Corinna's body as the
figure of Elysium (but an Elysium of sense, not of regenerate
life); and in stanza 110 Ovid touches her. He laments, as usual

disingenuously, that he must with Touch, 'a fleshly engine', unfold 'a spirituall notion' (111) by which disability the difference between men and beast is obscured; the latter part of what he says is true. Despite this deficiency in the sense, he praises Touch:

> Sweete touch the engine that loues bowe doth bend,
> The sence wherewith he feeles him deified,
> The object whereto all his actions tend,
> In all his blindenes his most pleasing guide,
> For thy sake will I write the Art of Love . . . (113)

We cannot expect much more clarity than Chapman gives us here. This love is blind; its end is the satisfaction of the lowest sense; to celebrate it Ovid will write a handbook of amorous seduction.

Tactus is the fifth course of the Banquet, and the fourth Point of Love. The *quinque lineae* scheme supervenes, and Coitus should succeed Tactus. But Ovid is forced by the arrival of other ladies to leave the garden. He grieves, like Alexander, 'that no greater action could be done' (116).

> But as when expert Painters haue displaid,
> To quickest life a Monarchs royall hand
> Holding a Scepter, there is yet bewraide
> But halfe his fingere; when we understand
> The rest not to be seene; and neuer blame
> The Painters Art, in nicest censures skand:
> So in the compasse of this curious frame,
> *Ouid* well knew there was much more intended,
> With whose omition none must be offended.

Intentio, animi actio. Explicit convivium. (117)

This figure occurs in *The Rape of Lucrece*, in Shakespeare's description of the 'imaginary work' in the Troy picture; it amounts to a claim on the part of the poet that he is able, as well as the painter, to suggest more than he describes. We are, in fact, invited to suppose the completion of the *quinque lineae* scheme, imagine Ovid's love consummated, taking the will for the deed. *Explicit convivium*; a Banquet of Sense indeed, with the full moral implication we have found in the scheme elsewhere. Ovid is not to be counted among the *castissimi convitati*. Chapman's use of the theme is perhaps intended as an ironical comment on erotic poets (notably Shakespeare) whose works in his view have dishonest moral pretentions. His Ovid represents such poets, as Jonson's does; and he abuses philosophy for erotic ends, indeed involves himself in the impossible task of dressing up the Banquet of bestial love to look like the true *convivium*.

So, 'if we can but spell and join his sense', Chapman falls into line with the others; according to his habit, however, he obscures that sense, and allows us to misinterpret him as making an Ovidian celebration of 'love's sensual employ'. As in *Hero and Leander* his warnings are obscure (the portents, Ceremony) so here he is willing to allow folly to convert his work to its own purpose. But he himself remains the well-inspired moralist; and the poem from whose title I borrow mine is not in its theme exceptional.

5

JOHN DONNE

I

To have read Donne was once evidence of a man's curious taste; now (though the vogue may be fading) it is a minimum requirement of civilized literary talk. We have seen the history of English poetry rewritten by critics convinced of his cardinal importance. This change was partly the effect of the reception into England of French Symbolist thought, and its assimilation to the native doctrines of Blake, Coleridge and Pater. Poets and critics were struck by the way Donne exhibits the play of an agile mind within the sensuous body of poetry, so that even his most passionate poems work by wit, abounding in argument and analogy; the poetry and the argument cannot be abstracted from each other. And this was interesting because the new aesthetic was founded on a hatred for the disembodied intellect, for abstract argument, for what the French called *littérature*. A series of poets, culminating in Mr. Eliot, proclaimed their affinity with Donne. They also searched the past in order to discover the moment when the blend of thought and passion that came so naturally to Donne, and with such difficulty to themselves, developed its modern inaccessibility. One answer was that this occurred during the lifetime of Milton, who helped to create the difficulties under which modern poetry labours. This very characteristic Symbolist historical myth is usually called by the name Mr. Eliot gave it, the 'dissociation of sensibility'. Mr. Eliot has altered his views on Donne and Milton, but his new opinions have been less powerful than the older ones; and it remains true that to write of the fortunes of Donne in the past seventy years is, in effect, to write less about him than about the aesthetic preoccupations of that epoch.

Donne has been distorted to serve this myth; but it is true that earlier criticism had treated him harshly. As Ben Jonson suggested, his kind of poetry runs the risk of neglect, especially in periods that value perspicuity. Dryden thought of him as a great wit, rather than as a poet, and a normal late seventeenth-century view of Donne was that this 'eminent poet . . . became a much more eminent preacher'. Johnson's brilliant critique occurs more or less accidentally in his *Life of Cowley*. Coleridge and Lamb, Browning and George Eliot admired him, but Gosse, in what was long the standard biography, is patronizing about the poetry and calls Donne's influence 'almost entirely malign'. The revaluation of Donne has certainly been radical. The present is probably a favourable moment for a just estimate. The past fifty years have provided the essential apparatus, and though the time for partisan extravagance has gone, so has the time for patronage.

II

Donne was born early in 1572, of Roman Catholic parents. His mother was of good family; and since she numbered among her kinsmen Mores, Heywoods and Rastells, Donne could well claim, in his *apologia* at the beginning of the anti-Jesuit *Pseudo-Martyr*, that his family had endured much for the Roman Doctrine. His own brother was arrested for concealing a priest, and died in prison. His father, a prosperous City tradesman, died when Donne was not yet four, leaving him a portion of about £750. A more enduring legacy was his early indoctrination by Jesuits. To his intimate acquaintance with their persecution under Elizabeth he attributes his interest in suicide (*Biathanatos*) and his right to characterize as mistaken the Jesuit thirst for martyrdom by the hostile civil power (*Pseudo-Martyr*). In fact, his whole life and work were strongly affected by this circumstance of his childhood. He suffered materially; for example, as a Roman Catholic he was disabled from taking a degree at Oxford. But, more important, his mind was cast in the mould of learned religion. We know that during his years at the Inns of Court, in the early nineties, he read much besides law; that he explored many fields and many languages, and—though described as a great visitor of ladies—rose at four every morning and rarely left his chamber before ten. Much, if not most, of this reading must have been theological in character.

Donne travelled in Italy and Spain, and in 1596 and 1597 took part in naval expeditions. In 1598 he became secretary to the influential Sir Thomas Egerton; but his secret marriage to Lady Egerton's niece, Ann More, in December 1601, put an end to his hopes of worldly success. Her father had Donne imprisoned and dismissed his post; he even tried to have the marriage annulled. Donne's dignified apologies prevailed, but he did not achieve reinstatement, and for some years lived somewhat grimly and inconveniently in what he called 'my hospital at Mitcham', burdened and distracted by illness, poverty, and a growing family. A letter describes him writing 'in the noise of three gamesome children; and by the side of her, whom . . . I have transplanted into a wretched fortune'. He complained, in dark and memorable phrases, of his hated inactivity. He sought patronage, and had it of the Countess of Bedford, of the King's favourite, Carr, and of Sir Robert Drury. He worked as assistant to Morton, later Bishop of Durham, in anti-Romanist polemic, but refused to take orders when Morton requested it. The belated payment of his wife's dowry gave him a period of relief, in which he wrote more and published for the first time—*Pseudo-Martyr* in 1610, *Ignatius his Conclave* in 1611, the two poems for Elizabeth Drury's death in 1611 and 1612. *Biathanatos*, which he forbade 'both the press and the fire', belongs to this time, and the *Essayes in Divinity* were written in 1614.

When the King had made it plain that he would advance Donne only within the Church, the poet finally took Orders (January 1615). In 1616 he was appointed Reader in Divinity at Lincoln's Inn, where, over the years, he both gave and received great satisfaction. A learned audience suited Donne, although this one must have been well-informed about those youthful indiscretions concerning which the lack of evidence has never impeded warm speculation; he was accepted as the penitent he claimed to be, and the audience would remember St. Augustine. Donne had found his true *genre*.

His wife died in 1617, her memory celebrated by a fine sonnet and a great sermon; Donne was left with seven children. He was made Dean of St. Paul's in 1621, and became the most famous of preachers, invested with a sombre sanctity, and happy in the rejection of 'the mistress of my youth, Poetry' for 'the wife of mine age, Divinity'. In 1623 he was seriously ill, and during his illness wrote *Devotions upon Emergent Occasions*, a series of religious meditations on the course of his disease which is striking evidence of his continuing ability to be witty on all topics; with all its solemnity it has a macabre playfulness and hospital wit.

His sermons are often surprisingly personal; we learn of his family anxieties (the death of a daughter, a son missing in action, his own departure abroad in 1619) and his remorse for past sins. In the end he brought his own death into the pulpit (having wished to die there) and preached the appalling sermon called 'Deaths Duell' before Charles I in Lent, 1631. His ordering of the monument which survived the Fire and is still in St. Paul's, and his almost histrionic composure on his deathbed, Walton has made famous. This aspect of Donne has perhaps been overstressed; he and death are a little too closely associated. This can be corrected only by prolonged reading in the sermons, or perhaps by reminding oneself of his marked interest in life: his desire for success, which made him the dependent of the dubious Carr, or his rich and varied friendships—with Goodyere, with the scientist Earl of Northumberland, with Lady Danvers and her sons, George and Edward Herbert, with Jonson and Wotton— many of them central to the intellectual life of their time. But it is still true that he was a sombre man, a melancholic even, and that at a time when this quality was associated with the highest kind of wit.

III

Wit is a quality allowed Donne by all critics, of all parties. In his own time people admired his 'strong lines', and perhaps the best way of giving a general account of his wit is to try to explain what this expression meant. Donne is notoriously an obscure poet—in fact his obscurity is often overestimated, but he is never easy— and this is often because his manner is tortuous and, in his own word, 'harsh'. Carew's famous tribute emphasizes the strain he put on language: 'to the awe of thy imperious wit Our stubborn language bends'. Carew speaks of his 'masculine expression';

Donne himself of his 'masculine persuasive force'. There was a contemporary taste for this kind of thing, related probably to an old tradition that it was right for some kinds of poetry to be obscure. And Donne was not writing for the many. He expected his readers to enjoy difficulty, not only in the scholastic ingenuity of his arguments, but in the combination of complicated verse-forms and apparently spontaneous thought—thought that doubled back, corrected itself, broke off in passionate interjections. This kind of writing belongs to a rhetorical tradition ignored by much Elizabethan poetry, which argued that language could directly represent the immediate play of mind—style as the instantaneous expression of thinking. And this is why Donne—if I may translate from Mario Praz what I take to be the best thing ever said about Donne's style—will always appeal to readers 'whom the *rhythm of thought* itself attracts by virtue of its own peculiar convolutions'.

Obviously this is a limited appeal. Ben Jonson, himself not a stranger to the strong line, was only the first to accuse Donne of overdoing it. He recommended a middle course between jejune smoothness and a manner conscientiously rough. But for a while 'strong lines'—applied to prose as well as verse—was a eulogistic term; so Fuller could praise those of Cleveland, saying that 'his Epithetes were pregnant with metaphors, carrying in them a difficult plainness, difficult at the hearing, plain at the considering thereof'. But there was opposition to what Walton called 'the strong lines now in fashion'; witness, for example, Corbet's good nonsense poem 'Epilogus Incerti Authoris', a heap of paradoxes beginning 'Like to the mowing tone of unspoke speeches', and ending:

> Even such is man who dyed, and yet did laugh
> To read these strong lines for his Epitaph—

which not only parodies Donne, but foretells the fate of the strong line: it degenerated into a joke, and until recently recurred only in comic poetry. Hobbes, legislating for a new poetry in the fifties, called them 'no better than riddles'. The taste for strong lines is not universal; nor are the powers they require of poets.

As strong lines directly record mental activity, they contain concepts, or, in the contemporary form of the word, 'conceits'. The meaning we now attach to this word is a specialization

directly due to the vogue for strong lines. The value of such lines
obviously depends on the value (and that is almost the same thing
as the *strangeness*) of the concepts they express, and these were
usually metaphors. A high valuation was placed on metaphor, on
the power of making what Dr. Johnson, who understood without
approving, called the *discordia concors*. The world was regarded as a
vast divine system of metaphors, and the mind was at its fullest
stretch when observing them. Peculiar ability in this respect was
called *acutezza* by the Italians and, by the English, Wit. But
although the movement was European in scope, it is unnecessary
to suppose that Donne owed much to its Spanish and Italian
exponents; they were known in England, but they conspicuously
lack Donne's colloquial convolution, and his argumentativeness.
Johnson's mistake in reporting Marino as a source has often been
repeated. Marino has strength, but not harshness, not the masculine persuasive force. We cannot think of Donne without thinking
of relentless argument. He depends heavily upon dialectical
sleight-of-hand, arriving at the point of wit by subtle syllogistic
misdirections, inviting admiration by slight but significant per-
versities of analogue, which re-route every argument to parodox.
Still, in view of the lack of contemporary English criticism on
these points, it is wise to learn what we can from Continental
critics of witty poetry, and the most important lesson, brilliantly
suggested by S. L. Bethell, is that they regarded the conceit of
argument—making a new and striking point by a syllogism concealing a logical error—as the highest and rarest kind of conceit.
This is Donne's commonest device. Of course we are aware that
we are being cleverly teased, but many of the love-poems, like
'The Extasie' or 'The Flea', depend on our wonder outlasting our
critical attitude to argument:

> Marke but this flea, and marke in this,
> How little that which thou deny'st me is;
> It suck'd me first, and now sucks thee,
> And in this flea, our two bloods mingled bee;
> Thou know'st that this cannot be said
> A sinne, nor shame, nor losse of maidenhead,
>   Yet this enjoyes before it wooe,
>   And pamper'd swells with one blood made of two,
>   And this, alas, is more than wee would doe.

Oh stay, three lives in one flea spare,
Where wee almost, yea more then maryed are.
This flea is you and I, and this
Our marriage bed, and marriage temple is;
Though parents grudge, and you, w'are met
And cloysterd in these living walls of Jet.
 Though use make you apt to kill mee,
 Let not that, selfe murder added bee,
 And sacrilege, three sinnes in killing three.

Cruell and sodaine, hast thou since
Purpled thy naile, in blood of innocence?
Wherein could this flea guilty bee,
Except in that drop which it suckt from thee?
Yet thou triumph'st, and saist that thou
Find'st not thy selfe, nor mee the weaker now;
 'Tis true, then learne how false, feares bee;
 Just so much honor, when thou yeeld'st to mee,
 Will wast, as this flea's death tooke life from thee.

This poem, which was enormously admired by Donne's contemporaries, is cited here merely as an example of his original way of wooing by false syllogisms. So in 'The Extasie': the argument, a tissue of fallacies, sounds solemnly convincing and consecutive, so that it is surprising to find it ending with an immodest proposal. The highest powers of the mind are put to base use, but enchantingly demonstrated in the process.

Part of Donne's originality lies precisely in the use of such methods for amorous poetry. Properly they belong to the sphere of religion (of course there is always much commerce between the two). This human wit suggests the large design of God's wit in the creation. It is immemorially associated with biblical exegesis and preaching, sanctioned and practised by Ambrose and Augustine, and blended in the patristic tradition with the harshness of Tertullian, as well as with the enormous eloquence of Chrysostom. The Europe of Donne's time had enthusiastically taken up witty preaching, but the *gusto espagnol*, as it was called, though associated with the Counter-Reformation, is essentially a revival of what Professor Curtius would call the 'mannerism' of the patristic tradition. Now this tradition was venerated by the

Church of England, a learned Church which rejected the Puritan aphorism 'so much Latin, so much Flesh'. And the Fathers could provide not only doctrine but examples of *ingenium*, that acuity of observation by which the preacher could best illustrate and explicate the Word. Donne's youthful examination of 'the whole body of divinity controverted between the Churches of England and Rome' provided him not only with a religion but with a style. Some aspects of his Jesuit training would help him in the business of analogy; but primarily the conceit of his secular poetry is derived from his later religious studies. It is, in fact, a new, paradoxical use, for amorous purposes, of the *concetto predicabile*, the preacher's conceit. As usual, we see him all of a piece, yet all paradox; Donne the poet, with all his 'naturalist' passion, knowingness, obscenity indeed, is *anima naturaliter theologica*. What made him a poet also made him an Anglican: the revaluation of a tradition.

IV

It is for this reason that the old emphasis on the 'medieval' quality of Donne's thought, though in need of qualification, is more to the point than the more recent stress on his modernity. A great deal has been made of his interest in the 'new philosophy', and the disturbance supposed to have been caused him by such astronomical discoveries as the elliptical movement of planets, the impossibility of a sphere of fire, the corruptibility of the heavens, the movement of the earth, and so on. Certainly, as we know from *Ignatius* and elsewhere, Donne was aware of such developments, aware that it was no longer humanly satisfactory to look at the heavens through the spectacles of Ptolemy. But it is the greatest possible misunderstanding of Donne to suppose that he took this as any more than another proof, where none was needed, of the imperfection of human intellect. Mutability reached higher towards heaven than one had thought; but this only shows how unreliable human knowledge must always be. In *Ignatius*, Donne does not recount the new discoveries for their own sakes, but only as part of the sneering. '*Keppler* . . . (as himselfe testifies of himselfe) *euer since* Tycho Braches *death, hath receiued into his care, that no new thing should be done in heauen without his knowledge.*' Kepler

himself called this 'impudent', not 'flattering'. When the Devil
sees that he can find no worthy place in Hell for Ignatius, he
decides to get Galileo to draw down the moon (an easy matter
for one who had already got close enough to see its imperfections) so that the Jesuits can get on to it—they will 'easily unite
and reconcile the *Lunatique Church* to the *Romane Church*', and a
hell will grow in the moon, for Ignatius to rule over. Sometimes
he uses 'new philosophy' more seriously, to illustrate some moral
or theological assertion. The new astronomy, for example, is
'applicable well' because it is right that we should move towards
God, not He to us. Or, the Roman Church is like Copernicanism
—it 'hath carried earth farther up from the stupid Center' but
carried heaven far higher. When he wants, for the sake of some
argument, to disprove the sphere of fire, he does not use the new
scientific argument from optics, but the old-fashioned opinion of
Cardan (God would not make an element in which nothing could
live). In serious mood he often forgets that the earth moves: 'the
Earth is not the more constant because it lies stil continually'
(*Devotions*), or: it is a wonderful thing that 'so vast and immense a
body as the Sun should run so many miles in a minute' (Sermon of
1627). The famous passage in 'The First Anniversary':

> And new Philosophy calls all in doubt,
> The Element of fire is quite put out;
> The Sun is lost, and th'earth, and no mans wit
> Can well direct him where to looke for it,

is merely part of the demonstration of 'the frailty and decay of
this whole World' mentioned in the title of the poem—a theme
enforced by many illustrations taken from a wide variety of subjects, including the 'old' philosophy. And this is Donne's way
with new or old knowledge. It would be very unlike him to be
much affected by the new philosophy: 'if there be any addition to
knowledge,' he says in a sermon of 1626, 'it is rather new knowledge, than a greater knowledge'. For, if you know as much as
Socrates, you know nothing, and 'S. Paul found that to be all
knowledge, to know Christ'. There is always an antithesis, in
Donne, between natural and divine knowledge, the first shadowy
and inexact, the second clear and sure. New philosophy belongs
to the first class. What we really know is what is revealed; later
we shall know in full:

Up into the watch-towre get,
And see all things desployl'd of fallacies:
Thou shalt not peepe through lattices of eyes,
Nor heare through Labyrinths of eares, nor learne
By circuit, or collections to discerne.
In heaven thou straight know'st all, concerning it,
And what concerns is not, shalt straight forget.

V

A mind habituated to such discriminations between the light of
nature and 'light from above, from the fountain of light', as
Milton calls it, may, in some spheres of knowledge, earn the
epithet 'sceptical'. Donne deserted a Church which, as he and
Hooker agreed, had mistaken mere custom for law. Liberated
from the tyranny of custom, he turns, in his erotic poetry, a professionally disenchanted eye on conventional human behaviour.
We may speak confidently of a 'libertine' or 'naturalist' Donne
only if we use the terms as applying to literature and thought
rather than to life; but it remains true that the *Songs and Sonets* are
often (though without his shocking coolness) akin to the franker
pronouncements of Montaigne. Consider, for example, his essay
'Upon some verses of Virgil', where he professes his contempt for
'artised' love: he prefers the thing itself, and in accordance with
his preference argues that amorous poetry also should be 'natural',
colloquial, 'not so much innovating as filling language with more
forcible and divers services, wrestling, straining, and enfolding it
. . . teaching it unwonted motions'. This is Donne to the life:

Who ever loves, if he do not propose
The right true end of love, he's one who goes
To sea for nothing but to make him sick.

Donne openly despises the ritual and indirection of Platonic love;
he will follow Nature and pluck his rose (or roses; for Love's
sweetest part is variety). The enemies of nature are such fictions
as Honour; in the good old times, before Custom dominated
humanity, things were very different: see 'Loves Deity' and
Elegy xvii:

How happy were our Syres in ancient times,

> Who held plurality of loves no crime! . . .
> But since this title honour hath been us'd,
> Our weake credulity hath been abus'd;
> The golden laws of nature are repeald . . .

This is the sense in which Donne often celebrates the passion of love—as immediate and natural, but constricted by social absurdities:

> Love's not so pure and abstract, as they use
> To say, which have no Mistresse but their Muse.

But of course we must allow for an element of formal paradox. Donne found this very congenial—it is in a way a theological, a liturgical device—and his *Juvenilia* contain such joke paradoxes as a defence of woman's inconstancy, an argument that it is possible to find some virtue in women, and so on, worked out with the same half-serious, half-ribald ingenuity that we find in some of the *Songs and Sonets*:

> Goe, and catche a falling starre,
> Get with child a mandrake roote,
> Tell me, where all past yeares are,
> Or who cleft the Divels foot,
> Teach me to heare Mermaides singing,
> Or to keep off envies stinging,
>> And finde
>> What winde
> Serves to advance an honest minde.
>
> If thou beest borne to strange sights,
> Things invisible to see,
> Ride ten thousand daies and nights,
> Till age snow white haires on thee,
> Thou, when thou retorn'st, wilt tell mee
> All strange wonders that befell thee,
>> And sweare
>> No where
> Lives a woman true, and faire.
>
> If thou findst one, let mee know,
> Such a Pilgrimage were sweet;

> Yet doe not, I would not goe,
> Though at next doore wee might meet,
> Though shee were true, when you met her,
> And last, till you write your letter,
> > Yet shee
> > We bee
> False, ere I come, to two, or three.

To take these poems too seriously, as moral or autobiographical pronouncements, is to spoil them; though some are clearly more serious than others.

VI

This may suggest the possibility of dividing the secular poems into groups other than their obvious *genres*; but it is a highly conjectural undertaking. There is a similar difficulty about their chronology; attempts to determine this depend on hypothetical links with events (and women) in Donne's life. We can say the Satires were written in the 'nineties; we can place many verse-letters over a twenty-year period; epithalamia and obsequies are datable; one or two references in the love-poems hint at dates. But in these last the evidence is scanty. Jonson's testimony, that Donne did his best work before he was twenty-five, depends on what he thought good—all we know is that he admired 'The Calm' and 'The Storm' (verse-letters) and Elegy xi, a frantically witty poem, but not among the most admired today. Only exceptionally can we say with certainty that this poem is addressed to his wife, that to another woman; this is witty with a stock situation ('The Flea', for example, or 'The Dream') while that is drawn from life. Gosse actually invented a disastrous affair to explain some poems, and absurdly supposed Elegy xvi to be addressed to Donne's wife; another critic has argued passionately that 'The Extasie' is a husband's address to his wife. Even Sir Herbert Grierson supposes that the 'Nocturnall' must be connected with the Countess of Bedford, whose name was Lucy; and a whole set of poems, some of them full of racy *double-entendre*, has been associated with Lady Danvers, ten years Donne's senior and the mother of his friends the Herberts. All we may be sure of is that Donne, with varying intensity, passion, and intellectual conviction, exercised his wit on the theme of sexual love, and that he was inclined to do this in a 'naturalist' way. We need not concern ourselves with dates, or with the identities of mistresses celebrated, cursed or mourned

The *Songs and Sonets* were read only in manuscript in Donne's lifetime, and so by a small and sophisticated circle. They certainly exhibit what Donne, in the little squib called *The Courtier's Library*, calls 'itchy outbreaks of far-fetched wit'; and the wit is of the kind that depends both upon a harsh strangeness of expression and upon great acuity of illustration and argument. We are asked to *admire*, and that is why the poet creates difficulties for himself, choosing arbitrary and complex stanza forms, of which the main point often seems to be that they put tremendous obstacles in his way. Without underestimating the variety of tone in these poems, one may say they all offer this kind of pleasure—delight in a dazzling conjuring trick. Even the smoothest, simplest song, like 'Sweetest love, I do not goe', is full of *mind*. Donne would have despised Dryden's distinction between poets and wits. True, some of these poems deserve the censure that when we have once understood them they are exhausted: 'The Indifferent', 'The Triple Fool', and a dozen others fall into this class. Others, like 'The Flea' and 'A Valediction: of my name, in the window', are admired primarily as incredibly perverse and subtle feats of wit; yet others, like 'The Apparition', as examples of how Donne could clothe a passion, in this case hatred, in a clever colloquial fury. This is the inimitable Donne: sometimes, as in 'The Broken Heart', we might be reading Cowley's sexless exercises.

One should here dwell at rather more length on one or two poems. I almost chose 'The Dampe', a fine example of Donne's dialectical wit (the main argument is attended by a ghost-argument, supported by slang double-meanings); and 'Farewell to Love', which would have pleased Montaigne by its grave obscenity; and, for its wide-ranging metaphor and brilliant far-fetched conclusion, 'Loves Alchymie'. 'Lovers Infinitenesse' has the characteristic swerving argument, its stanzas beginning 'If . . . Or . . . Yet . . .' —compare 'The Feaver', with its 'But yet . . . Or if . . . And yet . . . Yet . . .' For his best use of 'the nice speculations of philosophy', 'Aire and Angells' and 'The Extasie' commend themselves:

Where, like a pillow on a bed,
A pregnant banke swel'd up, to rest
The violets reclining head
Sat we two, one anothers best.
  Our hands were firmley cimented
With a fast balme, which thence did spring,
Our eye-beames twisted, and did thred
Our eyes, upon one double string;
  So to'entergraft our hands, as yet
Was all the means to make us one,
And pictures in our eyes to get
Was all our propagation. . . .

But O alas, so long, so farre
Our bodies why doe wee forbeare? . . .

  As our blood labours to beget
Spirits, as like soules as it can,
Because such fingers need to knit
That subtile knot, which makes us man:
So must pure lovers soules descend
T'affections, and to faculties,
Which sense may reach and apprehend,
Else a great Prince in prison lies.

But 'The Curse' is both characteristic and neglected, and 'A Nocturnall upon S. Lucies Day' is Donne's finest poem; so there
follow some scanty remarks on these.

'The Curse' has the usual complex rhyme-scheme, and rather
more than the usual energy in that Irish ingenuity of malediction
which reminds us that Donne was one of the early satirists:

Who ever guesses, thinks, or dreames he knowes
    Who is my mistris, wither by this curse;
        His only, and only his purse
        May some dull heart to love dispose,
  And shee yeeld then to all that are his foes;
        May he be scorn'd by one, whom all else scorne,
        Forsweare to others, what to her he'hath sworne,
        With feare of missing, shame of getting, torne . . .

The syntactical conciseness of lines 3–5 is remarkable: 'May he win only a mercenary love, yet may he have to spend all he has to get her (and may she be dull into the bargain). Then, wretched mistress though she be, let her betray him—and do so with everybody who dislikes him (presumably a large number of people).' This only begins the cursing. 'May he suffer remorse, not of conscience because he has sinned (too noble a passion for him) but because the reputation of the only woman he was able to get makes him everybody's butt' . . . and so on. The poem ends with an inventory of hatred and poison, provisions for further additions to the curse as they may occur to the poet, and finally—as often in Donne—a light, epigrammatic couplet to place the poem on the witty side of passion: you can't curse a woman more than she is naturally 'curst' (forward, fickle, uncertain of temper) already:

> The venom of all stepdames, gamsters gall,
> What Tyrans, and their subjects interwish,
>   What Plants, Mynes, Beasts, Foule, Fish
>   Can contribute, all ill which all
> Prophets, or Poets spake; And all which shall
>   Be annex'd in schedules unto this by mee,
>   Fall on that man; For if it be a shee
>   Nature before hand hath out-cursed mee.

So much of the effect depends on the control of syntactical and rhythmic emphasis, on devices like the repeated 'all' (28–9), on the impressive catalogue, the compression of meaning in 26 which calls forth the neologism 'interwish', the formal streak of legal diction, and the minatory solemnity of 'Fall on that man'—that paraphrase breaks down into inoffensive jesting a poem that gets its effect by an impression of qualified but dangerous loathing. This is pure Donne; as a matter of opinion good, as a matter of fact unique.

This last is true, *a fortiori*, of the 'Nocturnall', which has the additional interest of involving some of his known intellectual problems and convictions. The imagery is predominantly alchemical; the argument goes in search of a definition of absolute nothingness; yet the *cause* of the poem is grief at the death of a mistress. This is the most solemn and the most difficult of Donne's poems, superficially slow in movement, but with a contrapuntal velocity of thought. It begins as a meditation on the

vigil of his saint: Saint Lucy's day is chosen because it is the dead
day of the year, as midnight is the dead hour of the day:

> Tis the yeares midnight, and it is the dayes,
> *Lucies*, who scarce seaven houres herself unmaskes,
> The Sunne is spent, and now his flasks
> Send forth light squibs, no constant rayes;
>   The worlds whole sap is sunke:
> The generall balme th'hydroptique earth hath drunk,
> Whither, as to the beds-feet, life is shrunke,
> Dead and enterr'd; yet all these seeme to laugh,
> Compar'd with mee, who am their Epitaph.

That which preserves life, the 'generall balme', is shrunk into the
frozen earth. Darkness, which is Nothing to light's All, and
death, which is Nothing to life's All, reign in the great world; yet
the little world, the poet, is far deader and darker, an abstract of
death, an epitaph. The world will be reborn in Spring, and there
will be lovers; but he is 'every dead thing'. His deadness is
enforced by a remarkable alchemical figure, based on the idea
that the alchemist deals in the quintessence of *all things*, 'ruining'
—abstracting form from—metals in order to reconstitute them as
gold, by means of the quintessence. But this 'new' alchemy, on
the contrary, works with a quintessence of *nothing*, privation, and
imposes on the poet's 'ruined' matter the 'form' of absolute
nothingness—'absence, darkness, death'. Alchemical and theological figures come as it were naturally to Donne; he uses
alchemy to push the notion of absolute privation beyond human
understanding. The poet has less being than the primaeval Nothing that preceded Chaos, which preceded Creation; he is a quintessence of Nothing: 'I am None.' The internal rhyme with
'Sunne' (meaning light, and All, as well as the woman responsible
for his state of non-being) brings us back, at the end, to the
commonplace lovers whose activity will be restored in Spring,
when the commonplace sun returns:

> But I am None; nor will my Sunne renew.
> You lovers, for whose sake, the lesser Sunne
> At this time to the Goat is ninne
> To fetch new lust, and give it you,
>   Enjoy your summer all;

> Since shee enjoyes her long nights festivall,
> Let mee prepare towards her, and let mee call
> This houre her Vigill, and her Eve, since this
> Both the yeares, and the dayes deep midnight is.

The witty sneer about the object of the sun's journey to the Tropic of Capricorn helps to distance these inferior loves; and we return to darkness, the perpetual sleep of the other Sun, and the propriety of this saint's day as the type of darkness and lifelessness.

This is a very inadequate account of a marvellous poem. My main object is to make a point about Donne's use, in poetry, of ideas he clearly regarded as important. The general balm, the alchemical ruin, the violent paradoxes on All and Nothing, belong to Donne's mental habit. There is, for instance, a fine examination of the All-Nothing paradox in the exegetical passages on Genesis in *Essayes in Divinity*, and it occurs in the sermons. As he extracted the notion of absolute privation in alchemical terms, Donne must have been thinking of the Cabbalistic description of God as the nothing, the quintessence of nothing; here a keen and prejudiced ear might discover one of his blasphemies. But it is more interesting, I think, that Donne the poet is claiming what Donne the theologian calls impossible; he constantly recurs to the point that man cannot desire annihilation. So the wit of the poem (using the word in its full sense) really derives from its making, by plausible argument, the impossible seem true. And he does it by the use of figures from alchemy, an art traditionally associated with the resurrection of the body, the escape from annihilation—he spoke in his own last illness of his physical decay as the alchemical ruining of his body before resurrection; here, with vertiginous wit, he uses the same analogy to prove the contrary. It is not inappropriate that the finest of the *Songs and Sonets* should also be the most sombrely witty, and the most difficult.

Of Donne's twenty Elegies I have room to say little. They are love-poems in loose iambic pentameter couplets, owing a general debt, for tone and situation, to the *Amores* of Ovid; the Roman poet loses no wit, but acquires harshness, masculinity. These poems are full of sexual energy, whether it comes out in frank libertinism, or in the wit of some more serious attachment. 'The Anagram' (ii) is an example of the wit that proved all too imitable, all too ready to degenerate into fooling—it is a series of paradoxes on somebody's foul mistress, a theme current at the time. Elegy viii is a similar poem, comparing one's own and another's mistress, with plenty of unpleasant detail. But the Elegies have a considerable variety of tone, ranging from the set pieces on Change and Variety (iii and xvii) which are paralleled by several of the *Songs and Sonets*, to the passionate xvi and the sombre xii, on the theme of parting:

> Nor praise, nor dispraise me, nor blesse nor curse
> Openly loves force, nor in bed fright thy Nurse
> With midnights startings, crying out, oh, oh
> Nurse, ô my love is slaine, I saw him goe
> O'r the white Alpes alone . . .

The Elegies have always had a reputation for indecency, and they certainly exploit the sexual puns so much enjoyed by Elizabethan readers. Among the poems excluded from the first edition is the magnificently erotic Elegy xix, 'Going to Bed': too curious a consideration of some of the metaphors in this poem (such as the passage about 'imputed grace') has led critics to charge it with blasphemy, a risk Donne often runs by the very nature of his method. Montaigne might have complained that Donne here substitutes a new mythology and metaphysics of love for those he had abandoned, new presbyter for old priest. But it is impossible not to admire the translation of sexual into mental activity. Elegy xix was later regarded as the poet's own epithalamion, a fancy as harmless as it is improbable, except that it has perhaps resulted in the acceptance of a very inferior reading in line 46.[1] One beautiful and exceptional poem is Elegy ix, 'The Autumnall' to Lady Danvers; but even this would not, I think, quite escape Sir Herbert Grierson's criticism, that Donne (especially in the Elegies) shows 'a radical want of delicacy'; for it has the wit and fantastic range of reference that mark the erotic Elegies.

The Satires belong to the same phase of Donne's talent as the work I have been discussing. They are, as Elizabethan satire was

---

[1] 'There is no pennance due to innocence', the reading of 1669, is represented in most manuscripts by 'There is no pennance, much less innocence'. The received reading makes the poem slightly more appropriate if the woman is a bride. But clearly she is no more innocent than she is penitent, and ought not to be wearing the white linen which signifies either innocence or penitence.

supposed to be, rough and harsh, written in that low style that Donne so often used, though here it is conventional. Satyre iii I shall discuss later; of the others we may say that they have the usual energy, a richness of contemporary observation rather splenetic, of course, in character. Pope thought them worth much trouble, but it is doubtful if, except for iii, they play much part in anybody's thinking about Donne. The same may be said of the epicedes and obsequies, funeral poems which in this period were often, when they were not pastoral elegies, poems of fantastically tormented wit. So Donne proves, in the elegy on Prince Henry, that 'wee May safelyer say, that we are dead, then hee'. The form suited him only too well. The same cannot be said of the epithalamion; Spenser is the poet to thrive here. Yet there are fine things in Donne's poem for the marriage of the Princess Elizabeth in 1613:

> Up, up, faire Bride, and call,
> Thy starres, from out their severall boxes, take
> Thy Rubies, Pearles, and Diamonds forth, and make
> Thy selfe a constellation, of them All,
> And by their blazing signifie,
> That a Great Princess falls, but doth not die.

Donne could not speak without wit; it is this naturalness that often redeems him.

Of the occasional verse included under the title 'Letters to Severall Personages' a word must suffice. There is a mistaken view that they are negligible because they occasionally flatter. They were written over many years, and not for all profit: notice the little-known verses to Goodyere (Grierson, I. 183) which have the strong Jonsonian ring; the charming 'Mad paper, stay' to Lady Herbert before her re-marriage. The best, probably, are to the Countess of Bedford, dependant though Donne may have been; and the poem beginning 'You have refin'd mee' is a great poem, certainly no more 'blasphemous' in its compliment than Elegy xix in its persuasions.

This matter of blasphemous allusion comes to a head in the two 'Anniversaries', written for Sir Robert Drury on the death of his daughter Elizabeth, and published in 1611 and 1612. These are amazingly elaborate laments for a girl Donne had never seen. The first he called 'An Anatomy of the World', announcing in his full title that the death of Elizabeth Drury is the *occasion* for observations on the frailty and decay of the whole world, and representing the dead girl as Astræa, as the world's soul, as the preservative balm, and so on, her departure has left it lifeless, and he dissects it. The second, describing 'the Progresse of the Soule' after death, is similar: 'By occasion of the Religious death of Mistris Elizabeth Drury, the incommodities of the soule in this life, and her exaltation in the next, are contemplated.' From Jonson forward, critics have complained of the faulty taste of such hyperbolical praise of a young girl, and Donne defended himself more than once, though without much vigour; he would have little patience with this kind of misunderstanding. All we may say here is that these poems—now known to be planned in a highly original way as a series of formal religious meditations—are essential to the understanding of Donne; they come near to giving us a map of the dark side of his wit. The deathbed meditation in the second poem is comparable with the Holy Sonnets on the same topic:

> Thinke they selfe labouring now with broken breath,
> And thinke those broken and soft Notes to bee
> Division,[2] and thy happyest Harmonie.

> Thinke thee laid on thy death-bed, loose and slacke;
> And thinke that, but unbinding of a packe,
> To take one precious thing, thy soule from thence.

The 'Anniversaries' lead us into a consideration of Donne's religious life. But we shall find that the poet and the religious were the same man.

VII

Donne's acceptance of the established Church is the most important single event of his life, because it involved all the powers of his mind and personality. His youthful sympathies must have been with the persecuted Romanists, and his Satires contain bitter allusions to 'pursuivants', tormentors of Jesuits; the odious Topcliffe is mentioned by name in some manuscripts. But he was

[2] A musical term, meaning a variation on a melody, made by dividing each of its notes into shorter ones.

familiar with the fanaticism as well as with the learning of Jesuits; and later he decided that the first of these was the hardest affliction of Christendom, though the second was to serve him well. No one can say exactly when he left one Church for the other; it was a gradual process. According to Walton, he was about nineteen when, 'being unresolv'd what religion to adhere to, and, considering how much it concern'd his soul to choose the most Orthodox', he abandoned all studies for divinity. Donne himself, in *Pseudo-Martyr*, claims to have done this with 'an indifferent affection to both parties'. Particularly, he consulted Bellarmine, 'the best defender of the *Roman cause*' (Walton), and Hooker, whose *Laws of Ecclesiastical Polity* appeared in 1593, when Donne was 21—though his famous sermon 'Of Justification', which must have appealed to all moderate Romanists, had long been available. Hooker triumphed; but as late as 1601 the unfinished satirical extravaganza, 'The Progress of the Soul', treats the Queen as the last of a line of arch-heretics, and more dubious references suggest that Donne's recusancy persisted in some form up to the time of *Pseudo-Martyr*. When Walton says he treated the problem as urgent, he is paraphrasing the remarkable Satyre iii, which must belong to the 'nineties. What makes this poem odd is the brisk impatience of its manner, an exasperated harshness proper to satire but strange in a deliberative poem about religion. It has often been misunderstood. The main theme is simply the importance of having a religion; without that one is worse off than 'blind (i.e. pagan) philosophers':

> Shall thy fathers spirit
> Meete blinde Philosophers in heaven, whose merit
> Of strict life may be imputed faith, and heare
> Thee, whom hee taught so easie wayes and neare
> To follow, damn'd?

But which religion? Rome is loved because true religion was once to be found there; Geneva out of a perverse love for the coarse and plain; the English church from inertia. Such divisions encourage on the one hand abstinence from all, and on the other a mistaken belief that they are all true. It is necessary to choose one; and the best course is to 'Aske thy father which is shee, Let him aske his'. Above all, do not rest; no business is as important as this. This is a tentative assertion of the Catholic tradition invoked by all Anglicans—the *true*, not the *Roman*, Catholicism. Donne had in fact to choose only between these two Churches; though he was to develop a great respect for Calvin, he was never concerned with extreme Protestantism. Of the two communions—'sister teats of his graces' he called them, 'yet both diseased and infected, but not both alike'—he was to choose the one truer to the Catholic tradition as he understood it. Like his learned contemporary Casaubon, he found this to be the Church of England—episcopal and sacramental, but divested of the Romanist accretions. Satyre iii is a poem about his search, not about its end. He had still much to do before he could think of 'binding his conscience to a local religion'.

One consequence of this deliberation was that Donne was unusually moderate in later allusions to Rome. In *Pseudo-Martyr* he speaks frankly of its long hold over him, and is charitable to 'all professors of Christian Religion, if they shake not the Foundation'. All his animus is against the Jesuits, for incalculating a false doctrine of martyrdom, and for opening up, by their intransigence, deplorable breaches in the Church. He attacks and satirizes them as enemies of tolerance: 'that Church,' he says in *Essayes in Divinity*, 'which despises another Church, is it self no other then that of which the *Psalm* speaks, *Ecclesia Malignantium*'. Here we are at the heart of his religious position. Donne had convinced himself that Reform had made the English Church more truly Catholic than any other. It was not only a middle way, but the ground on which, he hoped, the longed-for reunion of the Churches might be accomplished. Given tolerance, given an abatement of 'that severe and unrectified Zeal of many, who should impose necessity upon indifferent things, and oblige all the World to one precise forme of exterior worship, and Ecclesiastick policie', Donne saw a chance of ending the division of the Church.

In this aspiration he was at one with James I, though the prospect of success was much smaller than it had been when the Gallican party in France hoped for something from the Council of Trent. With the King, and his friend Wotton, Donne had expected much of the dispute between Venice and the Papacy in 1606; Wotton, as English Ambassador in Venice, had played an active part, and there was for a while excited speculation about the chance of Venice turning to a sort of Anglicanism. Wotton was acquainted with Paolo Sarpi, the canonist who conducted the Venetian case; and Sarpi's *History of the Council of Trent* was published first in London. In it he deplores the rigidity and extremism of that Council, and, as Miss Frances Yates has said, 'indirectly suggests that if the right course had been pursued at Trent, the Church as a whole would have been reformed somewhat on the model of the Anglican reform'. Wotton sent home several portraits of Sarpi for his English admirers; and it was presumably one of these that hung, as Donne's will testifies, in his study. It was an emblem of his hopes, and Donne completely accepted Sarpi's view of Trent. Preaching before the new King in April, 1926, on the text 'In my Father's house are many mansions', he deplores its intolerance, its coming 'to a finall resolution in so many particulars': as a result the Scriptures themselves are slighted and reduced in authority; and men are the readier to call each other heretics, 'which is a word that cuts deepe, and should not be passionately used'. Both these consequences are disastrous. The priest is ordained to preach the Word—Donne's favourite quotation is St. Paul's *vae mihi si non*, woe unto me if I do not so: 'Nothing', he says in 1618, 'is to be obtruded to our faith as necessary to salvation, except it be rooted in the Word', and he constantly complains that Rome 'detorts' the Word, as the Puritans do. As for the frequent charges of heresy, he warns his own congregation to 'be not apt to call opinion false, or hereticall, or damnable, the contrary whereof cannot be evidently proved'. Early and late, Donne the preacher insists upon the prime importance of the Word, and on the great need for tolerance; only thus may the Church in England be the matrix of a new universal Church. So, in an early sermon: 'For all this separation, Christ Jesus is amongst us all, and in his time will breake downe this wall too, these differences among Christians, and make us all glad of that name . . .' And in 1627 he prays that God 'in his time bring our adversaries to such moderation as becomes them, who doe truly desire, that the Church may bee truly *Catholique, one flock in the fold, under one Shepherd*, though *not all of one colour*, of one practise in all outward and disciplinary points'. This last was after the set-back to the cause in 1626, when the defeat of the Elector of Bohemia elicited from Donne the sonnet 'Show me, dear Christ, thy spouse'.

Donne, then, accepted the Church of England because it was

truly Catholic. He rejoiced to discover a Reformed Church which cultivated the Fathers and was slow to come 'to a final resolution' in 'particulars'. He wanted tradition but without its errors: Aquinas, but not the scholastic nonsense; the Fathers, but not their mistakes. The Catholic heritage was enormously more important to him than any 'new' knowledge, theological or physical, and he has little distinction as a speculative theologian, though his age is one of dogmatic controversy. He detested, for instance, the Calvinist teaching on Predestination, which had the intellectual presumption to dishonour God by suggesting that He could 'make us to damn us'; when it was necessary to pronounce on the matter he fell back on Aquinas ('God has appointed all future things to be, but so as they are, that is necessary things necessarily, and contingent things contingently') but he disliked the whole argument: '*Resistibility*, and *Irresistibility*, of grace, which is every Artificers wearing now, was a stuff that our Fathers wore not, a language that pure antiquity spake not.' 'The best men', he says, 'are but Problematicall, only the Holy Ghost is Dogmaticall.' Though by no means a complete Sceptic, he knew the limits of reason, and often defined its relation to faith (in *Essayes in Divinity, Biathanatos*, a verse-letter to the Countess of Bedford, the Christmas sermon for 1621). His position is not dissimilar from Hooker's (e.g. *Laws* I. 8). The limitations of human learning he sets forth in the famous Valediction Sermon of 1619, and the contrast between natural and heavenly knowledge (see the passage quoted earlier from 'Anniversaries') is developed in a splendid passage of the 1622 Easter sermon: 'God shall create us all Doctors in a minute.' Obviously the fierce certainties of some contemporaries were not for Donne. 'It is the text that saves us', he says. 'The interlineary glosses, and the marginal notes, and the *variae lectiones*, controversies and perplexities, undo us.' He was content with his Church's restoration of a good, lost tradition, just as, in his capacity as poet, he had used a traditional but neglected style that had its roots in the same great body of learning, the teaching of the Fathers.

VIII

No one, then, will read Donne for theological novelties; even in the *Essayes*, which are full of curious applications, Donne's regard for authority puts him at the opposite pole from the radically speculative Milton. And whatever may be offered by the vast array of sermons, it is not that kind of excitement.

It is not easy to give a general account of the sermons. They were preached on all manner of occasions, over fifteen years, and they take their colour from the audience, and from Donne's mood, as well as from the text and from the ecclesiastical occasion. Some were for a great audience, some for a small; some for lawyers, some for the Court; some for Lent and some for Easter; some were preached when the preacher had private reason for joy, some when he was miserable. The tone varies widely. There is truth in the often-repeated charge that Donne was preoccupied with sin and death; he confesses his melancholy temperament (calling it 'a disease of the times') and constantly quotes St. Paul's *cupio dissolvi* (Phil. i. 23), 'having a desire to depart and be with Christ'. 'If there were any other way to be saved and to get to Heaven,' he says, 'then by being born into this life, I would not wish to have come into this world.' There are terrible sermons on death, full of the poetry of charnel-house and worm. There are lamentations for the sins of youth: 'I preach the sense of Gods indignation upon mine own soul.' There are even rather grim sermons on apparently joyous occasions; a wedding sermon for personal friends is a forbidding, though orthodox, account of the Church's teaching on marriage, with many gloomy strictures on women. But one can overdo this aspect of the sermons. Death and Sin are fully presented; but perhaps not inordinately. And, to balance them, there is a massive insistence on the theme of Resurrection, and far more humanity than one is led to expect— see, for example, the moving passages on the death of Augustine's son, and that of his own daughter, in the superb Easter sermon for 1627:

> He was but a Heathen that said, If God love a man, *Iuvenis tollitur*, He takes him young out of this world; And they were but Heathens, that bestowed that custome. To put on mourning when their sons were born, and to feast and triumph when they dyed. But thus much we may learne from these Heathens, That if the dead, and we, be not upon one floore, nor under one story, yet we are under one roofe. We think not a friend lost, because he is gone into another

roome, nor because he is gone into another Land; And into
another world, no man is gone; for that Heaven, which
God created, and this world, is all one world. If I had fixt
a Son in Court, or married a daughter into a plentifull
Fortune, I were satisfied for that son and that daughter.
Shall I not be so, when the King of heaven hath taken
that son to himselfe, and married himselfe to that daughter,
for ever? I spend none of my Faith. I exercise none of my
Hope, in this, that I shall have my dead raised to life againe.
    This is the faith that sustaines me, when I lose by the
death of others, or when I suffer by living in misery my
selfe, That the dead, and we, are now all in one Church,
and at the resurrection, shall be all in one Quire.

There is no possible doubt that the sermon suited Donne's
talents perfectly. That patristic learning which had settled his
Anglican convictions and given him his style as a poet equipped
him also with the matter and the manner of his preaching; and
for the style he adopted he needed all his mastery of the techniques
of wit. The preacher's basic duty was simply, as Augustine said,
'to teach what is right and refute what is wrong, and in the performance of this task to conciliate the hostile, and rouse the
careless'. This was to be done according to a general scheme
which both preacher and congregation took for granted. But
within this scheme there could be enormous variation. Donne
was of the party that cultivated 'the learned manner of preaching'; not for him the doctrinal plainness of the Puritan. He
was, as hostile witnesses put it, 'a strong-lin'd man' and 'a bad
edifier'.
    How did 'strong lines' go with the preaching of the Word?
First: their cultivation did not mean that the Word was neglected.
It was stated, divided, illuminated, fantastically explicated. For
example, Donne makes much of the expression 'let us make man'
(Gen. i 26): no other act of creation involved a conference:
therefore, the Trinity was concerned in this one alone. Secondly;
the Word itself gives warrant for all the devices of the learned
preacher. The style of the Scriptures is 'artificial'; indeed the
Psalms are poems. 'There are not in the World so eloquent Books
as the Scriptures..they mistake it much, that thinke, that the
Holy Ghost hath rather chosen a low, and barbarous, and homely

style, then an eloquent, and powerfull manner of expressing himselfe.' The Scriptures use metaphor of 'infinite sweetnesse, and infinite latitude', though they have, when necessary, concision as well as eloquence, simplicity as well as highly-wrought wit. All these qualities are found in the Fathers whom the Reformed Church revived. Ambrose and Augustine—to whom Donne owed most—are ancestors of mannerist wit; Tertullian Christian- ized the Latin strong lines of Seneca. Nearer in time to Donne was the continental revival of witty preaching, which, as I have said, had much to do with the new poetic wit; but ultimately all depended on the Fathers, and on the wit and eloquence of the Holy Ghost in Scripture.

One famous and passionate page must serve to illustrate Donne's habitual eloquence:

Let me wither and weare out mine age in a discomfortable, in an unwholesome, in a penurious prison, and so pay my debts with my bones, and recompence the wastfulness of my youth, with the beggery of mine age; Let me wither in a spittle under sharpe, and foule, and infamous diseases, and so recompence the wantonnesse of my youth, with that loathsomenesse in mine age; yet if God withdraw not his spirituall blessings, His Grace, his Patience, If I can call my suffering his Doing, my passion his Action, All this that is temporall, is but a caterpiller got into one corner of my garden, but a mill-dew fallen upon one acre of my Corne; The body of all, the substance of all is safe, as long as the soule is safe. But when I shall trust to that, which wee call a good spirit, and God shall deject, and empoverish, and evacuate that spirit, when I shall rely upon a morall constancy, and God shall shake, and enfeeble, and enervate, destroy and demolish that constancy; when I shall think to refresh my selfe in the serenity and sweet ayre of a good conscience, and God shall call up the damps and vapours of hell it selfe, and spread a cloud of diffidence, and an impenetrable crust of desperation upon my conscience; when health shall flie from me, and I shall lay hold upon riches to succour me, and comfort me in my sicknesse, and riches shall flie from me, and I shall snatch after favour, and good opinion, to comfort me in my poverty; when even this good opinion shall leave me, and calumnies and misformations shall prevaile against me; when I shall need peace, because there is none but thou, O Lord, that should stand for me, and then shall finde, that the wounds that I have, come from thy hand, all the arrowes that stick in me, from they quiver; when I shall see, that because I have given my selfe to my corrupt nature, thou hast changed thine; and because I am all evil towards thee, therefore thou hast given over being good towards me; When it comes to this height, that the fever is not in the humors, but in the spirits, that mine enemy is not an imaginary enemy, fortune, nor a transitory enemy, malice in great persons, but a reall, and an irresistible, and an inexorable, and an everlasting enemy, The Lord of Hosts himselfe, The Almighty God himselfe, the Almighty God himselfe onely knowes the waight of this affliction, and except hee put in that *pondus gloriae*, that exceeding waight of an eternall glory, with his owne hand, into the other scale, we are waighed downe, we are swallowed up, irreparably, irrevocably, irrecoverably, irremediably.

But in addition to such tremendous sentences we find a hopping Latin wit, as of Tertullian: 'He came, and *veni in mundum*, He came into the world; it is not *in mundam*, into so clean a woman as had no sin at all, none contracted from her parents, no original sin. . . yet *per mundam in mundum*, by a clean woman into an unclean world.' And we find enormous conceits and paradoxes. Can man be the enemy of God, even as the mouse is of the elephant? Man is nearly nothing, but God is 'not onely a multiplied Elephant, millions of Elephants multiplied into one, but a multiplied World, a multiplied All. . . Man cannot be allowed so high a sinne, as enmity with God.' But Donne can also be simple, like the parables. So on Irresistibility of Grace: 'Christ beats his Drum, but he does not Press men; Christ is serv'd with voluntaries.' For 'no metaphor, no comparison is too high, none too low, too triviall, to imprint in you a sense of Gods everlasting goodnesse towards you'. To such a preacher the 'metaphysical conceit' was a natural mode of thought. Laud, addressing from the scaffold a hostile crowd, spoke of 'going apace. . .towards the Red-sea. . .an argument, I hope, that God is bringing me into the Land of

Promise': here, at such a moment, we have precisely those qualities of deliberate false argument to the wit of Donne's poems.

As a preacher Donne is guilty, by modern standards, of pedantry. His style is artificial; he would have been angry to have been told otherwise. The pedantry was partly a matter of fashion, but also a token of his confidence in a truly Catholic tradition. The sermons are inconceivable without it, so is Donne himself. And if he makes our flesh creep, that was still part of his duty; if he almost ignores the ecstatic religion that flourished in his day, that was a defect of his central merit. If we want Donne as a modern poet we may find it tiresome that he was capable of so much archaic quibbling, so much jargon and flattery. But, while it is perfectly proper to read the *Songs and Sonets* and ignore the sermons, it is improper to construct an image of Donne without looking at them; and many such caricatures still circulate.

IX

It was Donne's habit, in later life, to speak slightingly of his poetry; and although he considered, for a brief moment before his ordination, the possibility of publishing his poems, it seems he did not even possess copies of them. There are signs that it was regarded as slightly improper, after his ordination, for 'a man of his years and place' to be versifying, and indeed Donne wrote little verse as a priest. The Elegies on his death often allude to the exercise of his great wit in both secular and religious spheres —'Wit he did not banish, but transplanted it'—but Chudleigh in these lines, has in mind not verse but sermons:

> Long since, ô Poëts, he did die to you,
> Or left you dead, when wit and he tooke flight
> On divine wings, and soard out of your sight.
> Preachers, 'tis you must weep.

In fact it now appears that the bulk of the divine poems belongs to 1607–15. These years produced the 'Corona' sequence, most of the Holy Sonnets, the 'Litanie', 'Upon the Annunciation and Passion', 'Goodfriday, 1613', and probably 'The Crosse'. The poem addressed to Tilman, the 'Lamentations of Jeremy', the lines on Sidney's 'Psalms', the three great Hymns, three Sonnets, and 'An hymne to the Saints, and to Marquesse Hamylton', which Donne wrote reluctantly in 1625, make up the extant poetical work of the priest. Most of the religious poetry, therefore, belongs to the period of many of the verse-letters, and the *Anniversaries*.

It is verse of remarkable originality. Satyre iii shows that even in his youth Donne considered the language of passionate exploration and rebuke appropriate to religious themes; and even when he is working in strict forms like the sonnet, and on devotional topics, we recognize at once that turbulent diction which spontaneously records the pressure of fervent and excited thought. But though he rejected some of the formalities in his secular poetry, Donne was habituated in matters of devotion to certain schematic disciplines. He had been taught to pray; and when his poems are prayers they are formed by this early training. When he undertook 'a serious meditation of God', he tended to do so by employing these meditative techniques.

Here a learned man committed to the reformed religion occupies himself with Papist devotion; but we should not exaggerate the paradox. Donne's Church did not reject what it found good in the tradition; many devotional practices were retained, and some were revived. Donne's 'Corona' sonnets are an ingenious adaptation of an old Dominican system of meditation, based on an obsolete type of rosary called the *corona*. A Puritan might condemn this, but to Donne it was, theologically, an indifferent matter, and good in that it concentrated the devotional powers of a man easily distracted from prayer. More remarkable, perhaps, is the fact that some of the Holy Sonnets, and the *Anniversaries*, are indebted to meditative techniques defined and propagated by Ignatius Loyola and the Jesuits; yet these were so widely disseminated, and apparently so fruitful, that it was by no means exceptional for enemies of the Order to adopt them.

The 'Corona', with its linked sonnets and carefully balanced ingenuity, may strike us as 'mixt wit'; the Ignatian method is more interesting. The purpose of the technique is to concentrate all the powers of the soul, including the sensual, in the act of prayer. So a man might present as vividly as possible to himself the scene of the Nativity or the Crucifixion, or his own death-bed. There is no doubt that this technique, the most considerable contribution of Jesuit piety to European art, affects the Holy Sonnets; Miss Gardner presents twelve of them as a sequence, the first six being a formal meditative series on the Last Things. The method is to achieve a vivid image, enforce it with appropriate similitudes, and then to pray accordingly. So, in 'O my blacke Soule! now thou art summoned', Donne imagines his deathbed in the octave, and compares the sinful soul to an exile afraid to return to his country, or a prisoner afraid to be freed; then in the sestet he prays for grace to repent, so that death may not, after all, be like such miseries. The meditation is here forcefully assimilated to the sonnet form, which Donne uses with virtuosity; and the complexities of the form coexist with that sense of immediate and poignant spiritual effort, that tormented natural diction, which was his great, and sometimes abused, discovery. The sonnets are not reports of spiritual exercises; they are the exercises themselves. There is little sense of contrivance, 'artificial' though the form is; Donne reconciles the prescribed form with the true word, just as he reconciles ecclesiastical tradition with the supremacy of Scripture. It is true that the wit of these poems occasionally ventures where we are reluctant to follow, as in 'Show me, dear Christ, thy spouse'. This last complaint for the division of the Church is couched in terms of a traditional image carried to the point where we feel uneasy about its taste:

> Betray kind husband thy spouse to our sights,
> And let myne amorous soule court thy mild Dove,
> Who is most trew, and pleasing to thee, then
> When she' is embrac'd and open to most men.

Perhaps we dislike this metaphor (Christ as *mari complaisant*) because the image of the Church as the Bride is no longer absolutely commonplace; but having accepted the image we are still unwilling to accept its development, even though we see that the main point is the *glorious* difference of this from a merely human marriage. Something is asked of us that we can no longer easily give. Many of the Holy Sonnets have this perilous balance; their wit is always likely to seem indelicate as well as passionate. So in one of the greatest, 'Batter my heart, three person'd God':

> Batter my heart, three person'd God; for, you
> As yet but knocke, breathe, shine, and seeke to mend;
> That I may rise, and stand, o'erthrow mee,' and bend
> Your force, to breake, blowe, burn and make me new.

I, like an usurpt towne, to'another due,
Labour to'admit you, but Oh, to no end,
Reason your viceroy in mee, mee should defend,
But is captiv'd, and proves weake or untrue,
Yet dearely'I love you, and would be lov'd faine,
But am betroth'd unto your enemie,
Divorce mee,'untie, or break that knot againe,
Take mee to you, imprison mee, for I
Except you'enthrall mee, never shall be free,
Nor ever chast, except you ravish mee.

This is a great poem, certainly; but what, we wonder, has 'three person'd' to do with the passion of the opening? Yet the poem is another of Donne's exercises in the paradoxes of his religion, and the Trinity is one of the greatest of them. The epithet is obliquely justified by the intensity of the rhythmical conflicts throughout; in the opposition between the heavy 'Batter' and the weak, cadential 'knocke, breathe, shine and seek to mend'; in the divine absurdity of Heaven troubling to take the sinner by storm, laying him low that he may stand; finally by the imagery of rape. Love is figured as lust because it is to be rough and irresistible; God is a monster of mercy (but the Scripture compares him to a thief). The powerful paradoxes of the last couplet suggest an infinite series of such: God as infant, God as malefactor, Justice as mercy, Death as Life, and so forth. We respond crudely to this kind of challenge, and such a reading as this is clumsy and over-explicit. Similarly we are inclined to think of a poem that celebrates the coincidence of Lady Day and Good Friday as a toy; but for Donne it was a motive to reverence, a piece of calendar wit that challenged a Christian poet to prayer. We are usually content to be cleverer about the love of women than the love of God; therefore the *Songs and Sonets* keep better. But Donne was clever about both, and sometimes in much the same way; our awkwardness here leads us to charge Elegy xix with blasphemy, and 'Show me, dear Christ' with indelicacy. Donne himself was not blind to some of the dangers of his method: in the 'Litanie' he writes, 'When wee are mov'd to seeme religious Only to vent wit, Lord deliver us'.

The finest of the other pre-ordination poems is 'Goodfriday, 1613'. Here too Donne starts from a paradox; on this day of all days he is turned away from the East. This plunges him into that paradoxical series where he moves with such assurance; and his wit binds up the paradoxes, with just the neatness and passion of the love-poems, in a fine conclusion:

> I turne my backe to thee, but to receive
> Corrections, till thy mercies bid thee leave.
> O thinke mee worth thine anger, punish mee,
> Burne off my rusts, and my deformity,
> Restore thine Image, so much, by thy grace,
> That thou may'st know mee, and I'll turne my face.

Of the poems written after ordination, only the sonnets of the Westmoreland MS. and the three Hymns are of the best of Donne. The little group of sonnets includes the moving poem about the death of his wife, and 'Show me, dear Christ'. The Hymns are justly admired. 'A Hymn to Christ, at the Authors last going into Germany' records a moment of intense personal feeling, and is a companion to the beautiful Valediction Sermon of 1619. The other two belong to the period of Donne's serious illness in 1623, when he also wrote *Devotions*. 'Thou art a metaphysical God,' he says in that work, 'full of comparisons.' And although these poems abjure harshness in favour of the solemnity proper to hymns, they nevertheless live by their wit. 'A Hymn to God, my God, in my sicknesse' is founded on a favourite conceit; the poet is a map over which the physicians pore.

> As West and East
> In all flatt Maps (and I am one) are one,
> So death doth touch the Resurrection.

The 'Hymn to God the Father' contains the famous play on the poet's name (but so does the inscription on the portrait of the author in his shroud, prefixed to 'Deaths Duell'); what in our time would be only a puerile joke is thrice repeated in this solemn masterpiece.

Donne's wit, of course, depends on the assumption that a joke can be a serious matter. Wit, as he understood it, was born of the preaching of the Word, whether employed in profane or in religious expression. 'His fancy', as Walton says, 'was unimitably high, equalled only by his great wit...He was by nature highly passionate.' It will never be regretted that the twentieth century, from whatever motive, restored him to his place among the English poets, and wit to its place in poetry.

6

THE PATIENCE
OF SHAKESPEARE

The reason why we are all here this evening is that we are content to believe that Shakespeare was born on 23rd April, 1564. We all love a century, and four centuries we love even more; so this has struck us all, without serious question, as a good moment to honour him. In coming together to do so, we follow—though perhaps more sedately—the example of earlier generations. I do not know whether the publishers of the Third Folio in 1664 were inspired by a rudimentary centennial piety, though they were true to type in some respects, since they obscured the canon of Shakespeare's work with a number of falsely attributed plays. A century later (in fact five years late, since the opportunities of 1764 were frittered away) the most famous of all the celebrations brought Garrick to Stratford, and the proportion of nonsense was higher but gayer. Milton had formerly observed that Shakespeare did not need the labour of an age in piled stones, but Garrick, in his Ode, disagreed:

> To what blest genius of the isle
> Shall gratitude her tribute pay,
> Decree the festive day,
> Erect the statue, and devote the pile?

The chorus answered, 'Shakespeare!' An octagonal pile was erected; fireworks and routs, declamations and processions, entertained not only the quality who came down from London but Shakespeare's incredulous townsmen. On the second day drizzle hampered festivity, and later a solid downpour put out fireworks and raised the Avon to flood. This apocalyptic conclusion may or may not have appeared to bear out the ironic account of the programme given by a hostile commentator: 'The whole will conclude with the apotheosis of Shakespeare.' Better luck attended the celebrations of 1864, at least so far as the weather went, and there was a Will Shakespeare train to bring devotees from London; but the planning had been mismanaged, huddled into three months, and the American support already considered essential to the maintenance of due splendour in the celebration of Shakespeare had not been sought in time. Nevertheless a large dodecagonal building was erected—an advance from Garrick's octagon in the direction of circularity—and Germany not only sent a delegation to Stratford but founded the Deutsche Shakespeare Gesellschaft, which in due time added its heavy tribute—the labour of an age in piled tomes. As a voluntarily exiled Englishman one hardly knows whether to laugh or cry at being remote from Stratford on the fourth centennial. However, I am sure we shall all do our best here.

Clearly, then, it is a well-established custom to regard every hundredth April 23rd as singularly important. Yet it has its curious aspects. We are clear that we are celebrating Shakespeare's birth, not his death; but although we are quite sure he died on April 23, 1616, we have no evidence that he was born on April 23, 1564. I shall seem to yield, in this talk, to the persuasion that Shakespeare was human; that he differs from other writers rather less than is sometimes assumed. But I concede that in one respect he is on his own, and that is in his enormous *patience*, his ability to answer to anything and everything, to absorb speculation. So let us speculate upon the reasons for our insistence that he was born on a particular day. Two facts are relevant: the first is that he died on that day, as I have mentioned. The second is that April 23rd is St. George's Day.

As to the first of these, it need only be said that the motive for desiring this degree of circularity in Shakespeare's life is a magical one. As Donne might have said, our firmness makes his circle just, and makes him end where he begun. The circle is the perfect figure, and an ancient emblem of eternity. As Ben Jonson observed, Shakespeare is not of an age but for all time. He closes the cycle of the year, dying and being born in the spring.

St. George, we recall, was struck off the Roman calendar, but the English have sturdily ignored this. He slew the dragon and delivered the princess. Not only was he patron of the Order of the Garter and hero of the first book of the *Faerie Queene*; he was the prototype of more vulgar dragon slayers in popular romances, and the central figure in the English folk play, where he kills Slasher, the dragon-figure who represents winter. So he had theatrical connections. You can discern Shakespeare in the words of the Presenter as he introduces St. George:

> Activity of youth,
> Activity of age,
> The like was never seen
> Upon a common stage.

The point is not that these mumming plays have a tragic action and very low characters, such as Jack Finney and Belsey Bob, and the mysteriously babbling Big Head or Fool, though this is Shakespearian enough. It is rather that these odd plays seem to remember remote pagan origins; they tell you, as it were, to seek their explanation in Frazer or in some more sophisticated treatment of the hero, such as Lord Raglan's or Eliade's. The English hero whose day is celebrated on April 23rd complies with the heroic archetypes. He is susceptible to mythography. Formerly he might have been called a sun-god, or in the famous phrase of Max Müller, a disease of language—certainly he contorted the language and gave it a variety of developments verging on the pathological. And when Shakespeare took upon him the divine attributes (if we had to say when, the estimate would be, strangely enough, in the early eighteenth century) he also became subject to sceptical or euhemerist interpretations: some say he was that more civil hero Bacon, some Oxford, and some Marlowe, who is by others considered the rival poet, or Slasher.

But for most of us he is everything that St. George had been; even a saint. There is the case of his mulberry tree, the invention of which is attributed to Sir Hugh Clopton in 1742. Clopton died in 1751 and the new owner of New Place, an irascible and iconoclastic clergyman called Francis Gastrell, chopped down the tree. But Mr. Thomas Sharpe bought it and made it into knickknacks, 'curious toys and useful articles', so many of them indeed that some suspicions were aroused and he had to swear an affidavit that all the wood had come from the true tree. But scepticism could not prevent the growth of this secular piety, and men of feeling, none of whom exceeded in demonstrativeness James Boswell, would fling themselves on their knees before a relic, and kiss it. Boswell, shown the Ireland papers, remembered his *Nunc Dimittis* and said he would now die contented, having lived to witness the present day. Francis Webb, on the same occasion, observed that 'All great and eminent Geniuses have their characteristic peculiarities and originality of character, which not only distinguish them from all others, but make them what they are. These none can rival, none successfully imitate. Of all men and Poets, perhaps Shakespeare had the most of these. He was a peculiar Being—a unique—he stood alone. To imitate him... were impossible.'

Now it is of interest that the Ireland Papers which prompted this encomium, and before which not only Boswell but almost everybody else prostrated himself, were clumsy forgeries. For it is the desire, or need, of honest men to venerate the new St. George, without sceptical enquiries as to authenticity. The whole has concluded, as our eighteenth-century sceptic prophesied, with the apotheosis of Shakespeare. And, as visitors to Stratford are aware, the sale of pious art and relics continues.

So it may be said that there is a large admixture of superstition in our veneration of the Bard. It is not merely that we choose a day such as this, a climax of annual and centennial mysticism, and surround ourselves with relics. It is not even that, to judge by 1962, when there were nearly 1,200 of them, we shall lay at least four votive offerings daily before the shrine, in the shape of books and articles on Shakespeare. What we do is to make him in our own image and then call him unique. The Ireland forgeries began with business papers mostly, as if the main business of the pious forger was to show that Shakespeare was a respectable member of the new commercial class. It is hardly a worse fault than our modern producers commit when they give you a Shavian or a Brechtian Shakespeare. These are pious frauds. They could not happen if we did not venerate their victim. Nor should we be afflicted by heresiarchs—Baconians, disintegrators, and so forth —nor should we have developed out of Biblical criticism such fantastically elaborate bibliographical tools for the determination of texts. Behind the whole effort there is this superstitious awe of Shakespeare the peculiar Being, the unique, the inimitable who is yet so like us; who contrives like a god to be and to provide us with anything and everything.

It is sometimes said to be a characteristic of our time that we undo the spiritual structures of our ancestors; whatever they sacralized we desacralize. They retreated from the evident unholiness of the world into images which stored up the strength of those moments when it seemed holy or terrible in a different way. They built in order to make space sacred, and in their rites they abolished the terrors of time, as spring kills winter and St. George the dragon. They made books which were compact of all the world and of all its history, syllabically inspired and, like nature itself, signed with the secret meanings of a god. We build to serve human functions, and not to make models of a divine world; cathedrals that were living bibles, churches proportioned as the music of the spheres. We live, more than any of our ancestors, in a time become linear and patternless. Our books inform or divert in a purely human sense. Where a book continues to be venerable, we attribute its power to different causes: we demythologize, find reasons in nature for its being as it is; we see it as figuring not the whole world of knowledge but dead men's knowledge of the world. It sinks into history, becomes the victim of our perspectival trick, falls under the rule of time. So we desacralize the world.

And yet there are enormous exceptions. Shakespeare has not escaped the processes of analytic criticism, high and low, but he preserves a numinous quality; in a strange modified way he is a sacred book; he is one of those foci of significance, one of those objects in which reside the largely unquestioned criteria of our civilization. He is major man. 'He is the transparence of the place in which | He is, and in his poems we find peace.' It is appropriate that Shakespeare offers wisdom—or, rather, that wisdom must be sought in Shakespeare—not in completed formulations, not in detachable logia, but in the dynamic tumult of action and dramatic utterance. We cannot use him in a Virgilian *sortes* game. It is part of our literary holism—the device by which we try to maintain a semblance of the sacred in our literary lives—that we cannot treat him otherwise than as we treat the great books of our own time. And it is the mark of his perpetuity and patience that he can tolerate this treatment. Every age, so far at any rate, has been able to find in Shakespeare whatever it needed to maintain contact with him, considered as a focus of given, natural meaning, a source of order and civility. So far as we can see it is usually possible to discover in this presence that 'interior sensitization' of which theologians speak in relation to the Bible. We may not always find it. Everybody knows that one can read, even see, *King Lear*, and find it, not the charged and numinous experience it can be, but a flat, overemphatic extravaganza. These are moments without grace. But they are, genuinely, not common. The power is, more usually, there.

But let me try to banish magic or mysticism, if not from Shakespeare, at any rate from my own language. The simple fact is that, by common consent, others abide our question but Shakespeare is free. The great modern classic of my own youth was T.S. Eliot; but he now abides the question of the young. The changes he effected in our view of the relative importance of earlier poets were considerable: Milton was 'dislodged', Donne given major status. Shelley, after a century of authority during which he became virtually a type of lyric poet, no longer seems to warm, console, or give meanings to experience. It would be a mistake to call these mere changes of fashion; deeper cultural rhythms are involved. But they do not touch Shakespeare. Tolstoi, we are sure, was not speaking in the fullness of his own immense gifts when he rejected Shakespeare: we know his condemnation as a passing fit of heresy. And the reason for this immunity is not hard to find. It is the product of a conspiracy; we are all members of a secret society, of which the principal ritual is to speak well of Shakespeare. We may fall from grace; the drug may not take. Or we may try to deprive him of his privilege. But it is nearly impossible for us to stand quite clear of the circle. We should find the search for a real outsider—someone really able to approach Shakespeare without the faintest awe; a really *profane* critic in fact—a long and hard one. Shakespeare thus escapes the operation of criticism, and exhibits the quality I attributed to him at the outset—patience.

It may sound curious to speak of his escaping criticism, in view of those four daily offerings. How does criticism normally operate in respect of great reputations? There are two things to be said about that. First, criticism—conceived as ungrandly as possible— is the medium in which past art survives. It is the activity of the schoolmaster in the classroom, even of people chattering at parties. It is simply the way the news gets about that X, having this or that to be said for him, belongs to what we talk or should care about. At a higher level it may provide ways of talking and caring, adapting the old to our newer requirements, showing that there are aspects of the old which can be dealt with by signalling-systems based on the new. In the respect that now concerns me, that is what criticism does. And the second point is simply that it is not only a humble but an uncontrolled and inexact science. This is especially true of the evaluative phase of criticism—when it is telling us what is worth our love or veneration. So it is clear that when the picture alters, when we cease to read Browning or turn with interest to William Alabaster, when we see Spenser not as a great poet and a great source of poetry but as an unquenchable bore, it is not because somebody has been able to *prove* that our fathers were wrong, but because of turns in the tide of comment, the causes of which we should have to seek elsewhere. And the reputations of our poets are subject to this apparently random movement. And when I say Shakespeare escapes criticism I mean simply that his is not; he has a sacral quality; there is a conspiracy into which we are all seduced, on his behalf. The first thing we think of is his difference from the others: he is unique, inimitable, yet somehow very like us.

Let us look at the way in which this conviction of Shakespeare's 'peculiar Being', his uniqueness, is made consistent with what one thinks it necessary to attribute to a poet who has a special relation to oneself. We can do it by looking at earlier centennials. In 1664 Margaret Cavendish, Duchess of Newcastle, a lady of great charm and enterprise, had just been reading the new Third Folio. She congratulated Shakespeare on his power to metamorphose himself from man to woman in order to create Cleopatra. She also found him very comical—not as comical as her husband, but more comical than anybody else. Furthermore, he 'had a Clear Judgment, a Quick Wit, a Spreading Fancy, a Subtil Observation, a Deep Apprehension, and a most Eloquent Elocution'—like her husband.

For the next century I shall have to cheat a bit in order to have Dr. Johnson, whose edition appeared in 1765. His Preface is the most resonant and perhaps the best general essay ever written on Shakespeare, and I need hardly do more than remind you of some of the counts upon which he determines the greatness of his author. His first sentence deals resoundingly with those who refuse Shakespeare his due. I quote only half of it: 'That praises are without reason lavished on the dead, and that the honours due only to excellence are paid to antiquity, is a complaint likely to be always continued by those, who, being able to add nothing to the truth, hope for eminence from the heresies of paradox.' And he proceeds to praise the antique Shakespeare. 'Nothing,' he observes, 'can please many, and please long, but just representations of general nature.' Pursuing this ideal, expressed as universally valid but very much of its century, he makes the remarkable observation that Shakespeare's characters are species rather than individuals. This encomium he borrowed, we should notice, from the scholastic doctrine of angels. He adds that these characters have a way of speaking which, because it is derived from that permanent language which exists between the transience of grossness and the transience of refinement, is also immutable, sempiternal, angelic. He turns now to Shakespeare's faults, which, he says, are so great that they would overwhelm an ordinary man. So we must think of him as angelic in the same way that we think of the earth as spherical, despite its protuberances and cavities. He lists these faults, having earned the right to speak 'without superstitious veneration'; and who can say that the nobility of his praise is not thereby enhanced? 'If we owe everything to him', observes this great critic, 'he owes something to us…if much of his praise is paid by perception and judgment, much is likewise given by custom and veneration.'

This is hard for the nineteenth century to match, even if I cheat again and choose for the third centennial David Masson's lectures of 1865. They are an attempt to derive from the plays a biographical image of Shakespeare. The figure that emerges is certainly complex enough; but where have we seen him before? He is upright, shrewd in business, careful to maintain respectability, shunning publicity. He avoids what Masson calls the Poetry of Occurrence: 'in the heart and bustle of London we see Shakespeare sitting by himself, not only silent, non-obtrusive, non-opinionative, but absolutely proof against the wiliest lure or the fiercest explosion of contemporary incident that would draw an utterance from his pen."*Aiunt: Quid aiunt! Aiant*," we hear him saying to himself'—as if running through some of that Latin grammar he may have learnt at Stratford Grammar School. He saw the world, says Masson, as 'on the whole, gracious and likeable...with a manifest rule of good and evil and a power of calm and beneficent order through all its perturbations; and Shakespeare's own preferences and affinities in it are for what is high, divine, beautiful, honourable, lovely, and of good report'. His principal characteristics are 'magnanimity and moral observation'. Of course he had a complicated interior life, and perhaps needed the sonnets as safety valves; but after a lively, witty youth, he passed through the severity of middle age to the 'contemplative serenity' of his last years. (How old, by the way, this view makes Shakespeare seem! I reflect with some puzzlement that I myself do not feel entitled either to severity or to serenity, yet I am older than Shakespeare was when he wrote *Lear*, and within two years of my *Winter's Tale*.)

Here, then, are three centennial comments. The first, Margaret Cavendish's, attributes to Shakespeare all the qualities she would wish to find in a heroic poet, and found in her husband: judgment, wit, fancy, elocution are the criteria of the moment, and he does well by them all. But she writes before the true apotheosis; the element of veneration is largely absent from this seventeenth-century Shakespeare. The Duchess prefers her husband. Johnson dwarfs the others; living in the age of the natural artless Shakespeare, he nonetheless manages to distinguish between the homage of perceptive judgment and that of superstitious veneration. But he himself slips unawares into a kind of idolatry; he speaks of Shakespeare's characters as angels. Perhaps this is not so injudicious as it appears; perhaps we have made of Shakespeare a substitute for older and inhuman mediators between heaven and earth. Descartes, we are told, brought the powers of scholastic angels down to men; Johnson brought them down to Shakespeare. And we find Shakespeare more venerable, more angelic, more properly sempiternal, than our own cogitations. Certainly we can still say, less grandly, less certainly, less humanly than Johnson, that 'the stream of time, which is constantly washing the dissoluble fabricks of other poets, passes without injury by the adamant of Shakespeare'. It is thus, in the schoolmen, that the stream of time washes past the angels.

In Masson's image, as I suggested, we see a somehow familiar figure, not an angel, but perhaps some large man, a Provost of

Eton maybe, erect at his desk, emblem of rectitude and intellectual labor. His household accounts are impeccable, his unspoken thoughts expressed in Latin subjunctives. Once, long ago, he got drunk at a college feast, perhaps, like Wordsworth, by toasting Milton. He is aware of evil; Lyell and Chambers have disturbed his faith; but he trusts, if only faintly, the larger hope. As to the sonnets, they are as inexplicable as Victorian pornography. I am not saying that Masson's book is ridiculous; only that he wants to make Shakespeare very eminent, and the way he understands eminence is the Victorian way. With much scholarship and regard for fact, even with some delicacy of inference, he establishes Shakespeare as the most eminent of Victorians. The Duchess made him a lively Restoration gentleman, the Victorian professor made him a mutton-chop-whiskered, solidly benign nineteenth-century intellectual. Johnson certainly escapes period portraiture better than they; yet the assumption of the grandeur of generality and the celebration of just representations of general nature are of his time.

So much for the past centennials. I of course do not know what is going to have been said in 1964, except in so far as I am saying it. But we can be sure that the avatar of St. George will have assumed a twentieth-century shape. Such is the shape I give him now. For when I speak of Shakespeare's *patience*, his power to absorb our questions, I am already imposing upon him a twentieth-century conception. If he is another nature, why cannot we say of him, as Whitehead said of nature itself, that 'Nature is patient of interpretation in terms of laws that happen to interest us', for 'the truth must be seasonable'? It is not even necessary to suppose that, for us to understand and use such patience, we and nature must, in Wordsworth's phrase, be 'exquisitely fitted'. The mathematical physicist knows he can go with some confidence to nature for confirmation of something he himself has worked out that it must have or do; and we can go to Shakespeare with the same certainty. We may qualify the position in the words of Heisenberg: 'What we observe is not nature in itself but nature exposed to our method of questioning.' Shakespeare may not be subject to the rule of time; his fabric may not be dissoluble and subject to change; but our questions change with time, and so do the answers they presuppose.

Our questions, our seasonable truth, are not those of the Duchess of Newcastle, or of Masson, or of Johnson. What they have in common with such questions and such truths is merely an assumption of Shakespeare's patience. And where we differ from Johnson and especially from Masson is in our knowledge that truth may be thought of as seasonable, our fear of confounding the contingent (represented if you like by Masson's grave respectable gentleman writer) with the absolute. We know we can have any Shakespeare we want, but know also that the one we want will not do for another time, perhaps not even for another person.

As a consequence of this sophistication we have a multiplicity of Shakespeares, as we have a multiplicity of pasts; we could not have them if we were not sure of his superhuman patience, his angelic perpetuity. Consider a random selection of the Shakespeares we are invited in our day to grant existence. There are the Shakespeares associated with a particular line of thought: Senecan Shakespeare, Machiavellian Shakespeare, Shakespeare sipping at the mind of Montaigne. There are the sectarian Shakespeares: Catholic, Protestant, Rosicrucian, Neo-Platonist. There is a thinking Shakespeare with his own philosophy, and a Shakespeare who was a good poet because he knew it was not his business to think. There is a learned Shakespeare who read St. Thomas Aquinas before dealing with the murder of an old Scottish king, treatises on melancholy before tackling *Hamlet*, and emblem books as a preparation for *Lear*; who got Bottom's dream out of Macrobius. There is a Shakespeare who loved Essex so much that he could think of little else, and a Shakespeare who hated all great men. There is an official Shakespeare who dramatized the Homily of Wilful Disobedience, dutifully followed the Tudor propaganda line, and approved of the treachery of Prince John in *2 Henry IV*. There is a Shakespeare who sailed very near the wind on historical matters, risked the punishment of censors, liked Falstaff, and detested not only Prince John but perhaps Prince Henry as well. There is the Shakespeare who wrote the first existentialist play, *Hamlet*, and the one who could not find in that work an objective correlative to his emotions. There are Freudian Shakespeares, Jungian Shakespeares, Shakespeares whose plays were intended, like *Ulysses*, not to be read but to be reread—to be looked down on as shapes and patterns in space, not as narratives in time—symbolist, imagist, meta-physical Shakespeares, whose heroines had no girlhood and whose Lady Macbeths no children; Shakespeares heterosexual, and homosexual, healthy and diseased, ironic and simply rhetorical, proper and improper, legal, bird-loving, anti-Semite, liberal, musi-cal, allegorizing, problem-posing, seriously punning, anything and everything, prince and angel. There are plays and characters who share the same inclusive power, the same ability to contain multi-tudes. We know of a hundred Hamlets, and can always make another who will enable us to say with Coleridge, 'I have a smack of Hamlet'. We may say of the plays, as of their author, that they are patient. We may add that they are perpetual, or, to be more exact, sempiternal. We therefore allow, it seems, that Shake-speare is *sui generis*.

But let us try, for this quadricentennial, a Shakespeare who is not so. Let us make him a member of the class of poets, though *primus inter pares*. What we need is a lay figure rather different from Masson's mutton-chopped St. George. We can begin by trying on him some of the attributes we know from personal experience that poets tend to have. Thus we can ask whether he was lecherous, and it seems clear that he was, if the Dark Woman sonnets are anything to go by, Was he irresponsible, did he find it easier to be a good writer than a good husband? The evidence points that way; he was careless in his work and of his wife. There are hints of drink, and of a fondness for what must be officially rejected—for Falstaff and Lucio and Caliban and Shylock, for Richard III and Cleopatra, for the passion of Romeo and Juliet, for anything and everything that honest folk fear or despise. Like most writers who find themselves suddenly capable of making money, he liked money; as knighthoods were still not given for services to literature, he had himself made a gentle-man. Under pressure, with a deadline to make, he sometimes wrote very badly, and when he was unassailably top dramatist he was occasionally self-indulgent, in a way nobody has ever characterized as well as Johnson, who catches Shakespeare 'entangled with an unwieldy sentiment; which he cannot well express, and will not reject; he struggles with it a while, and if it continues stubborn, comprises it in such words as occur, and leaves it to be disentangled by those who have more leisure to bestow upon it.' Lecherous, negligent, ambitious, lazy: without looking at his virtues at all, we are halfway to trapping him in the class of poets.

There have been poets of great learning, Goethe, for example, and Milton, among the major; Gray and Coleridge among the lesser. But for the most part poets are widely and selfishly rather than deeply learned; they approach learning insolently, and make raids and rapes, not colonies. And surely this is what Shakespeare did. A flourish of formal scholarship in the Ovidian imitations of his youth was followed by a career of independence—eclectic reading, or rapid getting-up of subjects. It may be true, as Mr. Eliot once said, that he learned more Roman history out of the Plutarch *Lives* than another man might get out of the whole British Museum; but what we must attend to now is the arrogance, the selfish certainty, that animated those awe-inspiring raids on North, those absorptions of Holinshed, that marvellous theft from Sidney in *King Lear*: the distillation of voyagers in *The Tempest*, the transfiguration of his old enemy Greene in *The Winter's Tale*. We see he had the poet's habit: the world of learning owed him a living. When he uses learned themes he transforms them, makes them ambiguous. Are we to believe that Theseus on lunatics, lovers, and poets means exactly what it says (which was what it was conventional to say)? Is the right way to understand his interest in Empire—and he told the whole story of the birth of the Empire—to find out what others thought about Caesar and Rome, Antony and Egypt? Certainly not, not even when he seems to be saying the same things. When he handles some formal scheme, except in the poems, is he doing it as a dull man might, getting it right and depending on its intrinsic power? Never. The very processes of freely associative thought fascinated him, and they have nothing to do with formal schemes and tropes; when he uses such schemes he does so for his own purposes.

Shakespeare's speculative freedom gave us the late style, a style of thought in action, as of Cominius marvellously brooding on the banishment of his dangerous ally Coriolanus:

> Whether 'twas pride,
> Which out of daily fortune ever taints
> The happy man; whether defect of judgement,
> To fail in the disposing of those chances
> That he was lord of; or whether nature,

Not to be other than one thing, not moving
From th' casque to th' cushion, but commanding peace
Even with the same austerity and garb
As he controlled the war; but one of these—
As he hath spices of them all—not all,
For I dare so far free him—made him feared,
So hated, and so banish'd: but he has a merit
To choke it in the utterance.

It gave us that happy valiancy which Coleridge found in *Antony and Cleopatra*; the expression could be used as well of *Cymbeline*, and quite as well of the greater sonnets.

What is your substance, whereof are you made
That millions of strange shadows on you tend?

Many wrote of shadow and substance, Shakespeare himself somewhat obsessively; but only he knew that the gross hyperbole of *millions* would come right in that line, and perhaps nowhere else. And that is not even a famous sonnet. Equally wanton valiancies could be adduced from a dozen others. For wantonness in strength is a mark of the absolutely mature Shakespeare, as perhaps of all poets; it arises from a confidence that one has created the context in which one can be understood, and that such a context can be indefinitely enlarged, till nonsense and brutality—if necessary, as in *The Winter's Tale*—can oblige the tough and sensitive reader to a fine understanding. Indolent, lecherous, arrogant, wantonly speculative, cherishing the value of his own thoughts, humble only in respect of his own possibilities—you may be sure he knew the feeling that poets have: of estrangement welcomed, of a difference from other men but not from other poets.

Thus, precariously, we capture him, Johnson's angel, the prince of poets, for the class of poets as we know it: different, heroic, but, as the poet of the supreme fiction has it, 'part, Though an heroic part, of the commonal.' Yet all our heroes must have their roots in the commonal; and we have no sooner trapped him there than his uniqueness asserts itself again: he is the author of our most nearly supreme fiction,

walking by himself, crying
Most miserable, most victorious,

the one poet who 'can do all that angels can'. 'God is anything anyone believes in,' said Montaigne. But we do not need to say, even on the fourth centennial, that Shakespeare is God, or a god: only, as Johnson implied, an angel, or—by a slight hierarchal displacement—a saint, the Saint George whose feast falls on this day, and whose victory and triumph we celebrate with an exposition of carefully preserved relics and a transient flurry of praise.

He is an English saint; but Shakespeare is American English as well as English English. So I end by quoting an American poet, Delmore Schwartz, in celebration of *our* Shakespeare—I have had his words in mind and now will speak them out. The dragon is killed, the great age begins anew; we know where to look for our meaning and for our angel.

> ... sweet prince, black night has always
>   descended and has always ended,
> ... prince of Avon, sovereign and king
> Of reality, hope and speech, may all the angels sing
> With all the sweetness and all the truth with which
>   you sang anything and everything.

7

SURVIVAL OF THE CLASSIC

There can never have been a time when the question seemed more urgent. Classics are, roughly, works of art that survive; more exactly, those that belong to a shadowy, indefinite canon which is, for everybody concerned with survival from the lowly pastorate to the inspired theocrat—that is, from the working schoolmaster to the legislating critic—the best analogue we have to the less mutable canon of the church. The urgent question is, how does survival work? What are the chances of its continuing to do so after our own time? There are now a dozen ways of saying that the day of the classic is past. For Walter Benjamin, classics are beautiful unjust objects, each representing usurpations and exploitations impossible to justify in a world moving inevitably towards socialism and fully equipped with the means of mechanical reproduction. We must be content to lose the *aura* of the unique object because at the same time we lose its stains; and we have instead the new things, clean and capable of equitable distribution. For Marshall McLuhan, classics belong to a cultural epoch which is being technologically phased out. For the counter-culture they are simply a part of the past which they have abolished, or aspects of a gigantic confidence trick against human liberty which has now been exposed. Our ways of talking about them are equally obsolete; the old terms of praise are now terms of insult, as Mr. Robbe-Grillet remarks, imagining the stock commendations of nineteenth-century novels applied to his own. Our notions of form are not only inapposite but demonstrably wrong. Shock, discontinuity, silence, emptiness, succeed *rondure*, harmony, plenitude, order. And so on.

There are many ways of characterizing a situation which one need only hint at, since everybody knows about it and some people express it with marked exaggeration. There remains, though, a perfectly reasonable doubt about the fate of the classics after our day.

It isn't that change is new, that survival hasn't been constantly threatened by it. The question is whether what has worked hitherto can be expected to work henceforth. There is, anyway, some point in understanding how classics have survived, and so in what follows I glance at the well-documented history of what looks like a pretty flourishing classic, namely *King Lear*.

The authority and, so to speak, the canonicity of *King Lear* have not escaped all challenge; there was Tolstoi's emphatic dissent. So great was Shakespeare's authority in Russia that Tolstoi's animosity simmered for half a century before he gave it public expression. His dislike was at first founded on aesthetic principles, but these merged into social concerns; Shakespeare was coarsely decorative, given to fine writing rather than to the psychological realism that seemed necessary in any work that could be thought relevant to the important ideological and social conflicts of the sixties. If, as both Tolstoi and Chernyshevsky held, art should be directed towards 'changing the established order', and if it should always 'pronounce a verdict on life', then *King Lear*, which if anything appears to deplore such change and pronounces, according to the way you look at it, too many verdicts or none at all on life, lacked relevance. Shakespeare does not speak out.

Properly qualified, this is a true and interesting observation, though it could as well be used in the course of an argument sharply opposed to Tolstoi's. But by the time he wrote his essay on *Lear* Tolstoi was so committed to moralism that he had rejected *Anna Karenina*, and he could certainly see no case for Shakespeare; his rancour was such that he argued for the superiority of the old anonymous *Leir*, with its happy ending and simpler Christian ideals of justice, against the work of Shakespeare. He found *King Lear* so lacking in merit that he felt it necessary to speculate about the universal habit of calling it very good: was it mass hypnosis or 'epidemic suggestion', like the tulip mania of the Crusades or Darwinism? But in the end the survival of such a work can only be explained, Tolstoi says, by some correspondence existing between it and the irreligion and immorality of the upper classes in Shakespeare's time and ours.

There is some truth in this; it is merely a pejorative way of saying that whatever an individual makes of *King Lear*, and even the fact that he is in a position to make something of it, derives from the existence of a continuous tradition of valuation. This may not seem to be expertly critical, and often it sounds simply like lip-service, but it implies a general cultural agreement, regularly transmitted; and it further implies that to reject *King Lear*, which out of indifference or dislike one might be prepared to do, would be to reject a lot of other things one does mind losing. So Tolstoi is quite reasonable in saying that the whole culture that protects *Lear* is what ought to be rejected with the play; its values are immoral and irreligious, and the fact that it makes a treasure of such a play is merely evidence of this. It might have been, by a different chance, Dekker or Marlowe or Spenser who got cultural protection; it happened to be Shakespeare, and specifically *King Lear*, that qualified for preservation by a wicked society.

The usual way of getting round Tolstoi is to say how old he was, or how Russian he was; Russians, says Lawrence, are outside the culture, and when they are inoculated with it they are irritated into madness; for this or other reasons the old man was slightly crazy. George Orwell, however, having asked himself why Tolstoi reacted as he did, instituted one of his unprejudiced enquiries. Whatever else may be said of them, they are certainly from within the culture, or from the subculture of the common reader. Orwell is quite right to ask *why* Tolstoi should make such an attack, but, although his answers to that question are interesting in themselves, they are not my present concern. More to the point are certain concessions that Orwell himself feels he must make. Thus he admits without delay that in his view '*King Lear* is not a very good play, as a play. It is too drawn out, and has too many characters and subplots. One wicked daughter would have been quite enough, and Edgar is a superfluous character: indeed'—and here he warms to his task—'it would probably be a better play if Gloucester and both his sons were eliminated.' He goes on to invite the reader to do a simple exercise:

Shut your eyes and think of *King Lear*, if possible
without calling to mind any of the dialogue. [It is
interesting that he thought it not wholly or necessarily
impossible to do so.] What do you see? Here at any rate is
what I see: a majestic old man in a long black robe, with
flowing white hair and a beard, a figure out of Blake's
drawings (but also, curiously enough, rather like Tolstoi),
wandering through a storm and cursing the heavens, in
company with a Fool and a lunatic. Presently the scene
shifts and the old man, still cursing, still understanding
nothing, is holding a dead girl in his arms while the Fool
dangles on a gallows somewhere in the background. This
is the bare skeleton of the play....

It is not Tolstoi's skeleton—he thought the Fool redundant and
offensive—but it is certainly a skeleton. And it is very like
Orwell to say exactly what he thinks, even if it may sound a bit
absurd. His *Lear* leaves out the Gloucester plot, leaves out everything that requires two wicked daughters, including the great
scene where they quantify their father's needs and allow him his
great outcry: 'O reason not the need.' But although there may not
seem to be much left, it is clear that Orwell values it, that some
King Lear has found a place for itself in his reveries.

It might be interesting to do as he says: 'Shut your eyes...
What do you see?' That the answers will be very various is
likely to have something to do with the survival of *Lear*. I find
I can't keep the dialogue from intruding, but I also find that my
scenario is wholly different from Orwell's. First I see an old man,
blind and alone on the stage, while a battle is fought in the
distance. Then—and now I hear dialogue—this same old man
meets another old man as mad as he is blind, and they talk about
kingship, justice, punishment, sex. They don't push the story
along much, and one thinks of the whole passage as a kind of
dance, performed astride the frontier of sanity or across it; or at
the limits of the controlled creative intellect and across them. Or so
it seems to me, echoing the traditional cries; while to Orwell,
this scene and the other I spoke of were without importance
and might be omitted from the play.

The first of the scenes that came before my eye is very brief.
Gloucester comes on with Edgar, who calls him 'father', though

Gloucester does not know that his guide is his son. He does know that without this guide he is lost; and he believes also that the defeat of Cordelia's forces in the battle about to begin would be the worst thing that could happen to him—a mistake Edgar knows all about, and one which is often committed in this play. Edgar seats his father under a tree:

> Here, father, take the shadow of this tree
> For your good host. Pray that the right may
>   thrive.
> If ever I return to you again,
> I'll bring you comfort.

Gloucester: Grace go with you, sir.

And now there really is no dialogue for a while. The stage direction says '*Alarum and retreat within.*' The old man sits alone, listening. And this silence, or wordlessness, might strike you as the heart of the play, if the play has one. But Edgar comes back, bringing no comfort:

> Away, old man; give me thy hand, away!
> King Lear hath lost, he and his daughter ta'en.
> Give me thy hand; come on!

Gloucester, certain that this really is the end of his hope, answers:

> No further, sir; a man may rot even here.
> *Edgar:* What, in ill thoughts again? Men must endure
> Their going hence, even as their coming hither;
> Ripeness is all.

So, almost at the end of this extraordinary scene, we hear three words which nearly everybody remembers as part of the *seriousness* of *Lear*, part of the reason why it is conventional to esteem it: 'Ripeness is all'. What is Edgar telling his father? He has, though young, learnt from experience, in a world grown harder, what the old man had been privileged never to know. Ripeness for death, as for birth, is what must be patiently waited for; it is not subject to the will of the sufferer. So much, and more, we may take the words to mean, and so they are at the heart of many Lears and of many Shakespeares.

But we may look at this scene in another light if we supply the end of it, which I have so far withheld.

What, in ill thoughts again? Men must endure
Their going hence, even as their coming hither;
Ripeness is all. Come on.
                                        And that's true too.

Edgar has business, Gloucester thinks he has none. The young
man is impatient of his father's wish to sit and rot. His exasp-
eration shows in his words: 'O God, are you at it again? Stop
your moping.' He seizes his hand impatiently; and how the
famous *logion* sounds like a hastily spoken cliché. There's no
portentous pause on 'Ripeness is all'—the speech hurries on to
action: 'Come on!' And Gloucester's response is not really that
of somebody who has just been illuminated; so might the old
react to the impatient and assured advice of the young in whose
hands they find themselves. Perhaps the lesson isn't that 'ripeness
is all', but only that so long as you can still *say* that (or anything
else), you have to hurry along, get on with life. So the famous
words constitute merely one of a large number of statements
that for all their truth hardly affect the course of life, and are
properly followed by some such urgency as 'Come on!'—unless
they are selected by other criteria as cultural mottoes and their
contexts forgotten or neglected, as Tolstoi neglects the Fool and
Orwell, Gloucester.

So there was a version of.*Lear* seen behind closed eyelids, as
Orwell specified. It might, or so it seemed, contain the heart of
the work, but it could appear to do so only if one ignored that
what is given with one voice is taken away with another. To make
a talisman of 'Ripeness is all' one has to leave out something else:
'and that's true too.' We are quicker to notice what others have
omitted than to castigate our own selectivities. One more point
should be made: it seems to be true of *King Lear* that even after
one has left a lot of it out there is plenty left to work on. This, if
true, is important, and we shall return to it.

What others have seen when they shut their eyes and considered
Lear is, as I say, a well-documented story.[1] There is the celebrated
instance of Nahum Tate, who in 1681 published his version of
Shakespeare's play. For Tate, the play was a heap of uncut stones
which he could polish into jewels, a chaos into which he could

[1] See, especially, Maynard Mack's excellent survey in *King Lear in Our
Time* (1965).

introduce principles of regularity. He left out the Fool and the suitors of Cordelia, he made Edgar be Cordelia's lover and he restored the original happy ending. It is easy to ridicule Tate, but more useful to reflect on his purpose. The model of orderly drama by which he judged *Lear* was not derived from Shakespeare, and his wanting to make Shakespeare over into a form which complied with it is at least as strong testimony to an already existing desire to maintain some sort of contact with Shakespeare as it is to that *mauvaise foi* which imposes notions of regularity, justice and order at the expense of freedom. It used to be the case that official versions of the world rather successfully resisted subversion by fictional accounts of it. This meant that if *Lear* was to be a classic for Tate's time, it had to be made to comply with the paradigmatic requirements for a classic in that time. This is what Tate did to it: he rewrote it (as a great many of Shakespeare's plays were rewritten after the Restoration) in something like the spirit in which we might rewrite, say, *Middlemarch*, though we do it by offering new 'readings', critical essays which make it comply with our standards for novels, with paradigms that would hardly have interested George Eliot even if she could have known them. The success of Tate's enterprise is indicated by the well-known fact that his version held the stage for 157 years, until Macready, with some trepidation, restored the Fool, a character who seemed to Leigh Hunt, even in 1808, to be 'out of date'. It is true that people could read the Shakespearian version, but especially in the public playhouse the 'Tatefied' version was preferred; what seems to us an absurd and intemperate piece of meddling must have been accepted as a just reordering of a text that infringed natural notions of order and justice.

For even Dr. Johnson did not condemn the 'Tatefied' *Lear*. And to speak of Johnson is to speak of a truly great critic; he will not fail to inspect the assumptions underlying such approval. Tate's performance tells us something about the conditions of survival, but Johnson's view will tell us more. We know he had a certain dread of the play: 'I was many years ago so shocked by Cordelia's death, that I know not whether I ever endured to read again the last scenes of the play till I undertook to revise them as an editor.' And in the notes to his edition he called the death of Cordelia 'contrary to the natural ideas of justice, to the hope of the reader, and what is yet more strange, to the faith of the chronicles'. This famous sentence convinces me that Johnson had really, so to speak, deeply *scanned* the play. He saw in it not primitive ignorance but a disregard of publicly endorsed and acceptable answers which terrified him because it did *not* arise out of incompetence or carelessness. The shocks and discontinuities, which Tate saw as irregularities that his hand might eliminate, were for Johnson as deliberate as they were gratuitous. Shakespeare could have 'saved' Cordelia and Lear; in fact he had to go out of his way not to do so. But he makes the old man out-Job Job; he restores him in order to destroy him more completely, makes him watch his daughter's death and imagine her recovery. When Johnson finds in poetry an easy departure from the canons of nature and sense he calls it 'disgusting'; but he does not use that word of *Lear*; *Lear* is almost unendurable. The discontinuity between decent expectation and what occurs wounds him, whereas the pastoral only exasperated him. Jenyns wounded him, but could be put down with a superior rhetoric and shown to be vain and callous. *Lear* is a deeper threat to his necessary fiction of the world, to whatever he hoped was 'natural'. There ought to be continuity between the laws of a play and the laws of a universe; if there is such a continuity in *Lear*—and why, if it were simply a mess, should it be unendurable rather than disgusting?—then it is not such that Johnson, having sensed it, could bear to accept it.

It might be argued that it is in such an understanding that the best criticism consists, since it will work for us regardless of divergencies between our view of the world and that of the critic. So, at a time like our own, when we might tend to suppose that our world view, more deficient in 'natural ideas of justice' than Johnson's, gives us easier access to such a work as *Lear*, it is worth remembering that Johnson read it deeply, though not easily. Fearing that the world might be thus, Johnson is responding to tragedy more deeply than we, who profess to be more easily persuaded; for like prophecy and apocalypse, tragedy may make us consider that which we, out of the habit of seeking comfort in the world, avert our eyes from; it legitimates death and pain. Perhaps this was already very private, a shock to be borne by a man in solitude because that is how he must now bear death; so Johnson condoned Tate, avoiding public encounters with the deep perversity of Shakespeare's text, but in private knowing its terror. Once, in a French sixteenth-century commentary on the book of Revelation, I came on this passage, here given in the English of a contemporary translator, about the fate of good men and bad men at the latter day: 'The godly are afflicted to their own profit: namely that they may be murthered into patience; but the ungodly are consumed.' That accounts for everybody, and so does *Lear*. Johnson's ambivalence is remarkable only in that he understood it well. Faced with such comprehensive terrors, those who respond to it at all will both accept and avoid, will select, concede and amend.

The history of *Lear* criticism is a history of acceptance, avoidance, selection: Swinburne's eyes were closed to all but cruelty; Bradley passionately asserted that a 'sense of law and beauty' dominates the play and that its evil is negative and self-limiting —and that's true too. But I cannot here recount it. Nor is this the time to survey the huge variety of modern readings, all partial, accepting and avoiding.

I must, however, say something about one characteristic modern *Lear*, the version of Peter Brook, which owed much to the criticism of Jan Kott. It was probably the best of our time, but I can't here dwell on its great merits. What was immediately striking was the determination of the director to eliminate as much as he could of human kindness. Thus, in his programme note, he explained that he had omitted the passage where the servants of Cornwall tend Gloucester after the blinding, bringing him flax and eggs for his bleeding face. He did so in order 'to remove the tint [taint?] of sympathy usually found in this place'. Curiously enough, this passage is omitted in the Folio text, but Mr. Brook was not going to use a bibliographer's excuse. So Gloucester is pushed off the stage. The King's knights are represented as rustic brawlers, deserving the censure of the daughters; the gentlemen who comes for the King in IV.vi answers the lines 'I am a king. My masters, know you that', with the true text, 'You are a royal one and we obey you', but makes the line a sneer, which Shakespeare's context apparently forbids. Brook's version is a Fool *Lear* and a Gloucester *Lear*, a play which says 'And worse I *will* be yet', a world in which the hanged are cut down before they die so that they might suffer disembowelling. At the centre of it Gloucester snuffs the air as the battle goes on off-stage or rolls absurdly about as he tries to throw himself off an imaginary cliff. The old tragic is the new absurd.

It is a production for our world, continuous with what we apprehend of its order, adapted, like Tate's, to prior notions—this time negative—of order and justice. The madness, the gabble, are played up; the absurdities become central. Shakespeare took an old story and put into it madness and death, which it had largely lacked; his having done so is our cue. We do not have to imagine versions of Shakespeare which rewrite as much as Tate did; they already exist, though Mr. Brook chose not to add to them. A *King Lear* in which Cordelia cuts her father down and carries him from the gallows, having killed the slave that was a-hanging him, is conceivable. It may occur to you that such a version would have the authority of Freud. Certainly it would be in the tradition of 'saving Lear', legitimating it, as some sociologists might say; preserving, at whatever cost to the body of the play itself, its live relation to our world, as the Stoics allegorized Homer and as theologians demythologize the Bible. Relevance is not a new demand. At some point some people will cease to be able to say, 'And that's true too'. Scholars tend to say it early, but scholars do not, unaided, ensure the survival of the classics; *la cour et la ville* have a strong hand in it and are more liberal. Hence Tate and Brook. Meanwhile the play is very patient, takes a tremendous amount of punishment; we depend on that, require it of our true classics.

Of course it's not enough merely to say that if a work is 'patient' it will survive, nor is it enough to say that our wanting to keep it—perhaps because we are, as Tolstoi thought, immoral—is a sufficient explanation of the ways in which we try its patience. We need to go a bit deeper than that.

It is true that we have to want it, and that to do so is some sort of commitment, which Tolstoi abstained from, to a cultural tradition. Cultural survival is always problematical simply because the information on which it depends is not transmitted genetically; positive and practical action is required of those who think it should not die between one generation and another; and they are the people in the very best position to judge the width of that gap and the degree of adaptation required if the information is successfully to cross it. Critics, teachers, adapters, all, however original, are committed to the transmission of the classic. Tolstoi was not; but Tate was, and so was Orwell, and so was Jan Kott. What each of them wanted *King Lear* to be differed enormously. But wanting it to be at all is to declare for continuity; it amounts to an assertion that, however the world changes, there are some elements in the cultural or human stock which one is not yet prepared to write off, even in the middle of a cultural revolution. So even the most adventurous and iconoclastic of the commentators and adapters would accept some form of this statement by W. H. Auden: 'Let us remember that, though great artists of the past could not change the course of history, it is only through their work that we are able to break bread with the dead, and without communion with the dead a fully human life is impossible.'

And yet it is of course possible to try for a fully human life without such communion. You need a wholly different concept of the historical mode of culture to replace the rather Burkeian assumptions of Auden; you need a new concept of human personality and of communications between persons. It would be presumptuous to say these cannot be had; certainly they are at present being sought after. And so it is clear that survival until now is no guarantee of survival hereafter; that in a new world Tolstoi never dreamed of *King Lear* will be forgotten like the tulip mania, since there will be no *Weltanschauung* to which the play could possibly be adapted, even if somebody felt like doing it. Such a world is totally unpredictable as to detail; but it seems, in principle, a possible world, and one with no place for *Lear* or the mechanism of survival. We can speak only of things as they still are, of survival till now, and continue, if we want to, with the business of non-genetic transmission while it still seems possible.

In doing so we assume that the classic has a peculiar power to remain in a condition of complementarity with one's view of the world. Eliot said it had a sort of imperial quality; it is in this respect that we are all provincial. The *imperium* persists through extreme temporal mutations, retaining in all circumstances some nuclear identity and purity; *imperium sine fine*, as Virgil says with what degree of poetic licence I don't try to determine. As the empire of Constantine lived on in partial and provincial substitutes, so Virgil gives way to the vernacular poets, to Dante and Shakespeare; but the *imperium* survives, patient of change, patient of interpretation. We know that when they depart the other gods go with them, so that we can say quite soberly that they have the quality also of the palladium, of which Arnold wrote:

> And when it fails, fight as we will, we die;
> And while it lasts, we cannot wholly end—

where 'we' means our sect, now sometimes disparagingly called humanist, with its heavy investment in a certain kind of value. Others would happily give away the palladium and have done with it, but we can't, because we have accepted it at an older valuation and are inextricably committed not only to that valuation but to that which has been and, we think, ought to be transmitted, and to communion with the dead who transmitted it. This remains true even if it is conceded that the choice of what is to be transmitted is in the last analysis arbitrary.

But that brings up a harder question. For it cannot be allowed that the choice is entirely arbitrary, even if one concedes an element of chance, luck or grace; it cannot be supposed that a choice could simply be entailed upon successive generations by propaganda. However great the inertia of the many, there would always, presumably, be some who resisted brainwashing and a Tolstoi to confirm their suspicion that this emperor really had no clothes. In short, there must be some quality in the work itself which encourages the regular confirmation of the choice, which consolidates its imperial patience. In trying to say what it is I shall call again on Johnson, and on Freud.

Johnson shows us that it is possible to respect a work which seems to give terribly wrong answers to what you take to be the right questions, and which contains a great deal of information which you do not seem able to handle because many of the clues seem to be pointing in some direction you cannot follow, or in a puzzling variety of directions. Even if it did more readily comply with one's particular demands upon it, there would still be a sense that there was too much of it for one's perception, or anybody else's, to organize, so that the work seems, if not a chaos, at least a system of potentialities beyond one's power to actualize them.

This, if true of *Lear*, is equally true of *Hamlet*, and in some measure of all the works of Shakespeare we value most highly.

How Shakespeare came to write as he did—with such reticence about how his clues ought to be read, about the importance of one set as against another—is hardly a question for a sane critic three parts of the way through a lecture; but the effect is certainly to defeat attempts to isolate some determinate meaning. Mr. Hirsch, in his book *Validity in Interpretation*, declares that determinate and reproducible meaning is the true object of the critical quest, that a text which lacks such meaning means nothing in particular, and that as meanings require a meaner it is Shakespeare's meaning alone that concerns us. But even if this were generally true, Shakespeare would have to be called exceptional because of his habitual withdrawals and confusions; the fact that one can't, in Mr. Hirsch's terms, 'discover' Shakespeare's 'most probable horizon' or, usually, his 'most probable context', suggests a connexion between horizonlessness and classic status. There is a difference between Shakespeare and the people who write *Lear* differently, saving Cordelia and making only consistent statements about the gods and justice, just as there is a difference between Shakespeare and all the critics who can tell us, on the evidence of other revenge plays or the laws relating to feud, exactly what *Hamlet* means. This is not to say that either play means nothing or anything, though I suppose it may imply that it means nothing *in particular*, if we take the sense of this to be that no particular set of answers to the questions asked will seem, to a good observer, to make these questions appear to be the only proper ones, or even to be proper questions at all. These classics are certainly, in some sense, indeterminate as to meaning, lacking any clearly delineated semantic horizon. The noise that accompanies whatever information the questions elicit will suggest that there is much more to be had, and that without it the information you have got is in some measure false. This is a manner of speaking about Johnson's experience of the play.

Freud began by getting simple answers to simple questions. He observes, rather in Orwell's manner, that *Lear* 'inculcates two prudent maxims: that one should not forego one's possessions and privileges in one's lifetime and that one must guard against accepting flattery as genuine'. But he adds, sensibly, that it would be absurd to suppose that 'the overpowering effect of *Lear*' arises from these propositions. And he recounts the climactic scene: '*Enter Lear with Cordelia dead in his arms.*' 'Cordelia', he says, 'is Death. Reverse the situation and it becomes intelligible and familiar to us—the Death goddess bearing away the hero from the place of battle, like the Valkyr in German mythology. Eternal wisdom, in the garb of primitive myth, bids the old man renounce love, choose death and make friends with the necessity of dying.' It is the situation adapted by the Christian *pietà*. All is explained: the division of the kingdom, the rejection of the silent daughter, the confrontation with Poor Tom, the tearing off of the lendings, the assault on a limited and venal justice. And most of us will be conscious of the beauty of the reading.

Of course such explanations, like all that depend on a recourse to mythical archetypes, assume that what is stated in the work is merely a cover for a real meaning which is hidden; Cordelia in Lear's arms is a lie, or a fiction, for Lear in Cordelia's. And this presupposes, as all such explanations must, that we have to penetrate a façade, or disregard the manifest content of the work, either calling it sophistical and mendacious, or commonplace and prudential, or, perhaps, irrelevant, as Lear is when he raves against the imagined lechery of the man in the furred gown. But this is contrary to experience, for the manifest content of *Lear* has been a matter of continuous interest and speculation and is clearly not in this way disposable. Freud's great discovery was that dreams yield their meanings to a form of inquiry which insists that their final or remembrable form is derived from their original purport by means of many displacements, condensations, acts of censorship; and in his work on literature he is making the assumption, which amounts to a brilliant hypothesis, that in this respect dreams are a subclass of the class of fictions; thus we may expect all fictions to be susceptible to similar modes of interpretation. Modern reductive or archetypal modes of analysis which have no direct contact with Freudianism nevertheless take over this hypothesis. But it has little reality for *la cour et la ville*, who still prefer archaic ways of reading and listening; and that alone is sufficient to establish that it is not universally valid. The surface is still alive, and it cannot be reduced to a set of maxims.

So we have somehow to get in both hypotheses: that there are meanings accessible and meanings to be dived for. I cannot imagine that any good critic would be so doctrinaire as to decline all assent to Freud's beautiful reading, and I would trust none who thought it exclusively right. We certainly need Cordelia in

Lear's arms, and perhaps also the shadowy possibility of Lear in Cordelia's. We do not want to lose ourselves in a sort of dream, in purely subliminal scanning, but we don't, either, choose meanings so obvious that only a *mauvaise foi* could be satisfied with them. It is useful to hypothecate a chaos of potentialities which, without sacrificing its secrets, can satisfy the demands which are rightly made of all texts whose expectation of life is that of the culture itself—say, for prudence, justice, probability. It is what we ask of classics, and it is a demand that few works can consistently meet. To do so, a work may expose itself to a rancorous levelling eye as muddled; to a marvellously good reader, such as Johnson, it may be the occasion of profound and despondent concern, and even lesser men may be left with a sense that it is full of answers beyond their power to elicit. A classic is required, in short, to be a piece of wisdom literature, but also to be a nature susceptible to an indefinite number of physics, some rational, some not. Or, to put this in a quite different way, it has to show some kind of explicitness: 'this shows you are above, you justicers'; or, 'Ripeness is all'; in short, to be sharp and clear, yet at the same time to exhibit some of the signs of overdetermination and condensation which characterize dreaming. Clarity coexistent with condensation, the façade consistent with the meaning of the dream: here, crudely, tentatively, are some of the qualifications for the classic patience.

To simplify this requirement, one could say that a classic, surviving, will have in some measure an obsessed, dreamlike quality, which nevertheless does not resist sharp and simple demands for significance. My belief is that Shakespeare, at his most powerful, supplies just this kind of thing, having devised public expressions for the deepest and most obsessed of his meanings. It is, in the circumstances, naturally rather hard to be sure; but to take a single example we may, I think, say that there is some evidence that he was obsessed with the image of the king's body, and with all the related problems of human authority. *King Lear* is his twenty-sixth play, or thereabouts; and it is the fifteenth in which he concerns himself with such problems, with the right of the ruler and with justice as dispensed by a poor forked thing. Nor is this by any means the only obsession we can confidently attribute to Shakespeare; it might be said, for example, that he was more than usually interested in vicious sexuality and madness. Long before we get down to the displaced archetypes, we have to contend with this extraordinary, reticent, obsessed person, who knew a world of dream, vision, madness, and yet talked sense, sense that satisfies the undemanding whose franchise the classic requires, nearly all the time.

And that is a way of explaining why his works are, or have been until now, patient and responsive, in the manner of classics. Classics have somehow to fit; not only must they, by some institutional adjustment, be helped to do so, but they must, in themselves, contain that which can satisfy not only the relatively unconsidered demands—the moralistic, the prudential—but all or many of the others, harder to describe: our interest in death, in madness, our darker purposes in sex, which we do not formulate ourselves because we are afraid to do so. Part of the business of fitting is to hint at some sort of undertaking that, if we choose, or are somehow impelled, to go below the sane surface, we may encounter material relevant to us, and then, by techniques of adaptation, anamnesis or distortion, put it to our use.

So there seem, now, to be at least two necessary conditions for the survival of a classic. First in my order, though not logically first, we have to want it to survive, take a great deal of trouble over it out of a kind of instinct for self-preservation, perhaps. And here we may be particularly aware of the threat of social revolution, and the knowledge that our wanting it to survive will not, in all conceivable circumstances, be enough. Secondly, whatever will bear the stress of our demands upon it will, in all probability, be complex, superficially confused, resembling a dream in its condensations and overdeterminations, yet not like a dream in speaking with disarming immediacy to our waking concerns. Meanings are visible in sharp profile, but we know how many of them there are, and how multiple, complex and mysterious the object must be that affords them. There is a quality of pre-allegory, so called by Mr. A. D. Nuttall,[2] who notes it particularly in *The Tempest*: the work invites and absorbs, but cannot exclusively endorse any 'reading' because it has not itself settled into a shape hinting at one dominant allegorical interpretation. And this is a way of speaking about the shifting, obsessed text of *Lear* and the way in which it challenges and defeats our power of

[2] *Two Concepts of Allegory* (1967).

penetration, and at the same time sustains the demands made of it by all who have wanted and want it to survive.

So it fits us as nature fitted Wordsworth, more or less exquisitely, so long as one keeps the faith that it never will betray the heart that loves it. As that faith involves emotional and intellectual operations of much complexity, so must the nature that calls for it be obsessed, multiple, full of answers waiting for questions that may or may never be asked.

These, the qualities needed for imperial survival, may be sought and found in the classics we elect from later literature—in, for example, the pre-allegorical Kafka, in the overdetermined, condensing Joyce and in Proust, the multiple and occultly obsessed. *Their* survival also depends upon their accessibility to *la cour et la ville*, but we try to assure that by setting up a class of exegetes, people who continually say, in a hundred different accents and with all the authority they can muster, 'This is valuable; this endures as long as we do.' Much that they say in the course of their duties may strike us as ridiculous or banal; in so large a profession it is hardly to be expected that all the practitioners will be ingenious and persuasive. But it is to be hoped that some of them succeed in transmitting their valuations across the generation gap. Once that is done it hardly matters that the young will reject the old rhetoric and the old interpretations; indeed, it could be said that they must do so; to survive, the work must change. The necessary change may be measured in terms of interpretations which we elders find repellent. Yet when the young propose an impatient and alien wisdom, as Edgar did to Gloucester on the battlefield, we can at least imitate his dazed tolerance and say with him, 'And that's true, too.' We may even suppose that what strikes us as wanton or schismatic could be the alteration of attitude necessary, amid rapid change, to the preservation of the *imperium*, an attempt, now necessarily radical, to ensure a continuing connexion with a past that recedes too rapidly for gentler adaptations to succeed. So, at any rate, we may hope. But the only certainty is that our ingenuities and persuasions, like the obscure depths of the classic itself, belong to a world that can end; one of the surest indications of so great a mutation would be precisely the failure of the classic to survive into the next one.

8

SHAKESPEARE'S LEARNING[1]

Like most Shakespearian topics, this is a very old one; the first
critic to imply that he was more learned than Shakespeare was
probably his angry contemporary, Robert Greene. A little later,
when it had to be conceded that the Stratford man could write,
people at once began to exclaim upon his power to do so without art or study. Of all the stock requirements for a poet as set
forth in Ben Jonson's *Discoveries*, Shakespeare, it seems, had only
the one nature provides: *ingenium*, wit or wits. Again and again
it was remarked that his 'strength and nature' made 'amends for
art'. 'Those who accuse him to have wanted learning', argued
Dryden, 'give him the greater commendation.'

It is partly a question of how you can praise him best: by
saving his scholarly reputation or triumphantly denying that he
had one. If you want him to have some kind of training in the
humanities, you can work on the hints that he read Ovid in Latin,
perhaps Boccaccio in Italian, more probably some books in
French. Rowe, the first biographer, thought he could do some of
these things, and that he remembered, from Stratford Grammar
School, a tag or two of Horace. Others claimed that he was so
clever that having studied the ancients he refused to imitate them.
Others again treated him as divinely ignorant. Here is a subject
on which a man can find some sort of authority for whatever he
cares to believe, so long as he means to praise Shakespeare.

In the eighteenth century Upton made him learned and Farmer
a mere genius. 'Solicitous only for the honour of Shakespeare',

[1] See Preface.

Farmer is amazed that 'any *real* friends of our immortal POET should be still willing to force him into a situation which is not tenable: treat him as a learned man'.[2] And he claims, with some justice, to have 'removed a deal of *learned Rubbish*' from Shakespearian commentary. Farmer rightly attached importance to the testimony of the poet's contemporaries, which is strongly on the side of Nature against Art. And we should not forget that to these men poetry was (as indeed it remains) a learned art; it has always been worth notice that a man of only ordinary education should master it. So Farmer deserved Jonson's commendations for his labour in finding sources for Shakespeare more probable than the original texts of Greek and Latin (it was he, for example, who first showed that Shakespeare read Plutarch in North's translation). It was no longer possible, if you thought that learning was a matter of imitating ancient authors, to think Shakespeare very learned. And nobody will ever again try to make Shakespeare into the eighteenth-century idea of a classical scholar. Whether or not D'Avenant is speaking the truth in his scurrilous account of how Shakespeare amused himself when passing through Oxford, it seems unlikely that he went into Bodley to read. For that matter, you do not hear in his *Henry VI* of the Library of Duke Humphrey, or of certain colleges established during those troubles; or in *Sir Thomas More* that the hero was the modern Socrates and a great scholar. Shakespeare's scholars are not a great company —they are pedants mostly, or magicians, men of power like Prospero, or men trained, like Horatio, for spiritual emergencies: 'thou art a scholar, Horatio, speak to it'. The only sustained academic effort represented in the plays is that of the courtiers in *Love's Labour's Lost*; and it is thwarted by life and love. Shakespeare's own most obviously learned work—*Venus and Adonis*, *Lucrece*—belongs to the periods when he was young and *désœuvré* and trying a different role from the one he settled in; or when he was indulging the inscrutable whims of his last phase in *The Tempest*. He was first a scholar to please patrons, and last a scholar to please himself; in between he was a scholar to please no one.

Let us then happily abandon hope of one kind of learned

[2] 'An Essay on the Learning of Shakespeare', in *Eighteenth Century Essays on Shakespeare*, ed. D. Nichol Smith (1903), p. 162. See Nichol Smith's Introduction for an account of the controversy.

Shakespeare. Not that we can afford to neglect what modern enquirers tell us of his education. Once allow—as we must—the probability of his having attended Stratford Grammar School, and it will follow that the description 'schoolmaster among the playwrights'—acceptable to Professors Smart and Baldwin—is an apt enough description. Then we shall go on to admit that 'he read Ovid as well as Golding's Ovid, some Seneca and Virgil as well as English Seneca and Virgil'.[3] Nor will it be possible to contend that he avoided books; we can catch him looking through books on Popish impostures, on the law of honour, on travel, on history, on law. He must have read deeper in Holinshed than his plots required, and gone into Plutarch beyond the Lives he was using. He knew something of the commentators on Terence; he knew Palingenius, emblem books, and of course the Bible. We must allow that his school reading helped to form his mind,[4] but also that he underwent some process of self-education, as we all do; and this justifies Professor Whitaker's feeling that as time went on he experienced an intellectual and ethical development in part caused by his mature reading.

What it comes to is this: there was nothing freakish or extreme about Shakespeare's learning habits. Though no scholar, he was a reading man, and since he was also a writing man, it shows. But there are two qualifications to be made here. The first is obvious: Shakespeare was a fantastically *good* reader because he was a person of enormously superior intelligence. The second is that he belongs not only to the class 'Elizabethan' but to the class 'poet', and he read not merely as one but as the other.

On the general topic of Shakespeare's intelligence I will spare you platitudes, but it is only proper to be reminded now and again that it was a superior one. Mr. John Wain, somewhat like Carlyle before him, has observed that 'one of Shakespeare's achievements was to demonstrate just how strong, how wide-ranging, how

---

[3] F. P. Wilson, 'Shakespeare's Reading', *Shakespeare Survey*, 3 (1950), p. 14.

[4] In addition to T. W. Baldwin's series of books: *William Shakespere's Petty School* (1943), *William Shakespere's Small Latin and Lesser Greek* (1944), *Shakespere's Five-Act Structure* (1947), *On the Literary Genetics of Shakespere's Poems and Sonnets* (1950), and *On the Literary Genetics of Shakespere's Plays* (1959)—these last for arguments as to Shakespeare's methods of imitation—see also V. K. Whitaker, *Shakespeare's Use of Learning* (1953), and J. A. K. Thomson, *Shakespeare and the Classics* (1952), which disputes many of Baldwin's conclusions.

subtly adjusted the intelligence of a great poet has to be'.[5] But perhaps the second point, that Shakespeare's mind, and his learning, were those of a *poet*, is less obvious. Mr. Wain's formula was devised to meet the need of describing Shakespeare's power to synthesize—his rapidity of mind, his control of linguistic as of dramatic situations; one is repeatedly surprised—and more and more frequently in the later work—by the sheer extent of the possibilities envisaged in some grammatical ellipse or some conceit. But I wish to speak of another aspect of the poet's intelligence, and it is at this point that it becomes inseparable from the question of his learning. There are poets who read as philosophers or as theologians—Coleridge and Milton, for example—and with these poets one can—dangerous and difficult though the practice undoubtedly is—hypothecate *some* structure of learning in their poetry analogous to their non-poetic thought. In the other poets one cannot do this: Yeats is an instance, Shakespeare is another. Of course people do it, but they nearly always go wrong. There is no 'philosophy' of Shakespeare, though there are prevailing intellectual moods and plural *philosophies* in plenty. What we should remember is their status. If I say that Shakespeare read, learnt, listened in much the same frame of mind as Yeats attended to his 'instructors'—'they give me metaphors for poetry'—I shall certainly be misunderstood. Such labours as those of Miss Doran and Mr. Baldwin and Miss Tuve should by now have prevented such mistakes. Yet I cannot avoid the feeling that there is something in it. There is a brooding Shakespeare, a Shakespeare sometimes excited, sometimes possessed by, sometimes merely playing with, learning, or with schemes of a learned sort.

Consider, for example, his treatment of the motif or *topos* of the banquet of sense. I have studied this at length elsewhere;[6] Shakespeare uses it in Sonnet 141, in *Timon* (I. ii. 123), and in *Venus and Adonis*, 427–46; it is a theme iconographically associated with that of Hercules at the Crossroads, and Shakespeare remembered this when he wrote *Antony and Cleopatra*. Now this topic is not uncommon, even on the stage; Massinger develops it in *A New Way to Pay old Debts* (III. i), and Ben Jonson treats it several times, once, in *The New Inn*, at considerable length and very seriously. Is Shakespeare then merely following a fashion? The longest of the passages, in *Venus*, is the most straightforward

[5] *Essays on Literature and Ideas* (1963), p. 70.   [6] See Chapter 4, above.

because here the poet's learning is on show. In the Sonnet the theme is presented in simple inversion, for the text says 'In faith I do *not* love thee with mine eyes', etc. In *Timon* the context is the masque of ladies; the choice of theme is ironical and tells us something about the nature of Timon's feast. In *Antony* all is glancing allusion. Only in the earliest example (1593) does Shakespeare use the idea 'straight', as Jonson was still doing in 1634.

Here, then, is a simple instance of the *obliquity* of the poet's intelligence. The Banquet of Sense, like the 'quinque lineae amoris', 'to see, to hear, to touch, to kiss, to die', also used in *Venus*,[7] was a piece of stock learned equipment for poets, and Shakespeare acquired and used it when he launched his fashionable Ovidian poem. In the *Venus* and the *Lucrece* you can watch him at work with many such devices, and he uses them with more skill and originality than he often gets the credit for. But when they occur in plays more than a decade later they are subtilized, sunk into the mind, mere hints and invitations. The degree to which Shakespeare's whole manner of dramatic proceeding was shaped by normal expectations, and by the body of ethical and emblematic lore held in common with his audience, should certainly not be underestimated.[8] But if we sacrifice to this perception all sense of the more curious or subtle or even perverse aspects of Shakespeare's mind, we shall be left with a wonderfully articulate *bien pensant*; and this, if only from the sonnets, we know Shakespeare was not. Our experience is of a mind pursuing ideas beyond the point where they yield to poetry.

Of this one might offer many instances. There is, for instance, the learning of *Macbeth*. When we think of a performance of that play we hardly recall what scholarship has established, as to its intellectual basis. Yet one of the permanent modern Shakespearian achievements was W. C. Curry's cautious and qualified book on the Augustinian and Thomist patterns in *Macbeth*;[9] and H. N. Paul's exhaustive speculations on the play[10] should at least convince us that Shakespeare embodied in his text metaphysical questions fit for a learned king. Nor is this exclusively

[7] See Baldwin, *Literary Genetics of Shakespeare's Poems* (1950), p. 16.

[8] See Russell A. Fraser, *Shakespeare's Poetics in Relation to King Lear* (1962).

[9] W. C. Curry, *Shakespeare's Philosophical Patterns* (1937).

[10] H. N. Paul, *The Royal Play of Macbeth* (1950).

a matter for tragedy. The comedies—from *Love's Labour's Lost*, *A Midsummer Night's Dream* and *The Merchant of Venice* through the 'problem comedies' and up to the philosophical romances of the final period—are full of thought; and the thought is poetic but sets out from existing 'patterns'.

When, therefore, we are considering Shakespeare's learning, we ought not entirely to neglect this habit of curious brooding upon ideas; not that one wants to make him a philosopher—only a poet capable of intense intellectual application, dealing in the excitement of speculative thought. It is an excitement that can seem perverse, wanton even; it has a privacy denied to public propositions. An instance which explains part of what I mean is the treatment of time in *Macbeth*.

When Lucrece apostrophizes Time she nobly utters commonplaces; what she says derives in an orthodox way from two famous places in Ovid (*Met*. xv. 234, 'tempus edax rerum . . .' and *Tristia*, IV, vi) and from Horace's 'exegi momentum', also laid under contribution in the sonnets. Shakespeare may have remembered also a frequently quoted scrap from the *Timæus*; certainly he had looked up Time in the emblem books. In short, he wrote, in the manner of his time, a variation on a set theme.[11] Traces of the same theme may be found elsewhere, not only in the Sonnets but as late as the comic set-piece on Time in *As You Like It*. The first hint of a personal, perhaps obsessive, treatment of the theme may be in *Henry IV*. There the Prince is 'redeeming the time'; this meant, in the devotional language of the period, to make 'the activity of the passing moment a contribution to a man's most vital duty, that of saving his soul'.[12] The Prince seeks ways 'to frustrate prophecies', and is accordingly attentive to the flow of time which brings their realization nearer; and his attention induces attention, notably in Hotspur, but also in others: 'We are Time's subjects.' In Act 3 of the Second Part the king introduces a passage which is as much a poetic dialogue on Time as a comment on innovation in the state; it opens with his own weary poetry, his wish to see time's end, and leads to Warwick's remarkable speech on the historical search into the seeds of time—'the hatch and brood of time' (III. i. 80 ff.).

[11] See, for example, S. C. Chew, *The Virtues Reconciled* (1947).
[12] Paul A. Jorgenson, *Redeeming Shakespeare's Words* (1962), pp. 52–69.

These variations on Time—as leveller, as pattern, as the medium of prophecy, as brooding over event and character like some malign dove—may not be a scholar's learning, but they sound like poet's learning; they have the effect of providing for the whole play and series of plays a dimension additional to that of mere chronicle. We should not characterize this dimension as philosophical; it is rather a matter, shall we say, of a fruitful unease of intellect (which is one of the conditions of a certain kind of poetry). The historical pattern, the action of prophecy (which the Prince cannot entirely prevent) are structural elements which have given rise to this controlled irrelevance, this disturbance in the texture, if you like those terms. The royal house is under a curse; the truth that slow time will bring, before it ends, is the return of a legitimate monarch. In the history plays, a century of time erodes justice and then injustice, and brings on the Day, the accesssion of the Tudors; Richmond is an imperial figure, reminding us of the strange relation in the mind of Europe between Empire and Apocalypse. And, working with such themes the poet agitates other figures of time, immersing the characters deeper in its element.

So too in *Troilus* the Trojan apocalypse lies ahead, its seeds sown in time; and we encounter time as the medium of human achievement and its destroyer, that which gives back the light of virtue but is also the porter of oblivion and the provider of Occasion. In *Lear* time is under the shadow of the promised end. And in *Macbeth* this vortex in Shakespeare's mind is deepest and strongest; the word itself tolls through the play as 'world' does in *Antony and Cleopatra*.

Time is the medium in which human desires are translated into actions; the interval between them is the phantasma of Brutus, the hideous dream. The first part of *Macbeth* is about that terrible time; and what seems characteristic of Shakespeare in his insistence on the excitement, the complexity of it. The prophecies tempt a man to jump over that interim and 'feel now | The future in the instant', or be 'transported | Beyond the ignorant present'. But one need not take the leap, which is the same thing as to 'jump the life to come'. Lady Macbeth taunts her husband with his inability to proceed directly from desire to act; and through the scenes ticks the dramatic clock which is the word 'time' itself: time beguiled, time mocked, time running. The second act begins with Banquo simply asking Fleance the time; the bell tolls, the owl signals midnight, the knocking at dawn ends a blessed and begins a woeful time. 'By the clock 'tis day.' Thenceforward the word is introduced—you might almost say, intruded—like a ticking clock: 'fill up the time'; 'let every man be master of his time'; 'the perfect spy o'th' time'; 'the pleasure of the time' (spoilt says Lady Macbeth, by her husband's terror at Banquo's apparition!) the glimmering west and the timely inn. .

Meanwhile time changes, contracts. 'The time has been', says Macbeth, 'that when the brains were out the man would die.' In this new time, guilt has reduced the interim between desire and act; the firstlings of the heart become the firstlings of the hand. And time anticipates Macbeth's dread exploits. Since he would not use it for protection against evil, it offers him no defence against the equivocal fiend and the prophecy literally fulfilled. Now each minute teems a new grief. For his enemies, 'the time' approaches; but for Macbeth it has become meaningless; no moment a moment of grace, to the last syllable of recorded time. The last speech of the play uses the word three times; but the most remarkable and Shakespearian use is to have Macduff enter with the tyrant's head and announce that 'The time is free'.

Shakespeare has used the family of meanings which characterize this word, including those the New Testament distinguishes as *chronos* and *kairos*. The passion with which this game is played properly, I think, reminds one of the greatest of all Christian meditations on time, in the eleventh chapter of the *Confessions* of Augustine. 'If it were done when 'tis done' is based on a proverb; but Shakespeare finds in it a wish that a moment in time should have no succession, that is, be eternity. 'But the present, should it always be present, and never pass into time past, verily it should not be time but eternity', says St. Augustine. Macbeth cannot have the future in the instant; he deceives himself, saying 'If the present were eternity we need not bother about eternity'. As Augustine puts it, 'we generally think before our future actions, and . . . forethinking is present, but the action whereof we forethink is not yet, because it is to come.' It is precisely the difficulty over which Macbeth broods. 'My soul is on fire to know this most intricate enigma', says the saint. The enigma also, it appears, engaged Shakespeare.[13]

[13] There is more discussion of this in *The Sense of an Ending* (1967), pp. 84-9.

Now the difference is that Shakespeare is not seeking to *know* an enigma. He is rather, with deep excitement, assembling a family of contexts. The deep penetration of the text by the 'time' of ordinary language, as we might say, makes it impossible to offer the barest paraphrase, let alone some solution of a problem. What we may be sure of is that the nobly correct and learned exercises we remember from *Lucrece* have given way to deeper tones, to a poetry at once dramatic and, in a Coleridgean sense, philosophical. At any rate, the simply learned treatment of a topic lies far in the past.

To speak in this way is not to deny the important truth that some at least of Shakespeare's plays have a fundamental thematic interest which is reducible to a learned *topos*. The whole structure depends on some central ethical issue, as in *Love's Labour's Lost* or *Two Gentlemen*. There is the conflict of Truth and Opinion in *Troilus*, of Equity and Justice in *Measure for Measure*; Fortune in *As You Like It*, or Nobility in *Cymbeline*. There are many other such instances. His freedom and variety in handling such themes speaks for Shakespeare's power to make commonplaces impinge on us like elements in immediate but unnaturally beautiful life.

But I am trying to describe something subtler, even perhaps more *wanton*. I'm speaking of a Shakespeare *not* conventional, not an inspired illustrator of homily or commonplace—from the eccentric, even *louche* Shakespeare of certain late sonnets, from the Shakespeare who so abused his sources. Brooke's interpretation of the moral of *Romeo and Juliet* is used, in Shakespeare's version, as the partial opinion of the Friar. So, in *Othello*, the only characters who share Cinthio's view of the moral of the story are Iago and Brabantio. And in *Antony and Cleopatra* Shakespeare builds up the structure of conventional moralization the story had long before attracted, only to bless the immoral opposition with the unanswerable argument of poetry.

It is this *perversity* I want to trace in certain aspects of Shakespeare's intelligence as it operated on learned subjects. *Antony and Cleopatra* provides notable instances in the cases I have mentioned, and in its treatment of such subjects as Empire. *Cymbeline* is a monument to such brilliant perversions. A more familiar and concrete instance might be the entirely idiosyncratic development of the Christian-Aristotelian difference over the doctrine of creation 'ex nihilo' in *King Lear* which raises, quite deliberately I think, if you consider the apocalyptic patterns of the play, the old philosophical dispute on the eternity of the world. But perhaps I can state my views on this, and on the related issues I have introduced, by asking you to think of a specific theme, centrally stated in one short poem.

The most direct challenge to people who suppose Shakespeare to have been a 'natural' arises from the poems, above all from 'The Phoenix and the Turtle'. The imagery of this poem, however interpreted, is certainly in some way learned; and to deny Shakespeare this kind of learning you must say he was not the author of the poem. This has indeed often been done; but the external evidence in favour of his authorship happens to be unusually strong. It can also be said, I think, that the learned interests it reflects—and its mode of reflecting them—are Shakespearian.

Let us retreat a few years from 1601, the undoubted date of the poem, to *Richard II*. It would not be difficult to show, with the help of Ernst Kantorowicz, the degree to which Shakespeare was affected by certain ideas on perpetuity having their origin in medieval philosophy and law. I have already commented upon his preoccupation with time; if one wished to place that in the context of the history of ideas one would doubtless label it 'Augustinian'. Time began with the creation and will have a stop. Its course is marked by acts of will, by sin, senescence, and mutability. Against it may be placed for instance, such glory as derives from poetry, if not from honour, as existing not in time but in some perpetual duration. But what of the great *continuities* of earthly life? The most obvious of them is kingship: the king never dies; or rather, he dies in his body natural, not in his body politic. Kantorowicz has shown[14] that the theory was associated with the scholastic concept of *aevum*.

This was originally an angelological concept, a third order between time and eternity. I believe that both Spenser and Shakespeare had a deep and exploratory interest in this concept. In so far as it relates to the kingship, Shakespeare put it into *Richard II*. This aspect of the doctrine is summed up in Kantorowicz's title: the king has a mortal body and also a dignity which does not die, and which is represented by ceremonies. The painful separation of the two bodies is part of Lear's experience also; he

[14] *The King's Two Bodies* (1957).

gives away the *dignitas* and is left with his natural body, subject, as the lawyers said, to all infirmity. He sees the lost *dignitas* as adhering to the natural body only by means of ceremony and ceremonial clothing. When he curses the robed justice he curses the ironical antithesis between the Dignity and the erring man within the robe—a contrast as great as that between the decaying body in the coffin and the robed effigy of the king that was placed upon it in royal funerals. Lear in the storm is realizing the loss of the *dignitas*, tearing off the last fragments of the clothing that have come to symbolize it, as his daughters have stripped away lands, knights, servants; only in madness is he a mockery king, every inch a king, with his fading regalia of wild flowers. But when Gloster kisses the hand of his body natural 'it smells of mortality'. And throughout Lear we are made to share (with Kent and Gloster and Lear) the sense that such dissolution means the end of time, 'the promised end'. But—and this is the strange power of the conclusion—the truth is different. The Dignity falls on Edgar, in all the misery of regal mortality and the death of good men and women, life continues; we see that continuity must be accounted for even in tragedy. Aquinas says that without revelation (and revelation is excluded from *Lear*) we could not know that the world ever had a beginning; without it we should be sure enough of misery, but not of an end. What we have in *Lear* is not an end but a bleak perpetuity of the dignity.

Now kingship, a topic which so preoccupied Shakespeare, is not the only instance of his application of the concept of *aevum* to continuity in human affairs. We have seen that he applied it also to the justice: he dies but his office does not. Above all, perhaps, it applied to the Empire. The Virgilian *imperium sine fine* began with Augustus, sometimes called the first vicar of Christ, and the Empire thenceforward was coeval with the Church. Since the power of *imperium* was held to be conferred by the Roman people, the people also never died; its *maiestas* was continuous, transmitted to the peoples of every kingdom which claimed the rights of the Roman *imperium*.[15] Thus, in England, which had not the Roman law but which under Elizabeth carefully imported the main elements of European imperial mythology, it was held that the Queen wore the *dignitas* of Augustus and of Constantine. In two plays Shakespeare interests himself deeply, but with some

[15] Kantorowicz, Chapter VI.

obliquity, in the nature of Empire. In *Antony and Cleopatra* we may take the hint from Caesar's prophecy of the 'time of universal peace' (IV. vi. 4) his reign will begin; indeed it brought the birth of Christ and the extinction of pagan time, represented by Antony and Cleopatra in their masks as Isis and Osiris (for Shakespeare knew more Plutarch than the *Lives*).[16] *Cymbeline*, set at the time of the birth of Christ, describes the reception into Britain of Roman civility and establishes as from the earliest possible moment the British share of the Roman *maiestas* now devolving upon the imperial James.

I do not mean to imply that Shakespeare unambiguously celebrates these regal and imperial continuities. In fact, the situation of the incumbent of the *dignitas* strikes him rather as humanly appalling, and no one could say that he tried to make the founder of the imperial dignity humanly attractive; the majesty that *dies* is what we remember from *Antony and Cleopatra*. The point is that these are poetic meditations on a learned theme, a philosophico-legal complex.

Now the twin-natured incumbent of the *dignitas* was held to be unique, in that he was both species and individual. The nearest analogues were in the Trinity, in angelology, and in the bestiary, from which was drawn, as emblem of the doctrine, the Phoenix. This bird was both mortal and immortal, its own father and son.[17] It stood for perpetuity in mortality, and had a long connection with the idea of perpetual dignity. Coins of Valentinian II (375–392) show a phoenix and the legend *Perpetuetas*.[18] The same emblem served the French and English dynasties in Shakespeare's time; it had a special propriety in the case of Elizabeth, since it

[16] In Plutarch's account of the myth, Isis is the material female principle, receptive of all form, and Osiris is form. They are like Venus and Adonis in Spenser's Garden of Adonis (*F. Q.*, III. vi). She is Egypt, and he the fertilizing Nile-water. Typhon, the destroyer, is dryness. But as crocodile he is both Sun-emperor and destroyer (like Octavius). Crocodiles are also predictors of the future. Osiris Plutarch assimilates with Dionysus (and in the *Lives* he compares Antony with that god). In the play Antony and Cleopatra think of Octavius as dry and destructive, and as the minister of *Chance* (Here there is also an allusion to the theme of *fortuna imperatoris*). We are expected to see him as the agent of providence, the herald of a new era and, incidentally, the first incumbent of the *Dignitas* currently enjoyed by James I.

[17] Kantorowicz, pp. 388–401. Claudian calls the Phoenix 'felix heresque tui' (*Phoenix*, line 101).

[18] M. C. Kirkpatrick, ed., *Lactanti de Ave Phoenice* (1933), p. 29.

also stood for virginity. The Phoenix was sexless or hermaphrodite, according to Lactantius, the great source of its lore: 'femina seu mas sit seu neutrum seu sit utrumque'; he also insists on its virginity: 'felix quae Veneris foedera nulla colit'.[19] The use of the Phoenix in the propaganda of the later Elizabeth—'semper eadem' —has been illustrated by Miss Frances Yates.[20] And half a century later the medal struck by English royalists to commemorate the death of Charles I showed the dead king on the obverse, and on the reverse a phoenix rising from its ashes and representing the immortal dignity.[21] Later the bird became the emblem of the British and American insurance house, signifying an *aevum* (sustained by your premiums) in which property, mortal in individual cases, achieves perpetuity as a species. This by no means exhausts the figurative significances of the phoenix; it stood also for 'felix renovatio temporum', as Elizabeth rememberd; and it was also the bird of the *saeculum*, the century—Milton's 'secular bird'.[22] It was the king or emperor of all the other birds, and is sometimes, as by Claudian, represented as receiving the praise and devotion of the others:

> conveniunt aquilae cunctaeque ex orbe volucres
> ut Solis mirentur avem.[23]

The Phoenix, then, concentrates clusters of learned themes. What did Shakespeare make of it? He was evidently preoccupied by problems of continuity and *dignitas*, and he alludes rather frequently to the Phoenix, sometimes with glancing familiarity, as when Iachimo calls Imogen 'the Arabian bird', meaning that she is unique, the most chaste of women. Cranmer's speech at the baptism of Elizabeth in *Henry VIII* makes James I the heir who will arise from the queen's virgin ashes; a prophecy by hindsight not only of her virginity but of the unusual transmission of the dignity to a new dynasty. But there is nothing greatly out of the

[19] *De Ave Phoenice*, lines 163, 164.

[20] F. A. Yates, 'Queen Elizabeth as Astraea', *Journal of the Warburg and Courtauld Institutes*, x (1948), 27–82. Also Roy C. Strong, *Portraits of Queen Elizabeth I* (1963), pp. 22, 60, 104, 109, 113, 114, 134, 156.

[21] Kantorowicz, p. 413. For the Phoenix as βασιλεύς see Jean Hubay and Maxime Leroy, *Le Mythe du Phénix* (*Bibliothèque de la Faculté de Philosophie et Lettres de l'Université de Liége*, lxxxii, 1939), p. 130; and Claudian, *Phoenix*, lines 83–88.   [22] Hubay-Leroy, p. 218.

[23] *Ad Stilichonem*, ii. 418–19; Hubay-Leroy, p. 129.

way in that passage, whether or not Shakespeare wrote it; whereas everybody agrees that 'The Phoenix and the Turtle' is out of the way.

I take it we should agree that there is not much to be learned about Shakespeare's poem from the other poems in *Loves Martyr*. Chester, of course, was responsible for introducing the Turtle into what might seem the self-sufficient life of the Phoenix. Nobody has ever succeeded in saying what Chester's poem is about. If he is really talking about the marriage of Sir John Salisbury, it follows, as Chambers observed, that Shakespeare did not read the poem closely, since the marriage was not childless.[24] In Chester the two birds discuss true love, and then, Turtle first, throw themselves on a pyre in the expectation of some even better Phoenix from the ashes. Before this, Nature, before bringing the birds together, offers the Phoenix a survey of English history, and especially of King Arthur's life (King Arthur was a notable Phoenix; he rose again as a Tudor king). At the end of the poem the Pelican confusedly argues that the Phoenix, though unique, is improved by union with a bird symbolizing constancy, which will give the new Phoenix what it surely should not have lacked, 'loue and chastitie'.[25] Chester's poem is obviously one which remains confused about its occasion, and for this reason (and, I suspect, his having cleared out his desk and fitted all the extraneous matter into the long poem) it is likely to remain a kind of Bottom's Dream. But some better poets added verses on the theme. The first, Ignoto, ignores the Turtle and stresses only the uniqueness and self-perpetuation of the Phoenix ('Her rare-dead ashes fill a rare-line urn').[26] The second is Shakespeare. Marston, following him, briefly mentions the turtle, but then embarks on a crabbed celebration of the new Phoenix, 'God, Man, nor Woman',[27] (recalling the passage of Lactantius already quoted). Chapman, though celebrating 'the male Turtle', dwells only on the perfection of his beloved 'Whome no prowd flockes of other Foules could moue, But in her selfe all companie concluded'.[28] Jonson lengthily celebrates voluntary chastity, and the constancy of 'a person like our *Doue*'[29] to his phoenix. None of them needed

[24] E. K. Chambers, *William Shakespeare* (1930), i. 549–50.
[25] Robert Chester, *Loves Martyr*, ed. A. B. Grosart (1878), p. 132.
[26] Grosart, p. 181.   [27] Ibid., p. 185.
[28] Ibid., p. 188.   [29] Ibid., p. 193.

more than the title and a hazy idea of the contents of Chester's poem. Some of Marston's hyperbole suggests that he must be thinking of the queen, though one cannot be certain of that in the age of Donne's *Anniversaries*; and if one wanted to develop the point one would have to use the Pelican's speech, since the Pelican was another of Elizabeth's birds. I doubt, indeed, whether all the contempt poured on Grosart's theory, that the poem has to do with the queen and Essex, is justified; Chester could just have been talking about the death of Essex and the almost mortal grief of the queen, and the other poets could have had it in mind.

But we had better not depend on the other contributors. It seems likely enough, of course, that writing at the end of a reign (and the end of a century) the poets, invited to reflect for whatever occasion on the Phoenix, would remember the old queen, her body natural in decay, her dignity seeming all too mortal in the uncertainty of the succession (she would hardly, like Shakespeare's Cranmer, think of James of Scotland in that way). Yet the only one of these learned men who really did meditate the Phoenix emblem, consider all its deep meanings, was Shakespeare.

> Here the Antheme doth commence:
> Loue and Constancie is dead;
> *Phoenix* and the *Turtle* fled
> In a mutuall flame from hence.
>
> So they loued, as loue in twaine,
> Had the essence but in one;
> Two distinct, Diuision none;
> Number there in loue was slaine.
>
> Hearts remote, yet not asunder;
> Distance, and no space was seene,
> 'Twixt the *Turtle* and his Queene:
> But in them it were a wonder.
>
> So betweene them Loue did shine,
> That the *Turtle* saw his right,
> Flaming in the *Phoenix* sight;
> Either was the other's mine.

Propertie was thus appalled,
   That the selfe was not the same:
   Single Natures double name
Neither two nor one was called.

Reason in it selfe confounded,
   Saw Diuision grow together,
   To themselues yet either neither,
Simple were so well compounded,

That it cried, how true a twaine
   Seemeth this concordant one,
   Loue hath Reason, Reason none,
If what parts, can so remaine.

How did he go about it? He must have known Lactantius, as T. W. Baldwin argues, and he would also remember the parrot in Ovid (*Amores*, II. 6).[30] Baldwin says that the poem is about married chastity, and a charming variation, in the Lactantian vein, on Ovid's parrot and the sparrow of Catullus. And certainly the old phoenix is there, with its 'wondrous voice,' inimitable even by the nightingale or the dying swan; its lack of sex, its chorus of birds. Above all, Lactantius is present, in the poem, when it says that 'the selfe was not the same'; 'ipse quidem sed non eadem est, eademque nec ipsa est'.[31] Translating this, Shakespeare rather characteristically plays on the two parts of the English word *selfsame*, achieving by a sort of pun what Lactantius does by profuse repetition. On these words of Lactantius, quoted by Shakespeare, depends most of the traditional emblematic quality of the phoenix as continuity in the *aevum*.

So we are here very close to a large and difficult body of learning, one in which, as we have seen, Shakespeare elsewhere showed some interest. And his language in the poem is obviously learned. No one has written about it so well as J. V. Cunningham;

[30] See, for a lengthy analysis, T. W. Baldwin, *Literary Genetics of Shakespere's Poems*, pp. 363 ff.

[31] *De Ave Phoenice*, line 169. As elsewhere in the poem, there are many variant readings, including 'Est eadem sed non eadem, quae est ipsa nec ipsa est', which is preferred by Hubay-Leroy.

indeed, his is the best essay ever written on this poem.[32] He shows that the terminology is borrowed from scholastic enquiries into the Trinity, where you have to go to find 'distinct persons' with only one essence. 'Two distincts, Diuision none'—as Aquinas observes, 'to avoid the Arian heresy . . . we must avoid the terms *diversity* and *difference* so as not to take away the unit of essence; we can, however, use the term *distinction* . . . we must [also] avoid the terms *separation* and *division*, which apply to parts of a whole . . .' (*S.T.*, I, 31. 2). 'Number' is 'slain' because plurality is a consequence of division; as the mathematicians said, 'One is no number'. 'Distance and no space' is from the argument for the co-eternality of the Persons of the Trinity. 'Property' (the *proprium*) is the quality that distinguishes separate persons; it is 'appalled' in Shakespeare because what ought to characterize only one person here characterizes two. But the English word can hardly be used purely in this sense, and the less technical reference to matters of *meum* and *tuum* is here also present, outraged because of this ideal commonwealth ('either was the other's mine'). 'Reason' is confounded because it has to work by division, and in these 'distincts' there is no 'division'. Love has achieved what Reason cannot.

So St. Thomas is also behind the poem. Cunningham refers to the *Summa Theologica*, I. 31, 'de his quae ad unitatem vel pluralitatem pertinent in divinis'. The Thomist paradoxes and distinctions become strained, even tragic, because of the difficulty of making such points in English. Aquinas can develop distinctions between *alium* and *alienum*, *alius* and *aliud*, the first relating to a difference *secundum personas*, the second to a difference *secundum essentiam* (I. 21. 2). For the momentary establishment of such distinctions Shakespeare torments English terminology; it is a learned and sombrely witty torture.

Yet even granting that, we may be reluctant to think of Shakespeare as working with the *Summa* open before him. How, then, did he know about this? The answer is that this scholastic terminology persisted and was in common enough use. To speak of the Father and Son as distinct Persons with but one essence

---

[32] J. V. Cunningham, 'Idea as Structure: *The Phoenix and the Turtle*', in *Tradition and Poetic Structure* (1960), pp. 76 ff. There are some useful insights in A. Alvarez, 'The Phoenix and the Turtle', in *Interpretations*, ed. J. Wain (1955), pp. 1–16.

was familiar theology—Hooker, as Cunningham reports, even says that 'their distinction cannot admit separation'.[33] And when Bacon wanted for a legal purpose to argue that 'it is one thing to make things distinct, another to make them separable', he clinches the point with a scholastic tag: 'aliud est distinctio, aliud separatio.'[34]

Bacon's argument occurred in a plea of 1608. The question was whether natives of either Scotland or England, born after the accession of James I, should be naturalized in both kingdoms. The King's natural body, reasons Bacon, operates upon his body politic, so that although his bodies politic as King of England and King of Scotland 'be several and distinct, yet nevertheless his natural person, which is one ... createth a privity between them'.[35] Because of this privity, a Scots subject of the king's natural person must also be a subject of his English body politic. His person and crown are 'inseparable though distinct', like the persons of the Trinity. The language which a contemplation of the Phoenix educes from Shakespeare is, in short, a language based upon certain paradoxes still indispensable to theology and constitutional law. Spenser, as I have argued elsewhere, was interested in them; and now it seems clear that Shakespeare, invited to dwell upon the Phoenix, related it to precisely this complex of paradoxes concerning continuity, number, property, and so forth. They derive from scholastic thought, but are variously associated with the figure of the Phoenix, which makes them available in many contexts: dynastic, imperial, legal, constitutional. They can suggest the Tudor renovation, the virginity of the last Tudor, the end of a century and a dynasty. Who can say whether some particular aspect of all this was in Shakespeare's mind? It seems almost impossible that he shut out from his mind all the broader implications of the theme: the end of the century, for which the secular bird could stand; the decay of the Phoenix Elizabeth, with no certainty, in 1601, of the survival of her Dignity. Perhaps he uses the strange intrusive dove, as a figure for the hermaphroditic relation of the Queen's two bodies.

And yet for our present purposes it is enough to say that he

---

[33] Cunningham, p. 87.

[34] 'Case of the Postnati of Scotland', in *Works*, ed. Spedding, Ellis and Heath (1861), xv. 234.

[35] Ibid., p. 227.

gave in this poem a rather strict metaphysical expression to concepts—the *aevum*, the dignity, the double name of natural beings—which had long interested him. Perhaps he *was*, after all, as the editions say, thinking of a chastely married pair, and that from such a point of departure all the rest was made to follow. But this sequel is what concerns us. It is learned, but not so learned that only a scholar could possess the materials of which it is made; its language, though wrought from a technical vocabulary, is freestanding, the language of a poet and not of a scholar, the language of a man whose craft is learned but not scholarly.

I have gone a long way about to make this point, which is the centre of my argument. We do not need to think of a very learned Shakespeare, but we do need to think of a Shakespeare who was capable of an intense interest—intense, yet sometimes at the same time wanton or even perverse—in the formulae of learning: a strong-minded, wilful, private, reading man. This is at any rate a way out of the old dilemma; if you measure his learning or his mind by some entirely inappropriate calculus, he emerges as a natural, all wit and no art, or, on the other hand, as the slave of familiar text books and homiletic commonplaces, all art and no wits. What we shall have instead is a plausible representation of a great poet: a speculative, interested man, a man of great intellectual force, who employs that force in poetry.

9

THE MATURE COMEDIES

The purpose of this chapter is briefly to characterize the mature comedies; and more, to suggest that they are the best of the comedies and that they do not often have the common good luck to be read decently. Nobody will want a demonstration that *Twelfth Night* and *As You Like It* are better plays than *Two Gentlemen of Verona* and *Comedy of Errors*, but the view that this group is in important ways superior to the 'Romances' is unorthodox, and it might be useful to start with a few remarks on *Cymbeline*. I speak only of an isolated aspect of *Cymbeline* but believe my conclusions to be applicable also to *The Tempest*.

Few would disagree that the plot of *Cymbeline* is monstrous—and it might even be called a fantastic design made by a past-master for the sake of showing that he could do pretty well anything. Some of the difficulties of *Cymbeline* can best be explained on that supposition. Much of the verse in the play has undoubtedly that special harsh excellence which goes with what Mr. John Wain has called Shakespeare's 'mature manner of kinaesthetic unification'.[1] But sometimes it is very strange; it draws attention to its own opacity. An example of this is the performance of Iachimo, who first approaches Imogen with such energetic obliquity that she cannot catch his drift (I. vii). Cloten is also addressed in verse so difficult that he can only strain feebly after its meaning. Thus his mother counsels him:

> Frame yourself
> To orderly soliciting, and be friended
> With aptness of the season; make denials

---

[1] 'The Mind of Shakespeare' in *More Talking of Shakespeare*, ed. J. Garrett (1959), pp. 159-72.

> Increase your services; so seem as if
> You were inspired to do thos duties which
> You tender to her; that you in all obey her,
> Save when command to your dismission tends,
> And therein you are senseless.
>
> (II. iii. 51)

Cloten, imagining some insult, replies only with 'Senseless? Not so'. Less than a hundred lines on Imogen repulses him in these terms:

> His meanest garment,
> That ever hath but clipp'd his body, is dearer
> In my respect than all the hairs above thee,
> Were they all made such men.
>
> (138)

and again Cloten hangs on to the insult, a real one this time: he seizes one expression, 'His mean'st garment', and will not let it go. 'His garment! . . . His garment! . . . His meanest garment! . . . His mean'st garment! Well!' The object of this is not to inform us of Cloten's stupidity; he often talks pretty kinaesthetically himself. But out of his failure to understand Shakespeare's mature verse there develops a remarkable bout of dramaturgical juggling. Posthumus' clothes begin to usurp the stage. It is true that they connect with a certain thematic interest in the play—the relation between nature and nurture, and between truth and seeming. Metaphors from clothes are commonly used for these purposes. But the way in which they are used here does not, I think, contribute to our understanding of those themes, if only because they are so wantonly complicated. For instance: the physique of Posthumus is that of a nonpareil; but that of Cloten equals it. Finding the headless body of Cloten dressed in the clothes of Posthumus, Imogen identifies the corpse as her husband's not only by the garments but by the physique:

> A headless man! The garments of Posthumus!
> I know the shape of's leg; this is his hand;
> His foot Mercurial; his Martial thigh;
> The brawns of Hercules; but his Jovial face—
>
> (IV. ii. 308)

The clothes fit him. All his difference from Posthumus is concentrated in his head, which is accordingly given specially rough treatment by the King's sons. The moral of this is obviously not that 'Thersites' body is as good as Ajax | When neither are alive'; indeed it is hard to see any moral at all. And the more one looks at all the to-do about clothes, the more difficult it becomes. Cloten dressed himself as Posthumus in order to satisfy a curious desire to enjoy Imogen in her husband's clothes and then 'cut them to pieces before her face'. He declares this intention first in III. v. to Pisanio, and then in a strange soliloquy:

> Why should his mistress, who was made by him that made
> the tailor, not be fit too? the rather—saving reverence of the
> word—for 'tis said a woman's fitness comes by fits. Therein
> I must play the workman. I dare speak it to myself—for it
> is not vain-glory for a man and his glass to confer in his own
> chamber—I mean, the lines of my body are as well drawn as
> his; no less young, more strong, not beneath him in fortunes,
> beyond him in the advantage of the time, above him in
> birth, alike conversant in general services, and more
> remarkable in single oppositions.
>
> (IV. i. 3)

But he is overcome by the true princes, dressed in skins. Shortly afterwards Posthumus, who on his departure was movingly described as waving a handkerchief, enters carrying a bloody handkerchief, and informs us that he proposes to change his clothes:

> I'll disrobe me
> Of these Italian weeds and suit myself
> As does a Briton peasant.
>
> (V. i. 22)

This will enable him to exhibit 'more valour . . . than my habits show' and set a new fashion 'less without and more within'. In this garb he defeats the astonished Iachimo, seeming to be only 'a very drudge of nature's' (V. ii. 5). Iachimo's error is that of the other characters; the King himself confesses that he had mistaken his queen, and 'thought her like her seeming' (V. v. 4). It is a small mouse to come of such labour. The whole thing has an air of wilful contrivance. It is a long way round to explain how Cloten is inferior to both Posthumus and the princes; the effect is

entirely different from that of the use of clothes in *Lear*, and forces
one to regard it as a deliberate technical excess: a bravura piece, an
example of the master doing something difficult—the intertwining
of a theme in texture and structure—with very great ease and for
its own sake. The same disinterested mastery is, I think, equally
evident in *The Tempest*; Strachey was wrong, but not as wrong as
it is pleasant to believe. Shakespeare was at this time less interested
in the great issues which had touched him and called forth incom-
parable technical resource; now he was more interested in the
technical means than their end.

That the Shakespeare of the last plays should have developed an
intense preoccupation with formal problems, a remarkable sophistication of means, is not surprising if one thinks of the demands
on his technical equipment during the early years of the new
century: he had worked out the incredibly original movement of
Macbeth, the revolutionary plotting of *Hamlet*, the contrapuntal
mazes of *Lear*. The apparatus *was* fascinating in his own right.
Perhaps, if we looked carefully for marks of this peculiar detachment, we should find them to a lesser degree in *As You Like It*
and in *Twelfth Night* also—at the point where, with *Hamlet* and
Troilus, radical new experiment ended a period of his work. But
one may still think of those plays as belonging to a time when
Shakespeare in comedy was capable of doing extraordinary and
beautiful things *at full pressure*; the cause of his inventions being
not technical display but the true comic theme. And this is the
sense in which one could legitimately say that the best of the
'mature' comedies are technically superior to all that came later;
I should myself be prepared to maintain that *A Midsummer
Night's Dream* is Shakespeare's best comedy.

With this play, and with *Twelfth Night*, criticism—inhibited
from the start by an historical failure to take the comedies seriously
—has been curiously slow to take the hint of the titles. From
the normal licence of St. John's Eve to the behaviour of Shakespeare's young lovers in the dark wood is a short step; Hardy
must have been aware of it when he wrote the twentieth chapter
of *The Woodlanders*, but only recently have critics taken their cue
from Frazer and seen something of the full import. What one
needs to add to this naïve theme is the recognition of an intense
sophistication. It is still probably too much to expect many
people to believe that the theme of *A Midsummer Night's Dream*

can be explained by references to Apuleius, to Macrobius and Bruno and so forth, and this is not the place to defend such modes of explanation, though they need defending as much as any others, including the view that the play means nothing much at all. Let us, for the sake of argument, assume that it is a play of marked intellectual content; that the variety of the plot is a reflection of an elaborate and ingenious thematic development; and that simple and pedestrian explanations of such developments have some value.

A Midsummer Night's Dream opens with a masterly scene which, as usual in the earlier Shakespeare, establishes and develops a central thematic interest. The accusation against Lysander is that he has corrupted the fantasy of Hermia (32), and the disorders of fantasy (imagination) are the main topic of the play. Hermia complains that her father cannot see Lysander with her eyes; Theseus in reply requires her to subordinate her eyes to her father's judgment (56–7) or pay the penalty. She is required to 'fit her fancies to her father's will'. All withdraw save Lysander and Hermia, who utter a small litany of complaint against the misfortunes of love: 'So quick bright things come to confusion'. This recalls not only *Romeo and Juliet* but also *Venus and Adonis* (the whole passage from l. 720 to l. 756 is related to *Midsummer Night's Dream*). This lament of 'poor Fancy's followers' gives way easily to their plot of elopement. Helena enters, in her turn complaining of ill-fortune; for Demetrius prefers Hermia's eyes to hers. Hermia leaves: 'we must starve our sight | From lover's food till morrow deep midnight'. Lysander, remembering that Helena 'dotes | Devoutly dotes, dotes in idolatry' (108–109) on Demetrius, departs, expressing a wish that Demetrius will come to 'dote' on Helena as she on him (225). The repetition of the word 'dote', the insistence that the disordered condition of the imagination which is called 'love' originates in eyes uncontrolled by judgment; these are hammered home in the first scene, and the characteristic lamentations about the brevity and mortality of love are introduced like a 'second subject' in a sonata. Finally Helena moralizes emblematically:

> And as he (Demetrius) errs, doting on Hermia's eyes,
> So I, admiring of his qualities:

Things base and vile, holding no quantity,
Love can transpose to form and dignity:
Love looks not with the eyes, but with the mind;
And therefore is wing'd Cupid painted blind:
Nor hath Love's mind of any judgment taste;
Wings and no eyes figure unheedy haste;
And therefore is Love said to be a child . . .

(230)

In love the eye induces 'doting', not a rational, patient pleasure like that of Theseus and Hippolyta. Helena is making a traditional complaint against the blind Cupid;[2] love has nothing to do with value, is a betrayal of the quality of the high sense of sight, and is therefore depicted blind, irresponsible, without judgment. Later we shall see the base and vile so transformed; love considered as a disease of the eye will be enacted in the plot. But so will the contrary interpretation of 'blind Love'; that it is a higher power than sight, indeed, above intellect. *Amor . . . sine oculis dicitur, quia est supra intellectum.*[3]

The themes of the play are thus set forth in the opening scene. Love-fancy as bred in the eye is called a kind of doting; this is held to end in disasters of the kind that overtook Adonis, Romeo, Pyramus; and the scene ends with an ambiguous emblem of blind love. The next scene introduces the play of the mechanicals, which, in a recognizably Shakespearian manner, gives farcical treatment to an important thematic element; for Bottom and his friends will perform a play to illustrate the disastrous end of doting, of love brought to confusion. Miss Mahood has spoken of Shakespeare's ensuring that in *Romeo and Juliet* 'our final emotion is neither the satisfaction we should feel in the lovers' death if the play were a simple expression of the *Liebestod* theme, nor the dismay of seeing two lives thwarted and destroyed by vicious fates, but a tragic equilibrium which includes and transcends both these feelings;'[4] and in *Midsummer Night's Dream* we are given a comic equilibrium of a similar kind. The 'moral' of the play is not to be as simple as, say, that of Bacon's essay 'Of Love': there it is said to be unreasonable that a man, 'made for the contemplation of heaven and all noble objects, should do nothing but

[2] See E. Panofsky, *Studies in Iconology* (1939), pp. 122–3, and p. 122, n. 74.
[3] Pico della Mirandola, quoted in Wind, *Pagan Mysteries of the Renaissance* (1958), p. 56.   [4] *Shakespeare's Wordplay* (1957), p. 72.

kneel before a little idol, and make himself subject, though not of the mouth (as beasts are) yet of the eye, which was given them for higher purposes'. Shakespeare's conclusion has not the simplicity of this: 'Nuptial love maketh mankind; friendly love perfecteth it; but wanton love corrupteth and embaseth it.' Yet, for the moment, the theme is blind love; and the beginning of the second act takes us into the dark woods. If we are willing to listen to such critics as C. L. Barber,[5] we shall take a hint from the title of the play and attend to the festival licence of young lovers in midsummer woods. Also we shall remember how far the woods are identified with nature, as against the civility of the city; and then we shall have some understanding of the movement of the plot. Puck is certainly a 'natural' force; a power that takes no account of civility or rational choice. He is, indeed, a blinding Cupid; and the passage in which he is, as it were, cupidinized is so famous for other reasons that its central significance is overlooked:

> That very time I saw, but thou couldst not,
> Flying between the cold moon and the earth,
> Cupid all arm'd; a certain aim he took
> At a fair vestal throned by the west,
> And loosed his love-shaft smartly from his bow,
> As it should pierce a hundred thousand hearts;
> But I might see young Cupid's fiery shaft
> Quench'd in the chaste beams of the watery moon,
> And the imperial votaress passed on,
> In maiden meditation, fancy-free.
> Yet mark'd I where the bolt of Cupid fell:
> It fell upon a little western flower,
> Before milk-white, now purple with love's wound,
> And maidens call it love-in-idleness.
> Fetch me that flower; the herb I shew'd thee once:
> The juice of it on sleeping eye-lids laid
> Will make or man or woman madly dote
> Upon the next live creature that it sees.
>
> (II. i. 155)

The juice used by Puck to bring confusion to the darkling lovers is possessed of all the force of Cupid's arrow, and is applied with

[5] *Shakespeare's Festive Comedy* (1959).

equal randomness. The eye so touched will dote; in it will be engendered a fancy 'for the next live thing it sees'. Puck takes over the role of blind Cupid. The love he causes is a madness; the flower from which he gets his juice is called 'Love-in-*idleness*', and that word has the force of wanton behaviour amounting almost to madness. The whole object is to punish Titania 'and make her full of hateful fantasies' (II. i. 258); and to end the naturally intolerable situation of a man's not wanting a girl who wants him (260–1). Puck attacks his task without moral considerations; Hermia and Lysander are lying apart from each other 'in human modesty' (II. ii. 57) but Puck has no knowledge of this and assumes that Hermia must have been churlishly rejected:

> Pretty soul! She durst not lie
> Near this lack-love, this kill-courtesy.

> (II. ii. 76)

Lysander awakes, his anointed eyes dote at once on the newly arrived Helena. He ingenuously attributes this sudden change to a sudden maturity:

> The will of man is by his reason sway'd;
> And reason says you are the worthier maid . . .
> Reason becomes the marshal to my will
> And leads me to your eyes . . .

> (115)

But in the next scene Bottom knows better: 'Reason and love keep little company nowadays'.

It is scarcely conceivable, though the point is disputed, that the love-affair between Titania and Bottom is not an allusion to *The Golden Ass*. In the first place, the plot of Oberon is like that of the Cupid and Psyche episode, for Venus then employs Cupid to avenge her by making Psyche (to whom she has lost some followers) fall in love with some base thing. Cupid, at first a naughty and indecent boy, himself becomes Psyche's lover. On this story were founded many rich allegories; out of the wanton plot came truth in unexpected guise. And in the second place, Apuleius, relieved by the hand of Isis from his ass's shape, has a vision of the goddess, and proceeds to initiation in her mysteries. On this narrative of Apuleius, for the Renaissance half-hidden in the enveloping commentary of Beroaldus, great superstructures of

platonic and Christian allegory had been raised; and there is every
reason to suppose that these mysteries are part of the flesh and
bone of *A Midsummer Night's Dream*.

The antidote by which the lovers are all restored 'to wanted
sight' is 'virtuous' (III. ii. 367), being expressed from 'Dian's
bud' (IV. i. 70) which by keeping men chaste keeps them sane.
So far the moral seems to be simple enough; the lovers have been
subject to irrational forces; in the dark they have chopped and
changed like the 'little dogs' of Dylan Thomas's story, though
without injury to virtue. But they will awake, and 'all this derision |
Shall seem a dream and fruitless vision' (III. ii. 370-1). Oberon
pities the 'dotage' of Titania, and will 'undo | This hateful imper-
fection of her eyes' (IV. i. 66); she will awake and think all this
'the fierce vexation of a dream' (72) and Puck undoes the confusions of the young lovers. In the daylight they see well, and
Demetrius even abjures the dotage which enslaved him to Hermia;
his love for Helena returns as 'natural taste' returns to a man
cured of a sickness (126 ff.). They return to the city and civility.
All are agreed that their dreams were fantasies; that they have
returned to health. But the final awakening of this superbly
arranged climax (as so often in the mature Shakespearian comedy
it occurs at the end of the fourth act) is Bottom's. And here the
'moral' defies comfortable analysis; we suddenly leave behind
the neat love-is-a-kind-of-madness pattern and discover that there
is more to ideas-in-poetry than ideas and verse.

> I have had a most rare vision. I have had a dream, past the
> wit of man to say what dream it was: man is but an ass if he
> go about to expound this dream . . . The eye of man hath
> not heard, the ear of man hath not seen, man's hand is not ·
> able to taste, his tongue to conceive, nor his heart to report,
> what my dream was.
>
> (IV. i. 202)

It must be accepted that this is a parody of 1 Corinthians ii. 9 ff.:

> Eye hath not seen, nor ear heard, neither have entered into
> the heart of man the things which God hath prepared for
> them that love him . . .
> Which things also we speak, not in the words which man's
> wisdom teacheth, but which the Holy Ghost teacheth . . .

Apuleius, after his transformation, might not speak of the initiation he underwent; but he was vouchsafed a vision of the goddess Isis. St. Paul was initiated into the religion he had persecuted by Ananias in Damascus. What they have in common is transformation, and an experience of divine love. Bottom has known the love of the triple goddess in a vision. His dream is of a different quality from the others'; they have undergone what in the Macrobian division (*Comm. in Somn. Scip.*, I. 3) is called the *phantasma*: Brutus glosses this as 'a hideous dream' (*J. Caesar*, II i. 65). But Bottom's dream is *oneiros* or *somnium*; ambiguous, enigmatic, of high import. And this is the contrary interpretation of blind love; the love of God or of Isis, a love beyond the power of the eyes. To Pico, to Cornelius Agrippa, to Bruno, who distinguished nine kinds of fruitful love-blindness, this exaltation of the blindness of love was both Christian and Orphic; Orpheus said that love was eyeless; St. Paul and David that God dwelt in darkness and beyond knowledge.[6] Bottom is there to tell us that the blindness of love, the dominance of the mind over the eye, can be interpreted as a means to grace as well as to irrational animalism; that the two aspects are, perhaps inseparable.

The last Act opens with the set piece of Theseus on the lunatic, the lover, and the poet. St. Paul speaks of the 'hidden wisdom' 'which none of the princes of this world know', which must be spoken of 'in a mystery'; and which may come out of the learned ignorance of 'base things of the world, . . . which . . . God hath chosen' (I Cor., ii). Theseus cannot understand these matters. In lunatics, lovers and poets, the imagination is out of control; it is the power that makes 'things unknown', as, so this orthodox psychologist implies, these are the disordered creations of the faculty when reason, whether because of love or lunacy or the poetic *furor*, is not in charge of it. The doubts of Hippolyta (V. i. 23 ff.) encourage us to believe that this 'prince of the world' may be wrong. The love of Bottom's vision complements the rational love of Theseus; Bottom's play, farcical as it is, speaks of the disasters that do not cease to happen but only become for a moment farcically irrelevant, on a marriage day. 'Tragical mirth . . . hot ice and wondrous strange snow' are terms not without their relevance; and the woods have their wisdom as well as the city.

[6] E. Wind, op. cit., pp. 57 ff.

Thus, without affectation, one may suggest the *skopos* of *A Midsummer Night's Dream*—the thematic preoccupation, the characteristic bursting through into action of what seems a verbal trick only (the talk of eyes). Unless we see that these mature comedies are thematically serious we shall never get them right. And it might even be added that *A Midsummer Night's Dream* is more serious in this way than *Cymbeline*, because the patterns of sight and blindness, wood and city, phantasma and vision, grow into a large and complex statement, or an emblematic presentation not to be resolved into its component parts, of love, vulgar and celestial. I should here mention the excellent essay on this play by Paul A. Olsen[7] who interprets the Macrobian dreams differently, and pays no attention to Apuleius or the imagery of eyes; on the other hand he has much to say about Oberon, the themes of conventional marriage entertainments, and the contrast between sensuality and married love. My own feeling is that he sacrifices too much to the view that *A Midsummer Night's Dream* is a very courtly play, and I do not think that we ever find in Shakespeare the kind of allegory he is looking for; he makes *A Midsummer Night's Dream* a slightly more diffuse *Hymenaei*. At present, however, the comedies may stand to lose less by over- than by under-interpretation, and Olsen's is one of the best essays on a Shakespearian comedy I have ever read. One may hope that it will be influential, but that others may point to simpler meanings that are overlooked because of our bondage to an old tradition: the tradition of Shakespeare's 'natural' genius, still potent in respect of the earlier comedies, and still capable of preventing us from studying him as an artist.

It is my intention to write with equal simplicity of *Twelfth Night*, but it would be wrong to suggest that only in the festive comedies does one find these methods employed, and so I may be allowed briefly to make the point that *The Merchant of Venice* is similarly designed. The point is that all the comedies are 'problem' comedies; that *The Two Gentlemen of Verona* is a legend of Friendship

[7] '*A Midsummer Night's Dream* and the Meaning of Court Marriage' (*English Literary History*, 1957, pp. 95–119). Many of the points I make above are made by Mr. Olsen (I may mention that my own reading is one I have long developed in lectures; this is to some extent a concurrence of independent testimony).

(see, for instance, *Faerie Queene*, iv. 9. 2–3, which could be a prologue to Shakespeare's play), *A Midsummer Night's Dream* of love, *As You Like It* of courtesy, and *The Merchant of Venice* of justice. It is a much simpler play than *A Midsummer Night's Dream*. We are not likely, whether or not we share his high opinion of Shakespeare as a comic writer, to fall into Johnson's error when he dismissed the reiteration of the word 'gentle' in this play as only another example of Shakespeare's weakness for his 'fatal Cleopatra', the pun. 'Gentleness' in this play means civility in its old full sense, nature improved; but it also means 'Gentile', in the sense of Christian, which amounts, in a way, to the same thing. Here are some of the passages in which it occurs:

> Hie thee, gentle Jew.
> The Hebrew will turn Christian: he grows kind.
>
> (I. iii. 178)

> If e'er the Jew her father come to heaven,
> It will be for his gentle daughter's sake.
>
> (II. iv. 34)
>
> (Jessica is also called 'gentle' in l. 19)

> Now, by my hood, a Gentile [gentle] and no Jew.
>
> (II. vi. 51)

> . . . to leave a rich Jew's service and become
> The follower of so poor a gentleman.
>
> (II. ii. 756)

The Duke urges Shylock to be merciful; asking him not only to

> loose the forfeiture,
> But, touch'd with human gentleness and love,
> Forgive a moiety of the principal. . . .
> We all expect a gentle answer, Jew.
>
> (IV. i. 24)

Other 'gentle' objects are Antonio's ships, and Portia, many times over; and Portia speaks of mercy as a 'gentle rain'.

There is a straightforward contrast between gentleness, the 'mind of love', and its opposite, for which Shylock stands. He lends money at interest, which is not only unchristian, but an obvious misdirection of love; Antonio ventures with his ships, trusts his wealth to the hand of God (and so they are 'gentle' ships). It is true that a Jew hath eyes etc.; this does not reduce the difference between man and man, when one is gentle and the other not. To make all this clear, Shakespeare twice inserts the kind of passage he later learned to do without; the kind which tells the audience how to interpret the action. It is normal to cut these scenes in acting texts, but only because these plays are so grossly misunderstood. The first such is the debate on Genesis xxxi. 37 ff. (Jacob's device to produce ringstraked, speckled and spotted lambs) which occurs when Antonio first asks for the loan (I. iii. 66 ff.). The correct interpretation of this passage, as given by Christian commentators on Genesis (see A. Williams, *The Common Expositor*, 1950), is that Jacob was making a venture ('A thing not in his power to bring to pass, | But sway'd and fashion'd by the hand of heaven'; compare *Faerie Queene*, V. iv). But Shylock sees no difference between the breeding of metal and the breeding of sheep—a constant charge against usurers (see J. R. Brown's note on the passage in his Arden edition, where he rightly points out that this was commonplace). Later, in II. viii, we have a pair of almost Spenserian *exempla* to make this point clear. First Solanio describes Shylock's grief at the loss of daughter and ducats; he cannot distinguish properly between them, or lament the one more than the other. Then Solario describes the parting of Antonio and Bassanio; Antonio urges Bassanio not even to consider money; the loss of Bassanio is serious, but he urges him to be merry and not to think of Shylock's bond. When love is measured out, confused by the 'spirit of calculation' (R. B. Heilman's phrase in his discussion of the errors of Lear),[8] the result is moral chaos.

Bassanio's visit to Belmont is frankly presented as a venture, like Jason's for the Golden Fleece; and the theme of gentle venturing is deepened in the scenes of the choice of caskets. The breeding metals, gold and silver, are to be rejected; the good lead requires that the chooser should 'give and hazard all he hath'. Morocco (II. vii) supposes that Portia cannot be got by any casket save the golden one, tacitly confusing her living worth with that of gold, the value of gentleness with that of the best breeding metal.

[8] 'The Unity of *King Lear*' in *Critiques & Essays in Criticism 1920–1948*, ed. R. W. Stallman (1949), pp. 154–61; and see Heilman, *This Great Stage* (1943.)

Arragon (II. ix—the intervening scene contains the lamentation of Shylock over his daughter-ducats) rejects gold out of pride only, ironically giving the right reasons for despising the choice of the 'many', that they are swayed not by Truth but by Opinion, a mere false appearance of Truth, not Truth itself. (In this sense the Jews are enslaved to Opinion.) He chooses silver because he 'assumes desert', another matter from trusting to the hand of God; and his reward is 'a shadow's bliss'. After another scene in which Shylock rejoices over Antonio's losses and again laments Jessica's treachery, there follows (III. ii) the central scene of choice, in which Bassanio comes to 'hazard' (2) and 'venture' (10) for Portia. The point of the little song is certainly that in matters of love the eye is a treacherous agent, and can mistake substance for shadow. Bassanio, rejecting the barren metals which appear to breed, avoids the curse of barrenness on himself (for that is the punishment of failure); and he finds in the leaden casket Portia's true image. The scroll speaks of the 'fortune' which has fallen to him (133). Portia, in her happiness, speaks of Bassanio's prize as not rich enough, deploring the poorness of her 'full sum' (158); and Gratiano speaks of the forthcoming marriage as the solemnization of 'the bargain of your faith'. Bassanio the merchant has 'won the fleece'; but at the same moment Antonio has lost his (243–4). Bassanio is 'dear bought', as Portia says; but Antonio will not have him return for any reason save love: 'if your love do not persuade you to come, let not my letter' (322).

At this point the conflict between gentleness (Antonio's laying down his life for his friend) and a harsh ungentle legalism becomes the main burden of the plot. Shylock demands his bond; this is just, like Angelo's strict application of the law against fornication in the hard case of Claudio. It is, in a way, characteristic of Shakespeare's inspired luck with his themes that Shylock in the old stories will take flesh for money. There is no substantial difference: he lacks the power to distinguish gold, goat's flesh, man's flesh, and thinks of Antonio's body as carrion. The difference between this and a 'gentle' attitude reflects a greater difference:

Duke: How shalt thou hope for mercy, rendering none?
Shylock: What judgement shall I dread, doing no wrong?

(IV. i. 87)

There is no need to sentimentalize this; as Shakespeare is careful to show in *Measure for Measure* the arguments for justice are strong, and in the course of Christian doctrine it is necessarily satisfied before mercy operates. Mercilla has her blunted sword, but also the sharp one for punishment, and she 'could it sternly draw' (*Faerie Queene*, V. ix. 30). Shylock has legally bought his pound of flesh; if he does not get it 'there is no force in the decrees of Venice' (IV. i. 102). But as heavenly mercy is never deserved, it is an adornment of human authority to exercise it with the same grace:

> . . . . earthly power doth then show likest God's
> When mercy seasons justice. Therefore, Jew,
> Though justice be thy plea, consider this,
> That, in the course of justice, none of us
> Should see salvation.

(196)

But this plea does not work on the stony unregenerate heart; Shylock persists in the demand for justice, and gets it. Like any other human being, he must lose all by such a demand. In offering to meet the demands of strict justice (in accordance with the Old Law) Antonio will pay in blood the price of his friend's happiness; and it cannot be extravagant to argue that he is here a type of the divine Redeemer, as Shylock is of the unredeemed.

Shakespeare's last act, another 'thematic' appendix to the dramatic action, is motivated by the device of the rings. It begins with a most remarkable passage, Lorenzo's famous 'praise of music'. In this are treated 'topics' which, as James Hutton shows in an extremely important study,[9] are all evidently the regular parts of a coherent and familiar theme—so familiar indeed, that Shakespeare permits himself to treat it 'in a kind of shorthand'. The implications of this 'theme' are vast; but behind it lies the notion, very explicit in Milton's 'Ode at a Solemn Musick', of the universal harmony impaired by sin and restored by the Redemption. The lovers, in the restored harmony of Belmont, have a debt to Antonio:

> You should in all sense be much bound to him,
> For, as I hear, he was much bound for you.

(V. i. 136)

---

[9] 'Some English Poems in Praise of Music', *English Miscellany*, II (1951), 1–63.

In such an atmosphere the amorous sufferings of Troilus, Thisbe, Dido and Medea are only shadows of possible disaster, like the mechanicals' play in *A Midsummer Night's Dream*; Antonio on his arrival is allowed, by the *contretemps* of the ring-plot, to affirm once more the nature of his love, standing guarantor for Bassanio in perpetuity, 'my soul upon the forfeit' (V. i. 252). *The Merchant of Venice*, then, is 'about' judgment, redemption and mercy; the supersession in human history of the grim four thousand years of unalleviated justice by the era of love and mercy. It begins with usury and corrupt love; it ends with harmony and perfect love. And all the time it tells its audience that this is its subject; only by a determined effort to avoid the obvious can one mistake the theme of *The Merchant of Venice*.

One could perhaps not say so of *Twelfth Night*, a subtler play, and one in which Shakespeare's sophistication of method is already impressively evident. Pepys was fantastically wrong in calling it 'but a silly play, and not at all related to the name or day'; it is another 'festive' comedy.

Two aspects (at least) of Twelfth Night celebrations are relevant to the theme of this play: the licence of appetite beyond what is normal (licensed misrule), and the confusion of authority and identity consequent upon ritual observances akin to those of the Boy Bishop.[10] The second of these interests led Shakespeare (as John Manningham perhaps noticed) to write a play 'much like the Comedy of Errors, or Menechmi in Plautus, but most like and neere to that in Italian called *Inganni*'. In fact, Shakespeare's most immediate debt was to Riche's *Apolonius and Silla*; but, as G. Bullough says, 'adaptations of Plautus were many in Italy, and *Twelfth Night* belongs to a tradition in which the Plautine twins became differentiated in sex, thus affording a greater variety of intrigue'.[11] The interest of this pre-history lies in Shakespeare's preoccupation with the comedy of mistaken identity, first as a brilliant apprentice-imitator in *Comedy of Errors*, later with an increasingly deep brooding over the truth hidden in the dramatic convention; for, if it is accepted that all our dealings with reality

[10] Details of these customs are everywhere available and indeed well known from such works as Chambers' *Medieval Stage*, and Welsford's *The Fool* (1935).

[11] *Narrative and Dramatic Sources of Shakespeare*, II (1958), 270.

are affected by an inability certainly to distinguish between what
is said and what is meant, between things as they are and as they
appear to be, between Truth and Opinion, then the comic errors
develop a peculiar relevance to life itself.

Here follows examples of confusion:

> *Viola:* I am not that I play. Are you the lady of the house?
> *Olivia:* If I do not usurp myself, I am.
> *Viola:* Most certain, if you are she, you do usurp yourself.
>
> (I. v. 196)

> Thou canst not choose but know who I am.
>
> (II. v. 152)

[The postscript of the trick letter to Malvolio; he *can* choose, and
chooses wrong.]

> Who you are and what you would is out of my welkin.
>
> (III. i. 64)

[Feste to Viola, followed by her remarks on the wise fool.]

> *Viola:* You do think you are not what you are.
> *Olivia:* If I think so, I think the same of you.
> *Viola:* Then think you right: I am not what I am.
> *Olivia:* I would you were as I would have you be!
> *Viola:* Would it be better, madam, than I am?
>
> (III. i. 151)

> Youth, whatsoever thou art, thou art but a scurvy fellow.
>
> (III. iv. 161)

[Sir Andrew's challenge to Viola.]

> ... as the old hermit of Prague, that never saw pen and ink,
> very wittily said to a niece of King Gorboduc, 'That that is
> is'; so I, being master Parson, am master Parson; for, what is
> 'that' but that, and 'is' but is?
>
> (IV. ii. 15)

[Feste about to torment Malvolio, claiming to be what he is not.]

> No, I do not know you ... Nothing that is so is so (IV. i. 5)
> [Feste to Sebastian.]

> Be that thou know'st thou art. (V. i. 209)
> [Olivia to Viola.]

> One face, one voice; one habit and two persons!
> A natural perspective that is and is not!   (V. i. 223)
> [Orsino, at the confrontation of Sebastian and Viola. A
> 'perspective' was an optical toy; the picture was different as
> viewed from one side and the other.]

And so forth. This is not a mere verbal trick. It is reinforced in the
language: Sir Andrew's tautology, proved wrong by the other
revellers—'to be up late is to be up late' (II. iii. 5); the language of
the taunting clown, like that of the menacing Belsey Bob in the
Mummers' Plays: 'it hath bay windows as transparent as barri-
cados, and the clerestories toward the south north are as lustrous
as ebony' (IV. ii. 36).

The plot of the play turns, of course, on the errors arising from
the apparent sameness of Sebastian and Viola; what appears to
be so is not so. Similarly Orsino and Olivia are deceived by their
own appetites (see the opening speech and II. iv. 96 ff.; also the
clown's comment earlier in the scene). Orsino's love and Olivia's
mourning are, as the wise fool says, foolish. The wise fool himself is a centre of paradoxes, carefully pointed out by Viola:

> For folly that he wisely shows is fit;
> But wise men, folly-fall'n, quite taint their wit.
>
>   (III. i. 74)

Sir Andrew is a mock-knight, 'dubb'd with unhatched rapier and
on carpet consideration' (III. iv. 257), with none of the powers
he pretends to. Malvolio is a mock gentleman ('as I am a gentleman' IV. ii. 88). Viola ('I see you what you are' I. v. 269) and
Sebastian ('This *is* the air; that *is* the glorious sun; | This pearl
she gave me, I do feel 't and see 't; | And though 'tis wonder
that enwraps me thus, | Yet 'tis not madness', IV. iii. 1 ff.) retain
their grasp of reality; they each play shadow to the other's substance. Yet in the duel the mock knight challenges the mock
man; to be knight and coward, woman and man at once is no
more out of the way than to be at once wise and foolish, like
Orsino, Olivia and Feste. The only character who is held to be
precisely what he seems to be is Viola's captain:

> . . . though that nature with a beauteous wall
> Doth oft close in pollution, yet of thee
> I will believe thou hast a mind that suits

With this thy fair and outward character.
I prithee, and I'll pay thee bounteously,
Conceal me what I am . . .

(I. ii. 48)

The climactic scene is the tormenting of Malvolio; a mock-madman teased by a mock-priest, and in the language of twelfth-night madness, or, for that matter, 'midsummer madness', as Olivia says (III. iv. 61). Here, under the volley of nonsense, Malvolio, though deserving to be the butt of Misrule, achieves some dignity by his claim that he thinks 'nobly of the soul' and is no madder than the others; no madder, at any rate, than a fool.

Over this play, as over *As You Like It*, are the shadows of Fortune and Nature at strife; Fortune rules the outside ('Fortune forbid my outside have not charm'd her!') and Nature the true quality (II. iv. 83 ff.). To call *Twelfth Night* a play about self-knowledge or the possibility of it in a world where Fortune domineers and appetite confuses, would be to put it too simply; out of the comic errors, out of the Plautine twins, has come a comedy of identity, set on the borders of wonder and madness. It is a more subtle play than either *A Midsummer Night's Dream* or *The Merchant of Venice*; the work of a great artist engrossed in the examination of his medium. The ancient theme gives rise to profound technical experiment (much as the almost contemporary *Hamlet* is a fiercely experimental play on an old subject) and we can see how the same hand later would set itself master-problems in dramaturgy almost entirely for the sake of solving them, as in *Cymbeline*.

10

THE FINAL PLAYS

INTRODUCTION

After the tragedies Shakespeare, perhaps working in Stratford, seems to have discovered a new vein; and it is widely agreed that the Last Plays—the Romances, as they may with some accuracy be labelled—form a distinct group, being, in the words of Philip Edwards, 'more closely related than any other group of Shakespeare's plays'. The dates of their composition are conjectural, but reasonably secure for all except the first: *Pericles* (1607), *Cymbeline* (1609), *The Winter's Tale* (1610), *The Tempest* (1611). Loosely associated with the group are *Henry VIII* (1613), which is more profitably treated with the other Chronicle plays; and *The Two Noble Kinsmen* (1612), said by the publisher of the first edition (1634) to be the work of Fletcher and Shakespeare. Whatever we may say of Shakespeare's part in it, *The Two Noble Kinsmen* is predominantly Fletcher's play, and our business is primarily with the first four works named above.

It is salutary to recall that the differences between these plays are very great, and that to neglect them is to risk inventing problems and preferring myth to fact; but all the same it may be convenient to begin by summarizing the ways in which the Romances resemble each other. First, they all seem to be affected by a new disregard for psychological and narrative plausibility, by a metrical freedom which goes beyond anything in earlier plays, and finally —to quote the most notorious of their detractors, Lytton Strachey —by a failure of 'concentrated artistic determination and purpose'. Secondly, there are more positive resemblances. All the Romances treat of the recovery of lost royal children, usually princesses of great, indeed semi-divine, virtue and beauty; they all bring important characters near to death, and sometimes feature almost miraculous resurrections; they all end with the healing, after many years of repentance and suffering, of some disastrous breach in the lives and happiness of princes, and this final reconciliation is usually brought about by the agency of beautiful young people; they all contain material of a pastoral character or otherwise celebrate natural beauty and its renewal.

These resemblances have naturally given rise to a great many different explanations. For example, it is argued that the implausibility and looseness of the plays are evidence that the author was feeling very serene or rather bored or merely playful. There may be a grain of truth in this, but one would need to express it differently: there is an element of play in the Romances, as of a master examining his medium in an unusually detached, experimental way. Another group of interpreters, thinking more of the positive resemblances, provides more or less allegorical explanations, assuming that Shakespeare had, like Yeats in his last years,

> a marvellous thing to say,
> A certain marvellous thing—

but that, unlike Yeats, he left no prose work to tell us what it was, so that impassioned guesswork is our sole resource. There is a long tradition of allegorical interpretation. *The Tempest* perhaps encourages this kind of attention more than the others, and it has long been read as a veiled farewell to the stage, or to poetry, but also as—for example—an Eleusinian or crypto-Masonic ritual. Allegory flourishes anew in the epoch of modern mythography, with modern anthropology, psychology and typology to sanction it; and the other Romances no longer escape. For Wilson Knight says they are 'myths of immortality', and D. G. James calls them failed myths. *The Winter's Tale* has lately been elaborately explained in at least three different ways as a Christian allegory.

It is true that much more is known about allegory, and about the thought of Shakespeare's age, than in the nineteenth century, when people wrote so badly about *The Tempest*; but it is possible that we in our turn may be accused of falling into equally obvious errors, and that much interpretation of this kind will be condemned as both wanton and limiting. There is probably more

staying power in less ambitious, more empirical approaches, like
E. M. W. Tillyard's theory that Shakespeare was working out a
development of tragedy into a scheme 'of prosperity, destruction,
and reconciliation'; this partly accounts for the tragi-comic aspect
of the plays, and for their general similarity, without demanding
of the reader the suspension of his common sense.

An explanation of an entirely different sort is that which offers
theatrical reasons for the characteristic features of the Romances.
It is no longer considered likely that Shakespeare, in *Cymbeline*,
could have been imitating Fletcher's *Philaster*, though the two
plays are somehow related; yet it remains possible that the Romances were written, as earlier plays of Shakespeare had been, in
response to a specific public demand. The long life, and the revival
in 1610 by Shakespeare's company, of the battered old play
Mucedorus suggest a public interest in dramatized romance, and
Pericles at least has something in common with this archaic play.
But we need not suppose that Shakespeare was archaizing, or
following a fashion set by Fletcher, to see the relevance of the
point that Shakespeare's company, from about 1609. was beginning
to play at the Blackfriars, an indoor theatre, which catered for a
richer audience than the great public play house across the river.
This house would create a demand for plays which could exploit
its superior facilities for music, scenery, and machinery. The
audience, for this was the era of the great masques, might well
require that the private theatre reflect the elaborate displays at
Court; and the actors were, as the King's servants, professionally
familiar with these entertainments. (There is indeed evidence that
they introduced elements of these masques into their own plays.)
Under the necessity of finding plays suitable for these new conditions, the King's Men perhaps sought the services of Fletcher,
who had already written for the private theatre, hitherto the
province of boys' companies; his play *The Faithful Shepherdess*,
though not a popular success, had been an experiment in the
European genre of pastoral tragi-comedy, with which some of
his later plays, and Shakespeare's, have a remote affinity. Altogether, then, one must not too easily dismiss the opinion of G. E.
Bentley, that in these plays we see Shakespeare, as a professional
man of the theatre, turning his attention to a new kind of play
especially suited to the Blackfriars. But it must be remembered
that his company continued to play at the Globe, and that *Pericles*,

Cymbeline, and *The Winter's Tale* were certainly, and *The Tempest* probably, performed there. Simon Forman saw *Cymbeline* and *The Winter's Tale* at the Globe during the summer of 1611. But this does not overthrow Bentley's theory, since plays could be put on in different kinds of theatre: perhaps at the Blackfriars in winter, at the Globe in summer. Of course, all this is conjecture, and even if it were true it would not rule out explanations of quite other kinds.

I believe the most profitable explanation is that which postulates a revival of theatrical interest in romance, and seeks the reason for it not so much in the older drama as in the great heroic romances of the period, Sidney's *Arcadia* and Spenser's *Faerie Queene*.[1] These works belong as romances, to a tradition stretching back to the Greek novel, but as epics they have purposes relevant to the highest kind of poetry. If one bears in mind that these books are highly serious in their ethical and political intentions, it may seem less surprising that Shakespeare could blend the improbabilities of romance plots with intentions evidently as profound. In heroic romance, characterization is governed by other forces than psychological verisimilitude: the wicked will be very wicked, the good very good. In *The Tempest* the noble are beautiful and the base ugly, which is an extension of platonic realities into the phenomenal world. The royal children, as possessors of high nobility, cannot be mistaken, for this inward quality shines through their bodies like godhead. The gods themselves may intervene in the action, or a noble magician may use invisible spirits to serve the ends of justice. When the world is observed from such a height, reality shows clearly under the veil of appearance. The sea which sunders lovers and royal families is not, as it appears to be, a type of chaos, but of providence; time is not, as it seems to be, the destroyer, but the redeemer. The mood of all these plays, in short, is not that of some improbable old man who wants to make everybody happy, but rather that of the *Cantos of Mutability*:

> All things stedfastnes do hate
> And changed be: yet being rightly wayd
> They are not changed from their first estate;
> But by their change their being doe dilate:

---

[1] On this see the Arden *Tempest*.

> And turning to themselues at length againe,
> Doe worke their own perfection so by fate.

A dramatist meditating these romance themes in terms of his own medium might well decide that the dramaturgical weight must fall not so much upon that part of the story which describes the sudden change of some royal fortune, not so much upon the *peripateia*, as upon the recognition, the moment of restoration and reconciliation. In *The Tempest* Shakespeare does not even show Prospero's deposition and banishment on the stage. But he always attends, with the utmost seriousness, and in some cases with extraordinary ingenuity, to the moment of recognition. Peter Ure observed of the 'problem' comedies that 'energy and meaning in the theatre may spring from the attempt to embody in its forms the very resistance which life offers to being translated into the expressive modes of art'. I think that Shakespeare must, from the time he worked on *Pericles*, have quite consciously been thinking about the possibilities of releasing such energy and meaning from the comic recognition. *Pericles*, in its last three acts, has the key-pattern of disaster, suffering, regeneration and reunion, and its final scene is surely so extraordinary that we could say that it might have discovered to its author interests and attitudes he had not thought to possess, and which he would want to explore in the dramaturgical context whereby he had discovered them.

This is not to suggest that other explanations, whether grander or more workaday than this, are entirely wrong. Indeed I do little more than develop a remark of Northrop Frye: 'The spirit of reconciliation . . . is not to be ascribed to some personal attitude of his own, but to his impersonal concentration on the laws of comic form.' In the Romances, this act of concentration was focussed on the recognition, which was to be studied with a new intensity and thoroughness in relation to romance-plots; for it has a special force in these extensive tales of sundered families, wandering kings, and lost princesses. And *Pericles* began it.

PERICLES, PRINCE OF TYRE

It is particularly unlucky, in view of its evident importance, that *Pericles* raises a number of technical problems which have so far evaded solution.

It was not included in the First Folio of 1623, and is the only play omitted from that collection which has ever been generally accepted into the canon of Shakespeare's works. Heminge and Condell, the friends of Shakespeare who put together the First Folio, may have left out *Pericles* because of copyright difficulties; or because they thought another writer had too much part in it; or because they could find no copy except the corrupt published Quartos. The last of these is the most likely reason, though the second is also quite possible.

Even if the play were wholly Shakespeare's we should still have to reconcile ourselves to the fact that we have only a corrupt report of it. But it is, almost certainly, not entirely his; some critics think it has no more right to a place in the canon than *The Two Noble Kinsmen*. Discussion on this point of authorship must turn on certain historical facts. The publication of an unauthorized *Pericles* in 1619 was preceded by the registration, in the name of a different publisher, of a book of the same name, which may have been the authorized text of Shakespeare's play, though it could also have related to an earlier version used by him. This edition was never published. In 1608 there appeared a novel by George Wilkins, called *The Painfull Adventures of Pericles, Prince of Tyre*, which claimed to be, as it were, the 'book of the play'. Though it borrows from another novel, Twine's *The Pattern of Painfull Adventures* (1576, reprinted 1607), Wilkins' book is certainly related to *Pericles*, and may derive from the same original as the extant text of the play. But the relationship is difficult to interpret; there are puzzling discrepancies; and some scholars think Wilkins was working with a version earlier than Shakespeare's.

A more fundamental difficulty is raised by the great change which comes over the play at the end of the second act. Acts I and II are mostly very poor stuff, but Shakespeare is quite certainly audible, if not in the Prologue to Act III, then in its opening lines:

> Thou god of this great vast, rebuke these surges,
> Which wash both heaven and hell; and thou that hast
> Upon the winds command, bind them in brass. . . .[2]
>
> (III. i. 1–3)

Unfortunately the old explanation that Shakespeare took over at this point (though he may have written a few superior passages

[2] Text here, and throughout, of Peter Alexander's edition (1951).

in the earlier part) is no longer acceptable, at any rate in so simple a form. Philip Edwards, for example, has argued that the Quarto is based on the work of two reporters, the first one very bad and working on the first two acts, the second handling the rest of the play much more faithfully. Professor Edwards will not say outright that 'the different aptitudes of the two reporters are the *sole* cause of the difference in literary value between the two halves of the play', but he inclines to that view. If he is right, the whole is Shakespeare's though we see it as if through two curtains, one very opaque and one fairly flimsy. What Wilkins used was also pure Shakespeare.

But of course the hypothesis that Shakespeare revised an earlier play could stand whether or no Professor Edwards's two reporters existed; and the theory that fits best an extremely complicated set of facts seems to be Kenneth Muir's: Shakespeare revised an old play; Wilkins used Shakespeare's version and perhaps in places the old play also; the piratical publisher of the Quarto used a reported text and perhaps glanced at Wilkins. It may be added that no reporter can be blamed for the structural crudity of I. iv, in which Cleon explains to his wife that Tharsus, once rich, is now famine-stricken, a fact of which she is naturally aware: 'Our cheeks and hollow eyes do witness it,' she says. Shakespeare had done nothing like that for years. And the Gower Prologues, which are much better reported throughout than anything else in the play, suddenly improve after the first two acts. So that, leaving behind problems which can never perhaps be fully solved, we may say that Shakespeare's interest begins, substantially, with the third act.

There are many guesses as to the identity of his co-author, but in these textual circumstances it is impossible to see how this figure could be identified. Whoever he was, we must suppose that he was responsible for the device of using as presenter the poet Gower, whose version of the narrative is found in Book viii of *Confessio Amantis*, though there the hero is Apollonius of Tyre (he is re-named Pericles only by Wilkins and Shakespeare). The story is very old; the original version was one of those Greek romances which lie behind much Elizabethan fiction. Shakespeare knew and used this kind of story as early as *The Comedy of Errors*, in which Aegeon's family is scattered in a tempest and reunited, after much Mediterranean wandering, a generation later. The presence of Gower is essential to *Pericles*, which is structurally little more than dramatized episodes from the narrative; he supplies links between them.

The first scene of the play is a reasonable sample of the archaic, stilted, sententious verse of the non-Shakespearian part. Pericles, seeking the hand of the Princess of Antioch, is tested by a riddle, which he correctly reads as signifying an incestuous relationship between the princess and her father. He betrays his knowledge and flees, pursued home by an assassin. His counsellor Helicanus very morally explains to him how to tell a friend from a flatterer, and then he is off again, before the assassin arrives. We next see him relieving the famine at Tharsus. Much honoured there, he nevertheless decides that 'in Tharsus was not best | Longer for him to make his rest'. On the way to Tyre he is shipwrecked, succoured by fishermen (the best scene of the first half) and wins a tournament where the prize is the daughter of Simonides of Pentapolis. His marriage with the princess Thaisa concludes the bad part of the play.

The story of the remaining acts, badly told, might seem to be of much the same kind. There is a storm at sea; Thaisa seems to die in childbirth, and is thrown overboard in a caulked chest. Washed ashore, she is revived by the priest-magician Cerimon. Pericles names his daughter Marina, puts into Tharsus to renew his acquaintance with Cleon and Dionyza, and leaves the baby there to be brought up. Marina is so accomplished that she overshadows the daughter of the King and Queen, whereupon Dionyza plots her murder. But she is carried off by pirates and sold into a brothel in Mytilene. There she successfully resists corruption, encounters the governor of the town, and is reunited with her father when his ship arrives at Mytilene. Prompted by a vision of Diana they go to Ephesus, and are reunited with Thaisa.

What, beside the quality of the verse, distinguishes this part from the first two acts? Simply the authors' way of thinking about the plot. Shakespeare chose stories not merely because they were stage-worthy, but because they had themes he might develop; in *As you like it*, for example, he seems almost to be less interested in Lodge's narrative than in certain ethical hints included in it. In Pericles there is a pattern which does not start till the storm at the beginning of the third act. A queen apparently dies, a princess is betrayed, a king moves endlessly over the sea from grief to grief, and finally to reunion and a restoration of harmony. It is almost as if Cordelia had not died, as if Lear's suffering, which, it seems, can change only by increase, should end, the worst having at last been reached, in a happiness of a kind which—in moments of peculiar insight—a man might think the proper issue of human affliction. The restoration of harmony dominates the whole play; after those early acts we find ourselves in a familiar environment, the Shakespearian drama in which all the action and suffering has a centre, and the work is an imaginative unity.

It is this imaginative coherence, felt through the limbs of the plot, that makes possible the extraordinary poetry of Pericles' lament:

> A terrible childbed hast thou had, my dear;
> No light, no fire. Th'unfriendly elements
> Forgot thee utterly; nor have I time
> To give thee hallow'd to thy grave, but straight
> Must cast thee, scarcely coffin'd, in the ooze;
> Where, for a monument upon thy bones,
> And aye-remaining lamps, the belching whale
> And humming water must o'erwhelm thy corpse,
> Lying with simple shells.
>
> (III. i. 56-64)

This verse is certainly, if we can purge the pejorative sense of the word, artificial; what the poet seeks is certainly not to have Pericles speak as a man would in such a plight, but by every artifice to give grief a possible new music. That a poet is always, however he may change, one poet, is a reflection prompted by the recollection of Clarence's submarine fantasy in *Richard III*. But the sea is more devotedly studied in these last plays, especially here and in *The Tempest*.

Out of it comes Marina, and we are repeatedly reminded that she is sea-born, tempest-born, not 'of any shores'; that she lives in a world of storm 'whirring me from my friends'. Marina is a most deliberate creation. She rises from the sea, like Venus, but plays out her part in a brothel. When we first see her she is scattering the sea with flowers, and here she has behind her the elaborately wrought figure of Florimell in *The Faerie Queene*, whose union with Marinell was so long delayed. The brothel scenes, though badly confused in the only text we have, are a calculated interruption of the ideal continuity of the plot, comparable with the juxtaposition in *Measure for Measure* of high debate on justice and equity with scenes of suburban fornication. Love, in *Pericles* is, in the end, the love that moves the sun and the other stars; but it has to live in a world where 'diseases have been sold dearer than physic', in which it is 'abominable' to speak 'holy words to the Lord Lysimachus', and in which a procurer can better Virtue in an argument:

> *Marina:* Thou hold'st a place for which the pained'st fiend
> Of hell would not in reputation change;
> Thou art the damned doorkeeper to every
> Coistrel that comes inquiring for his Tib;
> To the choleric fisting of every rogue
> Thy ear is liable; thy food is such
> As hath been belch'd on by infected lungs.
> *Boult:* What would you have me do? Go to the wars?
>
> (IV. vi. 161-9)

In all the Romances there is some harshly presented baseness or brutality, to enhance the final harmony which is their *raison d'être*. This conversation with Boult is still fresh in our minds when the great scene of recognition opens. The sea brings together the almost demented king and his lost daughter. Pericles arrives at Mytilene with black sails, speechless with the sorrow of years; Marina, whom we are taught to think of as a second nature, with power to renew the world, arrives at his ship. Her song, fragment of a higher harmony, breaks Pericles' stupor. Every art is used to preserve the rapt tone, to draw out the recognition and load it with useless, painful doubt, until Pericles feels a 'great sea of joy' rushing upon him; then he hears the music of the spheres, token of the harmony which will be restored to humanity at the happy end. Shakespeare did nothing alien to the mental habit of his age in using the sea to represent what seems to be a chaotic activity of Fortune but is really the action of Providence. 'Though the seas threaten they are merciful. | I have curs'd them without cause.' Out of apparent chaos comes harmony.

This version of the themes of sundering and reunion, the suffering king and the princess of magic virtue, is the prototype of the Romances. Marina, like Perdita and Miranda, has that 'better nature' which defies corruption, however harsh the world. And

Pericles can help us with the later Romances in other ways. It is allegorical to the degree suggested by the foregoing, and not more. In the hands of Sidney and Spenser romance was a very flexible, but also an unstable, mode of ethical allegory. Spenser, whose poem Shakespeare knew perhaps as well as any other book, does not write allegory of unvarying intensity, but diversifies a master-allegory with subtle and even opportunistic figurations of a lesser kind. In Shakespeare there is a good deal of this kind of thing, but his master-themes are invariably explicit and not figurative. He writes for the stage. He cannot put the Blatant Beast on the stage; he puts instead slanderers and louts. Florimell is pursued by a spotted monster 'that feeds on womens' flesh', but Marina is sold into an actual brothel. The playwright cannot afford to neglect what Professor Danby calls 'the creaturely and existential'. In *Pericles* he comes nearer than anywhere else to a schematic presentation of themes inseparable from the very idea of romance-comedy, and there is in the nature of the case a strong element of parable. But it is wrong to impose detailed allegorical readings on the play. In the end, the theatre explains it; it is an act of concentration on the laws of comic form, a huge, perhaps inordinate, development of the comic recognition. The parabolic habit of romance touches it, more or less lightly, here and there. Truths, Truth itself perhaps, glint in the narrative, shiver and thrash in the net of language. But *Pericles* is, above all, the work of a great dramatist who had been much moved by a great poet, and who—not without a certain pride in easy mastery—wanted to do a new thing in the making of comedy.

CYMBELINE

Heminge and Condell placed *Cymbeline* with the tragedies. Perhaps the printing was held up by copyright difficulties; perhaps they were puzzled as to the category of so strange a play, by the unprecedented mixture of ancient Britain and modern Italy, comedy and tragedy, history and romance. Dr. Johnson was severe upon these inconsistencies:

This play has many just sentiments, some natural dialogue, and some pleasing scenes, but they are obtained at the expense of much incongruity. To remark the folly of the fiction, the absurdity of the conduct, the confusion of names, and manners of different times, and the impossibility of the events in any system of life were to waste criticism upon unresisting imbecility, upon faults too evident for detection, and too gross for aggravation.

Some criticism must, nevertheless, be wasted on the incongruities. *Cymbeline* is, under one aspect, a history play, and for the story of Cymbeline's disagreement with the Romans over the payment of tribute, and the subsequent war and peace, Shakespeare referred to Holinshed. But he was far less respectful of history than in the English Chronicle Plays, and the freedom of his treatment reminds one rather of *King Lear*, in which he had once before blended a romance-plot with an episode from British history. As a matter of fact, Holinshed is perfunctory, not to say hazy, about Cymbeline; he is not sure whether it was this king or his son who refused the tribute, or even whether the Britons won the war. Shakespeare eked out Holinshed from a poem in a supplement to *The Mirror for Magistrates*. In this work the Britons won, which suited him because there was a vogue for incredibly bold and warlike Britons, reflected a little later in Fletcher's *Bonduca*. Since the accession of James I, the English were British in name as well as by remote descent; they could think of Cymbeline as of their own nation, and perhaps find him especially interesting because he occupied the throne of Britain at the time of the birth of Christ and the Augustan peace.[3]

On the other hand, Shakespeare could assume that nobody wanted archaeological accuracy. Iachimo's conduct is, admittedly, un-Roman (though Shakespeare remembered his own Tarquin as he wrote). He is a Sienese, and his Italian manners are appropriate to the wicked Italy of the Jacobean imagination; it was no part of the dramatist's purpose to portray a Tuscan of the time of Augustus. Iachimo's treachery is there to touch another responsive note in the audience; as Dr. Brockbank shows, it was conventional to contrast the craftiness, the 'doubleness and hollow behaviour', of Italians with the 'great strength and little policie, much courage and small shift' of the British. But this gives rise to one of those

[3] See J. P. Brockbank's article in *Shakespeare Survey*, xi (1955), 42–9. Emrys Jones, *Essays in Criticism*, xi (1961), 84–99, argues for a close application to contemporary political opnion or mythology.

contradictions, or at any rate tensions, which abound in *Cymbeline*; for it was also accepted that the Roman occupation of Britain did us good because it provided an early dose of civility and associated us with the great Empire. 'Were not Caesars Britaines as brutish as Virginians?' asked Samuel Purchas. 'The Romane swords were best teachers of civilitie to this and other Countries.' So when Cymbeline has won the war he offers the tribute after all, blaming the Queen and Cloten for restraining him from doing so earlier. We are meant to conclude that the valour of the British royal family is 'gentle', and not simply a brute toughness which must set the nation against the forces of civility and religion. And we remember that the secular Empire was a preparation for Christianity, and that the England of Shakespeare was the home of the true religion.

For the wager between Posthumus and Iachimo Shakespeare drew, more directly, on Boccaccio.[4] This ancient and implausible tale goes well enough in romance, and Shakespeare stirs it up with the pseudo-history, the pastoral tale of the King's lost sons, the wanderings of Imogen in the deserts of Wales, the fairy-tale plot of the Queen's drugs, without the least apology:

> Howsoe'er 'tis strange,
> Or that the negligence may well be laugh'd at,
> Yes it is true, sir.
>
> (I. i. 65–7)

Granville Barker explains the theatrical craft needed to bring this off. As to why Shakespeare wanted to do it, we must assume a desire to experiment in a new kind of play, in which probabilities and personalities count for less than *coups de théâtre* which suggest with ideal clarity certain truths left obscure in the turbulence of real life.

---

[4] For details of this and other sources and analogues see the New Arden and New Cambridge editions of *Cymbeline*. An important source which seems to have been overlooked is the episode of Child Tristram in *Faerie Queene*, vi. ii. Tristram, like Guiderius, is 'a Briton borne, Sonne of a king,' and like him is a great hunter. More important, it was easy to see at a glance that he was 'of noble race', and 'borne of some Heroicke sead'. He is anxious to learn 'the use of arms', and so are the sons of Cymbeline. As Guiderius kills the discourteous Cloten, Tristram kills the boorish knight who wronged Priscilla. These parallels are further testimony to the importance of the relation between the Romances and *The Faerie Queene*, especially Book VI.

Not that *Cymbeline* is a lucid play; its language prevents it being that. The romance plot is not matched by any assumed simplicity of diction, but set off against tough late-Shakespearian verse; and this produces an effect almost of irony, so that several critics, among them Professor Danby, have tried to convey their sense that the dramatist is somehow *playing* with the play. I think this is true. For example, *Cymbeline* is the only play in the canon which has characters given to such tensely obscure ways of expressing themselves that not only the audience but the other characters find it hard to make out what they mean. Add to this the extra-ordinary complexity of the plot, the wanton rapidity of the mul-tiple dénouement, and certain other complications to be mentioned later, and you have a play very remote in tone from *Pericles*. But it is a superb play nevertheless, and in some ways perhaps it shows more of the difficult, tortuous, ironical mind that made the Sonnets, than other greater works in which the main effort goes into the making explicit of some more public theme.

The opening scene is a good example of the obliquity that will prevail throughout. The two anonymous gentlemen constitute a simple device for telling the audience what it needs to know about the situation. The explanations of the First Gentleman to his guest do indeed cover a lot of ground in only 70 lines, but there is nothing simple in the way he goes about it. 'Everybody looks angry because the King is' becomes:

> You do not meet a man but frowns; our bloods
> No more obey the heavens that our courtiers
> Still seem as does the King's.
>
> (I. i. 1–3)

The reason for the King's anger is that his daughter and his only child Imogen has married Posthumus instead of the Queen's son Cloten; but there is room amid all the narrative detail for a com-parison between Cloten and Posthumus, with much tortuous praise of the latter:

> *First Gent.* He that hath miss'd the Princess is a thing
> Too bad for bad report; and he that hath her—
> I mean that married her, alack, good man!
> And therefore banish'd—is a creature such
> As, to seek through the regions of the earth

For one his like, there would be something failing
In him that should compare. I do not think
So fair an outward and such stuff within
Endows a man but he.
Second Gent. You speak him far.
First Gent. I do extend him, sir, within himself;
Crush him together rather than unfold
His measure duly.

(I. i. 16–27)

From this energetic, indeed violent dialogue—and it is the energy
of the writer rather than of the First Gentleman—we certainly
learn a number of facts necessary to the progress of the action;
but we are also left with the sense that some undoubtedly hectic
sequel will unfold the importance of this contrast between Cloten
and Posthumus. But Posthumus, of course, departs; though he
encounters Cloten on the way, we are merely told of this. There
is an angry scene between Imogen and her father, in which the
young men are again contrasted: 'I chose an eagle,' says Imogen
in reply to his angry accusations, 'and did avoid a puttock.' The
noble Posthumus sails away, waving a handkerchief: the base
Cloten is carefully exposed to us as a braggart and a coward. Is
Shakespeare once more treating a favourite theme, the matter of
nobility in birth and nobility in conduct? Apparently not, since
we next see Posthumus in Italy, Cloten forgotten, contracting his
wager with Iachimo; and all our attention is directed to the attempt
on Imogen, with only a scene essential to the plot—the substitu-
tion of a harmless drug for the Queen's poison—intervening
between the wager and the arrival of Iachimo at the British court.
There follows the great scene in which Iachimo disgustingly
expresses the disgust he feigns at the loose life of Posthumus
in Italy; this is verse of an hysterical virtuosity, recognizably
from the author of *Coriolanus* and *The Winter's Tale*, yet proper to
Cymbeline:

Iachimo: It cannot be i' th' eye, for apes and monkeys,
'Twixt two such shes, would chatter this way and
Contemn with mows the other; nor i' th' judgment,
For idiots in this case of favour would
Be wisely definite; nor i' th' appetite;
Sluttery, to such neat excellence oppos'd,

Should make his desire vomit emptiness,
Not so allur'd to feed.
Imogen: What is the matter, trow?
Iachimo: The cloyed will—
That satiate yet unsatisfied desire, that tub
Both fill'd and running—ravening first the lamb,
Longs after for the garbage.
Imogen: What, dear sir,
Thus raps you? Are you well?

(I. vi. 38–50)

She does not understand him; but even when she does she is not
equal to his Italian cunning, and allows him to send his chest to
her room.

The scene of Iachimo's intrusion in Imogen's chamber is a
carefully prepared set piece, and its power quite disarms the criticism that it is inherently ridiculous. Imogen is a lucky Lucretia,
reading the tale of Tereus; Iachimo knows how to value the beauty
he betrays:

> 'Tis her breathing that
> Perfumes the chamber thus. The flame o' th' taper
> Bows toward her.

(II. ii. 18–20)

Iachimo departs; Cloten (after receiving advice from his mother
which is too obscurely expressed for his understanding) returns
to the suit of Imogen.

The plot is developing fast; there is an embassy from Rome;
yet our attention is suddenly returned to the Cloten–Posthumus
contrast by a violent scene between Cloten and Imogen. Imogen
is straightforward enough:

> Wert thou the son of Jupiter, and no more
> But what thou art besides, thou wert too base
> To be his groom.

(II. iii. 125–7)

But then she puts the point of Posthumus' superior nobility in a
figure:

> His mean'st garment
> That ever hath but clipp'd his body is dearer

234

> In my respect than all the hairs above thee,
> Were they all made such men.
>
> (II. iii. 133-6)

And Cloten, affronted, four times repeats, 'His meanest garment!'
This is very devious. We discovered from the First Gentleman
that Posthumus was meritorious both outward and inward, and
this might explain Imogen's high valuation of his clothes. But
Shakespeare makes far more of this episode than can be explained
in terms of a conventional reference to the outer and inner man.
Imogen's insult rankles; Cloten procures a suit of Posthumus'
clothes, and sets out in pursuit of her when she goes off to Milford
Haven to find her husband with the Roman invasion force. His
intention is to ravish her, wearing her husband's suit:

> He on the ground, my speech of insultment ended on his
> dead body, and when my lust hath dined—which, as I say, to
> vex her I will execute in the clothes that she so prais'd—to the
> court I'll knock her back, foot her home again.
>
> (III. v. 143-6)

And Cloten can wear the clothes of Posthumus; the garments of
this nonpareil fit him exactly. After an insulting conversation
about clothes and tailors, the young prince cuts off Cloten's head
(for the true prince, even dressed in skins, is Cloten's superior);
and when Imogen awakes out of her drugged sleep and discovers
his corpse, she identifies it as that of Posthumus, by the clothes
and the unmatchable physique:

> A headless man? The garments of Posthumus?
> I know the shape of's leg; this is his hand,
> His foot Mercurial, his Martial thigh,
> The brawns of Hercules . . .
>
> (IV. ii. 309-12)

Shortly after this Posthumus, who, it will be remembered, left
Britain with a clean handkerchief, enters with a bloody one, and
declares his intentions of shedding his Italian clothes in favour of
the costume of 'a Britain peasant'. In this way he will be braver in
the battle than his clothes lead anyone to expect, and so set a new
fashion, 'Less without and more within.'

Clothes are a familiar figure for the false outward show; but there is far too much emphasis on this theme for so commonplace an explanation. It is not the first time Shakespeare has arranged for what begins as a verbal pattern to break through into the action; *Lear* is behind us. But why give Posthumus the body of a paragon, and then allow Cloten's to equal it, even in the eyes of Imogen? The point may be that, as Belarius says, 'Nature hath meal and bran, contempt and grace', and perhaps the physical identity merely stresses a moral discrepancy, as Shylock's most famous speech misses out on the sole but all-important difference between Jew and Christian. But however one looks at it, this thematic figure must seem, especially in a play so packed with plot, a wanton, decorative flourish. Admittedly the contrast between Cloten and Posthumus is related to other themes in the play— nature and nurture, barbarism and civility; but it is so far from the main issues of Roman tribute and the reunion of husband and wife, father and children, that for all its brilliance one feels it is not what Shakespeare would have allowed himself in the comedies of his middle period.

As to the historical theme, it thrives on the ambiguity of the situation of Briton *versus* Roman. The coward Cloten jeering at the Roman emissaries; Caius Lucius dignified under the threat of brutal British vengeance; the innate nobility of British princes and the victory of Posthumus over Iachimo—all these events exploit, and the final magnanimity of Cymbeline flatters, the prejudices of a contemporary audience. We may have changed preconceptions, but the play still has power to exploit and puzzle us with unexplained ambiguities. Another, perhaps, is the episode of Imogen at the cave of her lost brothers. Away from the intrigues of the court, Imogen—dressed as a boy, like earlier heroines in search of their lovers—speaks a different language; and so does Shakespeare. J. C. Maxwell suspects him of irony in his representation of the royal brothers, and certainly the tone alters, becomes appropriate to pure romance. Brought up as hunters, living in a cave, they are nevertheless bursting with natural nobility:

How hard it is to hide the sparks of nature!
These boys know little they are sons to th' King,
Nor Cymbeline dreams that they are alive.
They think they are mine; and though train'd up thus meanly
I' th' cave wherein they bow, their thoughts do hit

The roofs of palaces, and nature prompts them
In simple and low things to prince it much
Beyond the trick of others.

(III. iii. 79–86)

So their guardian Belarius. The boys are necessary to the plot, and
to the massive family reunion at the end; but in these pastoral
scenes Shakespeare apparently presents them with the simplicity
of Child Tristram or the noble savage in *The Faerie Queene*, VI:

O what an easie thing is to descry
The gentle bloud, how ever it be wrapt
In sad misfortunes foule deformity
And wretched sorrowes, which have often hapt!
For howsoever it may grow mis-shapt,
Like this wyld man being undisciplynd,
That to all virtue it may seeme unapt,
Yet will it shew some sparkes of gentle mynd,
And at the last breake forth in his owne proper kynd.

In the end they behave like princes before they are recognized as
princes, and save their father's cause. But the ambiguity lies in
such details of presentation as their brutality towards the body
of Cloten and their sentimental affection for Fidele; and the tone
of these scenes is somehow suspiciously simple and open, as if
Shakespeare were covertly parodying Fletcher.

The last act of *Cymbeline* includes not only the fighting but the
vision of Posthumus when prisoner, and the twenty-four-fold
dénouement. As to the vision, as Mr. Maxwell says, there seems
no reason why it should not be accepted as Shakespearian, and
none either why it should therefore be overvalued. Posthumus'
soliloquy before the vision is very fine; and so is the rapt speech of
Sicinius at Jupiter's departure—late Shakespeare of the kind
reserved for moments of awe:

He came in thunder; his celestial breath
Was sulphurous to smell; the holy eagle
Stoop'd, as to foot us. His ascension is
More sweet than our blest fields.

(V. iv. 114–17)

The prose of the gaoler is again very characteristic; and his hang-
man humour is a good enough introduction to the high-flown

royal recognitions of the last scene. Here is the untying of all knots, a 'fierce abridgement' indeed of the plot. The queen dies; Imogen turns up and wins the life of Posthumus; identities are established by ring or by mole ('It was wise nature's end in the donation | To be his evidence now'); condemnations, pardons, exposures, further condemnations and general forgiveness follow, and the tribute is promised which will 'let | A Roman and a British ensign wave | Together'.

The last scene is hard to bring off on the stage because the too rapid untying of all those knots awakens farcical associations. (This is to assume that Shakespeare did not want it to.) Yet this scene is very obviously the focus of the play; here all those separate plots and themes, so skilfully expounded through the play, are brought together straitly, in a multiple recognition which is, to put it at the lowest, a virtuoso exercise. However far Shakespeare got from the archetypal simplicity of *Pericles* in this remarkable 'historical-pastoral' tragi-comical romance, he was still thinking in dramaturgical terms about the recognition.

THE WINTER'S TALE

The story of his next play Shakespeare owed almost entirely to Robert Greene's novel *Pandosto: The Triumph of Time* (1588, reprinted 1607; Shakespeare used the first edition). Greene allows his Leontes (Pandosto) some ground for his suspicions of Hermione, who behaves towards Polixenes with what seems excessive familiarity. After a time the King's jealousy (without real foundation, but not, as in Shakespeare, merely fantastic) grows too much to bear, and he orders the poisoning of Hermione and Polixenes. When the latter escapes, he imprisons the Queen, and sends the newborn princess to sea in an open boat. After the trial he instantly accepts the word of the oracle; but his son dies, and then Hermione, of grief. Perdita is cast up on the shore of Sicily (for some reason Shakespeare changed Bohemia and Sicily about) and is brought up by the shepherds. Years later she is courted by Polixenes' son, Florizel, who escapes his father and carries her off to sea; they arrive at the coast of Bohemia and proceed to Leontes' court. Leontes imprisons Florizel, and himself pays court to Perdita; but when he hears the whole story from Polixenes he frees the prince and orders the execution of the shepherdess. By various tokens her true identity is discovered; Florizel and Perdita are married, and Leontes commits suicide.

Only in the scene of Hermione's trial does Shakespeare follow Greene's able but very mannered prose at all closely; and as usual he alters the story considerably. We need not ask why he refrained from making his mild and repentant Leontes seek the favour of his own daughter, or why he allows him to welcome the young lovers with warmth instead of severity. By making Camillo the agent not only of Polixenes' escape, but later of Florizel's, Shakespeare is practising a simple dramaturgical economy, though as usual extracting more than mere neatness from it. Similarly, by conflating the sheep-shearing feast with the Perdita-Florizel love-scene, and also with the discovery of the lovers by Polixenes, he is tightening the loose-knit narrative texture of the novel, but also creating an opportunity for suitable treatment of the very important topic which Polixenes and Perdita debate early in the scene. The story of Perdita's casting away by boat he puts aside for adaptation in *The Tempest*. (If we need a hint that all these plays were intimately associated in the mind of the dramatist, that the next one was perhaps growing during the composition of its predecessor, this might provide it; we remember also Imogen's foreshadowing of *The Winter's Tale* in the lines:

> Would I were
> A neat-herd's daughter, and my Leonatus
> Our neighbour shepherd's son!—
>
> (I. i. 148–50)

as well as the long shadows cast by Marina and Pericles.)

The two principal alterations, however, are that Shakespeare removes Leontes' motives for jealousy, and preserves Hermione for a reunion sixteen years on. As to Leontes, it is not the first time Shakespeare has reduced the plausibility of a source. He wants jealousy to burst upon and destroy a harmonious situation like a natural calamity, a terrible disease; to show the slow warping of a husband's mind was far from his purpose here. The recovery and concealment of Hermione is a greater problem. No other play of Shakespeare's keeps back information, as this one does, from the audience. There is some evidence in the text, and outside it— Forman's account of the play he saw in 1611 says nothing of the

statue-scene—that in an earlier version of the play Shakespeare
followed Greene and allowed Hermione to die. In such a version
the recognition of Perdita would necessarily have been the climax
of the play, whereas in the extant version Shakespeare deliberately
throws this scene away, and merely reports the rejoicing which
accompanied the King's recovery of his daughter; a great deal of
rewriting would have been necessary to convert the play into its
present form. At some stage, it seems, Shakespeare remembered
the survival of Thaisa, and decided on a conclusion which alters
the emphasis of *Pericles* by making the recovery of the Queen the
central moment, and subordinating the recognition of the Princess.
Having so decided, he hit upon the device of the statue, with its
great theatrical and poetic possibilities—there are several known
stories and plays from which he could have got the hint—and
worked out yet another elaborate variation on the basic recognition theme.

The Winters' Tale is structurally unique; the nearest analogue
to the almost wholly tragic quality of the first three acts is *Measure
for Measure*. These acts, with the sole exception of the scene in
praise of Apollo's oracle, are entirely devoid of romantic 'serenity'. The storm that divides a royal family is here he effect of
diseased emotion. The first scene speaks only of friendship and
love. The second, in which the disease strikes and the harmony is
shattered, is one of the most remarkable, for language and action,
in Shakespeare. The opening speech of Polixenes, though strong
with the conceits of the late manner, is in a vein of compliment
appropriate to a pastoral kind:

> Nine changes of the wat'ry star hath been
> The shepherd's note since we have left our throne
> Without a burden. Time as long again
> Would be fill'd up, my brother, with our thanks;
> And yet we should for perpetuity
> Go hence in debt. And therefore, like a cypher,
> Yet standing in rich place, I multiply
> With one 'We thank you' many thousands moe
> That go before it.

(I. ii. 1–9)

This is an indication that the audience will have to work, but it is
also calm and courtly; Hermione pleads gaily for an extension of

the visit and, in reminding her guest of his childhood friendship with her husband, prompts him to use a figure which brings into the context the idea of man's innocence before the Fall:

> What we chang'd
> Was innocence for innocence; we knew not
> The doctrine of ill-doing, nor dream'd
> That any did. Had we pursu'd that life,
> And our weak spirits ne'er been higher rear'd
> With stronger blood, we should have answer'd heaven
> Boldly 'Not guilty', the imposition clear'd
> Hereditary ours.
>
> (I. ii. 68–75)

This attribution to the blood of the motive to sin unconsciously prepares us for the onset of Leontes' sickness. He falls, like Othello into talk of beasts and diseases to express his disgust; the words 'infection' and 'disease' echo through the scene:

> Physic for't there's none;
> It is a bawdy planet, that will strike
> Where 'tis predominant; and 'tis pow'rful, think it,
> From east, west, north, and south. Be it concluded,
> No barricado for a belly. Know't,
> It will let in and out the enemy
> With bag and baggage. Many thousand on's
> Have the disease, and feel't not.
>
> (I. ii. 200–7)

This agitated speech combines the ideas of sudden infection and planetary influence (as Othello blamed 'the very error of the moon') in a kind of bawdy raving; and when Leontes confides his 'diseas'd opinion' to Camillo he does so in that verse which is the special property of the late Shakespeare, suggesting the involved, passionate language of a man intolerably tormented by his thoughts:

> Ha' you not seen, Camillo—
> But that's past doubt; you have, or your eye-glass
> Is thicker than a cuckold's horn—or heard—
> For to a vision so apparent rumour
> Cannot be mute—or thought—for cogitation

Resides not in that man that does not think—
My wife is slippery?

(I. ii. 267–73)

Polixenes, when Camillo informs him of the King's orders, combines in one horrified cry of rebuttal the ideas of the betrayer of Christ, and of diseased blood:

O then my best blood turn
To an infected jelly, and my name
Be yok'd with his that did betray the Best!

(I. ii. 417–19)

The question is often debated, whether Shakespeare meant Leontes' jealousy to have been long in the making or conceived and born simultaneously in this scene. Perhaps he did not care; his purpose is to show peace and courtesy destroyed by a storm of diseased passion comparable with the Fall, a betrayal like that of Judas. Disasters follow as Leontes, now a jealous tyrant, gives his cruelty rein. Hermione is imprisoned. But there is a beautiful suggestion that the regenerative force of nature exceeds even Leontes' power to destroy life and harmony; the child to which the Queen gives birth in prison

was prisoner to the womb, and is
By law and process of great Nature thence
Freed and enfranchis'd.   (II. ii. 58–60)

Leontes, however, can, and does, commit the child to the wildness of nature, and he entrusts Antigonus with its despatch.

In the third act Leontes pursues his cruel course; the Queen is tried; the oracle (and Shakespeare wrote a scene without narrative value simply to stress its happy sanctity) is ignored. At once Leontes is subject to the judgement which always attends on tyrants; his son Mamillius dies, and he recognises in this the anger of Apollo; but before he can change his ways the death of Hermione follows. The end of III. ii—about halfway through the play—is like the full close of a tragedy: Hermione and Mamillius dead, Leontes with nothing before him but reproach and repentance. There is little beyond the hint of the oracle ('if that which is lost be not found') and the romantic circumstance that babies abandoned in wilderness do not die, to suggest a comic issue to the plot. But although Antigonus is yet to be eaten by the bear, the tragic part of the play is now over; from prosperity and its destruction we pass to regeneration, love and continuance; the idea that all things 'Doe worke their own perfection so by fate'.

The story turns, as it must, to Perdita. III. ii. is a bizarre scene, a deliberate, near-farcical contrast with its predecessors. Before Time intervenes there must be a new note to make a suspension instead of a fully tragic cadence, to prepare for the entirely new tone of Act IV, which would otherwise seem to be another play. And in this scene occurs, almost casually, the pivotal line of the play: 'Now bless thyself: thou met'st with things dying, I with things new-born', as the old shepherd shows his son the rich child. Now Time himself can enter, maker and unfolder of error, destroyer and redeemer, agent both of change and of perpetuity, as he is in the Mutability Cantos:

> Let me pass
> The same I am, ere ancient'st order was
> Or what is now receiv'd.

> (IV. i. 9–11)

So sixteen years pass; and there follows the long episode of the sheep-shearers' feast. Its central action is slight enough; Polixenes interrupts the idyll of Perdita and Florizel, Camillo enables them to escape. But this, and the strange fortunes of Perdita's foster-father, are as long in the playing as the whole story up to the rejection of the oracle. Shakespeare finds room for an elaborately presented Autolycus, for rustic singing and dancing and revelry, for the pleasure taken by Polixenes in the pastoral scene, and much else. There were dramatic reasons for this enlargement of the Bohemian part of the play; it must have mass enough to balance the destructive Sicilian part. The mood of the rustic scene is innocence, like that of the 'twinn'd lambs' of which Polixenes spoke before the disaster. Autolycus, with his courtly pretences, is the blackest rogue available. Above all, there has to be an extensive natural setting for the better nature of the lost princess, for the inborn virtue which shines through her beauty; if the world is to be renewed, and the kings reconciled, she must be shown to have the power to do it. Unlike the lost Marina, and Imogen in Wales, Perdita does not know she is noble; but as she plays at being a queen her royalty speaks in her actions. She is endowed with strong suggestions of divinity, 'no shepherdess but Flora,' as Florizel says when she first appears on the stage. Here, with great deliberation, Shakespeare repeats the device by which Marina first appeared with flowers by the sea.

The arrival of the disguised Polixenes becomes the occasion not only for Perdita's famous flower-piece, but for a thematic passage of quasi-philosophical debate, which reverberates through the rest of the play:

> *Per.*   Sir, the year growing ancient,
> Not yet on summer's death nor on the birth
> Of trembling winter, the fairest flow'rs o' th' season
> Are our carnations and streak'd gillyvors,
> Which some call nature's bastards. Of that kind
> Our rustic garden's barren; and I care not
> To get slips of them.
>
> *Pol.*   Wherefore, gentle maiden,
> Do you neglect them?
>
> *Per.*   For I have heard it said
> There is an art which in their piedness shares
> With great creating nature.
>
> *Pol.*   Say there be;
> Yet nature is made better by no mean
> But nature makes that mean; so over that art,
> Which you say adds to nature, is an art
> That nature makes. You see, sweet maid, we marry
> A gentler scion to the wildest stock,
> And make conceive a bark of baser kind
> By bud of nobler race. This is an art
> Which does mend nature—change it rather; but
> The art itself is nature.
>
> *Per.*   So it is.
> *Pol.* Then make your garden rich in gillyvors,
> And do not call them bastards.
>
> *Per.*   I'll not put
> The dibble in earth to set one slip of them;
> No more than were I painted I would wish

This youth should say 'twere well, and only therefore
Desire to breed by me.

(IV. iv. 79–103)

At one level Perdita and Polixenes are, ironically, arguing against
and for the union of noble with base stocks, though Perdita accepts
the love of Florizel and Polixenes forbids it. The topic of their
discussion is more general, and a commonplace in the literature
of the period. it was one of these questions for which the arguments on both sides were familiar; Polixenes has the more favour-
ed case to put, yet even so late as half a century later Marvell could
argue Perdita's case in 'The Mower against Gardens'. On the
whole it seemed best to resolve the antithesis of Nature and Art
by saying that Art is, in the end, Nature's own agent; thus the
gardener, like all artists who seek to improve nature, is acquitted.
But Perdita herself is in fact the product of long and careful cultivation; and it is this concealed truth that really gives the passage its
full irony and justifies her refusal to act as Polixenes says she ought.
She turns the analogy from horticulture to cosmetics ('the gillyvors
are like painted women') and so averts an unjust analogy between
herself and the 'bark of baser kind'. Polixenes is apparently unconscious of it anyway. Shakespeare does not insert these set pieces—
compare both the discussion of Laban and the formal 'praise of
music' in *The Merchant of Venice*—without good cause, and we
are to think not only of the obvious dramatic ironies, but also of
the instructive 'better nature' of that 'gentler scion' Perdita, which
is fully expressed in the succeeding flower-speech and in the beautiful dialogues with Florizel: 'All your acts are queens.' The
pastoral 'intermezzo', as it has been called, acquires philosophical,
as the first act acquires theological, overtones. When Polixenes
has 'divorced' and Camillo' preserved the lovers, we return to
Sicilia and to Leontes, now chastened by sixteen years of penitence.

The whole business of this last act is recognition, which was
presumably Shakespeare's motive in choosing a story of prosperity
broken and restored, repentance and reunion; and not merely
choosing such a story but adding to it and giving central importance to supernumerary and wildly improbable recognition. Before
Time unfolds the errors, we have testimony of the genuine nature
of Leontes' repentance; and then Perdita arrives, 'the most peer-
less piece of earth', with her Florizel. They come to barren Sicily

like the spring, *renovatio mundi*; and Leontes, remembering the departure of Florizel's father, prays that 'the blessed gods | Purge all infection from the air whilst you | Do climate here'. The arrival of Polixenes himself precipitates the discovery of Perdita's identity, and all seems ready for a scene based on that between Marina and Pericles; but the King and his daughter are reunited off-stage, and we have to be content with the sprightly report of anonymous gentlemen. Thus the climatic moment is reserved for the scene in which the statue of Julio Romano moves, 'to forgive our illusion', as Auden puts it; to correct the opinion that mere art can match great creating nature, who works hand in hand with time. This scene, so moving in the theatre, so chastely alert to the possibilities of theatrical spectacle, as when Perdita stands statue-like in astonishment beside the image of her mother, transfigures the improbable by treating it with reverence. Yet it remembers that debate on art and nature. 'We are mock'd with art,' says Leontes; and later, 'What fine chisel | Could ever yet cut breath?' Then the art of the sculptor seems to him rather the art of the magus: 'If this be magic, let it be an art | Lawful as eating.' But the statue is the work of no artist, but of great creating nature; it falls under the rule of time, but a time that redeems as it makes wrinkles. The art that makes the beauty of the ageing Hermione is the same that made Perdita an evident queen in the sheepfold; a native royalty, the better nature of nobility.

The Winter's Tale has some marks of the new fashion for tragicomic romance, not only in its structure, but in the long pastoral episode, the satyr-dance, the grave, masque-like discovery of Hermione. But behind Perdita stand the lost princesses of higher romance and especially the Pastorella of *The Faerie Queene*, who sat among the shepherds 'upon a little hillocke'—

> As if some miracle of heauenly hew
> Were downe to them descended in that earthly vew—

and whose honest foster-father detested the vanity of gardens. Many attempts have been made to prove the whole play allegorical—to represent Hermione as Grace, and her passion, death and resurrection as Christ-like. It would be strange if the story raised no such echoes, or if the author never directed our attention to them; but here, as elsewhere in Shakespeare, the divine analogues are intermittently, not systematically, presented. Great subjects—

sin and death, repentance and love—cannot be spoken of by a poet in the Christian tradition without awaking such reverberations; but the poet has his mind upon 'the impersonal laws of comic form' in the first place, and only secondarily upon Christian doctrine. The greatness of the play is self-evident; it does not need the prestige of covert meanings.

THE TEMPEST

Much criticism of *The Tempest* stems directly from the fact that it is, in all probability, the last play Shakespeare wrote without a collaborator, so that it can be the focus of liberal speculation on the pattern of the poet's entire career. Indeed *The Tempest* does touch upon matters Shakespeare had treated earlier, and it has in particular much in common with the other Romances. But it remains very puzzling work.

Once more recognition is the heart of the piece; and once more Time is the unfolder of error and the servant of eternity, as chance is the servant of providence. The sea may appear to be random and cruel to these castaways, but it is the agent of purgation and reunion:

> Though the seas threaten, they are merciful;
> I have curs'd them without cause,

says Ferdinand on regaining his father. The sense of a mysterious movement of providence, which achieves its ends in spite of, and even through the agency of, human wickedness and the chances of life, is very strong in Gonzalo's rejoicing at the end. He thanks the gods, saying it is they 'that have chalk'd forth the way | Which brought us hither', and goes on:

> Was Milan thrust from Milan, that his issue
> Should become Kings of Naples? O, rejoice
> Beyond a common joy, and set it down
> With gold on lasting pillars: in one voyage
> Did Claribel her husband find at Tunis;
> And Ferdinand her brother, found a wife
> Where he himself was lost; Prospero his dukedom
> In a poor isle; and all of us ourselves
> When no man was his own.   (V. i. 205–13)

Here is that unmistakable flavour of Christian joy at the 'high miracle' which turns the discord of human tragedy into the harmony of divine comedy, at the renewal of the world after penitence and expiation.

If this was a familiar position to Shakespeare, so it was to the company of the *Sea Adventure*, which in 1609 ran aground off the Bermudas in circumstances of great danger; but they came out of the storm into what seemed an earthly paradise—'these infortunate (yet fortunate) Ilands', as Strachey, their spokesman, called the Bermudas. 'It pleased our mercifull God, to make even this hideous and hated place [the Bermudas had a reputation for fairies and devils] both the place of our safetie, and the meanes of our deliverance.' Shakespeare's indebtedness to Strachey and the other so-called 'Bermuda pamphlets' is clear. There is external evidence that he had more than a casual interest in the Virginian voyages, and he was well-read in travel literature. And his interest in the new world must have refreshed his interest in old problems. Although he knew not only the topical works of Strachey and others but Eden's *History of Travaile* (1577), he places his enchanted island in the Mediterranean, somewhere on the way from Tunis to Naples; and his Caliban is partly the savage of the New World, partly the wild man of European pageant, church-architecture, and poem. Some thought of the Indian as natural and therefore unspoilt; so Montaigne in the essay 'Of Cannibals' to which Shakespeare probably alludes in Gonzalo's speech on the commonwealth (II. i. 137 ff.). Others, and Shakespeare among them, thought him natural and therefore base, degenerate, lacking in cultivation and 'better nature'. Caliban is by no means the first wild man in drama, but he is the first to be affected by reports from America of natives who, though they 'knew no use of riches' and possessed useful mechanic arts such as building dams for fish, proved treacherous to the European who arrived in Virginia 'to be the lord on't'. Naturally, this information from the New World was made as far as possible to fit older preconceptions, and Caliban is basically the *homo salvaticus*, the savage man, of tradition; as Malone remarked, he ought to be dressed conventionally in skins, and not got up to look like a fish. Such a being, man without grace of civility, makes an interesting measure for art and cultivation, and he is the measure Miranda uses.

Apart from the travel literature, Montaigne, and Ovid (who is the source of Prospero's speech abjuring magic [V. i. 33 ff.]), there is no known source for *The Tempest*. That the plot has strong affinities with known romance themes is not in doubt; recently it has been shown how close is the resemblance between some elements of *The Tempest* and the *Daphnis and Chloe* of Longus.[5] It is often argued, though it cannot be demonstrated, that Shakespeare borrowed the plot from the scenario of some *commedia dell'arte*; later examples are extant which have some points of resemblance, and Shakespeare shows elsewhere that he knew something of these unscripted plays. One branch of the *commedia dell'arte* was called 'pastoral tragicomedy', and that is a genre to which in some ways *The Tempest* belongs. To academic pastoral tragi-comedy there is, whether or no through Fletcher, some indebtedness in all these plays; it was very fashionable on the continent, and there were some English examples, though the pervasive influence of Sidney and Spenser is really much more important.

Of the form of the play there are two obvious things to be said. First, in sharp contrast with the errant narrative of *Pericles*, the multiple plots of *Cymbeline*, and the unique design of *The Winter's Tale* (two counter-balancing masses and a final act), *The Tempest* confines its action to one place, to three hours, and to a closely related group of characters. It could be said to observe all the neo-Aristotelian unities. Secondly, it is much the most spectacular of all the plays, and includes a storm, a courtly entertainment, and a magic banquet interrupted by the apparition of a Harpy.

The obvious result of the choice of this very intensive form is to throw the whole weight of the play on to the recognition, for the preliminary disaster can only be talked about, not represented. To begin at the end, when Prospero can say 'lies at my mercy all mine enemies', is to change the role of Time in the play; there can be no pause at a seemingly tragic conclusion, no vivid contrast between the past and the present, to emphasize its destructive and redemptive power. It is as if *The Winter's Tale* had begun with the arrival of Perdita in Sicily. Furthermore, Prospero is clearly in charge of the whole action, so that there is no genuine uncertainty, little sense that Providence is wearing the mask of Chance. All the interest is in bringing together rather than in tearing apart. This is, in some ways, impoverishing. Prospero's account of his brother's treachery has none of the savage actuality of Leontes' outburst;

[5] See the article by Carol Gesner in *Shakespeare Quarterly* (1959), 531–44.

all those events in Milan—except in so far as the plot of Antonio and Sebastian recapitulates them—remain in 'the dark backward and abysm of time'; and it is worth noting that whereas Shakespeare could not risk sending Perdita to sea in a leaky fairy-tale cockboat, he could use the idea for Prospero and Miranda. As to the final recognition, there can be little of that sense of the marvellous—the drifting together through time, wind and weather—that impregnates the climactic scene of *Pericles*; and the omnipotence and omniscience of Prospero even preclude the excited dénouement of *Cymbeline*.

Yet Shakespeare is clearly just as interested as before in the Romance themes—guilt and repentance, the finding of the lost, forgiveness, the renewal of the world, the benevolence of the unseen powers. Only this time he gives them treatment at once more philosophical and more spectacular; he blends with the neoclassic design of his plot elements undoubtedly borrowed from the court masque.

This form had recently, as we have seen, reached new heights of allegorical spectacle in the hands of Ben Jonson. The main roles were played by courtiers, but professional actors often appeared in them, and dances, music and costumes borrowed from masques were sometimes used in public performances. Indeed, a new fashion followed; and the Blackfriars was capable of elaborate scenic and musical effects. *The Tempest* has much spectacle and music; it has also a more general resemblance to the masque. Prospero is like a masque-presenter, and the castaways wander helpless in an enchanted scene under his spell, until he chooses to release them, drawing back a curtain to display a symbol of aristocratic concord, Ferdinand and Miranda at chess. At the climax of each subplot there is a spectacular contrivance that owes something to masque: the rapacity of the 'three men of sin' is confronted with its own image in the allegorical figure of the Harpy; the disorderly desires of Caliban and his confederates are chastised, Actæon-like, by hounds; and the betrothal of Ferdinand and Miranda is marked by a courtly mythological entertainment (not strictly a masque, because it lacks an indispensable element, the dance of the masquers with the onlookers; Shakespeare probably ended this scene so abruptly because it could not be played out). Prospero's famous lament, 'Our revels now are ended', echoes the regret conventionally expressed at the ephemeral nature of the incredibly costly furnishings of court masques. If we take all this together with the close adherence to traditional five-act structures, we may conclude that Shakespeare was deliberately blending these 'tricks' with a conventional form that lent itself well to a necessarily intensive presentation of the material.

As in the other plays of the group, the focussing of attention on the moment of recognition, here carried a stage further, involves the illumination also of related ideas—the supernatural beauty of the princess, the contrast between the noble and the natural. *The Tempest* describes the healing of a political wound and the forgiveness of enemies; but it takes this theme of art and nature further than the other plays. It includes a 'natural' man, and an 'artist' who controls by super-natural means: and it conscientiously elaborates the parallel between Miranda and Caliban in respect of their 'nurture' or education. Hers is the good seed which benefits by nurture; he is the 'born devil on whose nature | Nurture will never stick'. That they were at first brought up together and educated alike by Prospero merely emphasizes this difference. She is astonished by the beauty of the brave new world; he comes to terms at once with new cruelty and foolishness. She is the cultivated plant, he the wild which rejects cultivation. Caliban is thus a central figure in the play, the wild man by whom civility is estimated; a 'saluage and deformed slaue' as the original 'Names of the Actors' in the Folio calls him. We know why he is called 'salvage'; he is deformed, like his mother Sycorax, because in romance ugliness within is platonically represented as ugliness without, just as the virtue of the heroines shine through their bodies; he is a slave because naturally inferior to European nobility. He is also the offspring of a witch by a devil, and so associated with a base natural magic, the antithesis of Prospero's 'Art', the product of virtue and learning.

This contrast Shakespeare develops in other ways. To bring off his experiment, Prospero must control his passions, and that is proof of civility and grace. Caliban attempts the virtue of Miranda; Ferdinand on the other hand can say, in response to Prospero's stern injunction:

> As I hope
> .For quiet days, fair issue, and long life,
> With such love as 'tis now, the murkiest den,

> The most opportune place, the strong'st suggestion
> Our worser genius can, shall never melt
> Mine honour into lust.

(IV. i. 23-8)

And so forth. Caliban is not, as this might suggest, a walking abstraction; Shakespeare cunningly varies the type of the lustful, angry wild man with material from the New World. He begins amiably, like the native Indians, but turns to treachery; like those 'wild men without any certaine language' reported by Peter Martyr, he is 'wonderfully astonied at the sweete harmony' of music. But so, according to Horace, were the beasts of the field. Caliban is not a diagrammatic character, but for all his unexpectedness he serves very faithfully the elaborate ethical scheme of *The Tempest*.

The design of the play—Prospero's experiment in Art—is the recognition, acceptance, and continuance of nobility, together, necessarily, with the exposure of baseness and the righting of political wrongs. Prospero makes the storm; the vivid opening scene does the work of acts, and precipitates the characters at once into the final crisis. But exposition is necessary, and the long second scene, in which Prospero impatiently tells Miranda of the past she has forgotten, is somewhat clumsy, though the nervous energy of Prospero's utterance sustains it:

> He being thus lorded,
> Not only with what my revenue yielded,
> But what my power might else exact, like one
> Who having into truth, by telling of it,
> Made such a sinner of his memory,
> To credit his own lie—he did believe
> He was indeed the Duke; out o' th' substitution,
> And executing th' outward face of royalty
> With all prerogative.

(I. ii. 97-105)

And whatever else may be said about this scene, Shakespeare has certainly not lost his power to dispose of a great quantity of business of all kinds very rapidly. We learn of the past, discover Prospero's magical powers, learn of Ariel's services past and his release to come; we not only meet Caliban but hear of his paren-

tage and his ugliness before he comes in and starts his flyting with
Prospero (nature against Art); and before the end of the scene
Ferdinand has arrived. In Ariel's songs and in Ferdinand's first
words we catch a new note in Shakespeare; the sea-music we know
from earlier verse, but this is the final rather faint, exotic development of it:

> Sitting upon a bank,
> Weeping again the King my father's wreck,
> This music crept by me upon the waters . . .
>
> (I. ii. 389–91)

Turning to Ferdinand after her recent encounter with the deformed
Caliban, Miranda says; 'There's nothing ill can dwell in such a
temple'; and, 'nothing natural | I ever saw so noble'. She may, as
Prospero later suggests, have to modify this platonic certainty;
but it is appropriate to the making of a brave new world. Ferdin-
and is likewise certain that Miranda is more natural, and retires
to his patient log-bearing.

The other castaways appear in the second act, and are soon under
Prospero's close management. First the royal party, in a strange,
desultory conversation, remind us that this is not an ordinary
shipwreck; the talk underlines the similarity of their voyage to that
of Aeneas, who sailed from Carthage to Cumae, as they from Tunis
to Naples; and according to their characters they comment upon
the utopian view of a natural commonwealth, such as Montaigne
found among savages. The plot against Alonso, invented by
Antonio and Sebastian, recapitulates the old usurpation, and
although we are aware of Ariel's presence, and the absolute control of Prospero, this is a fine, tensely written scene, economically
suggesting the depth of Antonio's baseness, and the feeble but
perhaps not irredeemable conscience of Sebastian. The plebeian
castaways Stephano and Trinculo join forces with Caliban in II. ii;
Caliban thinks they must be spirits, so grand are they, and, like
the Indians described by voyagers, supposes them to have dropped
from the moon. This scene is also recapitulatory, for Caliban offers
the newcomers the same service he had twelve years before given
Prospero:

> I prithee let me bring thee where crabs grow;
> And I with my long nails will dig thee pignuts;

Show thee a jay's nest, and instruct thee how
To snare the nimble marmoset; I'll bring thee
To clust'ring filberts, and sometimes I'll get thee
Young scamels from the rock. Wilt thou go with me?
(II. ii. 157–62)

With these groups moving about under Prospero's control, Shakespeare turns to Ferdinand and Miranda, and what Prospero calls
the 'fair encounter | Of two most rare affections'. But Caliban and
his friends, a miniature of any Shakespearian mob, go on with
their plot to kill Prospero and burn his books and the third act
ends with the spectacular frustration of the plot against Alonso.
The three guilty men 'stand to and feed'; but the banquet vanishes,
and they are confronted by their own guilt and the threat of
retribution:

You are three men of sin, whom Destiny,
That hath to instrument this lower world
And what is in't, the never-surfeited sea
Hath caus'd to belch up you; and on this island
Where man doth not inhabit, you 'mongst men
Being most unfit to live . . .
(III. iii. 53–8)

At this relatively early moment Prospero has already all his
enemies 'knit up | In their distractions', and the fourth act is
devoted—most unusually—to the entertainment celebrating the
betrothal of the young lovers, with its insistence on prenuptial
chastity (another mark of civility). The show does not reach its
conclusion because Prospero is, he says, much disturbed at the
thought of Caliban's conspiracy; not a very plausible reason for a
necessary intervention, but it enables Shakespeare to pass on to
the beginning of the end, *via* Prospero's famous speech, 'Our revels
now are ended.' Next we see the hunting of Caliban and his be-
draggled friends.

There remains the last movement, of recognition and forgiveness. First, Prospero, having used his art for the last time and
brought his great experiment to a head, abjures magic in a great
speech drawn from Ovid:

But this rough magic
I here abjure, and when I have requir'd

> Some heavenly music—which even now I do—
> To work mine end upon their senses that
> This airy charm is for, I'll break my staff,
> Bury it certain fathoms in the earth,
> And deeper than did ever plummet sound
> I'll drown my book.
>
> (V. i. 50–7)

Prospero's forgiveness of his enemies certainly lacks that gener-
osity which is prescribed as a part of courtesy in *Faerie Queene* VI,
and which is exhibited to some extent in *Cymbeline* and *The Winter's
Tale*:

> For you, most wicked sir, whom to call brother
> Would even infect my mouth, I do forgive
> Thy rankest fault,
>
> (V. i. 130–2)

he says to the unnatural Antonio. The discovery of Ferdinand
and Miranda at chess is a blessing to Alonso, and converts even
Sebastian: 'A most high miracle!' But Antonio seems to stand
unmoved outside the circle of the reconciled. Shakespeare is not
here interested in a high harmony such as he renders in *Pericles*,
though the happiness of that moment is registered by Gonzalo's
awed rejoicing, and Miranda's cry of pleasure at the beauty of the
more than natural world to which she is henceforth to belong
gives the scene its difference from the corresponding moments in
other Romances. It is hard to forget Prospero's sardonic qualification of Miranda's rapture at the brave 'new world': ' 'Tis new
to thee.'

The Epilogue, focus of much allegorizing, alludes to the parallel
between Prospero's abandonment of his art, and the actor's
abandonment of his role when he steps forward to ask for app-
lause. But Shakespeare will not often allow such things to be as
simple as they might, and the sense of the lines is altered and deepened by the final allusion to the Lord's Prayer.

The Tempest is in some ways the strangest of all Shakespeare's
plays; to return to it after a lapse of a year or two is to receive
with new force the impression that it has always eluded, and may
continue to elude, relevant comment. It deals in illusions—not
in theatrical illusions of reality, but in the reality of theatrical
illusions; as if Prospero in charge of the plot, spirits and machines,

were after all a figure of the playwright himself, showing what depths may be found in traps and flying-machines and music in the right places. Though its whole dramatic force is devoted to the arrangement of the romance-recognition, it has a coldness of tone not to be found in *The Winter's Tale*, and deliberately avoids a sustained employment of that note of solemn joy sounded in the closing scenes of *Pericles*. In a sense it is perhaps, a self-indulgence on the part of Shakespeare, a play for the theatre of his own mind; but if the mass of puzzled, barrenly ingenious commentary does nothing else, it shows that the world is in no danger of underestimating the value of such self-indulgence when the talent exercised is Shakespeare's.

THE TWO NOBLE KINSMEN

As Shakespeare grew older he necessarily associated with the younger playwrights who were to succeed him, and there is nothing improbable about the view that he collaborated with Fletcher in *The Two Noble Kinsmen*. I believe that he did so in *Henry VIII*, though the tide of opinion seems at present to be against this view, and certainly there is no external evidence for it, as there is for the attribution of both *The Two Noble Kinsmen* and *Cardenio* to both authors. *Cardenio* is lost, and we know only a little, and that very uncertainly, about it. *The Two Noble Kinsmen* was published in 1634 as the work of Fletcher and Shakespeare, when both had been dead for some time. Presumably Heminge and Condell could have got the play for the Folio had they wanted it; in the end it was included in the second Beaumont and Fletcher Folio of 1679 without mention of Shakespeare.

The question of authorship has dominated discussion of this play. The problem is not so much to distinguish Fletcher's part as to discover who wrote the rest, and Shakespeare is the favourite; though Massinger, always an imitator of his, was once a strong runner, he has now dropped behind. Beaumont is, of course, a candidate. Some argue for Shakespeare's sole authorship. Peter Ure, who completed most of his edition, told me that in his view the prosodic and lexical evidence, so far as established do not allow of a 'committee' theory of authorship, and he thought the sole authorship theory eccentric nonsense.

The source is Chaucer's *Knights' Tale*, and it is treated much in the manner of King's Men plays of the period, with a good deal of elaborate ceremonial, some spectacular effects, and a lot of Fletcherian posing on the topics of friendship, courtesy and love. There is a series of mad scenes in the subplot of the Gaoler's daughter which descend from Ophelia's, but have Fletcher's peculiar nastiness. In another disastrous passage the noble youths Palamon and Arcite break off urgent business to discuss old conquests with the vain salacity of saloon-bar amorists. This sorts ill with certain protestations Palamon later makes to Venus.

Two Noble Kinsmen, with its flippant Prologue and Epilogue, belongs in some ways to a later age than Shakespeare's. The first scene is always attributed to Shakespeare, but it is difficult to believe that he *planned* it, with its slow, falsely posed, ceremonial appeal by the three queens; indeed, the *ordonnance* of the whole work suggests the peculiar talent of Fletcher. There is an un-Shakespearian over-extension of the possibilities, as in the pretty lamentations of the young men in prison (II. ii.). The description of Emilia as a goddess in the same scene, though a Shakespearian theme, is grossly over-developed and mechanical. These examples are from a Fletcher scene, but they establish the tone of the whole work, which lacks the natural dynamism of a Shakespearian conception. The failure to distinguish Palamon from Arcite (Tweedledum and Tweedledee, Professor Muir calls them) and the weakly conception of Emilia; the absence of any attempt to develop, as Shakespeare would once have done, Chaucer's potent conclusion:

> Thanne may men by this ordre well discerne
> That thilke Moevere stable is and eterne—

support this view that although he probably wrote a great deal of the play Shakespeare had nothing to do with its plot.

Certain of the Shakespearian passages have that 'unearthly melody of a shattered blank verse rhythm', of which Middleton Murry spoke, and it would be hard to find any other author for Arcite's apostrophe to Emilia:

> O Queen Emilie,
> Fresher than May, sweeter
> Than her gold buttons on the boughs, or all
> Th' enamell'd knacks o' th' mead or garden; yea,

> We challenge too the bank of any nymph
> That makes the stream seem flowers; thou, O jewel
> O' th' wood, o' th' world, hast likewise blest a place
> With thy sole presence . . .

And Arcite's prayer to Mars in the last act transcends its fine original in Chaucer:

> Thou mighty one, that with thy power hast turn'd
> Green Neptune into purple, whose approach
> Comets prewarn, whose havoc in vast field
> Unearthed skulls proclaim, whose breath blows down
> The teeming Ceres foison, who doth pluck
> With hand armipotent from forth blue clouds
> The mason'd turrets, that both mak'st and break'st
> The stony girths of cities: me thy pupil,
> Youngest follower of thy drum, instruct this day
> With military skill, that to thy laud
> I may advance my streamer, and by thee
> Be styl'd the Lord o' th' day.

It may be that Theodore Spencer and Professor Ure were right in believing that where the Shakespearian parts of the play fall below what we expect of Shakespeare the explanation is simply that his powers were failing. So the splendour of the passages quoted above is less typical of his verse in this play than what Spencer calls a 'half-exhausted exaltation . . . the style of an old man'. But it is also possible that the 'faded, difficult magnificence' of the verse arises from the poet's lack of real interest in the play; he may have written perfunctorily, the fine things bursting out because of the pressure behind the pen. One guess seems no better than another. *The Two Noble Kinsmen* is of great interest to all students of Shakespeare but it is best thought of as a play by Fletcher to which Shakespeare contributed.

CONCLUSION

Conclusions, snatching all the plays together again for the sake of a neat generalization are dangerous. All that may safely be said is that the Romances form a distinct group, and are quite properly so called. They have connexions with earlier plays, but in them Shakespeare tried new things, and abstained from much that he had done very well before. They have, at moments, an astonishing simplicity and lucidity, yet never seem to be leaving life entirely out; their *naïveté* is a matter of art, yet could never be confounded with the *faux-naïf* of Fletcher. Because they are baffling in design and often in texture, and because we can love them and know them very well without feeling certain that we know why they are as they are, they may remind us of the works of other 'last periods', of Beethoven's, or perhaps of Yeats's—the 'little mechanical songs' and the noisy ballads coexisting with the obscure grandeur of, say, 'The Statues', the studied carelessness of some of the verse contrasting with the finish of masterpieces written fifteen years earlier.

So vague a concept as the 'last period'—it may properly be objected—is not very helpful if we are trying to understand the plays. True; and every attempt to treat the plays as if one key would unlock them all diminishes them. Each has its own peculiar greatness, each is to be understood in its own terms; and all impose upon the commentator limitations so severe that no reading, perhaps, will ever find general acceptance.

II

ADAM UNPARADISED

Molto è licito là, che qui non lece
alle nostre virtù, mercè del loco
fatto per proprio dell'umana spece.

It is no longer fashionable to use Raleigh's famous phrase, and call *Paradise Lost* a monument to dead ideas; but some such assumption underlies much of the modern hostility to Milton, however well concealed it may be. The proper answer to the charge is not that the ideas are, on the contrary, alive; but that the poem is not a monument to *any* ideas. And only an answer of that kind has much chance of being heard. The poem has had many ingenious and scholarly defenders; they have explained the habits of seventeenth-century readers, and shown that Milton was precise where he had been accused of imprecision; they have said a good deal about the poet's theology and even argued that literate Christians find no difficulty at all with his ideas. It is very good to have all this information; but it will not touch the quick of the objectors' position. No writer, so far as I know, has come so near to explaining what this is as the late A. J. A. Waldock did when he argued that the modern reader is really much too expert in fiction to put up with the crudity of Milton's narrative, and his imperfect control of its tone.[1] It is perfectly true that the modern reader, who thinks of novels when he thinks of long narratives, and who thinks of novels in post-Jamesian terms, will not find Milton 'thinking with his story' in the modern way; and he may assume that the reason for this failure is that Milton's mind was, on a great many

---

[1] A. J. A. Waldock, *Paradise Lost and its Critics* (1947).

points, made up for him in advance. And Waldock finds a damaging conflict between the official significance of what happens, and the natural bent of the narrative. This is held to limit the poem, to prevent it being what Lascelles Abercrombie nobly said epic poetry ought to be, an exhibition of 'life in some great symbolic attitude'.[2] I myself think this phrase precisely appropriate to *Paradise Lost*, and in a sense what I have to say is an indirect answer to Waldock. In fact, modern reader as I am, I find *Paradise Lost* wonderfully satisfying; not because of an odd taste for verse which has the qualities called by the Greek critic magnificence, sweetness and gravity, but because Milton's poem seems to me enduringly to represent, or better to embody, life in a great symbolic attitude.

THE NAÏVE

It is after all perverse of the modern reader to affect distaste at Milton's dependence on naïve materials; he ought to be properly conditioned to their use in art, not only by certain books of prime importance to him, but by the force of the whole Romantic tradition which always worshipped the primitive and became very explicit about the cult long before the end of the last century. It is to be studied anywhere from Herder to Nietzsche and Cassirer, from Rousseau to Jung, from Wordsworth to Pound; and when Gilbert Murray said that 'for full mental health the channels between primitive and sophisticated must be kept open' he spoke not only for a group of Cambridge scholars but for everybody. If there is one paramount requirement for major modern literature, it is that it should have a 'naïve' topic; that it should have found its myth; for only thus can everything be got in, and the whole truth presented, which would, under the conditions of sophisticated discourse, merely rattle endlessly on. So Mr. Eliot, with *Ulysses* in mind, spoke of myth as 'a way of controlling, of ordering, of giving a shape and a significance to the immense panorama of futility and anarchy which is contemporary history'; and Mr. Forster refers to the artist's power to do this as 'love', the power that can 'keep thought out'.

[2] *The Epic* (n.d.), p. 56.

Yet the world that these works confront is neither controlled by love nor free of 'thought'; and thought concerns itself, in *A Passage to India* and in *The Waste Land* as well as in *Paradise Lost*, with the conditions created by love's absence or corruption. There is a myth at the root of the work, and it contains all possible explanations; but the poem has to make it new and make it relevant. As much as any 'barren philosophy precept'—to adapt Greville's expression—it must be turned into 'pregnant images of life', whether it is the Grail or Paradise. The truth of the poem depends upon this process, not upon the special power of its theme. The modern reader has to agree not to indulge a special disrespect for Milton's myth; he should not despise it more than any other that accounts for the origin of death; but he must not be asked, on the other hand, to have a special respect for it, or for Milton's theology or his epic style. He owes them no more than he owes the story or the Hindu theology of *A Passage to India*, though of course he owes them no less.

Here, perhaps we arrive at an obstacle; it may appear that there is some confidence trick to be on one's guard against. Admirers of Milton do not often use the word 'myth' in this connexion, or offer full (though not licentious) freedom of interpretation. It may be that Waldock himself, having claimed this liberty, was afraid to use it; for he seems to call the poem wrong wherever he finds it pulling against what he assumes to be Milton's intention. It is important that one should be clear at this point, and understand that there is nothing in Milton's myth, nor in his own attitude to it so far as we can know what that was, to forbid the degree of liberty here proposed.

BIBLE TRUTH

As Johnson saw, Milton 'chose a subject on which too much could not be said'. Already in its primitive form it showed life in a symbolic attitude; to exhaust its implications you would have to say everything about everything. Of its nature, indeed, it would appear differently to different men, and to the same man at different times, so that no one man could ever say enough about it. A great many men had already had their say, and Milton knew a lot about his predecessors, and about the wide differences in their opinions as to the significance of the biblical narrative in later times.

A society whose sacred book is primitive closes the gap time has made by various devices of sophisticated explanation, of which allegory is the most important; with it the Stoics built a bridge between Homer and themselves, and generations of exegetes brought the Old Testament into conformity with a contemporary view of life.[3] Milton, though he is sparing of allegory, naturally had to think of his subject in something like this way, and obviously supposed that whatever the inconsistencies and difficulties it presented to the modern poet—many of them were as clear to him as to his commentators—this myth, precisely because of its inclusive quality, its containing the truth in little, could certainly be established as fully relevant to the here and now. Longinus said of certain parts of Homer that they were utterly indecorous unless taken allegorically; Milton has to stretch his literalism beyond breaking point to accept the Bible when it says that God laughed or repented (*De Doctrina Christiana*, I. ii); and for all that he found the Bible 'plain and perspicuous in all things necessary to salvation' he also held that it accommodated itself to the needs of its readers, 'even of the most unlearned' (*De Doctrina Christiana*, I. xxx). A perception of allegory or of 'accommodation' is the prelude to a certain liberty of interpreting, however restrained.

With a tradition of various interpretations behind him, all assuming that this myth embodied the whole human condition and could accordingly be endlessly explicated, Milton, though respecting the actual text of Genesis, thought himself entitled to handle it with a certain freedom, precisely in order to establish its universality. He would not have liked the word 'myth', at any rate in the sense here used; yet he does, in a way, treat his central topic rather as he does all those other related myths, mostly classical, which he is always bringing in. There is the important difference that these are usually rejected as erroneous fictions; but what makes them worth mentioning is that they contain (though only by natural light) ancient wisdom, worth remembering, recording and correcting. It is curious that Cowley, a pioneer whom Milton admired, had a decade earlier pronounced the whole repertory of classical myth to be exhausted; Milton suggests, with

[3] See, e.g., Beryl Smalley, *The Bible in the Middle Ages* (1941), pp. 2-3.

far more delicacy, and in the tradition of Christian Platonism, that in so far as these myths contain truth, it cannot be different from Truth itself; and he therefore uses this mythology to give both density and precision to the true story he is telling. In doing so he enriches his central myth, not of course in a way that sharpens its appeal to the *intelligence*; but that is not the primary purpose of poetry. He is constantly disclaiming these heathen fancies, but as constantly putting them in; in poetry all *buts* are partly *ands*, and an elaborate demonstration of the total difference between *x* and *y* is undertaken only if they are in some occult manner very alike. This is commonly admitted; no passage in *Paradise Lost* is more admired than that in which Milton explains that Proserpina's 'faire field | Of *Enna*' (iv. 268–9) was not Eden; and everybody remembers such references as those to Mulciber, and the fabled Hesperidean fruit. A less famous but very brilliant example of the method is in Raphael's greeting of Eve in Book V:

> but *Eve*
> Undeckt, save with her self more lovely fair
> That Wood-Nymph, or the fairest Goddess feignd
> Of three that in Mount *Ida* naked strove,
> Stood to entertain her guest from Heav'n; no veile
> Shee needed, Vertue-proof, no thought infirme
> Alterd her cheek. On whom the Angel *Haile*
> Bestowd, the holy salutation us'd
> Long after to blest *Marie*, second *Eve*.
>
> (v. 379–87)

The first thing we notice is the 'feignd', which puts this myth of the Judgement of Paris in its place. Allegorically the Judgement was normally used to illustrate the disastrousness of a young man's choosing the voluptuous rather than the active or contemplative ways of life; but Milton, by emphasizing the difference between Venus and Eve, is able to dispense with such excuses for paganism. Paris, not Venus, entertained guests from heaven, and he was not virtue-proof. But the real point is to associate Eve with both Venus and the Virgin: first the charged negative comparison with the goddess, then the *Ave* proper to Mary. As Mary is the second Eve, so is Eve the second Aphrodite, with all her contradictory attributes: her beauty is perpetually renewed, as Milton himself says in the fifth Latin elegy (1. 103); she is the patroness of fertility; she is dedicated under one aspect to order, and under another to voluptuous disorder and temptation. Under both characters she presides over the Garden of Love.[4] It is impossible that plain discourse should say so much about the Eve of the poem as this Venus–Eve–Mary triad suggests, especially if one remembers how wonderfully it is augmented by Adam's chastened echo of it after the Fall:

> the bitterness of death
> Is past, and we shall live. Whence Haile to thee,
> *Eve* rightly calld, Mother of all Mankind.
>
> (xi. 157–9)

Here is Mary's *Ave*; but here too the *Venus genetrix* of Lucretius: *per te quoniam omne animantium concipitur*. This is Milton's way of exploiting the sensuous illogic by which poetry makes its unparaphrasable points.

Milton, one may safely suggest, was no more naïve about his naïve subject than we are. If the style of the Scriptures is plain and perspicuous, his is not. If they assume that we can best understand the truth in a chronological arrangement, he does not. If they contain all things necessary to salvation, his poem contains both less and more, including a good deal that Milton doubtless believed to be true, but also a good deal that he did not. He sophisticates—or, with Schiller's sense in mind, 'sentimentalizes' might be better—his naïve subject; he is writing for the corrupt and intelligent. The original story, of inexhaustibly various significance for every individual, was there and known; and it would be absurd to suppose that Milton believed himself, in treating it, to be in full control of its affective power, no matter how much he might assume the right of the epic poet to intervene —to comment, to point out (Waldock found this distressing), that Adam was here being fondly overcome with female charm, or that Satan was there glozing. The more vitality he gets into the embodiment of the myth, the less adequate these comments will be; nothing he could say *about* Adam at that wonderful moment could seem adequate to the situation realized in the poem—a man's first glimpse of corruption and mortality, life in a great symbolic attitude.

---

[4] See, e.g., E. G. Kern, 'The Gardens of the Decameron Cornice', *Publication of the Modern Language Association of America*, xvi (1951), 505–23.

All this by way of opposing the notion that Milton's known views of scriptural inerrancy need prevent his myth working as it ought in a poem. His invention was not restrained by it; if he could not think with *his* story he could perfectly well think with *this* story. And his freedom to do so may be asserted yet more convincingly by a moment's consideration for what Milton thought to be the province of poetry—what he thought poems were for.

THE PROVINCE OF POETRY

To start from an obvious point: why does he not grind his formidable array of theological axes in the poem? For he certainly does not. The answer cannot be that he considered doing so and then rejected the notion as indecorous, nor as Rajan thinks,[5] that he put heresies into the poem only in veiled and oblique passages. In fact, it would not have occurred to Milton that poetry was a suitable medium for theological dispute. By an exercise of tact which, whether successful or not, is bold, he sets out the theological rules of the poem in Book iii as coming straight from God himself; there should be no room for argument so far as the poem is concerned about something very difficult and controverted which, though not at the heart of the work, had yet to be in it. He rather drily plots the whole course of human history according to the official point of view, and does it before we have even encountered Adam and Eve. This boldness is characteristic, and can also be seen at points where Milton does happen to think his own views relevant to the poem; there he puts them in, when many think he would have done well to leave them out, as for instance in his insistence on the materiality of angels. The reason is clear: this belief, like his mortalism and his rejection of creation *ex nihilo*, is related to his feelings about life in general. Thus, if he was to have angels he could afford to be pretty free with angelic lore in general (R. H. West has shown that Milton includes what he did not literally believe)[6] but not to hint at any discontinuity between body and spirit. This was more important to Milton than any other

---

[5] *Paradise Lost and the Seventeenth Century Reader* (1947), Cap. II, and especially p. 35.

[6] *Milton and the Angels* (1955), p. 101.

single belief, and he makes Raphael read a lecture on it (v. 469 ff.); it helped him to find the human situation tolerable and it infringed nothing in Scripture, so the angels eat and make love. He is risking a lot here, but not to make a theological or philosophical point. Milton wrote a theological treatise; but *Paradise Lost* is not it.

It could not have occurred to him to make it so; he would have thought merely commonplace Cowley's remark that 'if any man design to compose a *Sacred Poem*, only by turning a story of the Scripture, like Mr. *Quarles's*, or some other godly matter, like Mr. *Heywood of Angels*, into *Rhyme*; he is so far from elevating of *Poesie* that he only *abases Divinity*'.[7] From all Milton says about the way poetry works it is clear that he asks of it not that it should *immediately* instruct, but that it should immediately delight; and he presumably accepted some approximation of the Thomist gradations of logical discourse, which run from syllogistic certitude through dialectic, rhetorical probability and sophistic, down to poetry, which offers 'no better than a plausible estimate of the truth'.[8] Even in Hell, the song which suspends Hell and ravishes the audience is less sweet and elevated than the discourse, though fallacious, of the angels who 'reason'd high | Of Providence'; for, as Milton explains parenthetically, 'Eloquence the Soul, Song charms the Sense' (ii. 552-9).

Indeed, we shall always be standing at the wrong angle to *Paradise Lost* if we do not understand what Milton meant by his most celebrated critical observation, the remark that poetry is 'subsequent, or indeed rather precedent to logic' because it is 'less subtle and fine, but more simple, sensuous and passionate' (*Tractate of Education*). By 'simple' I take it Milton means what Fracastoro had in mind when he described poetry as the art *simpliciter bene dicendi*, of speaking well without other end; 'for the poet as a poet ... does not develop the matter enough to explain it ... all the others speak well and appropriately but not simply'.[9] The poet is concerned to transmit not explanations but delight, though there may be much benefit in this appeal to the senses,

[7] Preface to *Poems* (1656).

[8] W. J. Ong, 'The Province of Rhetoric and Poetic', *Modern Schoolman*, xix (1942), 25, quoting Aquinas; cited in W. K. Wimsatt, *The Verbal Icon* (1954), p. 223.

[9] Quoted in Madeline Doran, *Endeavors of Art* (1954), p. 28. See also pp. 87 ff.

since poetry has the power 'to allay the perturbations of the mind, and set the affections in right tune' (*The Reason of Church-Government*). The fundamental point is that poetry works through the senses; admittedly *dati sunt sensus ad intellectum excitandum*, but this is a more devious and uncertain route to the mind than logic and the other kinds of discourse. It is therefore entirely consistent, though still a little surprising, that Milton could say this: 'the words of a Psalm are too full of poetry, and this Psalm too full of passion, to afford us any exact definitions of right and justice; nor is it proper to argue anything of that nature from them' (*The Tenure of Kings and Magistrates*). Now for Milton the Psalms were the highest and most truthful of all poetry, 'to all true tasts excelling' (*Paradise Regained*, iv. 347); and he would apply this stricture, *a fortiori*, to *Paradise Lost*. He would, then, presumably deplore the amount of attention paid to its definitions of right and justice at the expense of its passion and poetry.

Poetry, since it works upon the passions, can obviously be dangerous if dishonestly directed or interpreted; and Milton speaks of the dangers to youth in libidinous poetasters and his own tactful handling of unchaste elegiac poets (*Smectymnuus*). He took the traditional view that a poet ought to be a good man, but he also thought that readers should be trained in virtue; his educational scheme allows the young men to study poetry only after they have been through the curriculum, and after they have reached the stage of *Proairesis*, that act of reason which enables them to contemplate upon moral good and evil. In short, he regards poetry, because of its predominantly sensuous nature, its working through the passions, as a force not of its nature entirely within the control of the author; the hearer's passions are under the control of his own reason, if of anybody's, and he can turn poetry to ill or to good. Milton would doubtless have considered those readers who heroise Satan to be either corrupt or imperfectly educated; but I do not think he would have argued that there was not, in some sense, an heroic Satan *in* the poem. To say that poetry appeals to the mind through the senses, and this is central to Milton's view of the function of poetry, is to admit that the poet's work can never be exactly regulated by his moral intention.

Nor is this doctrine isolated from Milton's more general ideas. As we shall see, his world, as *Paradise Lost* presents it, is unintelligible unless one gives due place to his remarkable insistence on the human capacity for pleasure—delight—and the relation of this to Man's possession of an immortal soul. The poem is primarily about the pleasures of Adam and their destruction by death; about the contrast between a world we can imagine, in which the senses are constantly and innocently enchanted, and a world of which this is not true. This is a contrast with which I shall be much occupied. It is responsible obviously, for much sophistication of the naïve material, and that in a manner very different from the theologian's or the philosopher's. It could not be presented in any other mode of discourse, and required the constant exercise of devices that may be called counterlogical. That *Paradise Lost* is in some sense counterlogical in presentation may strike anyone who has read the logical treatment of the Genesis passages in *De Doctrina* as self-evident; but it is worth mentioning because it is rarely mentioned. Milton in the poem is not aiming directly at the truth, but at the perturbed senses by means of delight; the planning of this circuitous route to the mind of the reader is an elaborate exercise in counterlogic.

COUNTERLOGICAL ELEMENTS

The syntax of the poem is a powerful counterlogical agent. I notice that Dr. Davie[10] decides that the dislocation of normal word-order works well in some places and not in others; and his demonstration is convincing. But he concludes that the practice itself betokens a failure to give proper value to a forward-moving narrative; when in truth movement in time is almost irrelevant to Milton's purpose. The syntax of the poem enables the texture of it to reflect the forces that govern its structure, the great contrasts which have nothing to do with chronological time because they are in the human condition as an inextricable pattern of dark and light, joy and woe, order and chaos, life and death, all making sense as a Latin sentence does, and also using the '. . . and then' as simply another form of emphasis.

One of the undoubted rediscoveries of the Renaissance was 'an awareness of syntactical process';[11] and only recently Professor

[10] In *The Living Milton* (1960), pp. 70–84.
[11] R. G. Faithfull, review of P. A. Verburg, *Taal en Functionaliteit*, in *Archivum Linguisticum*, vii (1955), 146.

F. T. Prince, in what is probably the most important book to have been written about Milton since the war, has made it plain that this rediscovery had a direct impact upon poetry. Milton's dislocations derive historically from Bembo's insistence on the latinization of the vulgar, so far as the vulgar could support this, as a means to gravity and pleasure; and Milton alone 'realized the dreams of Tasso and his predecessors'[12] by carrying to the necessary degree of 'magnificence' both the distortion of vulgar word-order and *asprezza* of diction and prosody—that disconnected speaking, *parlar disgiunto*, those tricks of elision and consonantal accumulation—thought proper to a topic seminally grave and pleasant. In treating his topic, the sample myth, in a manner so clearly conscious of the historical developments of human speech, Milton betrays the counterlogical complexity of his aim; for some purposes, not those of poetry, such complexity might be wickedness, but here it draws attention to the whole human experience under consideration. For in the fallen world pleasure is complex, and demands, as the price of its presence, that all routes to the reason be made difficult. The necessary deformation of language, which is both grave and pleasant, reflects the deformation of the faculty by which Adam named the beasts and Eve the flowers; it shows, though with delight, the difficulties under which we labour to repair the ruins of our first parents.

The most potent of counterlogical devices in verse is rhyme; and it may be asked why Milton, if bent on counterlogic, so unambiguously spurned it. Rhyme was, of course, inconsistent with the intention to achieve *latinità in volgare*; and in his note on the verse Milton calls rhyme 'no necessary Adjunct' of heroic verse, and labels it 'the Invention of a barbarous Age'; already it had been discarded by Italian and Spanish poets 'of prime note' as 'trivial and of no true musical delight; which consists only in apt Numbers, fit quantity of Syllables, and the sense variously drawn out from one Verse into another, not in the jingling sound of like endings'. To get rid of rhyme is to restore 'ancient liberty'.

Rhyme as a mark of bondage and inferiority is a notion likely enough to crop up in a post-Renaissance literature; yet even while its Gothic character was recognized, the possibilities it offered for counterlogical effects were most fully exploited. The special

[12] *The Italian Element in Milton's Verse* (1954), p. 13.

effects to be had from the collocation of ideas which, apparently totally heterogeneous, are momentarily exhibited, by the agency of rhyme, as possessing a magical resemblance, have been studied in Mr. W. K. Wimsatt's brilliant essay on Pope's rhymes.[13] Full rhyming (though the fullest, *rime riche*, was not licensed in England) is absolutely and intrusively illogical. Dr. Johnson thought rhyme should be intrusive, and disliked the remoteness of the rhymes in poems by Milton and Gray; and it may be that the rhyme of the *canzone*, which Milton imitates, is proper only to a language in which rhyme, because it is easier, is required to make less impact than it normally does in English. Later on there is great variety of rhyme in English—it is varied with half-rhyme, it is muted in different ways, it is employed internally and almost undetectably; but this comes in with poetry which is in other ways so clearly distinguished from logical discourse that there is no need to insist on its illogic. Milton might have found rhyme useful; but he had the failure of Cowley's biblical epic to warn him off, and he had all the resources of dislocated word order, of *parlar disgiunto*, in its place.

Nevertheless, there is more rhyming in *Paradise Lost* than people think,[14] and there is also a great deal of what may be called 'pseudo-rhyme'. It serves with all the other devices to distance logic. Milton, as F. T. Prince has shown, learned something of 'submerged rhyme' from the Italian Rota;[15] and, though I was writing out of the ignorance that prevailed before the publication of Prince's book, I still think there may be something in an old guess of my own that Milton was interested in a pretty widely held theory that the Psalms used rhyme and half-rhyme. Sometimes the rhymes in *Paradise Lost* may seem accidental:

> Thither let us *tend*,
> From off the tossing of these fiery waves,
> There rest, if any rest can harbour *there*,
> And reassembling our afflicted Powers,
> Consult how we may henceforth most *offend*

---

[13] 'Rhetoric and Poems: Alexander Pope', in *English Institute Essays* 1948 (1949); reprinted in *The Verbal Icon* (1953).

[14] See an elaborate study of the rhymes by J. S. Diekhoff, *P.M.L.A.*, xlix (1934).

[15] Op. cit., pp. 78–81.

> Our Enemy, our own loss how *repair*,
> How overcome this dire Calamity,
> What reinforcement we may gain from Hope,
> If not what resolution from *despair*.

> (i. 183–91)

I have here marked the full rhymes, but they only reinforce the
other conjunctions of opposites, such as the very characteristic
'hope-despair' of the last two lines quoted. This kind of antithesis, especially when strengthened by the placing of each term
at the end of a line, is a kind of pseudo-rhyming that goes on
throughout the poem. I open the work at Book v and find *all | all*
(470–1), *will | fate* (526–7), the short story of *will | fall | fall'n | fall |
woe*! (539–43), and the strong thematic triad *free | love | command*
(549–51). In the superb passage where Satan, having, 'stupidly
good', contemplated the beauty of Eve, bends himself to the task
of corrupting it, there is this fit of elaborate internal pseudo-
rhyming, brought to a close with a terminal half-rhyme.

> Shee fair, divinely fair, fit Love for Gods,
> Not terrible, though terror be in Love
> And beautie, not approacht by stronger hate,
> Hate stronger, under shew of Love well feignd,
> The way which to her ruin now I tend.

> (ix. 489–93)

And this whole passage echoes the lines describing Satan's first
sight of Eve, where there is this play with *delight, joy, woe* and *foe*:

> Ah gentle pair, ye little think how nigh
> Your change approaches, when all these delights
> Will vanish and deliver ye to woe,
> More woe, the more your taste is now of joy;
> Happie, but for so happie ill secur'd
> Long to continue, and this high seat your Heav'n
> Ill fenc't for Heav'n to keep out such a foe
> As now is enterd . . .

> (iv. 366–73)

The force of this comes generally from the conviction with which
the human predicament is stated ('for so happie ill secur'd') but
the impact depends upon the placing of 'woe' and 'foe', 'delights'

and 'joy', and also of 'nigh' and 'Ill'. There are a dozen other ways, rhetorical devices common and uncommon, of getting the effect of surprising rhyme without recourse to barbarous jingle: for instance, 'O fair foundation laid whereon to build | Thir ruin!' (iv. 521–2). This is, in the first place, a cruel paradox; one doesn't, or at this date didn't, build ruins. But there is also a pun-like effect using two senses of *ruin*, not only what is left after the destructive act, but also the fall itself—a sense which was still primary at the date of *Paradise Lost*. Another kind of pseudo-rhyming is found in some of Satan's close and fallacious argument, which not only gives the impression of being very tightly bound by phonetic repetitions but works like magic in deceiving Eve; consider, for instance, the brilliant lines ix. 694–702. If anybody doubts the truth of Richardson's well-known remark that the reader of Milton needs to be continually on duty, let him reread this passage and ask himself if he has always understood the argument by which Satan reaches his conclusion, 'Your feare it self of Death removes the fear' (702). His methods are rhetorical, but he is not interested in truth; this is a special kind of incantation aimed at the sense. One magic expression, 'death denounc't', continues hereafter to echo irrationally from this book of the Fall, through the next book, which is of despair: ix. 695, x. 49, 210, 852–3, 962.

It seems, then, that Milton did not abjure rhyme as an impediment to his dealing directly with the doctrinal substance of the theme, but because he had more complicated uses for it, more refined ideas about the way to achieve musical delight; his counter-logic is a vastly more subtle affair than a mere tagging of verses. And musical delight, before instruction, is his aim.[16]

We may conclude that there is reason to suppose that we shall miss the force of Milton's poem if we assume that he was strictly limited by the *naïveté* of his theme or the inerrancy of its biblical expression. His method is to affect the senses of his audience and not its reason directly. He could not have hoped for total control over the affective power of the poem, for that is not consistent with the nature of poetry; and in this particular poem the material is common property, so that there must be many aspects of it

---

[16] Here the reader might find it useful to be reminded of a remarkable passage on the rhetoric of irregular rhyming in Allen Tate's commentary on his own *Ode to the Confederate Dead*, 'Narcissus as Narcissus', *Reason in Madness* (1935).

which interest other people and not Milton, yet cannot be excluded. The original myth is a myth of total explanation, and therefore infinitely explicable; the poet can only say some of the things about it but the rest of it is still in men's minds, or indeed below them—Joyce's umbilical telephone line to Edenville. It is not of course doubted that Milton does offer interpretations, that he gets at the reader in many ways; the theology of Book iii, for example, is made to sound very dogmatic, though only to prevent irrelevant speculation; and we are always being told the proper way to think about Satan. As well as presenting the human predicament the poet suggests ways of understanding and accepting it. It should even be admitted that the general design of the poem is governed by this double purpose of presentation and interpretation; and that not only in the strategic theologizing of the third book and the loaded education of Adam between Books iv and ix. For although it is commonly said that Milton, on the ancient epic pattern, proceeds *in medias res*, he in fact strikes into his subject nothing like so near the middle as Virgil and Homer; he starts not in the Garden but with the fall of the angels, which is why some schoolchildren, having read Books i and ii, go through life thinking it was Satan who lost Paradise. The reason for this, one guesses, is that Milton wanted us to think of events in this order: the Fall from Heaven, the Fall from Paradise, and finally the effect of the Fall in the life of humanity in general, just in the manner of Ignatian meditation on these subjects.[17] But it is important that we should not allow considerations of this sort to lead to a conviction that there is at all times a design upon us. So deceived, we can easily miss something far more obvious and important to the structure of the poem: namely, that it is based on a series of massive antitheses, or if you like huge structural pseudo-rhymes, and the central pseudo-rhyme is *delight | woe*. The delight and woe are here and now, which is the real point of all the squeezing together of the time-sequences that Milton carries on in his similes, in upsetting allusions to clerical corruption, in using expressions like 'never since created man' or 'since mute'; in a hundred other ways, some of which I shall discuss later. The poem is absolutely contemporary, and its subject is human experience symbolized in this basic myth, and here made relevant in a manner

[17] See, e.g. *The Sermons and Devotional Writings of Gerard Manley Hopkins*, ed. C. Devlin (1959), pp. 131 ff.

not so different from that to which our own century has accustomed us.

THE THEMES

Miss Rosemond Tuve, in her magnificent and too brief book, has persuasively expounded Milton's treatment in the minor poems of certain great central themes. They lie at the heart of each poem and govern its secondary characteristics of imagery and diction; given the theme, the poet thinks in the figures appropriate to it, and in every case the theme and the figures have a long and rich history. 'The subject of *L'Allegro* is every man's Mirth, our Mirth, the very Grace herself with all she can include';[18] the *Hymn on the Morning of Christ's Nativity* proliferates images of harmony because its theme is the Incarnation. I now take a step of which Miss Tuve would probably not approve, and add that beneath these figures and themes there is Milton's profound and personal devotion to an even more radical topic, potentially coextensive with all human experience: the loss of Eden. In the *Hymn* there is a moment of peace and harmony in history—the 'Augustan peace', which looks back to human wholeness and incorruption, as well as forward to a time when, after generations of human anguish, the original harmony will be restored. The same moment of stillness, poised between past and future, is there in 'At a Solemn Musick', for music remembers as well as prefigures. In *Comus* too there is presented that moment of harmony, of reunion and restitution, that prefigures the final end, and in *Comus* as in the others there is an emphasis on the long continuance of grief and suffering; for in the much misunderstood Epilogue Adonis is still not cured of his wound and Venus 'sadly sits'. Only in the future will Cupid be united with Psyche and the twins of Paradise, Youth and Joy, be born. *Lycidas* tells of disorder, corruption, false glory as incident of life here and now, with order, health, and the perfect witness of God to come. All of them speak of something that is gone.

Paradise Lost deals most directly with this basic theme, the recognition of lost possibilities of joy, order, health, the contrast between what we can imagine as human and what is so here and

[18] *Images and Themes in Five Poems by Milton* (1957), p. 20.

now; the sensuous import of the myth of the lost Eden. To embody this theme is the main business of *Paradise Lost*; thus will life be displayed in some great symbolic attitude and not by the poet's explanations of the how and why. His first task is to get clear the human experience of the potency of delight, and its necessary frustration, and if he cannot do that the poem will fail no matter what is added of morality, theology or history.

My difficulty in establishing this point is that some will think it too obvious to be thus laboured, and others will think it in need of much more elaborate defence. What is rare is to find people who read *Paradise Lost* as if it were true that the power of joy and its loss is its theme; and though it is true that for certain well-known and important reasons Milton's poem is not accessible to the same methods of reading as Romantic literature, it is also true that this is the theme of *The Prelude*, and that we can do some harm by insisting too strongly upon differences at the expense of profound similarities. Anyway, I think I can make my point in a somewhat different way by a reference to Bentley, and in particular to his observations on the last lines of *Paradise Lost*, stale as this subject may seem.

Adam hearing Michael's promise of a time when 'Earth | Shall all be Paradise, far happier place | Than this of *Eden*' (xii. 463–5) is 'replete with joy and wonder' (468) and replies with the famous cry of *felix culpa*:

> full of doubt I stand,
> Whether I should repent me now of sin
> By mee done and occasiond, or rejoice
> Much more, that much more good thereof shall spring . . .
>
> (473–6)

Michael says that the comforter will watch over and arm the faithful; Adam, benefiting by Michael's foretelling of the future (in which 'time stands fixt' as it does in the poem) has now all possible wisdom (575–6); and Eve is well content with her lot. And thus matters stand when Eden is closed, and Adam and Eve move away:

> The World was all before them, where to choose
> Thir place of rest, and Providence thir guide:
> They hand in hand with wandring steps and slow,
> Through *Eden* took their solitarie way.
>
> (xii. 646–9)

'Why,' asks Bentley, 'does this distich dismiss our first parents in anguish, and the reader in melancholy? And how can the expression be justified, *with wandring steps and slow*? Why *wandring*? Erratick steps? Very improper, when, in the line before, they were *guided by Providence*. And why slow? even when Eve has professed her readiness and alacrity for the journey:

> but now lead on;
> In me is no delay.

And why their *solitarie way*? All words to represent a sorrowful parting? when even their former walks in Paradise were as solitary as their way now; there being nobody besides them two both here and there. Shall I therefore, after so many prior presumptions, presume at last to offer a distich, as close as may be to the author's words, and *entirely agreeable to his scheme*?

> Then hand in hand with *social* steps their way
> Through Eden took, *with heavenly comfort cheer'd*.'

Bentley assumes that he has exact knowledge of Milton's 'scheme', and quarrels with the text for not fitting it. He seems to be forgetting God's instructions to Michael—'so send them forth, though sorrowing, yet in peace' (xi. 117), and also Adam's knowledge of the events leading up to the happy consummation; yet it remains true that if Milton's 'scheme' was simply to show that everything would come out right in the end, and that this should keenly please both Adam and ourselves, Bentley is not at all silly here; or if he is, so are more modern commentators who, supported by all that is now known about the topic *felix culpa*, tend to read the poem in a rather similar way though without actually rewriting it, by concentrating on Milton's intention, somewhat neglected in the past, to present this belated joy of Adam's as central to the whole poem. There is, of course, such an intention or 'scheme'; the mistake is to suppose that it is paramount. It is in fact subsidiary, *Paradise Lost* being a poem, to the less explicable theme of joy and woe, which has to be expressed in terms of the myth, as a contrast between the original justice of Paradise and the mess of history: between Paradise and Paradise lost. The poem is tragic. If we regard it as a document in the history of ideas, ignoring what it does to our senses, we shall of course find ideas, as Bentley did, and conceivably the closing lines will seem out of true. But our disrespect for Bentley's Milton, and in this place particularly, is proof that the poem itself will prevent our doing this unless we are very stubborn or not very susceptible to poetry. The last lines of the poem are, we *feel*, exactly right, for all that Adam has cried out for pleasure; death denounced, he has lost his Original Joy. The tragedy is a matter of *fact*, of life as we feel it; the hope of restoration is a matter of faith, and faith is 'the substance of things hoped for, the evidence of things unseen' —a matter altogether less simple, sensuous, and passionate, altogether less primitive. We are reminded that 'the conception that man is mortal, by his nature and essence, seems to be entirely alien to mythical and primitive religious thought'.[19] In the poem we deplore the accidental loss of native immortality more than we can applaud its gracious restoration.

ADAM IMPARADISED

One of the effects of mixing up Milton with the Authorized Version, and of intruding mistaken ideas of Puritanism into his verse, is that it can become very hard to see what is made absolutely plain: that for Milton the joy of Paradise is very much a matter of the senses. The Authorized Version says that 'the Lord God planted a garden' (Gen. ii. 8) and that he 'took the man and put him into the garden of Eden to dress it and keep it' (ii. 15). But even in Gen. ii. 8 the Latin texts usually have *in paradisum voluptatis* 'into a paradise of pleasure'—this is the reading of the Vulgate currently in use. And the Latin version of ii. 15 gives *in paradiso deliciarum*. Milton's Paradise is that of the Latin version; in it, humanity without guilt is 'to all delight of human sense expos'd' (iv. 206), and he insists on this throughout. Studying the exegetical tradition on this point, Sister Mary Corcoran makes it plain that Milton pushes this sensuous pleasure much harder than his 'scheme', as Bentley and others might conceive it, required. For example, he rejected the strong tradition that the first marriage was not consummated until after the Fall, choosing to ignore the difficulty about children conceived before but born after it. For this there may be an historical explanation in the Puritan cult of married love; but it could not account for what

[19] E. Cassirer, *An Essay on Man* (1944), pp. 83-4.

has been called Milton's 'almost Dionysiac treatment' of sexuality before the Fall; Sister Corcoran is sorry that she can't even quite believe the assertion that 'in those hearts | Love unlibidinous reignd' (v. 449–50).[20]

In fact Milton went to great trouble to get this point firmly made; had he failed no amount of finesse in other places could have held the poem together; and it is therefore just as well that nothing in the poem is more beautifully achieved.

Why was innocent sexuality so important to Milton's poem? Why did he take on the task of presenting an Adam and an Eve unimaginably privileged in the matter of sensual gratification, 'to all delight of human sense expos'd'? There is a hint of the answer in what I have written earlier about his view of the function of poetry. Believing as he did in the inseparability of matter and form, except by an act of intellectual abstraction, Milton could not allow a difference of kind between soul and body; God

> created all
> Such to perfection, one first matter all,
> Indu'd with various forms, various degrees
> Of substance, and in things that live, of life;
> But more refin'd, more spiritous and pure,
> As nearer to him plac't or nearer tending
> Each in thir several active Sphears assigned,
> Till body up to spirit work, in bounds
> Proportiond to each kind. So from the root
> Springs lighter the green stalk, from thence the leaves
> More aerie, last the bright consummat flowre
> Spirits odorous breathes: flowrs and thir fruit
> Mans nourishment, by gradual scale sublim'd
> To vital Spirits aspire, to animal,
> To intellectual, give both life and sense,
> Fancie and understanding, whence the Soule
> Reason receives, and reason is her being,
> Discursive or Intuitive; discourse
> Is oftest yours, the latter most is ours . . .
>
> (v. 471–89)

---

[20] Harris Fletcher, *Milton's Rabbinical Readings* (1930), p. 185. *Paradise Lost with reference to the Hexameral Background* (1945), pp. 76 ff.

An acceptance of Raphael's position involves, given the cosmic scale of the poem, a number of corollaries which Milton does not shirk. Matter, the medium of the senses, is continuous with spirit; or 'spirit, being the more excellent substance, virtually and essentially contains within itself the inferior one; as the spiritual and rational faculty contains the corporeal, that is, the sentient and vegetative faculty' (*De Doctrina Christiana*, I. vii). It follows that the first matter is of God, and contains the potentiality of form,[21] so the body is not to be thought of in disjunction from the soul, of which 'rational', 'sensitive' and 'vegetative' are merely aspects. Raphael accordingly goes out of his way to explain that the intuitive reason of the angels differs only in degree from the discursive reason of men; and Milton that there is materiality in angelic spirit. It is a consequence of this that part of Satan's sufferings lie in a deprivation of sensual pleasure. Milton's thought is penetrated by this doctrine, which, among other things, accounts for his view of the potency of poetry for good or ill; for poetry works through pleasure, by sensuous delight; it can help 'body up to spirit work' or it can create dangerous physiological disturbance. Obviously there could be no more extreme challenge to the power and virtue of his art than this: to require of it a representation of ecstatic sensual pleasure, a *voluptas* here and only here not associated with the possibility of evil: 'delight to Reason join'd' (ix. 243). The loves of Paradise must be an unimaginable joy to the senses, yet remain 'unlibidinous'.

If we were speaking of Milton rather than of his poem we might use this emphasis on materiality, on the dignity as well as the danger of sense, to support a conclusion similar to that of De Quincey in his account of Wordsworth: 'his intellectual passions were fervent and strong; but they rested upon a basis of preternatural animal sensibility diffused through *all* the animal passions (or appetites); and something of that will be found to hold of all poets who have been great by original force and power . . .' (De Quincey was thinking about Wordsworth's facial resemblance to Milton). And it would be consistent with such an account that Milton also had, like Wordsworth, a constant awareness of the dangers entailed by a powerful sensibility. This gives us the short reason why, when Milton is representing the

[21] See W. B. Hunter, Jr., 'Milton's Power of Matter', *Journal of the History of Ideas*, xiii (1952), 551-62.

enormous bliss of innocent sense, he does not do so by isolating
it and presenting it straightforwardly. He sees that we must grasp
it at best deviously; we understand joy as men partially deprived
of it, with a strong sense of the woeful gap between the possible
and the actual in physical pleasure. And Milton's prime device for
ensuring that we should thus experience his Eden is a very
sophisticated, perhaps a 'novelistic' one: we see all delight
through the eyes of Satan.

POINTS OF VIEW

I shall return to this, and to the other more or less distorting
glasses that Milton inserts between us and the voluptuousness of
Eden; but first it seems right to say a word in general on a
neglected subject, Milton's varying of the point of view in this
poem. He uses the epic poet's privilege of intervening in his own
voice, and he does this to regulate the reader's reaction; but some
of the effects he gets from this device are far more complicated
than is sometimes supposed. The corrective comments inserted
after Satan has been making out a good case for himself are not
to be lightly attributed to a crude didacticism; naturally they are
meant to keep the reader on the right track, but they also allow
Milton to preserve the energy of the myth. While we are hearing
Satan we are not hearing the comment; for the benefit of a fallen
audience the moral correction is then applied, but its force is
calculatedly lower; and the long-established custom of claiming
that one understands Satan better than Milton did is strong
testimony to the tact with which it is done. On this method the
devil can have good tunes. Not only does his terrible appearance
resemble an eclipse which 'with fear of change | Perplexes Mon-
archs' (i. 598–9), but his oratory can include sound republican
arguments—God is 'upheld by old repute, | Consent or custom'
(639–40). This sort of thing makes its point before the authorial
intervention corrects it. Milton even takes the risk of refraining
from constant intervention and Satan-baiting in the first book,
where the need for magnificence and energy is greatest. It is in
the second that the intense persuasions of the angelic debaters are
firmly qualified; the speech of Belial is a notable case, for it is
poignantly and humanly reasonable, but hedged before and

behind by sharp comments on its hollowness and lack of nobility. We may find this argument attractive, but we ought to know that it has a wider moral context, and this the comment provides. At the other extreme, when God is laying down the law or Raphael telling Adam what he needs to know, the presentation is bare and unambiguous not because there is nothing the author wants to draw one's attention to but because these are not the places to start on the difficult question of how the reader's senses enhance or distort the truth; it is when the fallen study the deviousness of the fallen that corrective comment is called for, but even there sense must be given its due.

Of all the feats of narrative sophistication in the poem the most impressive is the presentation of the delights of Paradise under the shadow of Satan. He approaches out of chaos and darkness; a warning voice cries 'Woe to th'inhabitants on Earth' (iv. 5); he is 'inflam'd with rage' (9) as he moves in on calm and joy; and the consequences of the coming encounter are prefigured in the terminal words of lines 10–12: *Mankind* ... *loss* ... *Hell*. Before him Eden lies 'pleasant' (28); but we are not to see the well-tempered joys of its inhabitants before we have studied, with Uriel in the sun, the passionate face of Satan, marred by 'distempers foule' (118), a condition possible only to the fallen. He fares forward to Eden, 'delicious Paradise' (132); distemper and delight are about to meet. A good deal is made of the difficulty of access to Eden; not, I think, because Satan would find it difficult—he 'in contempt | At one slight bound high overleap'd all bound' (180–1)—but because *we* must find it so; we are stumbling, disorientated, with Satan into an unintelligible purity:

> And of pure now purer aire
> Meets his approach, and to the heart inspires
> Vernal delight and joy, able to drive
> All sadness but despair: now gentle gales
> Fanning thir odoriferous wings dispense
> Native perfumes, and whisper whence they stole
> Those baumie spoils. As when to them who sail
> Beyond the *Cape of Hope*, and now are past
> *Mozambic*, off at Sea North-East winds blow
> *Sabean* Odours from the spicie shore
> Of *Arabie* the blest, with such delay

> Well pleas'd they slack thir course, and many a League
> Cheerd with the grateful smell old Ocean smiles.
> So entertaind those odorous sweets the Fiend
> Who came thir bane, though with them better pleas'd
> Than *Asmodeus* with the fishie fume,
> That drove him, though enamour'd, from the Spouse
> Of *Tobits* Son, and with a vengeance sent
> From *Media* post to *Egypt*, there fast bound.
>
> (152–71)

This passage is preceded by praises of the colours of Paradise, and of delights directed at the senses of hearing, touch and taste; here the sense of smell is predominant, and Milton provides a remarkable association of fallen and unfallen odours. What becomes of the scents of Eden? They decay, and another smell replaces them, as Death himself will describe:

> a scent I draw
> Of carnage, prey innumerable, and taste
> The savour of Death from all things there that live . . .
> So saying, with delight he snuffd the smell
> Of mortal change on Earth.
>
> (x. 267 ff.)

At first Milton uses a lot of force to establish a situation lacking entirely this evil smell. 'Of pure now purer aire'—we are moving into the very centre of purity, delight and joy, where no sadness could survive save irredeemable hopelessness (a hint that even this purity cannot repel Satan). The breezes carry scents which betray their paradisal origin: 'baumie' is a key-word in the life-asserting parts of the poem, being used in the sense in which Donne uses it in the 'Nocturnall', as referring to the whole principle of life and growth; compare 'virtue', meaning natural vitality, in the same parts. The simile of the perfumes drifting out to sea from Arabia Felix refers to this breeze-borne odour, but also, with a characteristic and brilliant syntactical turn, to its effect upon Satan, the next topic treated; 'as when' seems at first to refer back, then to refer forward. This effect is helped by the Miltonic habit of boxing off formal similes with fullstops before and after. Satan checks himself at this influx of sensual delight; but we are reminded, with maximum force, of the difference between Satan and the sailors, by the emphatic 'Who came thir bane'. And this dissonance prepares us for the fuller ambiguities introduced by the reference to Asmodeus, a lustful devil who was driven away from Sarah by the stink of burning fish-liver. Why does Milton go about to fetch Asmodeus into his verses? The point is not that one he explicitly makes, that Satan liked the smell of Eden better than Asmodeus the smell of fish-liver; anybody who believes that will believe all he is told about Milton's sacrificing sense to sound, and so forth. The point is partly that Satan is also going to be attracted by a woman; partly that he too will end by being, as a direct consequence of his attempt upon her, 'fast bound'; but the poet's principal intention is simply to get into the context a bad smell. The simile offers as an excuse for its existence a perfunctory logical connexion with what is being said; but it is used to achieve a purely sensuous effect. As soon as we approach Eden there is a mingling of the good actual odour with a bad one, of Life with Death.

Another rather similar and equally rich effect is produced by another very long sentence, iv. 268–311. From the dance of 'Universal *Pan* | Knit with the *Graces*' (286–7) we pass on to negative comparisons between Eden and other gardens. All the negations work at an unimportant level of discourse; they are denials of similarity which would not be worth making if they did not imply powerful resemblances. Eden is not the vale of Enna, nor Eve Proserpina, nor Satan Dis, nor Ceres Christ. Though Daphne was saved from a devil by a divine act, her grove was not Eden, and though 'old *Cham*' protected in another garden the 'Florid Son' of Amalthea, this does not mean that the garden of Bacchus was the same paradise as that in which another lover of pleasure, almost divine, was, though inadequately, protected. In their unlikeness they all tell us more about the truth of Eden; yet it is upon their unlikeness that Milton is still, apparently, dwelling when his Satan breaks urgently in; they are all

> wide remote
> From this *Assyrian* Garden, where the Fiend
> Saw undelighted all delight. . . .
>
> (285–6)

Whereupon, having included the undelighted Satan in the enormous, delighted scene, Milton goes on, still without a full period, to an elaborate account of Adam and Eve.

THE GARDEN OF LOVE

The degree of literary sophistication in Milton's treatment of
the biblical account of Adam and Eve in Paradise is a reasonably
accurate index of his whole attitude to what I have called the
myth. I have already mentioned the incorporation of other
literary and mythological gardens in this Eden; they are significant
shadows of it. But the full exploration of the literary context of
Milton's Paradise would be a very large inquiry, and here there is
occasion only for a brief and tentative sketch of it, touching only
upon what affects the present argument.

When Milton comes to treat of the inhabitants of the garden he
plunges us at once into a dense literary context. The Bible says:
'And they were both naked, the man and his wife, and were not
ashamed' (Genesis ii. 25). According to Milton, however, they
were 'with native Honour clad | In naked Majestie' (289–90); and
a little later he moralizes this:

> Nor those mysterious parts were then conceal'd,
> Then was not guiltie shame, dishonest shame
> Of Natures works: honor dishonorable,
> Sin-bred, how have ye troubl'd all mankind
> With shews instead, mere shows of seeming pure . . .
> (312–16)

This is in open allusion to a literary topic so often treated in
Renaissance and seventeenth-century writing as to be unwieldy in
its complexity. First one needs to understand the general primi-
tivistic position which held that custom and honour were shabby
modern expedients unnecessary in a Golden Age society, with all
its corollaries in Renaissance 'naturalism'. Then one has to consider the extremely complex subject of literary gardens and their
connexion with the Earthly Paradise and the Golden Age, not
only in Renaissance, but also in classical and medieval literature.
Of the first of these I now say nothing. The easy way to approach
the second is through the *locus classicus*, the chorus *O bella età de
l'oro* in Tasso's *Aminta*. In the Golden Age, as in Eden, the earth
bore fruit and flowers without the aid of man; the air was calm

and there was eternal spring. Best of all, there was continual
happiness because—in the translation of Henry Reynolds—

> Because that vain and ydle name,
> That couz'ning Idoll of unrest,
> Whom the madd vulgar first did raize,
> And call'd it Honour, whence it came
> To tyrannize o're ev'ry brest,
> Was not then suffred to molest
> Poore lovers hearts with new debate. . . .
> The Nymphes sate by their Paramours,
> Whispring love-sports, and dalliance. . . .

It was Honour that ruined Pleasure,

> And lewdly did instruct faire eyes
> They should be nyce, and scrupulous . . .
> (*Torquato Tassos Aminta Englisht*, 1628)

This is the Honour, a tyrant bred of custom and ignorant opinion,
which inevitably intrudes into Milton's argument when he uses
the word in forcible oxymoron, 'honor dishonorable'. But he is
not using the idea as it came sometimes to be used in poetry
Milton would have called dishonest; his Honour is 'sin-bred', a
pathetic subterfuge of the fallen, and not, as it is in libertine
poems, an obstacle to sexual conquest that must yield to primitivist
argument.[22] Of these ambiguities Milton must have been fully
aware, since the poetry of his time contains many libertine attacks
on Honour which imply that reason and 'native Honour' will be
satisfied only by an absolute surrender to pleasure. Furthermore,
many of these poems are set in gardens, and we should not over-
look the difficulties Milton had to overcome before he could be
reasonably satisfied that his garden of love was the right kind. The
garden of love has a long history, and the topic nowadays called
the *locus amoenus*[23] is as old as the garden of Alcinoüs in the
Odyssey; the expression *locus amoenus* meant to Servius 'a place for
lovemaking', and *amoenus* was derived by a false etymology from

---

[22] I have said part of my say about this in 'The Argument of Marvell's
Garden', *Essays in Criticism*, ii (1952), 225–41.

[23] See E. R. Curtius, *European Literature in the Latin Middle Ages* (1952),
Cap. 10, especially pp. 195 ff. And among the growing literature on this
theme, E. G. Kern's article cited in note 4, p. 265.

amor. This tradition, mingling with the continuous traditions of the Earthly Paradise, and modified by the allegorical skills of the Middle Ages, sometimes conformed and sometimes conflicted with the garden of Genesis; gardens could be the setting for all kinds of love, just as Venus herself could preside over all kinds of love and all kinds of gardens. Milton needed a *paradisus voluptatis*, but it must not be the same as a 'naturalist' or libertine garden, and it must not be connected with 'courtly love'—hence the disclaimers in ll. 744 ff. and ll. 769-70. Whatever the dishonest and sophisticate, for that matter the falsely philosophical, might do with imaginary Edens, he was dealing with the thing itself, and must get innocent delight into it. So he uses these conventions, including the usual attack upon Honour, with his customary boldness, as if his treatment, though late, were the central one, and all the others mere shadows of his truth; the same method, in fact, as that used for pagan mythology. In Book ix, having risked all the difficulties of his contrast between love unlibidinous and love libidinous by showing them both in the experience of Adam and Eve, he is able to enlarge upon the oxymoron 'honor dishonorable', saying that

> innocence, that as a veil
> Had shaddowd them from knowing ill, was gon,
> Just confidence and native righteousness,
> And honour from about them. . . .
>
> (ix. 1054-7)

And Adam sees that the fruit of knowledge was bad, 'if this be to know, | Which leaves us naked thus, of Honour void' (1073-4); here the fig-leaves are assimilated to the literary tradition. As for *locus amoenus*, Milton also contrives to give two versions of it: in Book iv it is worked into the account of 'unreprov'd' love-making (see especially ll. 1034 ff.) as the scene of the first fallen act of love. Pope first saw another link between these two passages, and Douglas Bush has recently written upon this link a brilliant page of commentary:[24] each derives a good deal, and the manner of derivation is ironical, from a single episode in the *Iliad*, the lovemaking of Zeus and Hera in Book xiv.

So erudite and delicate, yet so characteristic a device might find, among fit audience, someone to value it for itself; but

[24] *Paradise Lost in our Time* (1948), pp. 105-6.

Milton's object was to exploit, with what force all the literature in the world could lend, the contrast between the true delight of love and the fallacious delight which is a mere prelude to woe; between possible and actual human pleasure. And however complex the means, the end is simply to show Adam and Eve as actually enjoying what to us is a mere imagination, and then explain how they lost it, and what was then left. In this sense their simple experience contains the whole of ours, including that which we feel we might but know we cannot have; and in this sense they include us, they are what we are and what we imagine we might be. This inclusiveness is given remarkably concrete demonstration in lines so famous for their unidiomatic English that the reason for the distorted word-order has been overlooked:

> the lovliest pair
> That ever since in loves imbraces met,
> *Adam* the goodliest man of men since born
> His Sons, the fairest of her Daughters *Eve*.
>
> (iv. 321–4)

The syntax may be Greek, but the sense is English, and inclusiveness could hardly be more completely presented; Adam and Eve here literally include us all. The illogic of the expression serves the same end as the illogic of those mythological parallels inserted only to be denied, or of those continuous reminders that the whole of history 'since created man' is somehow being enacted here and now in the garden. What must never be underestimated is the sheer absorbency of Milton's theme; everything will go into it, and find itself for the first time properly placed, completely explained. Todd has a note on the passage (iv. 458 ff.) in which Milton adapts to the awakening of Eve Ovid's account of Narcissus first seeing himself in the pool: he cites one commentator who enlarges upon Milton's enormous improvement of Ovid's lines, and another who adds that 'we may apply to Milton on this occasion what Aristotle says of Homer, that he taught poets how to lie properly'. Lying properly about everything is a reasonable way of describing the poet's achievement in *Paradise Lost*, if a proper lie is one that includes the *terra incognita* of human desires, actual love and possible purity.

That is why we see Adam and Eve in the garden of love not directly, but through many glasses; and the darkest of these is the mind of Satan. He looks at his victims with passionate envy and even regret:

> Ah gentle pair, ye little think how nigh
> Your change approaches, when all these delights
> Will vanish and deliver ye to woe,
> More woe, the more your taste is now of joy;
> Happie, but for so happie ill secur'd
> Long to continue, and this high seat your Heav'n
> Ill fenc't for Heav'n to keep out such a foe
> As now is enterd.
>
> (iv. 366–73)

He is reluctant to harm them; he pleads necessity (Milton calls this 'The Tyrants plea' (394) and neatly gives it to Adam in x. 131 ff.). But what he must take away from them is *delight*, physical pleasure in innocence; his dwelling in Hell 'haply may not please | Like this fair Paradise, your sense' (iv. 378–9). They are to 'taste' something other than Joy; and one remembers how frequently, at critical moments, the word 'taste' occurs in *Paradise Lost*, from the second line on. The shadow of Satan falls most strikingly over the pleasures of the garden when he watches Adam and Eve making love. It is not merely that the absolutely innocent and joyous act is observed as through a peep-hole, as if the lovers had been tricked into a bawdy-house; Satan himself acquires some of the pathos of an old *voyeur*. Pursuing his equation of delight with innocence, Milton boldly hints that the fallen angel is sexually deprived. He has forfeited the unfallen delights of sense. There is, we are to learn, lovemaking in heaven, but not in hell; the price of warring against omnipotence is impotence.

> Sight hateful, sight tormenting! thus these two
> Imparadis't in one anothers arms
> The happier *Eden*, shall enjoy thir fill
> Of bliss on bliss, while I to Hell am thrust,
> Where neither joy nor love, but fierce desire,
> Among our other torments not the least,
> Still unfulfilld with pain of longing pines . . .
>
> (iv. 505–11)

Satan is so sure of their sexual joy that he anticipates later love poetry in making the body of the beloved a paradise in itself—his 'happier Eden' is not the same as that promised later to Adam

(xii. 587)—and he uses a word, 'imparadis't' which was to have its place in the vocabulary of fallen love. But at this moment only Satan can feel desire without fulfilment, and Milton reminds us that he resembles in this fallen men; thus he actualizes the human contrast between innocence and experience, and between love and its counterfeits—the whole 'monstruosity of love', as Troilus calls it.

Milton, in short, provides an illogical blend of purity and impurity in the first delightful lovemaking. He does not present an isolated purity and then its contamination, as the narrative might seem to require, but interferes with this order just as he does with word-order, and for similar reasons. Not only does he show us the unfallen Adam and Eve in such a way that we can never think of their delight without thinking of its enemies; he also establishes such links between the fourth and ninth books that we can never think of his account of unfallen love without remembering the parallel passages on lust. It is here relevant to emphasize the unpraised brilliance of one of the linking devices, Milton's use of the theme of physiological perturbation. At the opening of Book iv Uriel observes that Satan is affected by unregulated passions, as the unfallen Adam and Eve cannot be; he is the first person on earth to experience this. But by the end of the Book he has established by an act of demonic possession that Eve is physiologically capable of such a disturbance (iv. 799 ff; v. 9–11); and the effect of the Fall in Book ix can be measured by the degree to which the humours of the lovers are distempered by the fruit:

> Soon as the force of that fallacious Fruit,
> That with exhilerating vapour bland
> About thir spirits had playd, and inmost powers
> Made err, was now exhal'd, and grosser sleep
> Bred of unkindly fumes, with conscious dreams
> Encumberd, now had left them, up they rose
> As from unrest. . . .

$$(ix. 1046-52)$$

We happen to know what Milton, as theologian, believed to be the significance of the eating of the fruit. He regarded the tree of the knowledge of good and evil as merely 'a pledge, as it were, and memorial of obedience'. The tasting of its fruit was an act that included all sins: 'it comprehended at once distrust in the

divine veracity, and a proportionate credulity in the assurances of
Satan; unbelief, ingratitude; disobedience; gluttony; in the man
excessive uxoriousness, in the woman a want of proper regard
for her husband, in both an insensibility to the welfare of their
offspring, and offspring the whole human race; parricide, theft,
invasion of the rights of others, sacrilege, deceit, presumption in
aspiring to divine attributes, fraud in the means employed to
attain the object, pride, and arrogance' (*De Doctrina Christiana* I.
xi, Sumner's translation). But none of this stemmed from the
intoxicating power of the fruit; God was testing fidelity by forbidding 'an act of its own nature indifferent'. In other words
Milton the poet establishes the theme of perturbation as a
structural element in the poem, using it as an index of fallen
nature, of the disaster brought upon Joy by Woe, by means which
must have earned the disapproval of Milton the theologian,
namely the attribution of intoxicating powers to the forbidden
fruit. Joy and Woe in the poem take precedence over theological
niceties; Milton's theology is in the *De Doctrina*, not in *Paradise
Lost*.

ADAM UNPARADISED

Joy and Woe, the shadow of one over the other, the passage from
one to the other, are the basic topic of the poem. We turn now
to Adam unparadised, to Joy permanently overshadowed by Woe,
light by dark, nature by chaos, love by lust, fecundity by sterility.
Death casts these shadows. It is not difficult to understand why
a very intelligent Italian, reading *Paradise Lost* for the first time,
should have complained to me that he had been curiously misled
about its subject; for, he said, 'it is a poem about Death'.

> For who would lose
> Though full of pain, this intellectual being?
>
> (ii. 164–7)

Belial asks the question, as Claudio had done; it is a human
reaction, and most of the time we do not relish the thought of
being without 'sense and motion' (ii. 151); nor can we help it if
this is to be called 'ignoble' (ii. 227). In the same book, Milton
gives Death allegorical substance, if 'substance might be calld

that shaddow seemd' (669); for it is all darkness and shapelessness, a 'Fantasm' (743), all lust and anger, its very name hideous (788). The only thing it resembles is Chaos, fully described in the same book; and it stands in relation to the order and delight of the human body as Chaos stands to Nature. So, when Satan moved out of Chaos into Nature, he not only 'into Nature brought | Miserie' (vi. 267), but into Life brought Death, and into Light (which is always associated with order and organic growth) darkness. At the end of Book ii he at last, 'in a cursed hour' (1055), approaches the pendant world, having moved towards it from Hell through Chaos; and the whole movement of what might be called the *sensuous* logic of the poem so far—the fall into darkness and disorder, the return to light and order—is triumphantly halted at the great invocation to Light which opens Book iii. But the return is of course made with destructive intent. We see the happiness of a man acquainted with the notion of Death but having no real knowledge of it—'So neer grows Death to Life, what e're Death is, | Som dreadful thing no doubt' (iv. 425-6); and then, after the long interruption of Books v–viii, which represent the everything which stretched between life and death, we witness the crucial act from which the real knowledge of Death will spring, when Eve took the fruit, 'and knew not eating Death' (ix. 792). The syntax, once again, is Greek; but we fill it with our different and complementary English senses: 'she knew not that she was eating Death'; 'she knew not Death even as she ate it'; 'although she was so bold as to eat Death for the sake of knowledge, she still did not know—indeed she did not even know what she had known before, namely that this was a sin'. Above all she *eats* Death, makes it a part of her formerly incorruptible body, and so explains the human sense of the possibility of incorruption, so tragically belied by fact. The function of Death in the poem is simple enough; it is 'to destroy, or unimmortal make | All kinds' (x. 611-12). There is, of course, the theological explanation to be considered, that the success of Death in this attempt is permissive; but in terms of the poem this is really no more than a piece of dogmatic cheering-up, and Milton, as usual, allows God himself to do the explaining (x. 616 ff.). From the human point of view, the intimation of unimmortality takes priority over the intellectual comfort of God's own theodicy, simply because a man can feel, and can feel the possibility of immortality blighted.

Milton saw the chance, in Book ix, of presenting very con-
cretely the impact of Death on Life; and it would be hard to think
of a fiction more completely achieved. The moment is of Eve's
return to Adam, enormously ignorant and foolishly cunning,
'with Countnance blithe. . . . But in her Cheek distemper flushing
glowd' (ix. 886–7). This flush is a token of unimmortality; and
then since, 'all kinds' are to be affected, the roses fade and droop
in Adam's welcoming garland. He sees that Eve is lost, 'Defac't,
deflowrd, and now to Death devote' (901). He retreats into Eve's
self-deception; but all is lost.

The emphasis here is on *all*; from the moment of eating the
fruit to that of the descent of 'prevenient grace' (end of Book x
and beginning of xi) Adam and Eve have lost everything, and are,
without mitigation, to death devote. If one bears this steadily in
mind the tenth book is a lot easier to understand; it seems often to
be misread. Adam, 'in a troubl'd Sea of passion tost' (718) cries
out 'O miserable of happie!' (720) and laments the end of the
'new glorious World' (721). He feels particularly the corruption
of love:

> O voice once heard
> Delightfully, *Encrease and multiply*,
> Now death to hear!
>
> (729–31)

and sums up in a couplet using the familiar pseudo-rhyme: 'O
fleeting joyes | Of Paradise, deare bought with lasting woes!'
(741–2). He has knowledge of the contrast between then and
now, but of nothing else. Deprived of Original Justice, he is now
merely natural; hence the importance of remembering that he is
here simply a human being in a situation that is also simple, and
capable of being felt naturally, upon our pulses. Deprived as he
is, Adam finds life 'inexplicable' (754); knowing nothing of the
great official plan by which good will come of all this, his speculations are by the mere light of nature. Rajan made something of
this in his explanation of how Milton got his heterodox theology
into the poem—mortalism, for example, is not very tendentious if
proffered as the opinion of a totally corrupt man.[25] But, much
more important, Adam is here for the first time true kindred to
the reader. The primary appeal of poetry is to the natural man;

[25] B. Rajan, *Paradise Lost and the Seventeenth Century Reader* (1947), Cap. ii.

that is why it is called simple, sensuous and passionate. When Eve proposes that they should practise a difficult abstinence in order not to produce more candidates for unimmortality, or Adam considers suicide (x. 966 ff.) we should be less conscious of their errors than of their typicality. Whatever the mind may make of it, the sensitive body continues to feel the threat of unimmortality as an outrage:

> Why is life giv'n
> To be thus wrested from us? rather why
> Obtruded on us thus? who, if we knew
> What we receive, would either not accept
> Life offerd, or soon beg to lay it down,
> Glad to be so dismisst in peace.
>
> (xi. 502-7)

Michael's treatment of the same topic that the Duke inflicts upon Claudio in *Measure for Measure* can only strengthen such sentiments:

> thou must outlive
> Thy youth, thy strength, thy beauty, which will change
> To witherd weak and gray; thy Senses then
> Obtuse, all taste of pleasure must forgo,
> To what thou hast, and for the Air of youth
> Hopeful and cheerful, in thy blood will reign
> A melancholly damp of cold and dry
> To weigh thy spirits down, and last consume
> The Baum of Life.
>
> (xi. 538-46)

Whatever the consolation offered by Death—no one would wish to 'eternize' a life so subject to distempers of every kind— it is not pretended that this makes up for the loss of the 'two fair gifts ... Happiness | And Immortalitie' (xi. 56-8). Most criticism of the verse of Book x and xi amounts to a complaint that it is lacking in sensuousness; but this is founded on a misunderstanding of the poem. *Paradise Lost* must be seen as a whole; and whoever tries to do this will see the propriety of this change of tone, this diminution of *sense* in the texture of the verse.

A striking example of this propriety is the second of the formal salutations to Eve, Adam's in xi. 158 ff., which I have already discussed in connection with v. 385 ff. (see p. 264 above). Here

Adam sees that Eve is responsible not only for death but for the victory over it; as she herself says, 'I who first brought Death on all, am grac't | The source of life' (xi. 168–9). This paradox, considered as part of the whole complex in which Milton places it, seems to me much more central to the mood of the poem than the famous *felix culpa*, because it is rooted in nature, and related to our habit of rejoicing that life continues, in spite of death, from generation to generation. Yet Adam is still under the shadow of death, and his restatement of the theme Venus-Eve-Mary is very properly deprived of the sensuous context provided for Raphael's salutation; and since the second passage cannot but recall the first, we may be sure that this effect was intended.

There is, indeed, another passage which strongly supports this view of the centrality of the paradox of Eve as destroyer and giver of life, and it has the same muted quality, casts the same shadow over the power and delight of love. This is the curious vision of the union between the sons of Seth and the daughters of Cain (xi. 556–636). The Scriptural warrant for this passage is extremely slight, though there were precedents for Milton's version. Adam rejoices to see these godly men united in love with fair women:

> Such happy interview and fair event
> Of love and youth not lost, Songs, Garlands, Flowrs
> And charming Symphonies attachd the heart
> Of *Adam*, soon enclin'd to admit delight,
> The bent of Nature. . . .
>
> (593–7)

And he thanks the angel, remarking that 'Here Nature seems fulfilld in her ends' (602). He is at once coldly corrected; these women, against the evidence of Adam's own senses, are 'empty of all good' (616), and nothing but ill comes from the 'Sons of God' (622) yielding up all their virtue to them. Milton remembered how much of Pandora there was in Eve. From women Adam is taught to expect woe; but, more important, this change in the divine arrangements means that the evidence of the senses, the testimony of pleasure, is no longer a reliable guide:

> Judge not what is best
> By pleasure, though to Nature seeming meet . . .
>
> (603–4)

Paradise Lost is a poem about death, and about pleasure and its impairment. It is not very surprising that generations of readers failed to see the importance to Milton's 'scheme' of Adam's exclamation upon a paradox which depends not upon the senses but upon revelation; I mean the assurance that out of all this evil good will come as testimony of a benevolent plan

> more wonderful
> Than that which by creation first brought forth
> Light out of darkness.
>
> (xii. 471–3)

The senses will not recognize that out of their own destruction will come forth 'Joy and eternal Bliss' (xii. 551). In that line Milton echoes the *Comus* Epilogue—Joy will come from the great wound the senses have suffered, but it is a joy measured by what we have had and lost. And the sense of loss is keener by far than the apprehension of things unseen, the remote promise of restoration. The old Eden we know, we can describe it, inlay it with a thousand known flowers and compare it with a hundred other paradises; throughout the whole history of loss and deprivation the poets have reconstructed it with love. The new one may be called 'happier farr', but poetry cannot say much more about it because the senses do not know it. The paradise of Milton's poem is the lost, the only true, paradise; we confuse ourselves, and with the same subtlety confuse the 'simple' poem, if we believe otherwise.

Shelley spoke of Milton's 'bold neglect of a direct moral purpose', and held this to be 'the most decisive proof of the supremacy of Milton's genius'. 'He mingled, as it were', Shelley added, 'the elements of human nature as colours upon a single pallet, and arranged them in the composition of his great picture according to the laws of epic truth; that is, according to the laws of that principle by which a series of actions of the external universe and of intelligent and ethical beings is calculated to excite the sympathy of succeeding generations of mankind.'[26] This passage follows upon the famous observations on Satan, and is itself succeeded by and involved with a Shelleyan attack on Christianity; and perhaps in consequence of this it has not been thought worth

[26] 'A Defence of Poetry', in *Shelley's Literary and Philosophical Criticism*, ed. J. Shawcross (1909), p. 146.

much attention except by those specialized opponents who contend for and against Satan in the hero-ass controversy. Theirs is an interesting quarrel, but its ground ought to be shifted; and in any case this is not the occasion to reopen it. But the remarks of Shelley I have quoted seem to me substantially true; so, rightly understood, do the much-anathematized remarks of Blake. I say 'substantially' because Milton himself would perhaps have argued that he accepted what responsibility he could for the moral effect of his poem, and that in any case he specifically desiderated a 'fit' audience, capable of making its own distinctions between moral good and evil. Yet in so far as poetry works through the pleasure it provides—a point upon which Milton and Shelley would agree —it must neglect 'a direct moral purpose'; and in so far as it deals with the passions of fallen man it has to do with Blake's hellish energies. And however much one may feel that they exaggerated the truth in applying it to Milton, one ought to be clear that Shelley and Blake were not simply proposing naughty Romantic paradoxes because they did not know enough. Indeed they show us a truth about *Paradise Lost* which later commentary, however learned, has made less and less accessible.

With these thoughts in my mind, I sometimes feel that the shift of attention necessary to make friends out of some of Milton's most potent modern enemies is in reality a very small one. However this may be, I want to end by citing Mr. Robert Graves; not because I have any hope of persuading him from his evident and irrationally powerful distaste for Milton, but to give myself the pleasure of quoting one of his poems. It is called 'Pure Death', and in it Mr. Graves speculates on a theme that he might have found, superbly extended, in Milton's epic:

> We looked, we loved, and therewith instantly
> Death became terrible to you and me.
> By love we disenthralled our natural terror
> From every comfortable philosopher
> Or tall grey doctor of divinity:
> Death stood at last in his true rank and order.[27]

Milton gives us this perception, but 'according to the laws of epic truth'; which is to say, he exhibits life in a great symbolic attitude.

[27] *Collected Poems* (1959), p. 71.

INDEX

Abercrombie, Lascelles, 261
Abessa, 46–7
Alabaster, William, 155
Aldington, Richard, 26, 50
Alexander III, Pope, 45
Allegory, 2–3, 12–32, 208, 220, 255, 263
  historical, 4–5, 22, 34–7, 42–3, 48, 58, 60
  moral, 3, 34, 36, 39, 50, 54–9, 228–229, 264
  mythological, 71–5, 77, 79
  religious, 46, 61–3, 68–71, 76–8, 83, 220
Alma, House of, 34, 60
Alpers, Paul, 6–9
Ambrose, St., 122, 142
Ananias, 209
Anti-Semitism, 23
Apocalyptism, 13–32
Aptekar, Jane, 5–6
Apuleius, 207, 209, 210
Aquinas, St. Thomas, 38, 77–8, 80, 81, 139, 159, 191, 197
Archimago, 44–5, 48
Aristotle, 10, 49, 67, 68, 79–83, 85, 288
Arithmology, 2, 6
Arthegall, 38, 50, 56, 58
Arthur, King, 14, 16, 21, 30, 46, 48, 194
Astraea, 18–19, 22, 40, 49–50, 55, 57–8
Auden, W. H., 174, 246
Augustine, St., 14, 19, 69–71, 78–9, 85, 87, 118, 122, 141–2, 188

Augustus, Emperor, 105, 191

Bacon, Francis, 52, 54, 198, 205
Baldwin, T. W., 103, 183–5, 196
Bale, John, 40, 43
Banquet of Intellect, 95
Banquet of Sense, 10, 84–115, 185
Barbarossa, 45
Barber, C. L., 206
Barres, Barnabe, 10
Bartlett, P. B., 99n, 104, 109
Beaumont, Francis, 256
Becket, Thomas à, 18
Bedford, Countess of, 118, 127, 134, 139
Beethoven, Ludwig van, 259
Benedict XIV, 81
Beniveni, Girolamo, 35
Benjamin, Walter, 164
Bennett, J. W., 14–16
Bentley, G. E., 221–2
Bentley, R., 276–8
Berger, Harry, 67–8, 78
Beroaldus, 207
Bethell, S. L., 121
Bible, 15, 20, 24–5, 40, 41, 61, 69–70, 77, 85, 138, 140–2, 146, 173, 208–9, 212, 262–3, 267, 269, 278; see also Revelation, book of
Blackfriars Theatre, 221–2, 250
Blake, William, 12, 116, 297
Blavatsky, Mme, 23, 25
Boccaccio, Giovanni, 63, 181, 231
Bodkin, Miss, 12
Boethius, 35
Bohemia, Elector of, 138

Boniface III, Pope, 45–6
Boswell, James, 152
Bradbrook, M. C., 101
Bradley, A. C., 172
Brethren of the Free Spirit, 20, 27n.
Britomart, 38, 50, 56–8
Brockbank, J. P., 230
Bromley, Thomas, 5
Brook, Peter, 172–3
Brooke, A., 189
Brown, J. R., 212
Browning, Robert, 117, 155
Bullinger, Heinrich, 40
Bullough, G., 215
Buno, Cardinal, 44
Bunyan, John, 12
Bush, Douglas, 100, 287

Calvin, John, 137, 139
Cardan, J., 124
Carew, Thomas, 119
Carr, 118, 119
Cartari, 63, 75
Carter, Frederick, 25–6
Casaubon, Florence Etienne, 137
Castiglione, Benedetto, 95
Catullus, 196
Cavendish, Margaret, 155, 157–9
Chambers, E. K., 158, 194
Chapman, George, 1–2, 7–8, 38, 61,
    63, 87, 101, 194
  Coronet for his Mistress Philosophy,
    101–2
  Hero and Leander, 10, 115
  Ovid's Banquet of Sense, 10–11, 62,
    84, 99–115
  Shadow of Night, 100, 101
Charlemagne, 21
Charles I, of England, 193
Charles V, of Spain, 19, 49
Charles, R. H., 26, 31
Chaucer, Geoffrey, 257–8
Chernyshevsky, N. G., 165
Chester, Robert, 194–5
Christ, 14, 16, 43, 47, 69–70, 77, 78,
    82, 124, 143, 147
Christianity
  heresies, 43, 48, 138, 266

origin of English, 17, 40, 41, 43
  sects, 20–1
Chrysostom, 122
Chudleigh, 144
Church, as Bride of Christ, 146–7
Church of England, 16–19, 40–3, 45,
    46–7, 123, 135–9
Claudian, 71, 75, 193
Clement of Alexandria, 74–6
Cleveland, John, 120
Clopton, Sir Hugh, 151
Cohn, Norman, 19–20
Coleridge, Samuel Taylor, 12, 116–
    117, 160, 161, 184
Collaert, Adrian, 87–8
Comes, N., 72–3, 104–5
Commedia dell'arte, 249
Condell, Henry, 224, 229, 256
Constable, Henry, 10
Constans I, 20
Constantine, Emperor, 16, 19, 41–2,
    44
Conti, 63
Corbet, Richard, 120
Corceca, 46
Corcoran, Mary, 278–9
Corke, Helen, 30
Cowell, Prof., 54
Cowley, Abraham, 128, 263, 267, 271
Cunningham, J. V., 196–8
Curry, W. C., 185
Curtius, E., 84, 103, 122

Danby, Prof., 229, 232
Dante, Alighieri, 18, 174
Danvers, Lady, 119, 127, 133, 134
D'Avenant, Sir William, 182
Davie, Dr., 269
Delbene, B., 51, 55
De Quincey, Thomas, 280
Descartes, René, 157
Dickens, Charles, 53
Donatus, 103
Donne, John, 117–19
  Amores of Ovid and, 132
  compared with Milton, 140
  compared with Spenser, 134
  elegies on his death, 144

Donne, John—*cont.*
  Jesuit training, 117, 123
  religious life, 117–19, 132, 134–9,
    141, 144, 148
  revaluation of, 116–17, 154
  as satirist, 129
  style, 119–23, 134, 139, 148
  works, chronology, 127
  Anniversaries, 124, 145, 195
  Biathanatos, 139
  'Corona' sonnets, 144–5
  Devotions, 124, 148
  Divine Poetry, 135, 144–8
  elegies, 125–7, 132–3, 147
  erotic poetry, 125, 133
  Essayes in Divinity, 132, 137, 139
  hymns, 148
  Ignatius, 123–4
  Juvenilia, 126
  Pseudo-Martyr, 136–7
  satires, 127, 129, 133–7, 145
  sermons, 119, 124, 132, 138, 139,
    140–4
  Songs and Sonets, 101, 121–2, 125–
    133, 144, 147, 283
  verse-letters, 127, 134, 139
Donne, Mrs., 118–19, 127
Donno, Elizabeth, 11
Doran, Madeline, 184
Dostoevsky, Feodor, 23
Drayton, Michael, 10
Drury, Elizabeth, 118, 134–5
Drury, Sir Robert, 118, 134
Dryden, John, 36, 79–80, 117, 128,
  181
Duessa, 17, 37, 40, 42–3, 46, 48, 58
Dunseath, T. K., 5

Ebreo, Leone, 102
Edward VI, 40
Edwards, Philip, 219, 225
Egerton, Sir Thomas, 118
Eleusis, 74–6
Eliade, Mircea, 20–3, 151
Eliot, George, 117, 170
Eliot, T. S., 30, 116, 154, 161, 261
Elizabeth I, 4–5, 22, 53–4, 58, 194–5,
  198

emperor cult of, 18–19, 40–2, 49,
  50, 191
Ellesmere, Lord, 54
Elyot, Sir Thomas, 52
Erasmus, 19, 62
Eroticism, 101, 114–15, 125, 133,
  204–6
Essex, Earl of, 195

Falls, Mary R., 46
Farmer, Richard, 181–2
Farrer, Austin, 24, 30
Ficino, Marsiglio, 35, 90, 93–5, 99,
  100, 102, 113
Fletcher, John, 219, 221, 230, 256–9
Forster, E. M., 261–2
Fowler, A. D. S., 2–3, 6–7, 8
Foxe, John, 16, 17, 19, 40–5, 49
Fracastoro, Girolamo, 267
Frederick I, *see* Barbarossa
Frederick II, 49, 51
Freud, Sigmund, 176–7
Frye, Northrop, 13, 24, 223

Gardner, Helen, 24, 30, 145–6
Garrick, David, 149–50
Gastrell, Francis, 151
George, St., 21, 150–3, 158, 163
Giraldi, 63
Globe Theatre, 221–2
Goethe, Wolfgang von, 12, 161
Gombrich, E. H., 13
Goodyere, 119, 134
Gordon, D. J., 63
Gosse, Sir Edmund, 117, 127
Gower Prologues, 225
Granville, Barker, 231
Graves, Robert, 297
Gray, Thomas, 161, 271
Graziani, René, 4, 5, 46
Greene, Robert, 161, 181, 238–40
Greenlaw, Edwin, 36–7, 40, 42
Gregory VII, Pope, 18, 41, 44–5,
  77
Grierson, Sir Herbert, 127, 133
Grosart, A. B., 195
Guyon, 34, 64–71, 74, 76–7, 78–9,
  81–3

Hamilton, A. C., 3, 37-8
Hankins, J. E., 14
Hardy, Thomas, 203
Hawthorne, Nathaniel, 13
Hazlitt, William, 12
Heilman, R. B., 212
Heisenberg, 158
Heminge, John, 224, 229, 256
Henri III, 19
Henri IV, 19
Henry IV, 45
Henry VIII, 17, 40, 52
Herbert, George and Edward, 119
Herbert, Lady, *see* Danvers, Lady
Hercules, 76-9, 85, 88, 184
Herod, King, 47
Heroic romance, 219-20, 222
Heroic virtue, 79-83, 85, 87, 89
Hieatt, Kent, 2
Hildebrand, *see* Gregory VII
Hirsch, 176
Hobbes, Thomas, 120
Holinshed, Ralph, 161, 183, 230
Homer, 71-2, 74-6, 159, 173, 261
    263, 274, 287-8
Hooker, Richard, 125, 139, 198
Horace, 186, 252
Hough, Graham, 37-9
Huizinga, Johan, 36
Hulme, T. E., 25
Hunt, Leigh, 170
Hutton, James, 214

Ignoto, 194
Imperialism, English, 41, 58; *see also*
    Elizabeth I
Ireland forgeries, 152
Isidore of Seville, St., 79
Isis, 55, 57, 207, 209
    Church of, 4-5, 34, 38-9, 49, 50,
    54-8, 60
Islam, 21, 45

Jacquot, Jean, 101, 103, 104
James I, 54, 137, 193, 195, 198
James, D. G., 220
Jesuits, 117, 123, 137, 145
Jewel, John, 15-17, 40, 43, 47

Joachim, 19
John, St., 15, 20, 25; *see also* Revela-
    tion, book of
John of Salisbury, 62
Johnson, Samuel, 117, 121, 155-60,
    162, 170-2, 175, 178, 211, 229, 262,
    271
Jonson, Ben, 10, 89-93, 95, 102-3,
    112, 115, 117, 119, 120, 127, 134-5,
    150, 181-2, 184-5, 194, 250
Joseph of Arimathaea, 17, 40-2
Joyce, James, 13, 23, 180, 274
Judas, 242
Justinian, Emperor, 41, 51

Kafka, Franz, 13, 180
Kantorowicz, E., 51, 190
Keats, John, 33
Keightley, Thomas, 17, 42
Kepler, Johann, 123-4
King, A. H., 102
Kirkrapine, 46-8
Knight, Wilson, 220
Kott, Jan, 172, 174

Lactantius, 193, 194, 196
Lamb, Charles, 117
Laud, Archbishop, 143-4
Laumonier, P., 103
Lawrence, D. H., 14, 24-6, 28-32
Lemaire, Jean, des Belges, 103
Lewis, C. S., 35
Longinus, 263
Longus, 249
Lorenzetti, Ambrogio, 57
Louis VII, 21
Loyola, Ignatius, 145
Lucas de Penna, 51
Lucius, King of Britain, 41, 55
Luther, Martin, 15, 17, 47, 51
Lyell, Sir Charles, 158

Machiavelli, 159
McLuhan, Marshall, 164
MacLure, Millar, 10
Macready, W. C., 170
Macrobius, 61, 80-2
Mahood, Miss, 205

Maitland, F. W., 52
Malory, Sir Thomas, 42
Manningham, John, 215
Marino, 121
Marlorat, Augustine, 44
Marot, Clément, 103
Marsilius of Padua, 18
Marston, John, 100, 194–5
Marvell, Andrew, 69, 71, 84–5, 87, 245
Mary Queen of Scots, 4–5, 34, 58
Massinger, Philip, 95, 184, 256
Masson, David, 156–9
Matthew of Paris, 43
Maxwell, J. C., 236–7
Mead, G. R. S., 25
Melville, Herman, 13
Mercilla, 49, 50, 56–8, 214
Meurs, J. (Meursius), 74–6
Michelangelo, 76
Miller, Henry, 23
Milton, John
  and Bible, 78, 262–6
  compared with Wordsworth, 280
  Eliot, T. S., on, 154
  learning, 161
  modern hostility to, 260–2, 297
  on poets and poetry, 116, 266–9
  rhyme and, 270–5
  Shakespeare and, 149
  Spenser and, 40, 67
  as theologian, 125, 184, 290, 292–3
  use of allegory, 263–4
  Comus, 96, 275, 296
  De Doctrina Christiana, 263, 269, 280, 291
  Hymn on the Morning of Christ's Nativity, 275
  L'Allegro, 275
  Lycidas, 275
  'Ode at a Solemn Musick', 214
  Of Reformation, 47
  Paradise Lost, 79, 260–97
  Paradise Regain'd, 69–71, 84, 89, 268
  Reason of Church-Government, The, 268
  Tenure of Kings and Magistrates, 268
  Tractate of Education, 267
Montaigne, Michel de, 125, 128, 133, 159, 163, 248, 253
More, Ann, *see* Donne, Mrs.
More, Henry, 38
Morton, Bishop, 118
Mucedorus, 221
Muller, Max, 151
Murillo, B. E., 88
Murray, Gilbert, 261
Murray, J. Middleton, 257
Myers, J. P., Jr., 10–11

Napier, John, 44
Nazism, 20, 23
Neo-Platonism, 35, 61–4, 76, 102
Newcastle, Duchess of, 155, 157–9
Newton, Sir Isaac, 15
Nietzcheanism, 20, 23
Northumberland, Earl of, 119
Nuttall, A. D., 179

Occultism, 25, 61, 76
Olsen, P. A., 210
Orwell, George, 166, 174, 176
Ovid, 11, 51, 72–3, 89–91, 101–2, 105, 107, 132, 181, 183, 186, 196, 248–9, 288; *see also* Chapman: *Ovid's Banquet of Sense*

Papacy, 44, 48, 49
Parker, Matthew, Archbishop, 42
Pater, Walter, 116
Paul, H. N., 185
Paul, St., 85–6, 138, 208–9
Pausanias, 73, 75, 105
Pepys, Samuel, 215
Peter Martyr, 252
Phaedria, 64, 67
Philotime, 66, 70
Phocas, Emperor, 46
Phoenix, 192–8
Pilate, Pontius, 66, 73
Placentinus, 51
Plato, 35, 63, 86, 91, 94
Platonism, 99, 101, 103, 264; *see also* Neo-Platonism
Plautus, 215

Plotinus, 80
Plutarch, 50, 55, 63, 161, 182–3, 192
Pole, Cardinal, 52
Pope, Alexander, 134, 271, 287
Potter, Peter, 88
Praz, Mario, 120
Prince, F. T., 270, 271
Proserpina, 8, 66, 68, 71–2, 74–5, 264
Protestantism, 16, 43, 58
Proust, Marcel, 180
Pryse, James, 25
Purchas, Samuel, 231

Radigund, 50, 57–8
Raglan, Lord, 151
Rajan, B., 266, 293
Raleigh, Sir Walter, 54, 260
Randolph, Thomas, 95–6
Red Cross Knight, 16, 43–6, 48, 67, 81–3
Reformation, 16, 18, 37, 40, 46–7, 139, 142
Renaissance, 35, 37, 38, 62–3, 84–5, 99, 269, 285
Renwick, W. L., 35
Revelation, book of, 13–16, 23–30, 36, 39–41, 43–4, 48, 172
Rhea, priesthood of, 55
Rhyme, 270–5
Riche, B., 215
Ripa, 87
Robbe-Grillet, Alain, 164
Roman Catholic Church, 15, 17, 43, 45, 47, 117, 123, 136–7; see also Papacy
Roman law, 52
Ronsard, Pierre de, 62, 103
Rowe, Nicholas, 181
Rubens, Peter Paul, 97

Salisbury, Sir John, 194
Sandys, George, 42, 46, 47, 79
Sarpi, Paolo, 138
Satan, 18, 44, 69, 265, 268, 272–4, 280–4, 289–92, 296–7
Schiller, J. C. F. von, 265
Schoell, 104
Schwartz, Delmore, 163

Scott, Sir Walter, 16, 42
Sea Adventure, 248
Seneca, 142, 159, 183
Senses, see Banquet of Sense
Seznec, 62–4
Shakespeare, William
  above criticism, 153–6
  as allegorist, 229–31, 246–7, 255
  anniversaries of, 149–50, 152, 156–157
  Banquet of Sense and, 96–8
  Chapman's hostility to, 101
  classic quality of, 178–9
  collaboration with John Fletcher, 219, 256–9
  compared with Spenser, 38–9, 61, 155, 190, 198, 212
  education, 182–3
  as erotic poet, 113–14, 204–6
  Faerie Queene, The, and, 151, 211–12, 214, 227, 237, 246, 249, 255
  hero worship of, 151–3, 157–8
  intellect, 184–99
  Milton and, 149
  multiple views of, 159–60
  primus inter pares, 160–3
  preoccupation with techniques, 203
  re-writing of, 170, 172–6
  St. George and, 150–1, 158, 163
  Tolstoi's animosity for, 165–7
  Antony and Cleopatra, 98–9n., 155, 162, 184–5, 187, 189, 192
  As You Like It, 186, 189, 200, 203, 211, 226
  Comedy of Errors, 200, 215, 225
  Coriolanus, 161–2, 233
  Cymbeline, 162, 189, 192, 200–2, 210, 219, 221–2, 229–37, 249–50, 255
  Hamlet, 159, 175–6, 203
  Henry IV, 186–7
  Henry VI, 182
  Henry VIII, 193, 219, 256
  Julius Caesar, 209
  King Lear, 154, 157, 161, 165–80, 187, 189, 190–1, 203, 236
  Love's Labour's Lost, 182, 186, 189

Lucrece, 111, 114, 182, 185, 186, 189

Macbeth, 185–8, 203

Measure for Measure, 189, 214, 228, 240, 294

Merchant of Venice, 186, 210–15, 236, 245

Midsummer Night's Dream, 186, 194, 203–11, 215

Othello, 189, 241

Pericles, 219, 221, 223–9, 232, 239, 240, 249–50, 255–6

'Phoenix and the Turtle, The', 190, 194–9

Richard II, 190

Richard III, 227

Romeo and Juliet, 189, 204–5

Sir Thomas More, 182

Sonnets, 96, 184–6, 232

Tempest, The, 161, 179, 182, 200, 203, 219–23, 227, 239, 247–56

Timon of Athens, 96–7, 184–5

Troilus and Cressida, 187, 189, 203, 290

Twelfth Night, 200, 203, 210, 215–218

Two Gentlemen of Verona, 189, 200, 210–11

Two Noble Kinsmen, The, 219, 224, 256–8

Venus and Adonis, 97–8, 100, 103, 182, 184–5, 204

Winter's Tale, The, 157, 161–2, 219, 220, 222, 233, 238–47, 249–50, 255–6

Sharpe, Thomas, 151

Shelley, Percy Bysshe, 154, 296–7

Sibylla, 20

Sidney, Sir Philip, 222, 229, 249

Sirluck, Ernest, 68

Smart, Prof., 183

Smith, Hallett, 77, 87, 101

Spens, J., 101

Spenser, Edmund
as allegorist, 1–2, 6, 12, 42, 64, 229
Banquet of Sense and, 10, 84
compared with Donne, 134

contrasted to Chapman, 7–8, 38, 61
guides to, 34
horror of libertine sects, 21
as learned man, 35, 59
Milton and, 40, 67
as myth-maker, 61
officer of Irish Court of Chancery, 5
style, 7–8
susceptible to historical analysis, 58
Faerie Queene, The
as allegory, 3, 12, 34–43, 48–51, 54–9, 61–3, 68, 71–9, 83
Alpers on, 6–7
apocalyptic imagery of, 13–16, 34–6, 39–41, 43, 49
Bower of Bliss, 78
'Cave of Mammon', 34, 60–83
compared with Aeneid, 83
compared with Lawrence's *Lady Chatterley's Lover*, 28–32
compared with Marvell's 'Pleasure offers Glory', 71
compared with Milton's *Paradise Regain'd*, 69–71, 84
Fowler on, 2
Garden of Adonis, 10, 34–5, 38, 60
imperial propaganda, 19, 52
Legend of Temperance, 60, 64
mentioned in Lawrence's *Apocalypse*, 31
Mutability Cantos, 10, 34, 222, 243
Nichomachean Ethics and, 68, 79–83
Shakespeare and, 38–9, 61, 151, 155, 190, 198, 211–12, 214, 222, 227, 231n., 237, 246, 249, 255
simplification of, 35–8
topicality, 4, 13
see also principal characters
Hymns, 95
Muiopotmos, 60, 71

Spenser, Theodore, 258

Sparrow, Warden, 29
Star Chamber, 53–5, 57
Starkey, 52
Strachey, Lytton, 203, 219, 248
Swinburne, A. C., 172
Sylvester II, 44
Symbolism, 12, 116

Tantalus, 66, 73
Tasso, 82, 285–6
Tate, Nahum, 169–71, 173–4
Taylor, Jeremy, 86
Tertullian, 15, 74, 76, 142–3
Theseus, 74–5, 161, 209
Thomas, Dylan, 208
Thomas, St., 77, 197
Thomson, J. A. K., 183
Tillyard, E. M. W., 221
Todd, H. J., 288
Tolstoi, Leo, 23, 154, 165, 173–5
Tomkis, Thomas, 95
Topcliffe, 135
Townely plays, 73–4
Trent, Council of, 137–8
Tuve, Rosemond, 3–4, 6, 184, 275
Twine, L., 224

Una, 14, 17, 37, 40, 42–4, 47–8
Upton, John, 36, 43, 48, 74, 83, 181
Urban VI, Pope, 48
Ure, Peter, 223, 256, 258

Valentinian II, 192

Venice, 137–8
Venus, 93, 207, 264, 287, 295
Virgil, 18, 22, 74, 83, 109, 174, 183, 274

Waddington, R. B., 11
Wain, John, 183–4, 200
Waldock, A. J. A., 260–2, 265
Walton, Izaak, 119, 120, 136, 148
Warburton, W., 74
Warton, Thomas, 71
Webb, Francis, 152
West, R. H., 266
Whitaker, V. K., 67, 183
Wheelwright, Philip, 12
Whitby, Synod of, 45
Wilfrid, Bishop, 45
Wilkins, George, 224–5
Wimsatt, W. K., 271
Wind, E., 62–4, 76
Winstanley, Lilian, 36
Winters, Yvor, 12
Woodhouse, A. S. P., 38, 58
Wordsworth, William, 158, 180, 280
Worringer, 25
Wotton, Sir Henry, 119, 137–8
Wyclif, John, 15, 45, 48

Yates, Frances A., 18, 43, 49, 50, 138, 193
Yeats, William Butler, 12, 23, 184, 220, 259

Xenophon, 86

Fontana Books

Fontana is at present best known (outside the field of popular fiction) for its extensive list of books on history, philosophy and theology. Now, however, the list is expanding rapidly to include most main subjects, such as literature, politics, economics and sociology. At the same time, the number of paperback reprints of books already published in hardcover editions is being increased. Further information on Fontana's present list and future plans can be obtained from: The Non-Fiction Editor, Fontana Books, 14 St James's Place, London S.W.1.

All Fontana books are available at your bookshop or news-agent; or can be ordered direct. Just fill in the form below and list the titles you want.

....

FONTANA BOOKS, Cash Sales Department, P.O. Box 4, Godalming, Surrey. Please send purchase price plus 5p postage per book by cheque, postal or money order. No currency.

NAME (Block Letters) _____

ADDRESS _____

_____

_____

Fontana Literature

Modern Essays Frank Kermode **75p**

Romantic Image Frank Kermode **50p**

The Brontë Story Margaret Lane **45p**

Sartre Iris Murdoch **30p**

Poems and Critics *Edited by* Christopher Ricks **50p**

Modern Poets on Modern Poetry *Edited by* James Scully **40p**

Axel's Castle Edmund Wilson **40p**

Fontana Modern Masters

General Editor: Frank Kermode

This series provides authoritative and critical introductions to the most influential and seminal minds of our time. Books already published include:

Camus Conor Cruise O'Brien **25p**
Chomsky John Lyons **30p**
Fanon David Caute **30p**
Freud Richard Wollheim **40p**
Gandhi George Woodcock **35p**
Guevara Andrew Sinclair **25p**
Joyce John Gross **30p**
Lenin Robert Conquest **35p**
Lévi-Strauss Edmund Leach **30p**
Lukács George Lichtheim **30p**
Mailer Richard Poirier **40p**
Marcuse Alasdair MacIntyre **25p**
McLuhan Jonathan Miller **30p**
Orwell Raymond Williams **30p**
Reich Charles Rycroft **30p**
Russell A. J. Ayer **40p**
Wittgenstein David Pears **40p**
Yeats Denis Donoghue **30p**

'We have here, in fact, the beginnings of what promises to be an important publishing enterprise. This series is just what is needed by the so-called "general reader" in search of a guide to intellectual currents that clash so confusingly in a confused world.'
The Times Literary Supplement

Many more are in preparation including:

Fuller Allan Temko
Eliot Stephen Spender
Lawrence Frank Kermode
Sherrington Jonathan Miller
Trotsky Philip Rahv
Weber Donald MacRae

Fontana History

Fontana History includes the well-known History of Europe, edited by J. H. Plumb, and the Fontana Economic History of Europe, edited by Carlo Cipolla. Other books available include:

The Nation State and National Self-Determination
Alfred Cobban   40p

American Presidents and the Presidency
Marcus Cunliffe   60p

The English Reformation   A. G. Dickens   60p

The Norman Achievement   David C. Douglas   50p

The Practice of History   G. R. Elton   40p

Debates with Historians   Pieter Geyl   40p

Russia 1917: The February Revolution   George Katkov   60p

Britain and the Second World War   Henry Pelling   50p

A History of the Scottish People   T. C. Smout   £1·25

Europe and the French Revolution   Albert Sorel   50p

The Trial of Charles I   C. V. Wedgwood   40p

The King's Peace 1637–1641   C. V. Wedgwood   60p

The King's War 1641–1647   C. V. Wedgwood   60p

The Fontana History of Europe

Renaissance Europe 1480-1520 J.R.Hale **50p**
The latest addition to the series.

Reformation Europe 1517-1559 G. R. Elton **50p**
'Not since Ranke has any historian described the religious and
political history of Central Europe during the Reformation with as
much insight and authority.' *History*

Europe Divided 1559-1598 J. H. Elliott **50p**
'John Elliott is no ordinary historian. He writes without fuss, but
with a sure instinct for words; he is always in command of his
material; always unprejudiced but never unfeeling. He is scru-
pulously fair in his tight allocation of space, and on every subject
he commands confidence and respect.' *J. P. Kenyon, The Observer*

Europe Unfolding 1648-1688 John Stoye **60p**
'A survey which is the best of its kind available in any language.'
The Times Literary Supplement

Europe of the Ancien Regime 1715-1783 David Ogg **50p**
'An excellent introduction to eighteenth-century Europe.'
The Times Literary Supplement

Revolutionary Europe 1783-1815 George Rudé **50p**
'A thoughtful and thought-provoking book. There have been many
reflections on the French Revolution since Burke's but few have
been as unprejudiced or as wise as Professor Rudé's.' *The Economist*

Europe Between Revolutions 1815-1848 Jacques Droz
50p
A work specially commissioned for the series from a distinguished
French historian.

Europe of the Dictators 1919-1945 Elizabeth Wiskemann
40p
'A model of succinctness and clarity.' *G. L. Mosse, Journal of
Contemporary History*

In preparation: volumes by J. S. Grenville, F. H. Hinsley and
Hugh Trevor-Roper.

The British Monarchy

This series describes the evolution of the British monarchy from the Saxon and Norman kings to George V—their personalities and lives, their influence on their ages. Six volumes, each with twelve pages of photographs.

The Saxon and Norman Kings Christopher Brooke **45p**
'An illuminating and imaginative reconstruction of what it really meant to be a king in Saxon and Norman times. The essential merits of this book are its lightness of touch and its firm grounding in scholarship.' *The Economist*

The Plantagenets John Harvey **45p**
'A portrait gallery of medieval English sovereigns, illustrated with many splendid photographs. Learned, informative and entertaining.'
Daily Mail

The Tudors Christopher Morris **45p**
'Brilliant . . . Mr. Morris's flair for the apt point or quotation is remarkable.' *History*

The Stuarts J. P. Kenyon **45p**
'A sardonic, witty, yet scholarly book, written with splendid gusto.'
Sunday Times

The First Four Georges J. H. Plumb **45p**
'The vitality and frankness of a literary Hogarth. He is never dull or merely derivative.' *The Economist*

Hanover to Windsor Roger Fulford **45p**
'As accurate as it is amusing, and conspicuously fair in its judgments.' *The Times Literary Supplement*